ESSAYS,

MILITARY AND POLITICAL

ESSAYS,

MILITARY AND POLITICAL,

WRITTEN IN INDIA.

SIR HENRY MONTGOMERY LAWRENCE, K.C.B.

GYAN

Published by

GYAN

Gyan Publishing House
5, Ansari Road
Daryaganj, New Delhi-110002
Phone: 011-47034999, 9811692060
E-mail: books@gyanbooks.com

Distribution Network
gyanbooks.com
India, USA, Canada, UK, Australia, France

ISBN: 978-81-212-9314-3 (PB)
First Published, 1859

2nd Impression 2023

Printed at: Gyan Press, Delhi.

ESSAYS, MILITARY AND POLITICAL
Author: SIR HENRY MONTGOMERY LAWRENCE

ESSAYS,

MILITARY AND POLITICAL,

WRITTEN IN INDIA.

ESSAYS,

MILITARY AND POLITICAL,

WRITTEN IN INDIA.

BY THE LATE

SIR HENRY MONTGOMERY LAWRENCE, K.C.B.,

CHIEF COMMISSIONER IN OUDE,

AND PROVISIONAL GOVERNOR-GENERAL OF INDIA.

LONDON:

W^M. H. ALLEN & CO., 7, LEADENHALL STREET.

1859.

TO

SIR GEORGE RUSSELL CLERK, K.C.B.,

UNDER WHOM

THE WRITER OF THESE ESSAYS

GRADUATED IN THE BEST SCHOOL OF INDIAN STATESMANSHIP,

THIS VOLUME

IS RESPECTFULLY INSCRIBED.

ADVERTISEMENT.

The Essays comprising this volume were contributed by Sir Henry Lawrence to the *Calcutta Review*. They are printed now with scarcely any alteration, beyond the correction of typographical or clerical errors, and an occasional excision or adaptation of those allusions to existing times and local circumstances, which are generally scattered, more or less, over our periodical literature, but which the lapse of years renders, if not unintelligible, unapprociable by the reader of to-day. It is not to be understood by this that there has been any attempt to adapt these Essays to the circumstances of the present times. It will be apparent after the perusal of a few pages, that there is much in them which, in one sense, may be described as "out of date." But to have expunged all references to a bygone state of things, and all recommendations of reforms which have been carried out, would have been but scant justice either to reader or to writer. For it would have diminished the historical interest of the volume, and would have obscured the services rendered by Sir Henry Lawrence to the cause of Military Reform. That many of his suggestions were acted upon, we know; that others were not, we can only deplore. That he saw clearly the rocks on which the vessel of the State was drifting, is to be gathered from many passages in this volume. The warning voice was lifted up in vain; but much still remains from which instruction may be gathered, very serviceable at the present time. The lessons which these Essays teach us are not all too late for profitable study. We have still an Indian army composed of all arms and of all classes. Upon the constitution of this army now turns, as on a pivot, the whole question of Indian government. We must keep up an efficient army, at a certain cost not to be exceeded, or we must cease to retain our hold of the country. Now, the great object of Sir Henry Lawrence, in his Military Essays, is to demonstrate that what India requires is an army deriving its strength, not from its numbers, but from its efficiency. And this is the great matter which it behoves us to ponder at the present time. What we want is, not men, not money—but mind. A hundred men may be made to do the work of a thousand; a hundred pounds, wisely spent, may contribute more to the strength of our empire than a thousand. Doubtless, the cost of an efficient army might be brought within the amount which the revenues of India can bear without exhaustion, and the State can furnish without bankruptcy. But to do this, we must look very gravely at the matter, and heed the pregnant utterances of such experienced, honest, plain-spoken instructors as Sir Henry Lawrence.

Of the Political Essays much need not be said in this place. One observation, indeed, will suffice. The reader will perceive how consistently opposed was Sir

Henry Lawrence to what is called the "Annexation Policy." He warmly advocated, on grounds alike of justice and expediency, the maintenance of the Native States of India, and deprecated all unnecessary interference with them. A different statement has been made, very ignorantly, and very unjustly, upon this point. It is of the more importance, therefore, that his opinions should be laid before the public in his own words, and that he should appear in his own proper character, not as an "annexationist," but as a teacher in that great school of which, in days gone by, Sir John Malcolm was the chief, and at the head of which, among living statesmen, now stands Sir George Clerk.

CONTENTS.

PAGE

Military Defence of our Indian Empire. [Written in 1844] 1

The Kingdom of Oude. [Written in 1845] 61

Mahratta History and Empire. [Written in 1845] . . 138

Lord Hardinge's Indian Administration. [Written in 1847] 225

The Indian Army. [Written in 1855–56] 362

Army Reform. [Written in 1856] 413

LAWRENCE'S ESSAYS.

MILITARY DEFENCE OF OUR INDIAN EMPIRE.

[WRITTEN IN 1844.]

In many learned volumes, more or less empirical, we have an infinite variety of "sure means of preserving health." New remedies for all the abundant evils to which frail flesh is heir, start into being every day, and doctors and disciples are so numerous in their diversities, and so strong in their convictions, that the marvel is, with so many infallible specifics, there is still so much human woe. The health which we are thus taught to preserve, after a variety of fashions so endless that it is difficult to escape following some one of them by chance, is the health of man as an individual unit; the health of man, in those thousands and tens of thousands and hundreds of thousands which constitute nations, is not so tenderly cared for; nor so assiduously watched; nor are such varied efforts made to preserve it. Still, ever and anon national remedies, for the cure of national diseases, are exhibited with an amount of confidence which we may call dogmatism; and whilst the wise men are quarrelling over their theories, the world is left very much to itself to suffer uncared for and unrelieved.

With the endless catalogue of ailments, which afflict a nation, as an individual, we have, in this place, nothing to do. In imitation of the medical writers of the present day, who now, for the most part, consider one organ and one disease, sufficient matter for an elaborate treatise, we direct our attention to one especial item of the great catalogue of national calamities. Peace is not in itself national health; but without it there can be no national health; and who will deny that the sage, who should write a treatise on the "true means of preserving peace,"—really exhibiting what it professes to exhibit—would entitle himself to a statue of gold in every city of the universe? There is no prospect, we fear, of such a consummation; but we have rival political schools, each propounding with an air of more or less infallibility its own profound dogmata; and often looking on with marvellous unconcern, whilst great battles are fought, and countries desolated in spite of their never-failing specifics. The two great schools may be described as the *irritative* and *sedative* schools. The former, proceeding upon the broad principle of the homœopathists, that *similia similibus curantur,* contend that war can only be cured by war—that it is necessary to make war in order to preserve peace. The other lays down, with no more misgivings than its antagonist, the more desirable and encouraging doctrine, that war does not check, but generate war; that peace ever engenders peace; that there is no security so certain as that which we purchase for ourselves, by creating a sense of security in the breasts of our neighbours.

We do not now purpose to examine these antagonist doctrines. On whichsoever side worldly experience may range itself, there is no disinclination on the part of either to appeal to it, as the standard whereby the question shall be settled. There is a better method of settlement; but it admits not of a conflict on equal ground, for one party is more inclined to that mode of adjustment than the other, whilst both are willing to appeal to human experience. The irritatives contend that there is no security without constant demonstrations of strength; that to be placid is to invite aggression; that to be ready to offend is the only way to escape being offended; that the birds of the air and the beasts of the field daily teach us this lesson; that we are instructed in it from our earliest youth, during which we learn by hard experience that we must fight our way up the school-boy ladder to peace, and thus alone avoid molestation; that this same principle is at work in the larger school of nations, and that the history of the world declares the fact, that if we would escape the injuries and insults of our neighbours we must show, by a few practical exhibitions of our strength, not only our readiness, but our ability to resent them. The sedatives, on the other hand, declare that to be tranquil and inoffensive is the surest means of inviting confidence, and thus of stifling the inclination to injure us; that the fear of being injured tempts to the commission of injury; and that, the converse of this being equally true, it follows that there is the utmost protectiveness in a peaceful and inoffensive character; and that so long as our neighbours consider themselves secure from our, we shall be secure from *their*, aggressions. Experience is said to demonstrate this: the man of peace is rarely insulted; the unarmed traveller walks more safely in the neighbourhood of the roving bandit, than he who goes armed to the teeth; that in troubled times, the man of peace and he alone escapes the perils of popular commotions; that with States, as with individuals, the one which never arms itself—which never prepares itself for aggression, or the resistance of aggression, is ever the last to be assailed; that as soon as there is a falling off from such practical proofs of a firm reliance on Providence, the protection is at once withdrawn, and we take up arms to have them turned against us. Such are the arguments derived from human experience—we are not at present to decide the contest.

Indeed, with regard to the matter now before us, it is not necessary that we should decide it. A resort to abstract speculation, however inviting, is no part of our career of duty, and we would rather, avoiding all controversies, build up our present structure on common admitted grounds. Our empire in the East is of so peculiar a nature, that we can scarcely make a just application of the principles of either one party or the other. It matters little what course would have been the best; we cannot now begin our work anew; or betake ourselves to new principles of action. We have reached an epoch, at which it would appear to be our only course to make a compromise between the irritative and the sedative systems—or rather we should say, an epoch at which it becomes our duty to allow the former to merge into the latter. The irritative system has been tried—has been carried out to its full extent. It has been our practice now for nearly a century; and it would seem that we had attained to that eminence, which has been compared to the status of the school-boy who has fought his way to the very summit of pugilistic renown. If it be necessary for a nation to preserve itself from injury and insult by demonstrating its power, surely the British in the East have done so in the most unmistakable manner. There is little call for fresh demonstrations; for the weight of our arm is still acknowledged, and many are yet reeling under the blows which it has dealt out. We can now, therefore, afford to be pacific—but we cannot afford to be weak. We have no occasion to put forth our strength; but we must not suffer ourselves to waste it. We must keep ourselves up to the athletic standard; and as we have made our election we must abide by it—as we have fought our way to power, we must show ourselves capable of retaining the lofty position we have assumed. The time may come when we shall find our best safeguard in the hearts of a grateful people—but that time has not *yet* come, nor is there a near prospect of its advent. The sword, whether in the hand or in the scabbard, has yet its work to do; and the philanthropist may labour to some good purpose, in endeavouring to show in what manner it may best be shaped, for the preservation of peace and the maintenance of that dominion, which we are justified in regarding as a means, under Providence, of advancing the happiness of the people who are compelled now to bear our yoke.

At first sight, bayonets and red coats do not appear to be precisely the instruments of Government which a philanthropist would advocate; but we belie or deceive ourselves when we declare or fancy that our Government is maintained otherwise than by the sword. And in pronouncing it to be so, we are far from admitting that it must therefore be one of oppression. The land that has for nearly a thousand years been held by the sword, and that has as often changed hands as that sword has been blunted, or the grasp that held it relaxed; the land that knows no principality of longer standing than our own;* that in its length and breadth, within the last fifty years, has seen Moguls, Patans, Mahrattahs, Pindarees; and mixed miscreants of every caste and clan rooting up the old families, and settling

* It is a curious fact, that not only has the power of the Nizam, the kingdom of Oude, and all the Mahratta States risen within the last century; but that the families of the three bordering States, Burmah, Nepal, and Lahore, have been established within that period.

themselves in their places—how could any Government, however beneficent, subsist for a day simply by its civil policy on the ruins of such a tempest-tost land? How in a day convert tribes who have lived only by war to habits of peace; how make cultivators, who for centuries have never paid a rupee, but under fear of the sword or the scourge—how induce them to pay their dues, unless they know that the civil officer has the power of calling in the military: and that the latter is prompt and bold? It has been the fashion to exalt the Mahommedan conquerors at the expense of the British Government; and some of those who have most benefited by the latter, and possibly have in their sphere oppressed the subject, against the views, opinions, and orders of their masters, have been loudest in vituperation of them; but let any impartial person turn over the pages of Dow—a violent hater of the system of his day, and we fear with too much reason—and see how little cause there is for singing the praises of the Moslem rule, beyond that of the Christian. War, eternal war, was then the sole business of royalty. Akbar made some laws for the protection of the people, but he is almost a solitary exception; and having spent the half-century of his reign in eternal battles and ceaseless marches, he could have had but little time to look to the improvement and cultivation of his empire. In the early days of his reign, every province was in rebellion, and with him, as with his predecessors and successors, while Guzerat was being subdued, Cashmere or Bengal would be in arms; and while the royal troops were employed against those States or in the Deccan, the Punjab or Delhi itself would be in revolt. A freak or favour to an individual would for a time remove the Hindoo capitation tax; while once in a century a tyrannical Governor would be trodden under the feet of the imperial elephants. Seldom was the honest Minister or Governor (when such rare creatures appeared) rewarded, whilst the bold and the unprincipled amassed treasure and bequeathed it to their children. Mark the fate of Akbar's great minister Byram—the man to whom he owed his throne; whilst the Saadut Allys and Nizams have left kingdoms to their descendants. Our only wonder is, when reading the Moslem annals, that such men as Asoph Jah, and his father, and Mohabat Khan, should have lived (generally) prosperously and died in their beds.

Utter selfishness was the Moslem motive; the high roads, the seraes, the plantations—were they for the people? Not at all, but for the royal progresses to Cashmere. The expense of one Badshahi serae would have built a dozen for the people. Throughout the country it was the same. In the direction the king was likely to travel there would be roads and conveniences; but elsewhere the people might sigh in vain for paths, for water, or for shelter. The Newabs of Oude, and Kings of Juanpore and of the Deccan did the same. They beautified the neighbourhood of their own favourite residences, made roads to their country seats, built bridges over the rivers in their way, sunk splendid wells and planted lines of trees. Some of our own magistrates in the times of the good old close-borough system did the same; and to this day European convenience is more regarded than native wants—the collector-and-magistrate being often considered more sacred than the thousands of poor around him.

Despotism, unchecked power, in whatever hands and in whatever quarter, produces the same fruit; and we would divest our minds of all clannish feeling in discussing its merits. Wars and their train of ills were not confined to the Mahommedan times or States, in

India. A glance at the old Hindoo annals will show that if the country so suffered in Moslem times, it was not more free from such distractions in what are called the bright days of Hindoo supremacy. Everywhere we see that the present occupants of the soil are not the aboriginals; and almost every district in India has its peculiar legend, how a Rajpoot, or other band, drove out, or enslaved the original holders; while another tale will perhaps tell of how the late conquerors were themselves overwhelmed; and how they eventually merged into another and bolder race. We doubt whether India was ever under an universal monarch; and the Kings of the Hindoo States of Oude, Kanouge, Muttra, Hustunapore (Delhi), &c., &c., played but the game that warriors of every age and every clime have ever played. They prospered, or sank; they conquered, or were themselves led captive; and then, as in later days, independent kingdoms disappeared, and small States rose into great ones. Not content with the usual and tolerably-sufficient grounds for war, we read that Prithora the brave, the hero of a hundred fights, amused himself with carrying off the brides of the several kings, of whose intended marriage he had information. He thus brought on himself many wars, and eventually thereby lost his throne—but he lost no credit, and is to this day the hero of Rajpoot Romance. It would seem, indeed, to be mere idleness to write and talk of the happiness and purity of a people, who deified the perpetrators of every crime, and whose very worship sanctioned every abomination. When we read of the hundreds of thousands that took the field with the Persian Kings and with the Moguls; and consider that they had no commissariat, we may imagine the frightful famines that such armies themselves experienced, and the more frightful afflictions they caused to the countries through which they passed. Dow, in his preliminary dissertation to Ferishta, writes of bazars, &c. in camp; but nowhere do we find that there were any regular establishments of the kind; Brinjaries (themselves plunderers of the worst description) carrying grain, followed the camp or did not, according to the individual genius and forethought of the monarch or general of the day; but when Dow goes on to tell us that each horseman received from sixty to two hundred rupees* per month, we can understand the value of his several dissertations. We doubt whether under any native ruler, in any age, Hindustani horsemen received all their pay in cash; or if our present rate of twenty rupees per month to Irregular Horse was ever materially and continuedly exceeded. And whatever was paid was in assignments on distant lands, or in at least half grain and food as rations for man and beast, and the small balance only in cash. Dow goes on to say (page xviii. preface) that on such high pay, the soldiery could afford to encourage the grain-dealers, &c., who flocked in from neighbouring towns and villages as armies advanced; but the traveller Bernier, with much more apparent truth, tells us that there were no towns worth mentioning between Delhi and Agra, and that the banks of the Jumna above Delhi, being the line of the imperial progress towards Lahore and Cashmere, were extensive hunting-grounds; that the imperial *cortège* usually left the high road, and sported through these Shikargahs, while the troops moved more directly forward.

We know that everywhere in the East, the track of an army is marked by desolation—that villages and towns are abandoned even at the intelligence of a coming hostile force. In the south of India, as the historian Wilkes tells us, such flights are called *wulsa*, the people burying their valuables, and carrying with them a few days' grain—flying to the hills or the

* Page 18, Preface to Dow's Hindustan.

nearest fortress, and when the enemy remained longer than their supplies lasted, famine and death ensuing.

While we should all endeavour, abstaining from idle self-congratulations, to soften the rigour of the British yoke, it is only fair to our country to show that the English in India are not the monsters they are sometimes represented; and that,—although much remains to be done; many improvements to be made; many legislative enactments to be set forth, and *acted on;* much to be done, much to be *undone*—much for us to do, more for us to let alone,—we have less to learn than is generally thought from either our Mahommedan or Hindoo predecessors.

Lord Valentia fifty years ago travelled in a palankeen to Lucknow, and wrote a book in which he stated that the Moguls had roads or causeways from one end of their dominions to the other. Mr. Buckingham a quarter of a century afterwards declared, and in his time not untruly, that there was not a good road in India above Barrackpore—and still more recently we have heard a somewhat similar declaration made at a great public meeting in Calcutta. But let the period of our rule be counted, and let it be considered that it does not materially exceed the united length of the reigns of Aurungzebe and Akbar, and then let it be remembered that we have a trunk road from Calcutta to Delhi; a better road than the Moguls or the Romans ever had; and that not a district in India but has its branch roads, all doubtless more or less defective, wanting more or less bridges, ghats, seraes, wells, &c.; but still showing that some attention is now being paid to the important subject. Let any impartial person visit the Punjab, where he will scarcely see such a vehicle as a hackery, or throughout the country alight upon a road;* let him then travel to Oude, where his experiences

* Written before its annexation to the British territories.

will be similar, and then let him cross the Gogra and enter the Gorruckpoor District, not half a century in our hands. At once he will find himself in a country abounding with good roads, many of them bridged—and every year the number of bridges and other improvements are increasing. In this one district alone we doubt whether there are less than a thousand miles of road. We say let these comparisons be fairly made, and then let England be exempted from the vituperations and unfair comparisons with which she is sometimes assailed; and rather let those who would so assail her, honestly do their own work; and, however humble be an individual's sphere, no one of us but has the opportunity, if not of making a road, building a bridge, or a serai; at least of planting a tree, or of preserving one that is planted. But if even this small means is denied us, no poverty can prevent us from setting a good example to those around us, by showing all that come within our influence, that a Christian is not to be recognised only by wearing a hat and coat, and by attending neither at the mosque or the temple; but by purity of life and honesty of conduct.

But though compelled, in candour, to admit that without sword-government the British in India could not maintain their position, we feel strong in our hearts the conviction that one good magistrate may be better than a regiment; one sound law, well administered, better than a brigade: that civilians must co-operate with the military; that neither unaided could maintain our empire, but that a happy admixture of a just civil administration with the strong hand will retain the country in peace and happiness as long as it is good that we should hold it; and it is not by believing either ourselves or our laws all purity, or all corruption, that we are likely to come to a right understanding of what is best for India, but by a close study of its past history; of the mistakes, and the injustice of former rulers, Hindoo, Mahommedan, and European; and then by setting ourselves down, each in his own sphere, and honestly working out the details of a code honestly and ably prepared; not shifting and changing from day to day, but founded on experience; and suitable to a rude and simple people, who, like all people under the sun, prefer justice to law, and the speedy obtainment of their ends to eternal dangling about the precincts of dilatory courts.

But it behoves us, under every view of the case, to keep up our strength. Debility, the result of apathy and negligence, would be nothing short of a state of crime. There are few national, as there are few bodily ailments, which have not their seat in debility; and any very apparent symptoms of weakness in the dominant power, would, under the present combination of circumstances, plunge the country into a state of terrible disorder, and gird about with desolation every province in Hindoostan.

Let us see then what is our military strength—what are our means of national defence. Glance at the map,* and see the enormous expanse which the Indian Army is employed to protect—from Cape Comorin to the Sutlej; from Kurrachee to the Gulf of Martaban—a tract of country, containing, according to the calculations of the Surveyor-general's department, a gross area of 1,076,590 square miles, to which must be added some 25,000 on account of our recent acquisitions on the banks of the Indus. Our army has not only to protect from foreign aggression this immense territory; but also

* We may avail ourselves of this opportunity strongly to recommend Allen's Map of India. It is distinguished by accuracy of detail and great typographical excellence; and is, on the whole, the best and most convenient of all the maps of India which have been published.

H. M. L.

to coerce a population of not less than a hundred millions—many of them men of strong military, and others of stronger predatory habits—twenty millions of them Mussulmans—all feeling that they are under the yoke of the stranger. And, however lightly that yoke be imposed, we must know that, differing in colour, caste, language, habits—everything; having indeed nothing in common with our subjects, our rule can scarcely be a loved one. It has been declared, in prophetic language, that "Japhet shall live in the tents of Shem;" but may we not attach to the figure more of a military than of a pastoral charactor?

But what is this Indian army, called upon thus to defend this wide expanse of conquered territory? It consists of 159 regiments of Regular Infantry; 21 of Cavalry; 5 brigades of Horse Artillery; 14 battalions of Foot Artillery; and three regiments of Sappers and Miners. To these must be added about 40 Irregular corps of Cavalry and Infantry, officered from the line, to the extent of a commandant, a second-in-command, and an adjutant—the commanders of troops and companies being Russaldars and Soobadars. In round numbers we may say that our Indian army is something very near the following:—

Regular Infantry (European) . .	5,600	
——— (Native)	184,000	
Cavalry (Native)	10,200	
Artillery (European) . .	5,600	exclusive of Lascars.
——— (Native)	4,600	
Sappers and Miners (Native)	2,500	
Irregular corps*	30,000	
Total .	242,500	

* This rough estimate does not include all the several components of the Nizam's force, the Gwalior Contingent, and the Police Battalions.—H. M. L.

To these regiments are attached, according to the latest Army Lists of the several Presidencies, 5850 European officers. Such, with some approach to accuracy, for perfect accuracy is not easily attainable, is the extent of the Indian army. By this we must be understood to signify only the troops of the East India Company—but in calculating our means of national defence we must consider, in addition to these forces, the very important item of some 20 or 30 regiments of European Infantry and Cavalry, belonging to the army of Great Britain. The number of regiments thus employed in India varies according to the exigency of the times; at present there are in the three Presidencies, under the Company's rule, 29 regiments of Cavalry and of Infantry detached from the army of the Crown.

But the strength of an army does not depend upon its numbers, but on its efficiency: and the matter now to be considered is the means of turning the troops at our disposal to the best possible account. Let us show, after some rough fashion of our own—suggesting rather than elaborating—how this is to be done.

Our Engineer Corps can scarcely be so called. It is a regiment of officers, perhaps not surpassed in ability by any equal number of officers in the world; but they are too much employed as Civil Engineers; too little engaged during peace in the functions that would best prepare them for war; and still less so their few subordinates. Barrack-building and repairing, and account-keeping, are not the best preparatives for a campaign; and we know no inducement that the sappers, (all natives, except four serjeants to each company,) have for exertion, for the enlargement of their minds, or the study of engineering. The trigonometrical survey of Ireland was almost entirely conducted by the Royal Sappers; Non-Commissioned officers and privates doing all parts of the work. An engineer officer used the theodolite, but it was as often used by common sappers, as was the microscope on the base operations; and much of the mapping was done by them. We do not mean to say that every sapper was a Colby or an Everest; but that many, nay the majority, could read, and use all the instruments, and understood the construction of maps;—Why should it not be so with us? and why should not at least every serjeant and every native Non-Commissioned officer in our sappers be able to do as much? Our trigonometrical and our revenue surveys show how easily natives are to be taught surveying, and, if looked after, how well they can survey. Why, then, should not our sappers be employed on the surveys, on the canals, on the roads; not as coolies but *as workmen*, until qualified as supervisors; and then, as such, in positions graduated to their conduct and abilities? A company or more could be employed in the same neighbourhood, so that, at a day's notice, they could be ready for field service—how much more easily when already in the field, than when summoned from Delhi; and how much better qualified would officers and men be for any duties that they might be called on to perform, than as now, when coming from perfect idleness or from mere bricklayers' work. Not that these labours in the Barrack-master's department are without their uses; or that we object to sapper companies taking their turn in cantonments; but we do contend that field work, surveys, laying out of canals and roads, especially in hilly countries, draining of lands and so forth, are the employments to call out the powers of engineers, and to habituate them to do readily and quickly what, on vital occasions, may be required of them in the field. Every engineer should not only be able to make an accurate map, but should be also accustomed to rapid sketching, and practise to take in the features of a country; so that at a glance he can comprehend the strong and weak points of positions, the distances of points and their bearings on the one he occupies, or that the army is to take up. His subordinates of every grade should be qualified for some work or other, beyond that of the shovel, and while none should be ashamed to employ himself in throwing up the trench or the battery, many should be able to trace them out and superintend their construction.*

We would double, nay treble or quadruple, the sappers, and we would attach every engineer officer to them; not simply, as at present, a captain and a few of the youngest subalterns. We should then, with the instruction and employment above suggested, have a most valuable staff corps; most useful in peace, invaluable in war; and when we think how little is yet known of India, how few the roads that are passable throughout the year; that are laid out on scientific principles or kept in order on any plan; how few the canals; and how much those in use pay in revenue, as well as what a blessing they are to the lands through which they pass—when we consider what is wanted for the commerce and for the military purposes of the country, in roads and bridges, we shall find profitable work for many corps of sappers. In short, we may make their peace employments as useful to the Government and to the country as to themselves.

While on this subject, we may incidentally observe that, two years ago, Lord Ellenborough promised us a

* We need not point out to those who have much *worked* with natives, how peculiarly their talents fit them for all such duties as we have mentioned; the trace of the road from Serinugger (in Gurhwal) to Kedarnauth, marked out by a native under Mr. Trail's eye, would do credit to any engineer; and it is our opinion that if their moral qualifications were equal to their intellectual, there are native *elèves* of the trigonometrical survey fully competent to complete the work.—H. M. L.

military road from Simla to Mussourie; and the result has been that a single engineer officer took a glance at the line, and no more has been heard of the project. A road such as was projected would possibly have been impracticable—that is, its expense would have far exceeded its advantages; but still there is no possible reason why there should not be a military road from Kumaon to the Sutlej, passable for guns on mules and elephants—why the intervening streams should not be bridged, instead of, as at present, that the only good bridge, nominally on the line (that over the Jumna), should be really not on the line at all, but several miles off—so placed, as we are credibly informed, because the bank at that place offered a better abutment. When we have good roads through and up to our Hills, we shall find the value of them for our European soldiery—but on this subject we shall presently enlarge.

Our artillery officers receive much the same education as the engineers; though their course of study is a less extensive one. They receive, however, sufficient preparation in England to enable them at Dum-Dum to become excellent artillerists, which many of them are; and we owe it to their early education, and perhaps to their having no loaves ready baked for them—to their being obliged to work their own way to anything beyond a subaltern's birth with a company for eighteen years, and then the command of a foot battery, that we see more names among the Artillery as Persian and Hindustani scholars than in any other branch of the service.

The men are, as material—as machines, excellent; but few are much more. Some few good laboratory men are to be found among them—perhaps three or four in a company. Thirty or forty per cent. can read and write; but not one in a hundred studies his duty scientifically; and the obvious reason is, that he has not the shadow of a motive for so doing. If he can read and write and is decently sober, he is sure to become a serjeant. If he is smart at drill and well-behaved and not too independent, he may rise to be a serjeant-major. Or if his liver is sound, he may live to be a conductor, or even, at the age of seventy, a deputy commissary of ordnance. And so in the Golundauze: if he has taken care of himself and not expended his vital energies as a young man, he will live to be an old one; and when physically and mentally disqualified, he will become a soobadar, or even a soobadar bahadoor; and all this even though he may be very little deserving of such promotion. He has the negative merit of having outlived the companions of his youth, who possibly got maimed, or killed, or lost their health, when he who gained the palm, was absent from his post or shirking at it; but we are strongly of opinion that old age is *but* a negative virtue, and should not without positive merit be rewarded in soldiers; but that the young man should have some motive to emulate the veteran.

There is little objectionable in the artillery system, except its locations, its system of patronage, and its utter sacrifice of the interests and usefulness of the Foot Artillery to those of the mounted branch—Native Artillery is stationed at Almorah in the Hills: they dislike it, and are out of their element there. They should be replaced by Europeans. Large bodies of Golundauze should not be kept at Dum-Dum and at Cawnpore, serving as Infantry, without guns and without officers. *At least* half the European Artillery should be located in hill stations; and the weakly and sick men of the other half should be with them. Cherra Poonjee, Dargeling, Kumaon, Mussourie, Sobathoo,

Kussoulie, and the immediate neighbourhood of those places, would amply accommodate them all.

To each company of Golundauze should be attached three European serjeants and three corporals; and to every company, European and Native, there should not be less than two officers when in cantonments and three in the field. At present, while a single troop of Horse Artillery has three or four officers, and they remain with it for years, a company is lucky if it possesses one; and that one is sometimes changed two or three times within a year. We have often and often seen lads of a year's or two years' standing, going on service with two or four guns, and even with a company. Indeed the exception to the rule is, when a company of artillery proceeds on service under a captain, and then the chances are ten to one that he has been taken from the staff, or suddenly drawn from another end of the country to command men, on perhaps an emergency, that he never saw before; to take charge of stores and guns that he has not a day to inspect; and where, as a stranger, he knows not the good from the bad men, and has not only to do his own duty, but to be the laboratory man, and the everything-else for a time himself. The consequence of all this is, that our Foot Artillery is not at all what it might be, and that the Foot Artillery officers, though harder worked and worse paid, are often better artillerists, more practical, rough-and-ready men, than their Horse Artillery brethren. But the reward they look to, for making a bad company a good one—for redeeming drunkards into respectability, slovens into smart soldiers—is, to be removed from the company into a troop; and to throw back the poor fellows who have learnt to appreciate their exertions, to the tender mercies of an old officer who cares not for them, or to a young hand who is learning his own duty, and each of whom will possibly have gone his way before the year has expired. Such a system is cruel in the extreme to the men themselves, and most injurious to the service.* The men, as material, are much the same in both branches; the officers are the same; but whether it be the Golundauze and the Native Horse Artillery, or the European Horse and Foot Artillery, there is a woeful difference between the two branches, entirely owing to the different footing on which the two are placed, the standing they occupy, and the way they are officered. It is a dogma very staunchly upheld by some Horse Artillery officers—generally not the wisest of them—that their branch should be a close borough. We have heard some captains, who spent most of their subaltern days in the Foot, forgetful of this fact, uphold the absurdity. We, as dispassionate observers, always thought that if the Horse Artillery were to be a matter of patronage and profit, it should be given to the best artillery officers—to those who were best acquainted with and best performed their duty; who could ride, who could see, and who could hear. But too frequently we have seen all these requisites neglected, and very bad officers appointed simply through local interest; and as this is likely to continue the case as long as man is man, we should be glad to see the Foot Artillery on a full equality with the Horse as to all emoluments, equipment, and officering. It would be materially to

* We cannot too strenuously insist on this point. We have known companies of Foot Artillery to be, in the course of three or four months, commanded by as many officers. We have known subalterns to command one after the other—or perhaps two at a time—all the four companies of a battalion within six months; and we have known a battalion to be so destitute of officers that the four (now five) companies have fallen to the command of the adjutant. It is impossible that, under such a system, the officers can take any interest in their men, or that the men should place any confidence in their officers, who necessarily trust everything—even the promotions—to the pay-serjeant, who really commands the company.

the benefit of the service and to the advantage of the artillery regiment at large. All artillery officers should have Horse allowance and Cavalry pay, after they have joined batteries, and as long as present with them. All batteries should be horsed; the additional expense to be covered by reducing two guns from each of the Horse Artillery troops. Three 6-pounders and a 12-pounder howitzer well horsed, with—as at present—a double set of horses, all picked ones, no roarers and man-eaters to stop the team and vitiate the powers of the other five; but all steady first-rate cattle, accustomed to work with Cavalry on all sorts of ground; with every horse willing to work either as leader or in the shafts. Such batteries on the out-rider system would, on a long campaign, tell more effectually than the six guns under the present system; and it is not the least merit of the plan we propose that it would put at the head of troops the young and active captains, or at least men who did not seek such commands simply for the extra pay.

Our Foot Artillery batteries would then be on their proper footing; they would be well horsed with slow but stout cattle; they would be as well officered as the Horse Artillery; the officers would have no motive for change, and their men would soon feel and appreciate the difference, and be as smart and efficient as are now their mounted brethren. Our 9-pounder batteries, instead of, as at present, being considered incumbrances, would always be up in action with the infantry; and would perform all the service they are capable of, but which they are now seldom permitted to do. It is at any rate a sheer waste of money, to keep the whole Foot Artillery of India inefficient; it is waste of *money* now, we say; for we look on two well-equipped guns as more to the purpose than six ill-found ones. But what is waste and folly now may, if not rectified, cost life and treasure hereafter; nay, may cost us India: and most absurd does it seem that the one arm which our enemies all dread; which alone, from the days of Hyder Ally to those of Akbar Khan, they all acknowledge they cannot match—the arm which our own sepoys look to and rely on—is the one we most neglect; the one that is in fact left to Providence. We could point out innumerable instances; we will satisfy ourselves with one—the state of the single battery at Ferozepoor when the Cabul outbreak took place. For the two previous years we all know how many reports there had been of Seikh inroads and invasions, and yet in November, 1841, when half that battery was ordered to Peshawur, it had to borrow bullocks from the commissariat, and was sent under an officer not three years in the service. The battery was then under one of its many transitions; it had twice had horses and once camels, and we believe twice bullocks within two years; and of course when wanted for the field had no cattle at all; and the young officer who went with the detachment had not joined the company a month. The sooner such matters are mended the better: we should at least know by this time whether camels, bullocks, elephants, or horses are best for draught; and at any rate if experiments are to be tried, our exposed frontier stations are not the ones to dismantle, while the periodical mutations are in progress.*

We are amused to hear that it has been determined, to add a captain to each Infantry Regiment, but not to the Cavalry. If any branches of the service require officers and good ones, they are the native cavalry and native artillery. Either is almost useless without

* We are glad to hear that a mountain train is again likely to be equipped, and should be glad to see an elephant battery of six pounders added to a strong one of three, all placed with a couple of companies of Europeans at a hill station.—H. M. L. (1844).

officers; and yet the latter has only half the number that the European branch has; whilst the former is not thought to require as many as the infantry. Had we our will, there should be, in addition to a full complement of officers, half a dozen or more Europeans in every troop of native cavalry; say three serjeants and three corporals; men promoted for smartness and gallantry from the Dragoons and Horse Artillery. Such men, with two officers to every troop, would bring up a cavalry corps to the charge in the style in which it should be done. We should have no pausing to count the enemy; nor would the few European officers have to be casting in their minds whether their men would follow them; nor when the critical moment came would they have a doubt that, wherever they led, the corps would be at their heels.

But our Infantry must ever be our main-stay; if it is indifferent, the utmost efficiency in other branches will little avail. We are inclined to advocate the presence of two European officers with each company of every regular sepoy corps; but we would divide the Native Infantry into three classes; have a fourth of the army on the footing of the Khelat-i-giljee corps; and say an eighth forming a third class somewhat similar to the Khelat-i-giljees and the several contingents, but the officers commanding companies being solely natives; and from them should be selected commandants, seconds in command, and adjutants, for the corps formed and commanded by natives, one of which should be in every brigade to cause emulation and prevent suspicion; and, by a mixture of interests, interfere with combinations. We will presently offer a scheme for doing away with native officers in the regular corps; but would desire that all promotions to command of companies in the corps of the 2nd and 3rd class should be made from the Infantry at large.

Native officers have long since been voted useless. They are great incumbrances in war; they are nonentities in peace. Occasionally a lion-hearted old fellow of seventy will keep up with his company in a charge or on a forced march; but he forthwith dies of exhaustion, after having, perhaps for a year or more during the campaign, put the commissariat to the expense of carrying grain for him, three or four servants, a pony, and half or a whole camel. In quarters they have nothing to do but to brood over their position; to feel that they are nominally officers, and yet that the serjeant-major is liable to command them, and that beardless boys are every day put over them. At Vellore and elsewhere, they did not prevent or give warning of intended massacre and insurrection; nor have they in the late cases of the 60th, 34th, 64th, and of the Cavalry and Artillery, either given a clue to their officers of what was the real motive of discontent, or do they appear to have striven to prevent insubordination.

We conceive that the motive of Government in having three native officers attached to each company and troop—who have nothing to do, and whose ages may be said to average sixty-two—must be their supposed moral influence with the sepoys, and the encouragement given to the latter by placing before their eyes their kinsmen promoted to such grades, and living comfortably and in honour among them. If such be the reason, how much more potent would this moral influence be, if the old men were comfortably seated under their own neem or mangoe trees, talking to their grandchildren and to the wondering villagers gathered around them, of the beneficence of the Honourable

Company, instead of toiling in the hot winds on treasure parties, or vexing themselves under young European officers in petty and discomforting duties unsuitable to their age, in which, though they are present in person, they can scarcely be called performers.

We would fain see every soldier, European and Native, and every native officer, appear before a committee at fifty years of age, and be at once sent to the invalids, or remanded for five years' further duty, according to his health, after which time—that is, at latest after fifty-five years of age—no man should be allowed to remain with a regiment. European officers are less exposed than their men; the waste of vital energy is not so great: but we are not sure that our commissioned ranks might not benefit by some such weeding.

Allahabad, Chunar, and other fortresses, as well as all treasuries and magazines—both of which should *invariably* be within forts, or redoubts of some kind or other—should be garrisoned by invalids, supported by small detachments of regulars for night and exposed duties. Invalids should be sent to their homes at sixty years of age, *at latest;* or, as at present, earlier periods, when disabled by sickness or wounds.

No sepoy, not considered qualified to rise to be a soobadar, should be promoted beyond the rank of naick. Havildars should be promoted, in their turn, to the rank of jemadar, and if considered unfit for the active duties of a lieutenant (jemadar) of a company or troop, to be transferred to the garrison or home invalids, according to age and strength. Jemadars should rise by seniority to the rank of soobadar; but no native officer should be promoted to second in command but for distinguished conduct. Seconds should rise to commandants by seniority, subject of course to proof of continued good conduct. The adjutants of these native corps might be promoted at once from the rank of naick and havildar; and as jemadars rise in their turn to command, naicks being steady soldiers, but passed over as not being sufficiently smart for native officers, might be invalided (when worn out, or beyond age) as havildars.

The Garrison Invalid corps should in all respects be paid as troops of the line; the Home Invalids as at present; and all ranks and orders should understand that rates of pay will not be altered, that invalids will not be remanded (as has been the case) to regimental duty; and the rates of pay, rations, foreign allowance, &c., &c., should be as distinctly and fully laid down as possible, so that no excuse could be given for error or miscalculation on the subject.

We should then have three descriptions of Native Infantry; the first class, regular infantry, officered by a full complement of Europeans; the second class, partially so officered; the third class, commanded and officered entirely by natives—but the two last always employed in brigade, or at least in concert with the regular corps.

The native officers would then have definite duties, and not be too old to perform them. The old and worn-out veterans would be comfortably located in quarters, or enjoying themselves quietly at home. There would be less clashing of interests, more contentment, and greater efficiency, at perhaps a less expense than at present; for a much less number than seventy regular infantry regiments would suffice for Bengal, if we were to establish an increased number of such as form the Gwalior Contingent, supported again by a few commanded by such soldiers as old Mahommed Issoof.*

* The reader of Indian History will remember the commandant of the English sepoys, the famous Mahommed Issoof, who in the worst times of the Carnatic wars under Lawrence was the only person who could safely conduct our convoys through the enemy's country. We commend his

Let us not be met with an outcry about the attendant decrease of European officers. We know their value very well, but we know that there are many bad as well as many good ones; and we know that although, where sepoys have been taught to follow only Europeans, there should always be enough of the latter to ensure vacancies being filled up in action, as leaders fall; yet where men have not been so habituated, we see not why our sepoys should not be permitted to use the senses and the courage they possess, without on every occasion relying on the leading and the life of an individual. Shah Soojah's regiments behaved admirably in Affghanistan; and the discipline of Captain Mitchell's regiment of the old Gwalior Contingent was the admiration of beholders. Clive's, Lawrence's, and Coote's battalions had seldom with them more than three or four officers; and yet the deeds of those days are not surpassed by those of the present.

Our regular issue of pay, and our pension establishment, are the foundation-stones of our rule; and there cannot be a doubt that for the lower orders our service is a splendid one. But it offers no inducement to superior intellects, or more stirring spirits. Men so endowed, knowing they can always gain their bread in any quarter, leave us in disgust, and rise to rank in foreign services. Did the times avail, they would raise standards of their own, and turn against us the discipline they learnt in our ranks. Rank and competence in our service would bind such men to our interests. It is a straw that turns the current. Such men as Nadir Shah and Hyder Ally did not, at the outset, aim at sovereignty; their ambition increased with their suc-

history as narrated by Wilkes to our readers, and especially the detail (page 326, vol. i.) of the effect of injurious treatment and unjust suspicions on the conduct of this fine old Native soldier.—H. M. L.

cess, and what, early in life, would have contented them, was, at a later day, despised.

There are many commandants in the Mahrattah and Seikh service, who were privates in our army. General Dhokul Singh, now at Lahore, was a drill naick in one of our sepoy corps; and Rajah Buktawar Singh, one of the richest and most powerful men in Oude, was a havildar in our cavalry. But is it not absurd that the rank of soobadar major and russaldar major is the highest that a native can attain in a native army of nearly 300,000 men,—in a land, too, that, above all others, has been accustomed to see military merit rewarded, and to witness the successive rise of families from the lowest conditions, owing to gallantry in the field?

There is always danger in handling edged tools, but justice and liberality forge a stronger chain than a suspicious and niggardly policy. We hold that no place or office should be absolutely barred to the native soldier, although the promotion of every individual should be grounded on his individual merits, and the requisite cautions be taken that he should not be tempted beyond his strength. The grandsons of the Gauls who opposed Cæsar, were senators of Rome; and the Jye Singhs and Jeswunt Singhs led the Mogul armies; but it cannot be said that it was to any such liberality the empire of either Rome or Delhi owed its fall.

Whenever sepoys and Europeans know and understand each other, the utmost harmony exists between them; witness the 35th B. N. I. and H.M.'s 13th at Julalabad; and we remember many such cases of old. Indeed, it was only the other day that we heard a sepoy of the 26th N. I. say, "If we go on service, send with us Number Nine" (H.M.'s 9th, with which they were brigaded in Affghanistan). Such a spirit should be encouraged; and it would be well to attach permanently to each European regiment, while in India, a couple of companies, or more, of picked men, chiefly Mussulmans, and the lower tribes of military Hindus —these companies to act as the Auxiliaries and Velites did with the Romans. Let them be Light Infantry; and, as picked and honoured troops, receive some additional pay. We know that Europeans cannot march in India without a detachment of natives accompanying them, and that such duty, as at present performed, is much disliked. But placed on some such footing as above proposed, the service might be made a duty of honour, and the sepoys of such companies, working well with Europeans, would be almost equal in value to the latter. The system has been found to work well with the gun lascars attached to the European Artillery, even though they have not been cared for and made much of, as we would propose all natives so employed should be.

And now a few words on the subject of enlistment. Our sepoys come too much from the same parts of the country; Oude, the lower Dooab and upper Behar. There is too much of clanship among them, and the evil should be remedied by enlisting in the Saharunpoor and Delhi districts, in the hill regions, and in the Malay and Burmah States. We laugh at our hill men; but they are much the same class as form Rajah Golab Singh's formidable Jumboos. But what inducement do we offer to any but coolies to enter into the Simoor or Nussuree battalions, when we give the men only five rupees per month, proportionably pay Native officers, and calling the corps local battalions, have them one day at Bhurtpoor, the next at Ferozepoor? Such policy is very bad; and we should rather encourage the military classes in the Hills to enter all our corps. We would have, too, some companies or regiments of

Malays; of China-men; of Mhugs and Burmese; and mix them up at large stations with our sepoy corps. We would go further, and would encourage the now despised Eurasians to enter our ranks, either into sepoy corps where one or two here and there would be useful, or as detached companies or corps. We are aware that they are not considered a warlike race. We might make them so, and we doubt not, with good officers, could do so. Courage goes much by opinion; and many a man behaves as a hero or a coward, according as he considers he is expected to behave. Once two Roman Legions held Britain; now as many Britons might hold Italy.

There is no doubt that whatever danger may threaten us in India, the greatest is from our own troops. We should, therefore, while giving no cause of discontent; while paying them well and regularly providing for them in their old age; while opening a wide field for legitimate ambition; and rewarding, with promotion, medals, jagheers, gallantry and devotion; abstain from indiscriminately heaping such rewards upon men undeserving of them; and we should at all times carefully avoid giving anything or doing anything, under an appearance of coercion, on the demand of the soldiery. The corps that under General Pollock misbehaved at Peshawur, should at least have been denied medals. Had they been so, possibly we should have been spared late events on the N. W. Frontier and in Scinde; and we should remember that every officer is not fitted for command, much less to command soldiers of a different religion and country; and that where, as has repeatedly of late years been shown, regiments were found to be going wrong through the weakness or the tyranny of their commanders—it matters not whether from too much strictness or too little—full enquiry should at once be made and remedial measures instituted. If commanders cannot manage their regiments, they should be removed from them, and that quickly, before their corps are irremediably destroyed. How much better would it be to pension, and to send to England, such men as we have in command of some corps, than to allow them to remain a day at the head of a regiment to set a bad example to their men. We could, at this moment, point out more than one commander answering our description; and we would seriously call the attention of those in high places to the injury that even one such officer may commit. He may drive a thousand men into discontent, and that thousand may corrupt many thousands—and all this may be done by a man without any positive evil in him; but simply because he is not a soldier, has not the feelings of a soldier; frets the men one day, neglects them the next: and is known by them all to care for nothing beyond his personal interests and his own hisab-kitab.

Before leaving this subject of the Native Army, we must devote a few sentences to one of its most important components, of which we have made no specific mention. The Irregular Cavalry is a most useful branch of the service, doubly so as providing for military classes that do not fancy our regular service. But we much doubt whether we adopt the best method of keeping up the efficiency of the Irregulars, which are our light horse; but which we encumber, as we do all other branches, with officers, and even privates, of sixty and even seventy years of age. We are not sure that we could not point out many native officers very much above seventy; and we once heard a commandant of one of these corps say his old men were his smartest—no great compliment to the quality of his young ones. But the fact is, that the purwustee system is more injuriously employed in the Irregular Horse than in any other branch of the army; though generally from kind and good motives. In times of peace these corps are little thought of, have nothing to do, are on small outpost duty, or, where collected, are entirely under their commander's authority and eye; but in service they are cruelly and often recklessly knocked about and exposed; no one has pity on them, and their own officers have therefore need the more to care for them. Mostly Patans or Rajpoots and Mahommedans of family, they are men of expensive habits, are almost all involved, and, from a system that has gradually crept in, they do not (generally) receive the pay allowed them by Government; that is to say, every man entering, in (we believe) seven out of the nine corps, has not only to purchase his horse and equipments, but to pay one hundred and fifty rupees or thereabouts to the estate or family of the man whose decease or invaliding created the vacancy. Such donation of course throws the recruit at once into the money-lender's hands, and often leaves him for life a debtor. If the man again has not the cash to purchase a horse, he rides one belonging to a Native officer or to some privileged person, and becomes what is called his bargeer—the soldier receiving only seven or eight rupees a month, and the owner of the horse the balance of the twenty allowed by Government.

There is much in all this and in the Kutchery and Banking system, prevalent in almost every corps (and without which, so deep-rooted is the evil, few Irregular regiments could now take the field), that requires gradual amendment, for while Government pays twenty rupees a month to each man, it is calculated, one with another, that the men do not receive above sixteen; and consequently, as far as efficiency is concerned, they are as if they received only that much pay; and when called on for service, instead of having a stock to draw on to render them efficient, they have to call on their banker; and enter more deeply into his books.

We have heard officers say that but for these bankers they did not know how they could have taken their corps on service; and we know how much trouble, vexation, and expense, has often been incurred by commanders, to render their regiments efficient. But whatever be the motive—and we believe that in the Irregular Horse it is a very good one—that makes close boroughs of corps, bringing into them only the sons and nephews of those already enlisted, when better men are candidates, the result is bad; and it is worse still, that such fines should be paid at starting as tend to shackle the troopers for life. So great is the evil that we consider that Government would do well to redeem all debts as they now stand and forbid the system for the future; and peremptorily order the service to be thrown open to candidates out of the several regiments, being men of respectability and bringing their own horses or able to purchase that of the man who created the vacancy. The fine we have mentioned is in some corps put on the price of the horse, so that the recruit, instead of one hundred and twenty-five rupees, has to pay two hundred and seventy for his charger.

The consequence of all this is, that we have not the horses, and often not the men, in the Irregular Cavalry, that we might have for the twenty rupees per month paid by Government. It is only justice to the Irregulars to say that it is wonderful what they have done on service, in spite of their old men and their small, poor horses; but having done well with little means, they would assuredly do better under a more encouraging system. The Poona Horse, we understand, receive thirty rupees per month, and they are a most efficient body. The matter of pay and equipment of the Irregulars requires serious attention; bad Cavalry are worth little, and we would prefer five regiments of first-rate, to ten of indifferent, quality.

As our army is constituted, the Irregular Horse is the only outlet for the native gentry. Every day it becomes less so, while recruiting is restricted to dependants of those already in the service. Lord Ellenborough's project of adding a portion of Irregulars, on increased pay, to the Body-guard was a wise measure; and we should be glad to see still further encouragement held out to gallantry and devotion. A Rassalah in each regiment might be formed from men who had distinguished themselves, each man of such troop receiving four or five rupees additional monthly pay. We would also give the command of half the Irregular corps to Native officers; such commanders, with their seconds and adjutants, to be selected for gallantry and good conduct; two brigades, each of two such corps, might be formed in the Bengal presidency; one stationed at Umbala, the other at Cawnpore; to be commanded by a brigadier under the Native title of Bukshee with a brigade-major under the designation of Naib—these two (European) officers not interfering in regimental details, further than paying the men and sanctioning promotions—the Bukshees and Naibs to be officers selected from present commandants. The system, we are convinced, would work well as giving objects of ambition to the more adventurous spirits. And having two good European officers with them, there would always be a check on the conduct of the Native commanders, who, we believe, would feel pride in keeping their corps in as efficient a state as those commanded by European officers.

But after all, what could we do without the European portion of the army?—useless of course by itself; but without which all else would soon pass from our hands. And yet how do we repay the gallant hearts that daily bleed for us, that daily sink and expire in a foreign land, uncared for and unpitied? We chiefly allude to the Company's European troops, but much will apply to Her Majesty's. How little is done, or at least how much more might be done, for the comfort and happiness of the men, and by the saving of their lives, for the pockets of Government!

In the first place, we consider that Fort William is about the worst station in India for Europeans,—especially for new comers. We would therefore see H. M. Regiments at once proceed up the country; and throughout India would have the Europeans, as far as possible, on the Hills, not keeping a man more than absolutely necessary on the plains. Three-fourths of the European Infantry and Foot Artillery and one-half of the Dragoons and Horse Artillery might easily be established on the Hills; and of the corps at Fort William, Madras, and Bombay, all the weakly men should be at Cherrah Poonjee or Darjeeling; or at the sanataria of the other presidencies. Nature has given us chains of hills in all directions, not only east and west, but through Central India, that would enable us to have moderately-cool stations in every quarter; and when the expense in life and in death of Europeans on the present system is considered; when it is remembered that every recruit costs the Government one thousand rupees, or £100; that barracks, with tatties and establishments and hospitals, must be kept up at great expense, and that with all appliances the life of an European is most miserable, how clear it is, that we should alter the old system, and, following the laws of nature, avail ourselves of the means and localities at our disposal that enable us, at a much less expense, to keep up our Europeans in double their present efficiency in the Hills; entailing, it is true, a certain first outlay, but which would be soon covered by the saving of life and the reduction in establishments, rations, &c. If Lord Ellenborough had done nothing else in India, he would deserve well of his country for establishing three European stations on the Hills. Three more may easily be so placed on the Bengal presidency; and the proportion of Artillery and Cavalry we have mentioned be posted there. But we must have good roads and ample means of conveyance on all the routes and rivers leading to such locations; we must have a certain proportion of carriage kept up; and have our rivers covered with boats, and among them many steamers.

We would advocate the employment, or permission to employ themselves, of half the Europeans on the Hills as handicrafts, in agriculture, trade, &c. A large proportion of the household troops are so employed in London; and yet the Guards of England have never been found wanting. Rations, establishments and barracks in half quantities would thus only be required; and perhaps a portion of the pay of men so employed would in time be saved. Small grants of land, too, might be given on the Hills or in the Dhoon to European invalids of good character, on terms of military service within a certain distance; or on terms of supplying a recruit, for seven or ten years, to a European corps.

Three-fourths of the European children, who now die in the barracks on the plains, would live on the Hills, and would recruit our corps with stout healthy lads, such as may be seen in Mr. Mackinnon's school at Mussouree, instead of the poor miserable parboiled creatures, that we see as drummer boys throughout the service.

The Chunar establishment bodily moved to the Mussourie neighbourhood would be an incalculable benefit and blessing. Indeed, it is marvellous that the cruelty of such a location as Chunar for European invalids has not been oftener brought to notice, and that the hottest rock in India has been permitted to continue to this day as a station for European invalids.

All that we have mentioned is not only feasible but easy; and we doubt not that all the expense which would be incurred by the change of locations and abandonment of barracks would be cleared by the several savings within seven years. We must walk before we can run; and we therefore only advocate roads, *metalled* roads, to each hill station; but we hope and expect soon to see railroads established on each line, so that in twelve hours the corps from Kussowlee, Sobathoo, and Mussourie could be concentrated at Delhi. Great as would be the first outlay on such rails, we are well satisfied that they would pay; and who can calculate the benefit of being at once able to keep our Europeans in a good climate, and, at the rate of twenty or thirty miles an hour, to bring them to bear upon any point? We should then realize Hyder Ally's notion, and really keep our Europeans in cages ready to let slip on occasions of necessity.

Every inducement should be held out to our European soldiers to conduct themselves as respectable men and good Christians. Reading-rooms and books in abundance should be provided: all sorts of harmless games encouraged; the children of all on the plains be sent to the Hills, and placed in large training establishments, where boys and girls might (separately) be instructed in what would make them useful and respectable in their sphere of life; and be taught from the beginning to stir themselves like Europeans, and not with the listlessness (as is usual in the barracks) of Asiatics.

We cannot write too emphatically on this most important branch of our subject. The morality of our European army in India is a matter which should engage the anxious attention not only of the military enquirer, but of every Christian man—every friend of humanity in the country. It is not simply a question of the means of making good soldiers; but of the means of making good men, and *therefore* good soldiers. We do not judge the European soldier harshly, when we say that the average standard of barrack morality is very low, for we cheerfully admit, at the same time, that the temptations to excess are great; the inducements to good conduct small; the checks wholly insufficient. It would be a wonder of wonders, if, neglected as he is, the European soldier were to occupy a higher place in the scale of Christian morality, but whatever he may have to answer for, it is almost beyond denial that the responsibilities of the officer are far greater than his own. The soldier's sins of commission are not so heavy as the officer's sins of omission, from which they are the direct emanations. The moral character of a regiment, be it good or bad, fairly reflects the amount of interest taken by the officers in the well-being of their men. The soldier wanders out of garrison or cantonment and commits excesses abroad, because he has no inducements to remain within the precincts of the barrack square. He goes abroad in search of amusement—and he finds not amusement but excitement; he makes his way to the village toddy-shop, or to the punch-house; he seeks other haunts of vice; and when both money and credit are gone, perhaps he takes to the high road. This would not happen, if regimental officers really did their duty to their men.* It is not merely the duty of an officer to attend parade, to manœuvre a company or regiment, to mount guard, to sanction promotions, to see the pay issued, to sign monthly returns, and to wear a coat with a standing collar. The officer has higher duties to perform; a duty to his sovereign; a duty to his neighbour; a duty to his God, not to be discharged by the simple observance of these military formalities. He stands *in loco parentis;* he is the father of his men; his treatment of them should be such as to call forth their reverence and affection; and incite in them a strong feeling of shame on being detected by him in the commission of unworthy actions. It is his duty to study their characters; to interest himself in their pursuits; to enhance their comforts; to assist and to encourage, with counsel and with praise, every good effort; to extend his sympathy to them in distress; to console them in affliction—to show by every means in his power, that though exiles from home and aliens from their kindred, they have yet a friend upon earth, who will not desert them. These are the duties of the officer—and duties too which cannot be performed without an abundant recompense. There are many idle, good-hearted, do-nothing officers, who find the day too long, complain of the country and the climate, are devoured with ennui, and living between excitement and reaction, perhaps, in time sink into hypochondriasis—but who would, if they were to follow our advice, tendered not arrogantly but affectionately, find that they had dis-

* The wives of the officers have also a duty to perform; and the moral influence which they might exercise is great. Some ladies are willing to acknowledge this, not merely in word, but in deed.—To all would we say "*Go and do likewise.*" It is possible that in a future article we may enlarge upon this subject.

covered a new pleasure; that a glory had sprung up in a shady place; that the day was never too long, the climate never too oppressive; that at their up-rising and their down-sitting serenity and cheerfulness were ever present—that in short they had begun a new life, as different from that out of which they had emerged, as the sunshine on the hill-top from the gloom in the abyss. Some may smile—some may sneer—some may acknowledge the truth dimly and forget it. To all we have one answer to give, couched in two very short words—*Try it.*

We need scarcely enter into minute details to show the manner in which this is to be done.' Every officer knows, if he will know, *how* it is to be done. The youth of a month's standing in the army, endowed with ordinary powers of observation, must perceive that there are fifty ways open to his seniors, by which they may advance the well-being and happiness of the inmates of the barracks. Let them see, think, and act, as men endowed with faculties and understandings; and we shall hear no more of that intense longing after transportation to a penal settlement, which has of late possessed many of our soldiers and urged them to the commission of capital offences. Does not this one fact declare trumpet-tongued the misery of a barrack life in India—does it not pronounce the strongest condemnation on those, who make no effort to shed a cheering light upon the gloomy path of the exiled soldier?

But we must do something more than alleviate the sufferings of the present—we must render him hopeful of the future; we must brighten up his prospects; animate him with a new-born courage; fill him with heart and hope that he may "still bear up and steer right on," until better days shall dawn upon him; and the wretchedness and humilitation of the past shall have a subduing influence in the retrospect, and shall lift up his soul with devout feelings of gratitude and love.

The commissioned ranks of the army should not be wholly closed against the deserving soldier in the Company's service, more than in the Queen's. There are no English regiments, which contain so many young men of family and education, as the few European corps and battalions in the army of the East India Company; and we should be truly glad to see the present great paucity of officers in the Native Army, in some degree, remedied by the appointment to each regiment of Cavalry and Infantry, and battalion or brigade of Artillery, and to the corps of Engineers, an ensign or second-lieutenant from the Non-Commissioned ranks; and that henceforth a fourth or fifth of the patronage of the army should be appropriated to the ranks.

For such promotion, we should select in some such fashion as the following. Let examination committees be held at Calcutta, Cawnpore, and two of the Hill stations twice a year; let any European soldier that wished appear before it; and having passed some such examination as is required at Addiscombe, substituting a course of history and geography, and what by late orders is required in Hindustani before officers can hold Companies, for some of the Addiscombe requisites; let such men be held eligible for commissions in the Engineers and Artillery, and those passing in Hindustani and in a more limited course of mathematics for the Cavalry and Infantry; but before any man received a commission, he should have served one year as a Sergeant Major, Quarter-Master Serjeant or Colour Sergeant, or as a Sub-Conductor, and produce a character for sobriety and good conduct and general smartness as a soldier.

With such a stimulus what might not our European soldiery become? The educated and unfortunate, instead of being our worst characters, would be inspired with hope, while many would wipe away the stain of early misconduct, and, by recovering their characters and position, bring peace to their bereaved families. By the infusion, too, of a different class into our covenanted service, we should all be more put on our metal; and in fact not only would the whole tone and position of the *Gora-log* be elevated, but their rise would in a certain degree raise the European character throughout the country. As Secretary-at-War, our present Governor-General * did much for the British soldier; he thoroughly understands their wants, and by his acts he has proved that he does not consider that they should be shut out from hope. We beseech his good offices on behalf of the European soldiers of India—the majority of them exiles for life; and when we consider the effect of character everywhere, the moral influence of one honest, of one good and zealous man, who would lightly discard any means of raising the tone of our Europeans? Too lamentable is the effect of their present misconduct, of their drunkenness, their violence, their brutality, for us to deny that the present system does not answer, and that it calls loudly for change. Every individual European, be he officer or private soldier, we look on as in his sphere a missionary for good or for evil. We have hinted that one indifferent commanding officer may ruin a whole corps. The experience of many will furnish an example. From violence, injustice, meanness, or indifference—from seeds of different sorts the equally baneful fruit is produced, discipline is undermined, discontent engendered, and misbehaviour and its train ensues.

On the other hand, what may not one Christian soldier do? However lowly his position, how much has he not within his power? The man who, a Christian at heart,

* The late Lord Hardinge.

devotes himself to his duties, and, vexing neither himself nor those under him with harassing frivolities, perseveringly acts up to what he believes his duty—not with mere eye or lip service, but as evincing his love to God by performing his duty to man—such a man will not be the one to quail in the hour of danger; his shoulder is ever at the wheel, whether it be in the dull duties of cantonment, the trying times of sickness and famine, or the exhilarating days of success; all will find him cheerful, all will find him at his post.

We fear there is still a very common under-estimate of military character and military duty. The philosophical moralist who calls the soldier a mere licensed murderer; the Epicurean who only wonders at the madness of men who consent to stand and be shot at, when they could get their bread in some pleasanter way; the narrow-minded Christian, who thinks of soldiers and their possible salvation in the same dubious tone as Corporal Trim, when he asked "a negro *has* a soul, an please your honour?" and the country gentleman who pronounces on the blockhead or blackguard among his sons, that "the fellow is fit for nothing but the church or the army," all, all, are equally wide of the mark. A soldier—it is a trite commonplace, we know, but, like many trite commonplaces, often forgotten—is not necessarily a man who delights in blood, any more than a physician is one who delights in sickness. Both professions will cease with human crime and misery. The prophecies that hold out to us a prospect of the days, when "nation shall not lift up sword against nation, neither shall they learn war any more," tell us likewise of that period, when "none shall say I am sick."

We may refresh our spirits by the contemplation of these promises, and pray for the coming of that kingdom; but our own personal duty lies under a different order of things. War is probably the sorest scourge with which our race is visited; but constituted as the world is, a good army is essential to the preservation of peace. Military discipline at large comes not within the province of individual soldiers; but if every man who enlists took care that there was *one* good soldier in the army, our commanders would have easy work.

No man attains to excellence in any design without setting before him a lofty standard, and Christianity, where it is more than a name, incites us always to take the highest. It is no easy slipshod system of shuffling about the world; but "up and be doing," is the Christian's motto. Cecil's opinion was that "a shoe-black, if he were a Christian, would try to be the best shoe-black in the whole town."

There is some grave defect in our religious instruction, which almost every one feels, when he awakens to the importance of the world to come. Somehow, the duties of time and the duties of eternity, instead of being inseparably blended, present themselves to the mind, as Dr. Johnson expresses it, "as set upon the right hand and upon the left, so that we cannot approach the one without receding from the other;" and the consequence is, that while some take one side, to the neglect of the other, the majority pass quietly between the two, on the broad road of self-pleasing. The great problem to be solved is, how we may put the soul of high principle and imperishable aim, into the body of our daily acts, small as well as great, as the quaint but delightful old poet George Herbert tells us—

> "The man who looks on glass,
> On *it* may stay his eye;
> Or if he pleaseth, through it pass,
> And then the heavens espy."

Applying these general remarks to military duties; we desire to see every soldier set before himself a lofty standard; remembering that if high qualities and high principles are requisite in the man who would lead and influence his countrymen, they must be more so in the European who would gain the affections of a race differing from him in colour, language, and religion. Mindful of their own religious observances, the Hindoo and Mahommedan soldier, far from despising their Christian officer, will respect him the more, on seeing that he has a religion; and the rudest of them will appreciate the man, who, first in the fight—first in the offices of peace—is staunch to the duty he owes to his God.

The Apostle Paul, of whom Paley, no bad judge, says, that "next to his piety he is remarkable for his *good sense*," when he speaks figuratively of the Christian warfare, gives some of the best maxims for the literal warrior; he lays down, "holding fast a good conscience" as indispensable to "warring a good warfare," and tells us that "a good soldier" must "endure hardness." That religion unfits a man to be a soldier, is a maxim that may be placed in the same category as that marriage spoils one. Both assertions arise from misapprehension of what a soldier, a Christian, and a married man, ought to be. We have quoted an Apostle, let us now refer to a Poet—

"Who is the happy warrior? who is he*
That every man in arms should wish to be?
* * * Who, doomed to go in company with pain
And fear and bloodshed, miserable train;
Turns his necessity to glorious gain;
In face of these doth exercise a power
Which is our human nature's highest dower;
Controls them and subdues, transmutes, bereaves
Of their bad influence and their good receives:
By objects which might force the soul to abate
Her feelings, rendered more compassionate;
Is placable—because occasions rise
So often that demand such sacrifice;
More skilful in self-knowledge, even more pure,
As tempted more; more able to endure,

* Wordsworth's Happy Warrior.

As more exposed to suffering and distress;
Thence also more alive to tenderness.
—'Tis he whose law is reason; who depends
Upon that law as on the best of friends;
Whence in a state where men are tempted still
To evil for a guard against worse ill,
And what in quality or act is best
Doth seldom on a right foundation rest,
He fixes good on good alone and owes
To virtue every triumph that he knows:
Who if he rise to station of command,
Rises by open means; and there will stand
On honourable terms or else retire;
And in himself possess his own desire;
Who comprehends his trust, and to the same
Keeps faithful with a singleness of aim;
And therefore does not stoop, nor lie in wait
For wealth and honours, or for worldly state;
Whom they must follow, on whose head must fall
Like showers of manna if they come at all:
Whose powers shed round him in the common strife,
Or mild concerns of ordinary life,
A constant influence, a peculiar grace;
But who, if he be called upon to face
Some awful moment to which Heaven has joined
Great issues good or bad for human kind,
Is happy as a Lover, and attired
With sudden brightness, like a man inspired;
And, through the heat of conflict, keeps the law
In calmness made, and sees what he foresaw;
Or if an unexpected call succeed,
Come when it will, is equal to the need.
He who, though thus endued as with a sense
And faculty for storm and turbulence,
Is yet a soul whose master bias leans
To home-felt pleasures and to gentle scenes;
Sweet images! which, wheresoe'er he be,
Are at his heart; and such fidelity
It is his darling passion to approve,
More brave for this, that he hath much to love.

* * * * *

Whom neither shape of danger can dismay,
Nor thought of tender happiness betray—

* * * * *

This is the happy warrior, this is he
Whom every man in arms should wish to be."

We would willingly quote the whole of this noble Poem, but as space forbids, we can but recommend every soldier to read it in the volume from which it is taken. We wish the same hand that drew the warrior had given us a picture of a fitting wife for him.

That neither piety nor domestic affection* spoil a soldier, we see in both classes and individuals. The Puritans and Covenanters fought and suffered as bravely as if they had owned their be-all and their end-all here, and the history of America testifies† to the fact that the Winthrops, the Williamses, and others, while most loveable in all the relations of life, were as brave, and daring as were the ruffian bands of Cortes and Pizarro. And where does History show such bright examples of genuine heroism, as in the persons of the royalists of La Vendée—in Lescure; in Henri Larochjacqueline; in their brave and devoted associates, who, with hearts full of love towards God and the tenderest domestic affections, rushed from the village church, or started from their knees on the greensward, to stem with their rude phalanxes the disciplined battalions of the National Guard, and met death on the field with the serenity and constancy of Christian martyrs?

Washington's life is better than a hundred homilies; it may offer an useful lesson to the martinet. How clearly it shows what integrity, good sense, and oneness of purpose may effect. The simple land-surveyor by his energy and honesty keeping together the ragged and unwilling militia of the States, training and accustoming them to victory, and, having performed his work, retiring to private life, is an example that even Britons may set before themselves; but we want not good and great soldiers of our own land,—who more

* Was Hector or was Paris the better soldier? There is no finer illustration—though unintentional—of the difference between the military husband and the military bachelor than in the pages of the Iliad. The hero of the Odyssey, too, is drawn as one eminent in all the domestic relations. Turning from Poetry to History, what character of antiquity, drawn in the breathing pictures of Plutarch, is more admirable than that of Agesilaus?

† See Bancroft's History of the United States, *passim:* a most interesting and instructive work, published at Boston.

so than Hampden, Colonel Gardiner, Admiral Collingwood, and a host of others?

But a soldier, though always ready for the fight, is not always fighting; and the beauty of right principles, and exalted aims, is, that they need not the stimulus of a concussion to arouse them, but are operative in the daily and hourly details of life. It is here that a Christian soldier shines, as much as in the conflict; and it would be difficult to overestimate the influence and utility of a *good* (using the word in its widest sense) commanding officer in the barracks and the field. Devoting himself to his profession, he will have an interest in every man under him; his example will check the dissolute, encourage the good, and confirm the wavering. A king among his subjects, a father among his family, a master among his pupils, a physician among his patients—the officer's position partakes of the power, the responsibility and the interest of all these positions. A living homily himself, he aids by his example and influence the labours of those appointed to teach and preach; having cultivated his own mind, he tries to bestow the blessings of intellect on those under him; having studied the feelings and circumstances of his men, he can estimate their temptations, and determine the best means of helping them out of vice, and into virtuous habits. Above all, he works not for self-gratification, or outward applause. He has before him a rule of right, a hope of reward, independent of present success; and therefore is he able to persevere against obloquy and failure, to go straight forward, "doing with all his might whatever his hand findeth to do."

But we must return to our military details. We had purposed to have offered some remarks on the different branches of the Staff: but our limits are already nearly exhausted. What we have said regarding the Engineers applies even more strongly to the Quarter-Master-General's Department; at best but the shadow of an Intelligence Corps, consisting as it does of eight or ten officers, and they not selected for peculiar qualifications, as linguists and surveyors, and not having any permanent establishment of non-commissioned officers or privates under them. In fact, it may be said that with more need for an Intelligence Department than any army in the world, we are worse supplied than any other. A handful of officers, however well qualified, does not form an establishment or department; and it is a cruelty to impose on officers important duties, involving often the safety of armies, without placing efficient means at their disposal.

When the Army of the Indus assembled at Ferozepoor in 1838, we are credibly informed that Major Garden, the deputy quarter-master-general, about to proceed in charge of his department with the expedition, had not a single European at his disposal; and not a dozen clashies. Three officers were then appointed, without any experience as intelligencers, and altogether it may be said that the army marched, as if it did not require information; as if the commander had perfect maps of the country, and had some special means, independent of the legitimate channel, for acquainting himself with what was going on in his front and on his flanks. The exertions of Major Garden are well known; and if he had been shot, as he possibly might have been any morning, the Bengal Division at least would have been without a Quarter-Master-General's Department. Colonel Wild, it is well known, was sent in December, 1841, on perhaps as difficult and hazardous an undertaking as has, for many years, been entrusted to an officer of his rank; with four Regiments of Native Infantry and one hundred Irregular Cavalry; a Company of Golundauze without guns, and one of Sappers (the two latter being under officers of less than two years' standing), and without staff of any kind—Quarter-Master-General's, or Commissariat Department. A regimental officer was for the occasion appointed brigade-major; and with him began and ended the staff of Brigadier Wild, who, had he had half a dozen guns and as many good staff officers, might have reached Jellalabad early in January, 1842; and have thereby, perhaps, averted the final catastrophe at Cabul. To this it may be added, that *two days before* the battle of Maharajpore, extra establishments were ordered for officers in the field.

These are recent instances of defects in our military organization, and misapplication of the means at our disposal; but the experience of our military readers will tell them, each in his own line and from his own reminiscences, how often an apparently trifling deficiency has vitiated the exertions of a detachment. Only last December, or January (1843–44), all Oude was alarmed by the report of a Nepalese invasion, and *then* individuals were called upon to lend horses to move the guns at Lucknow; and scarce twelve months before, when a small party was beaten at Khytul in the Seikh States within forty or fifty miles of Kurnaul,—one of our Army Division stations—it was three days before a small force could move; it was *then* found that there was no small-arm ammunition in store, and ascertained that a European corps could not move under a fortnight from Sobathoo.

At that time, when both Kurnaul and Ambala were denuded of troops; and every road was covered with crowds of armed pilgrims returning from the Hurdwar Fair; the two treasuries containing, we have heard, between them, not less than thirty lakhs of rupees, were under parties of fifty sepoys in exposed houses or rather sheds close to the Native towns; and, extraordinary as it may appear, *both* within fifty or a hundred yards of small forts in which they would have been comparatively safe; but into which, during the long years that treasuries have been at those stations, it seems never to have occurred to the authorities to place them.

The treasury at Delhi is in the city, as is the magazine; the latter is in a sort of fort,—a very defenceless building, *outside* of which in the street, we understand, a party of sepoys was placed, when the news of the Cabul disasters arrived. We might take a circuit of the country and show how many mistakes we have committed, and how much impunity has emboldened us in error; and how unmindful we have been that what occurred in the city of Cabul, may, some day, occur at Delhi, Benares, or Bareilly.

It needs not our telling that improvements are required in the Commissariat. We observe that Ramjee Mull, who was a man of straw in the department at Bhurtpoor in 1824, died at Delhi, the other day, worth twenty-four lakhs of rupees; and not long since one of the Calcutta papers gave a biographical sketch of Mr. Reid, who in 1838 was a hungry omedwar, and in 1843 died worth about two lakhs of rupees, having been in the receipt of a salary amounting to perhaps one hundred and fifty or two hundred rupees per month. We recollect being amused by the naïve expression that his gains were all honestly made. It is just possible that Ramjee Mull's were so: but we look on it as something highly improper that Mr.

Reid, a salaried public servant, should have made anything beyond his pay. He took contracts, but he should not have been allowed to do so; and in taking them he was only entering into partnership with Native Gomashtahs or Principals, such as Ramjee Mull, Doonee Chund, &c., who, by combining, raised their charges on Government; and it is clear that, in so participating or even in being a contractor on his own bottom, he became useless as an assistant to the Commissariat officer in checking fraud on the part of other subordinates.

We have repeatedly seen the charge of a batch of camels on ten rupees per month preferred by an indolent Mootusuddee to a quiet one of thirty or forty rupees; the inference is, that they have a percentage on the grain of the animals; and so it is throughout the establishment; and low rates of pay only are authorized. Commissariat officers are actually in the power of their subordinates; they have not the means of paying respectable men, and being generally called on suddenly, they are, in self-defence, thrown on their monied dependants or hangers-on.

The whole establishment requires reform. The few European officers are now no check on the subordinates; they are, indeed, often screens; and it sometimes occurs that a gentleman-like, inexperienced officer, considers it a personal offence to have it proved that his gomashta watered the grog, or served out short grain. Commissariat officers should be carefully chosen, and should then be armed with sufficient authority to do their duty efficiently. They have now just power enough to do harm—none to do good, unless they are bold enough to risk their own prospects, and even character. A commissariat officer may easily starve an army and yet bear no blame; but if he saves a detachment from starvation and loses his vouchers, or, under extreme difficulties, if he has failed to procure them, he is a ruined man. Oh, how much more in this, as in every other, department, are forms looked to rather than realities; and how much does Government seem to prefer being robbed according to the usual forms, than to act on the plain principles of common sense that would actuate the same Government taken individually instead of in its collective character!

But we must draw our remarks to a conclusion, first briefly recapitulating our recommendations:—

1st. To increase the Engineer regiment, and to make it the nucleus of a General Staff Corps, available in peace for all Civil Engineering operations—giving all ranks opportunities to qualify themselves for field duties, and by having acquired intimate acquaintance with the language, habits, and manners of the people, and the features of the country; by giving them habits of enquiry, and practice in such duties as they may be called on to perform during war.

An immediate increase to the Engineers might be made by volunteers from the Line and Artillery—all ranks of such volunteers passing an examination in the requisite scientific points. They might then, according to standing, be drafted into the present Engineer corps, or form a new regiment of two, three, or more battalions.

We advocate the more efficient officering of the Foot Artillery, its elevation to an equality with the Horse Artillery—or at least that the latter should not be unduly cared for to the neglect of the former.

The Regular Cavalry should have some smart European dragoons attached to each troop; the Irregulars should be paid in all cases the full twenty rupees per month; bargeers not being admitted, unless in the case of Native officers, who might each be allowed to have their own sons or nephews (failing sons) as bargeers; but their number should be limited to four to each officer.

We further desire that some regiments of Irregular Cavalry, and some of Native Infantry, should be commanded and officered by Natives, and placed in brigade under Europeans.

We would fain see the army, year after year, more carefully weeded of incapables. Age should no longer be the qualification for promotion; jemadars and soobadars should either be pensioned at their homes, or be real and effective lieutenants and captains. We have shown how the deserving old soldier, unqualified to be an officer, may be provided for by being allowed to return to his home as a havildar, on completion of his service. Our army being, in relation to the country it has to defend, a small one, it requires that every man should be effective; its subalterns and Native officers should not be hoary-headed invalids, but young and active men, and its field officers and commanders should not be worn-out valetudinarians. We need hardly say that, gallantly as the army has ever behaved, and much as it has done, more might often have been effected, at less expense of life and treasure, if a few years could have been taken from the ages of all ranks. We have all experience before us in proof that great military achievements have been generally performed by young armies, under young leaders; Hannibal and Napoleon had conquered Italy before they could have been brevet captains in the Company's army; at as early an age the victories of Cæsar were gained, and at an equally early age Alexander had conquered the world. Forty years ago the victories of the Great Duke were gained in India, and happily he is still (1844) at the head of the British army; and we doubt if the ages of all the generals commanding divisions under Wellington, or against him, in the Peninsula, would amount, in the aggregate, to the ages of an equal number of captains of the Bengal army; and this, be it remembered, in a climate where Europeans are old men at forty; and where, as there are but few of us, those few should be of the right sort, and full of energy, mental and physical.

The location in strength of Europeans in the Hills—having good roads and carriage by land and water for at least a portion of them always ready—is another of our schemes; as it is also our hearty desire to see the commissioned ranks of the army opened to them, and hope no longer shut out from the inmates of the barracks. The better education of European children, and colonization on a small scale, under restrictions, is a part of this scheme.

The attachment of Native Companies to European Regiments as posts of honour, or, at any rate, the permanent brigading of different classes of troops, seems to us highly desirable, as likely to enhance the good feeling of all, improve the tone of the sepoys and soften the asperities of Europeans.

The greater mixture of classes in our Native army we also hold to be desirable, so as never to give a designing Brahmin the opportunity of misleading a whole regiment. Instant and full enquiry into every case of discontent or disaffection we hold to be of vital moment—no glossing over to save individual feelings or what is wrongly considered to save the credit of the service. No army in the world has been at all times without taint; but where insubordination or dictation once was permitted—or donatives resorted to, where summary punishment should have been inflicted—that army soon mastered their Government.

We would make the Staff of the army, in all its

branches, efficient; keep it so and practise it, while opportunity offers during peace, so that it may be always ready for war. We would have a baggage train; and precise orders that *should be obeyed* as to the amount of carriage and servants and camp-followers, which under all circumstances on service should accompany our armies. We should not take mobs of hangers-on, or the luxuries of the capital, into the field; and it should be understood to be as much the duty of all ranks to obey orders in such matters, as in doing their duty when actually under fire.

We can see many advantages in having the three armies of Bengal, Madras, and Bombay, united into one Indian army, having one Commander-in-Chief and one General Staff; having rates of pay, equipments, and all else as far as possible, assimilated; and having *four* Commanders of the Forces with subordinate Major-Generals, all having sufficient authority to order and finally dispose of many matters of detail that now go to Army Head-quarters, and some that cannot now be there settled, with the power of bringing up the bulk of the Madras Cavalry and a portion of their other branches to our North-West Provinces; while the Bengal Presidency might send down a few Native Infantry Regiments to the central stations—all being on the same footing as to pay and batta, &c. Much good would thus accrue to the service. Emulation between the natives of different provinces would be excited and the danger of combination be greatly lessened.

We have necessarily but glanced at the various branches of our noble army. We have not forgotten our own deep personal interest in its honour and welfare; but as we hold that our presence in India depends, in no small measure, on the contentedness and happiness of our native soldiery, we have prominently put forth what has long been our opinion, that something more is wanted for the sepoy than that at the age of sixty he should, by possibility, reach the rank of Subadar Major, and with it the first class of Sirdar Bahadoor. Doubtless such hope and expectation is sufficient to influence nine out of ten of our sepoys; but it is for the tenth we want a stimulus; for the man of better education, the superior character, the bold and daring spirit that disdains to live for ever in subordinate place; and it is for such we firmly believe that is absolutely required some new grade where, without our risking the supremacy of European authority, he may obtain command and exert in our behalf those energies and talents which under the present system are too liable to be brought into the scale against us. Commands of Irregular Corps, Jagheers, titles, civil honours, pensions to the second and third generation, are among the measures we would advocate for such characters; while we would give the invalid pensions, at earlier periods and under increased advantages, to men who had distinguished themselves in the field or by any peculiar merit in quarters. For all such and such only there should be medals and orders, and not for whole regiments who may have happened to be in the field on a particular day.

Much reform is required in the Native Army, but still more in the European branch of the service. The system of terror has long enough been tried and been found wanting; the system that filled the American navy with British sailors and drove the flower of the French army into the ranks of their enemies, and that daily drives many Europeans in India, who under different circumstances might turn out good soldiers, to suicide, and to the high road, should at once be exploded. Under a better régime our Europeans, instead of enacting the part of highwaymen, might be rendered as available to purposes of peace as of war, and be as well conducted during one period as another. With commissions open to the ablest, and subordinate staff employment after certain periods to all the well-behaved; with aids to study and to rational amusement in barracks, instead of eternal drills, whose beginning and end is to torment and disgust men with a noble service, how much might be done with the materials at our command, and how much would our Government be strengthened and the value of every individual European's services be enhanced!

To raise men from the ranks, we feel, will be considered a terrible innovation, but we have not ourselves as a body of officers been so long emancipated from degrading restrictions that we should not have some fellow-feeling for our brother soldiers. Argument is not required in the matter; common sense dictates the measure. All history teaches its practicability; the Roman Legionary, nay the barbarian auxiliary, lived to lead the armies of the empire; almost every one of Napoleon's marshals rose from the ranks, and at this day and with all the preventions of aristocracy and moneyed interests, scarcely less than a fifth of Her Majesty's army, is officered by men who rose from the ranks. Indeed, since this paper was commenced we have observed not less than six staff-serjeants promoted to Ensigncies, Adjutancies, or Quarter-Masterships in a single gazette; but it is reserved to the army of a Company of merchants that her sentinels should be blackballed—should be driven with the lash instead of led by consideration and common sense.

Wonderful indeed is it, that this subject should have been left for our advocacy, and that, situated as we are in the midst of a mighty military population, we should fail to see the necessity—the common prudence—of turning our handful of Europeans to the best advantage; and that while we foster the Native, we degrade our own countrymen. Drive away hope from the former, make transportation, or death, a boon—a haven to the heart-broken or desperate sepoy; and then see whether the lash will be required in the Native army as well as the European. We would not abate a jot of discipline with the one or the other; each should be taught his duty thoroughly, which at present he seldom is: he should be a good marksman or swordsman according to the branch of his service, and until he is master of his weapon, he should be kept at drill; but there should be no after drill and parades to *keep men out of mischief*—to disgust them with their duty. They should have as much of exercise and instruction as should keep them practised and able soldiers, and their lives should be rendered happy, that they might remain willing and contented ones. The lash should be reserved for mutiny, desertion, and plunder—for Natives, as well as Europeans —and while the worthless and incorrigible are thus dealt with according to their deserts, the indifferent soldier should be encouraged to become a good one; and the best be rewarded according to their abilities by promotion to the non-commissioned Staff, and the commissioned ranks; and by comfortable provision in old age in climates suited to their constitution.

We cannot expect to hold India for ever. Let us so conduct ourselves in our civil and military relations as when the connection ceases, it may do so, not with convulsions, but with mutual esteem and affection; and that England may then have in India a noble ally, enlightened and brought into the scale of nations under her guidance and fostering care.

NOTE.—In an article on the military defence of the country, it is obvious that some detailed notice should have been taken of so important a point, as the means of rapid locomotion. We had not overlooked it; but the subject is too interesting and too important to be lightly touched upon in a rough desultory article, like the foregoing, which aspires not to teach but to suggest. A small force, which can be moved, at an hour's notice, from one part of the country to another, with a celerity that will disconcert the measures of an enemy—be the hostile demonstration from without or within—is of more real service in the defence of the country, than an overgrown, cumbrous army, which cannot be put in motion without much difficulty and much delay. To attain this great end, it is not only necessary that our troops should be prepared to move, but that they should have good roads along which to move. Now roads and bridges—we are uttering but a trite commonplace—are excellent things, not only as they strengthen our position, but as they conduce to the prosperity of the country—they are blessings to all, and no mean part of the real wealth of a nation. In a military point of view they are of incalculable value; and when the country is not only intersected with good roads, but boasts of at least one railroad along the main line, from the sea to the nor-western boundary; when our rivers are spanned at the most important points with bridges, and ever alive with magic steamships, then will it be found that our army of a quarter of a million is equal, in real strength, to an army of a million of men; and that, with this facility of transporting troops and stores to any given point—of concentrating a large army, with all the muniments of war, in a few hours—we have acquired an amount of military strength, the mere prestige of which will be sufficient to overawe our enemies, and to secure an enduring and honourable peace.

THE KINGDOM OF OUDE.

[WRITTEN IN 1845.]

No portion of India has been more discussed in England than Oude. Affghanistan and the Punjab are modern questions, but, for half a century, country gentlemen have been possessed of a vague idea of a province of India, nominally independent in its home relations, but periodically used as a wet nurse to relieve the difficulties of the East India Company's finances.* The several attacks that were made on Warren Hastings, Lord Wellesley, and the Marquis of Hastings, have all served to keep up the interest of the Oude question. Scarcely had the case of the plundered Begums and flagellated eunuchs been decided, and the folios of evidence elicited by Warren Hastings' trial been laid before the public, than proceedings scarcely less voluminous appeared regarding the territorial cessions extorted by Lord Wellesley. These were followed in turn by attacks on Lord Hastings' loan measures, with the several vindications of his Lordship's policy. We are among those unfashionable people who consider that politics and morals can never be safely separated; that an honest private individual

* "The King of Oude's Sauce" has found its way into London shops, and even Charles O'Malley's "Man for Galway" tells us that "The King of Oude is mighty proud."

must necessarily be an honest official, and *vice versâ;* but we confess that we have been staggered by a study of Oude transactions. Most assuredly Warren Hastings, Lord Teignmouth, Lord Wellesley, Lord Hastings, and Lord Auckland would never have acted in private life, as they did in the capacity of Governors towards prostrate Oude. Lord W. Bentinck, and Lords Cornwallis, Minto, and Ellenborough, appear to have been the only Governors-General who did not take advantage of the weakness of that country to dismember it or increase its burdens.

The earliest offender against Oude was Warren Hastings. Mr. Gleig undertakes to give a true and correct picture of Mr. Hastings' private character and public administration. With the former we have here nothing to do, beyond remarking that the very lax morality of the clerical biographer, when treating of domestic life, vitiates his testimony, and renders his judgment on questions of public justice valueless. Mr. Gleig's theory, moreover, that the wrong which is done for the public good is a justifiable wrong, tends to upset the whole doctrine of Right. When he vindicates his hero by asserting that, "if Mr. Hastings was corrupt, it was to advance the interests of England that he practised his corruption," and proceeds in a similar strain, of what he seems to consider exculpation, he asperses the illustrious person he would defend, far more than do Mr. Hastings' worst enemies. We have *a higher* opinion of Hastings than his biographer appears to have had, but we have *a very different* opinion from that of Mr. Gleig regarding the duty of à Governor-General. Thorough-going vindication, such as Mr. Gleig's, does far more injury to the memory of a sagacious and far-seeing, though unscrupulous, ruler like Warren Hastings, than all the vehement denunciations of Mill the historian. Oude affords but a discreditable chapter in our Indian annals, and furnishes a fearful warning of the lengths to which a statesman may be carried, when once he substitutes expediency and his own view of public advantage, for the simple rule of right and wrong. The facts furnished by every writer on Oude affairs, all testify to the same point, that British interference with that Province has been as prejudicial to its Court and people as it has been disgraceful to the British name. To quote the words of Colonel Sutherland, an able and temperate writer, "there is no State in India with whose Government we have interfered so systematically and so uselessly as with that of Oude." He most justly adds, "this interference has been more in favour of men than of measures; a remark, by the way, applicable to almost every case in which our Government has intermeddled with Native States." It is through such measures that Moorshedabad, Tanjore, and Arcot, have perished beneath our hands. Nagpoor we were obliged to nurse for a time; Hyderabad is again "in articulo mortis," and Mysore is under strict medical treatment. At Sattara, we are obliged to put down the puppet we had put up. Kholapore, another principality of our fostering, has, for nearly a twelvemonth, given employment for more troops than its revenues will pay in twenty years. Already, and almost before the ink of the subsidiary treaty is dry, the regular troops at Gwalior have been employed in police duties. The Minister of our selection has had his life threatened; and we are, again, in the predicament of being pledged to support a Government whose misdeeds we cannot effectually control. In short, wherever we turn, we see written in distinct characters the blighting influences of our interference.

The only unmixed advantage of despotism is its energy, arising from its indivisibility. An able and virtuous despot may dispense happiness; the same ruler, saddled not only with a Minister but with a Resident, can only diffuse wretchedness. He has no possible motive for exertion. He gets no credit for his good acts, and he is not master in his own country. Much casuistry was expended, some years ago, on the defence of the Dewani and Double-government system, which was, at best, but one of the poor cloaks of expediency, and was gradually thrown off as our strength increased. The subsidiary and protected system is, if possible, worse. If ever there was a device for insuring mal-government, it is that of a native ruler and minister, both relying on foreign bayonets, and directed by a British Resident. Even if all three were able, virtuous, and considerate, still the wheels of Government could hardly move smoothly. If it be difficult to select one man, European or Native, with all the requisites for a just administrator, where are three, who can, and will, work together, to be found? Each of the three may work incalculable mischief, but no one of them *can* do good if thwarted by the others. It is almost impossible for the Minister to be faithful and submissive to his Prince, and at the same time honest to the British Government; and how rarely is the European officer to be found who, with ability to guide a Native State, has the discretion and good feeling to keep himself in the background—to prompt and sustain every salutary measure within his reach, while he encourages the Ruler and Minister by giving them all the credit—to be the adviser and not the master—to forget self in the good of the People and of the protected Sovereign! Human nature affords few such men, and therefore, were there no other reason, we should be chary of our interference. From Tanjore to Gwalior the system has been tried, and everywhere has equally failed. In Oude each new reign has required a new treaty to patch up the system. Having little legitimate scope for ambition, the sovereigns have alternately employed themselves in amassing and in squandering treasure. The hoards of Saadut Ally were divided among fiddlers and buffoons: the penurious savings of the late King have been little more creditably employed by his successor; and the Government of Oude, like that of the Deccan, is now as bankrupt in purse as in character. And yet there are men who advocate interference with Native States! Satisfied as we are of the evils of the system, and desirous, by a record of the past, to offer a beacon for the future, we shall present a brief sketch of Oude affairs, and will then venture to suggest the policy which, under existing circumstances, appears fittest for our Government to adopt.

We will first briefly set before our readers a sketch of the kingdom of Oude, as it was and as it is.

Ajoodhya, or Oude, is celebrated in Hindoo legends as the kingdom of Dasaratha, the father of Rama, who extended his conquests to Ceylon, and subdued that island. The Mahommedan invaders at an early period conquered Oude, and it remained, with fewer changes than almost any other province of India, an integral portion of the Mogul empire until the dissolution of that unwieldy Government. Under the Delhi Kings, the Soubadaree, including what are now the British districts of Goruckpore and Azimghur, comprehended an area about one-fourth greater than the limits of the present kingdom. Abulfazel states, that "the length, from Sircar Goruckpore to Kinoje, includes 135 coss; and the breadth, from the northern mountains of Seddehpore to the Soobah of Allahabad, comprises 115 coss."

During the decadence of the Delhi empire, the Viziers Saadut Khan and Sufder Jung, each employed his power, as minister of the pageant King, to increase the bounds of the Oude viceroyalty. Both cast greedy glances on Rohilcund, and Sufder Jung made many attempts at its acquisition; but it was not till the time of Shooja-oo-dowlah that it became subject to Oude. The dominions of that prince, when he first came in contact with the British Government, extended over the greatest portion of Soubah Allahabad, including the districts of Benares and Ghazepoor. While our troops defended Allahabad and Oude proper, he took advantage of the absence of the Mahrattahs in the Deccan to seize and occupy the middle Doab, or districts of Futtehpoor, Cawnpoor, Etawah, and Mynpooree, close up to Agra. During the ensuing year, Colonel Champion's brigade, by the decisive battle of Kutterah, near Bareilly, placed the province of the Rohilcund at his feet, and enabled him to seize Furruckabad as a fief. Thus Shoojah-oo-dowlah not only owed his existence as a sovereign to the clemency, or perhaps to the fears, of his conquerors after the battle of Buxar, but his subsequent accessions of territory were the fruits of British prowess. He left his successor a territory paying annually not less than three millions of money, and capable of yielding double that sum. On the conquest of Rohilcund, in 1774, he at first rented that province at two millions; but it yearly deteriorated, so that not a quarter of that amount was obtained from it when ceded to the British in 1801. The cessions then made were estimated at 1,35,23,474 rupees, or, in round numbers, at one and a third million of money, being above half the Oude possessions; but, by improvement and good management, the Ceded Districts can scarcely yield, at the present time, less than two and a half millions. The area of the Oude reserved dominions is estimated to contain 23,923 square miles. They are bounded on the North and N. E. by the Nepal mountains; South and S. W. by the River Ganges; East and S. E. by the British districts of Goruckpore, Azimghur, Juanpoor, and Allahabad; and West by Rohilcund. The kingdom is very compact, averaging about two hundred miles in length by one hundred and twenty in breadth. Lucknow, the capital, in N. latitude 26° 51′, and longitude 80° 50′, is admirably situated on the navigable river Goomtee, nearly in the centre of the kingdom. The Oude dominions form an almost unbroken plain. The general flow of the rivers is towards the south-east. The Ganges, the Gogra, the Sai, and the Goomtee, are all navigable throughout their respective courses within the Oude territory; but owing to the long unsettled state of the country, and the impositions practised on traders, the last three are little used; and, even on the Ganges, few boatmen like to frequent the Oude bank, for fear of being plundered in one shape or another. The population is estimated at three millions, four-fifths of whom, perhaps, are Hindoos, and they furnish the best-disciplined infantry in India. Three-fourths of the Bengal Native Infantry come from Oude, and recruiting parties from Bombay are sometimes seen to the east of the Ganges.

A few remarks on the past and present capital of Oude, the only part of their dominions which Indian rulers much regard, will not be out of place here.

The ancient city of Ajoodhya, which either receives its name from the province, or gives its own name to it, must, even from present appearances, have been a place of prodigious extent, though we do not pledge ourselves to the *precise* accuracy of the dimensions given by Abulfazel, who states its length at 148 coss, and its breadth at 36 coss. Ajoodhya is a place of Hindoo pilgrimage, and is situated on the south side of the river Gogra, in N. latitude 26° 48′, and E. longitude 82° 4′. Its ruins still extend along the banks of the stream, till they meet the modern, but already decayed, city of Fyzabad. This last town, Shoojah-oo-dowlah made his capital, and adorned with some fine buildings; but it was abandoned by his successor, Asoph-oo-doulah, and has consequently fallen into decay, and bears little trace of any former magnificence. Lucknow, the present capital, consists of an old and a new city, adjoining each other; the former, like other native towns, is filthy, ill-drained, and ill-ventilated. The modern city, situated along the south bank of the river Goomtee, is strikingly different, consisting of broad and airy streets, and containing the Royal Palaces and gardens, the principal Mussulman religious buildings, the British Residency, and the houses of the various English officers connected with the Court. This part of Lucknow is both curious and splendid, and altogether unlike the other great towns of India, whether Hindoo or Mahommedan. There is a strange dash of European architecture among its oriental buildings. Travellers have compared the place to Moscow and to Constantinople, and we can easily fancy the resemblance. Gilded domes, surmounted by the crescent; tall, slender pillars; lofty colonnades; houses that look as if they had been transplanted from Regent Street; iron railings and balustrades; cages, some containing wild beasts, others filled with "strange, bright birds;" gardens, fountains, and cypress trees; elephants, camels, and horses; gilt litters and English barouches; all these form a dazzling picture. We once observed at Lucknow a royal carriage drawn by eight elephants, and another by twelve horses. Yet, brilliant and picturesque as Lucknow is, still there is a puerility and want of stability about it, characteristic enough of its monarchs. The Shah Nujoof, or royal Imam-bara, forms a striking feature in the group of buildings, half Frank, half Asiatic, that meets the eye, after passing through the Room-i-durwaza,* a gateway, said to be built on the model of one at Constantinople. The Imam-bara is a lofty and well-proportioned building. Hamilton gives the dimensions of the centre room as 167 feet long, by 52 wide; but its contents resemble those of a huge auction room or toy-shop, where the only object is to stow away as much incongruous splendour as possible. Mirrors, chandeliers, gigantic candlesticks, banners, manuscripts, brocades, weapons of all sorts, models of buildings, gaudy pictures, and a thousand other things, all bespeak a ruler who possesses wealth, without knowing how to employ it. That this is no mere vague assertion our readers will believe, from the fact that Asoph-oo-doulah expended £150,000 sterling on double-barrelled guns, a million of money on mirrors and chandeliers, and 160,000 gold mohurs, or £320,000, on a single taziah.†

The Fureed Buksh palace is a place of some interest. In 1837 it was the scene of the only insurrection which has occurred during our connection with Oude. The event, though recent, is comparatively forgotten, for the tumult was promptly crushed. With less energetic measures there might have been a rehearsal of the Cabul tragedy. On the night of the 7th July, 1837, when Nusseer-oo-deen expired, the Badshahi Begum

* Gate of *Room* or Constantinople.

† Model of the Tomb of the Martyr Hoossein.

forcibly placed on the throne the boy Moona Jan. During the twelve hours' tumult that ensued, the Resident, his suite, and the rightful heir to the throne, were all in the hands of an infuriated mob. Armed soldiers with lighted torches and lighted matchlocks in their hands, held possession of the palace, stalked throughout its premises, and spared no threats against the British authorities, if they did not assent to the installation of their creature, Moona Jan. The nearest succour had to come five miles from the cantonment. Five companies of sepoys, with four guns, however, soon arrived. The Resident managed to join his friends. He then gave the insurgents one quarter of an hour's grace. When that had expired, the guns opened,—a few rounds of grape were thrown into the disorderly mass, who thronged the palace and its enclosures. Morning dawned on an altered scene; the rioters had succumbed or dispersed; the dead were removed; the palace was cleared out; and, by ten o'clock in the forenoon, the aged, infirm, and trembling heir to the crown was seated on the throne that, at midnight, had been occupied by the usurper. The Resident placed the crown on the new king's head, and the event was announced to the people of Lucknow by the very guns which a few hours before had carried death and consternation among the Oude soldiery.

The Fureed Buksh palace is built close to the Goomtee, and, viewed from the opposite side of that river, has a very pleasing effect. But within, there is nothing to satisfy the eye or the mind. Enormous sums have been expended in decorating the rooms, but all these luxuries give the idea of having been collected from the love of possessing, not from the desire of using, them. The apartments are so crammed that there is no judging of their height or proportion. The room containing the throne is long and has a dismal appearance. It is laid out after the European fashion, with glass windows and scarlet cloth curtains, but these are dirty, musty, and moth-eaten. The throne itself must be of great value; it is a large, square seat, raised several steps from the ground. The sides are, if we remember rightly, of silver, richly chased, and gilt, set with a profusion of precious stones. Of these, many were plundered during the insurrection mentioned above; as they have not been replaced, the throne, with all its splendours, partakes of the prevailing air of incompleteness.

The neighbourhood of Lucknow, still more than its interior, differs from other cities of Hindoostan. At Delhi, Agra, and elsewhere, one is struck with the bleak, desolate aspect of the country, up to the very walls. Lucknow, on the contrary, is surrounded by gardens, parks, and villas, belonging to the King and his nobles. Besides these, there is the fine park and house of Constantia, the property of the late General Martine. The life and death of this soldier of fortune, are illustrative of Indian, and especially of Oude, politics. He bequeathed £100,000 to found a school at Calcutta to be called La Martiniere, and a sum nearly equal in amount for a like institution at Lucknow. Martine's will shows his estimate of Saadut Ali's conscience. He dreaded lest his estate of Constantia, where he intended the school to be built, should be seized by the Nawab after his death. A Mussulman might violate property, and even frustrate charitable intentions, but he would reverence a grave. The General, therefore, ordered that his own body should be interred in one of the underground apartments of his house, thus consecrating the whole building as a tomb. The buildings intended for the Lucknow charitable institution are now, after the lapse of nearly half a century, in progress of erection;

and we hope ere long to see the Lucknow Martiniere diffusing the blessings of education through the Oude territory.

The soil of Oude is generally fertile, though light; when properly cultivated and watered, it is capable of producing all crops. Not only are rice, wheat, barley, with the many kind of vetches and oil plants, grown, but opium, sugar-cane, and indigo are produced. From the numerous large rivers and numberless small streams, as well as the proximity of water in wells, irrigation, that first necessary to the Indian farmer, is easy and cheap. Indeed, in no division of India has nature done more for the people; in none has man done less. Elsewhere, famine, cholera, and the invaders' swords have reduced gardens to wastes; but to no such causes can the progressive deterioration of Oude be attributed. For eighty years the country has not known foreign war; the fertility of the soil and its facilities of irrigation have usually averted from this province the famines that have desolated other parts of the country; and its general salubrity is not to be surpassed by any portion of India. What then has laid waste whole districts, driven the inhabitants to emigration, or, still worse, compelled them, like beasts of prey, to take refuge in the forests, and abandon their habitations to the stranger and to the licensed plunderer? The answer is easily given. A double Government. An irresponsible ruler, ridden by a powerless pro-consul.

It may seem that we are exaggerating the evils of the system. Theoretically, it might be argued that a King, freed from all fear of foreign aggression, secured from domestic insurrection, and commanding a large, and what might be an unencumbered revenue, would have leisure for the duties of a good ruler, and would make it his ambition to leave some record of himself in the grateful remembrance of his people. Experience, however, proves that slavery, even though its fetters may be concealed or gilded, works the same mischievous effects on nations as on individuals. Independent freedom of action is as necessary to develope the powers of the mind as those of the body. The Roman system very much resembled that which has hitherto prevailed in British India. The Roman Provinces were gradually broken into the yoke. The subject Kings, shorn of their independence, and bereft of all means of good government, were continued for a time, until each voluntarily surrendered his load of care, or until the outraged people called aloud for absorption. That which was the result of a systematic plan with Rome, has arisen chiefly from a fortuitous combination of circumstances with Great Britain. During our weakness, we made treaties that have been a dead weight on our strength. These original arrangements have often dishonoured us, and have generally proved grievous to our protégés. Human nature is much the same in the East as in the West. The same principle holds good with nations as with individuals. The man, whether king or servant, who has no fears, has no hopes. The man who is not called on for exertion must be almost more than mortal if he bestir himself. We see the principle daily exemplified: the child born to competence seldom distinguishes himself in life, while the beggar stripling often reaches the top of the ladder. Subject States and guaranteed rulers, now as of old, verify the same remark; and no better example can be offered than that of Oude. It has had men of more than average ability, and of at least average worth, as rulers and ministers, who, if left to themselves, would have been compelled in self-defence, to show some consideration for the people they governed. Failing to do so, their exactions would have called into play the rectifying principle of Asiatic monarchies, and the Dynasty of Saadut Khan would long since have become extinct. But, protected by British bayonets, the degenerate rulers have felt secure to indulge in all the vices generated by their condition; sacrificing alike the welfare of their subjects and the character of the lord paramount.

Our arrangements, in Oude as elsewhere, have been the more mischievous because they have been invariably incomplete. Lord Wellesley's great measure was a most arbitrary one, but, if thoroughly carried out, in the spirit in which it was conceived, would only have injured one individual. Saadut Ali, alone, would have suffered; his subjects would have gained by it. But unhappily, in Oude, as in other parts of India, one Governor-General and one Agent decrees and others carry out, or rather fail to carry out, their views. Not only does no systematic plan of action prevail, but no such thing as a general system of policy is recognised. The only portion of Lord Wellesley's treaty that was thoroughly carried out, was that of increasing the subsidy to 135 lakhs, and seizing territory to cover this enormously-increased subsidy. In all other points, we played fast and loose, going on the usual seesaw practice which depends so much on the digestion of the local Resident and the policy of the Governor-General of the day. Saadut Ali, according to all report, was an extremely able, and naturally by no means an ill-disposed, man. Learned, intelligent, and studious, he was one of the few rulers of Oude who have been personally capable of managing their country, and yet, practically, he was more meddled with than even his silly predecessor, and very much more so than the silliest of his successors.

The British Government came to the reformation of Saadut Ali's administration with dirty hands. They commenced by depriving him of half his dominions, and could therefore hardly expect that their advice regarding the remainder should be kindly taken. Nor was it so; Saadut Ali's talents were henceforth employed in obtaining all the advantage he could from the Resident's presence, and in procuring from him the use of British troops to collect his revenues, while, at the same time, he treated him and his advice with all the neglect and dislike that he dared to show. The consequence was, that the British Government and its Agent were wearied out, and failed to enforce the very provision of the treaty which, at all hazards, should have been primarily attended to. In the acquisition of one-half the Oude territory we seemed to forget that we had become responsible for the good management of the other half. Having secured our subsidy, we not only abandoned the people of the reserved Oude dominions, but lent our bayonets to fleece them; and Saadut Ali, who, under a different system, might have consecrated his energies to the improvement of his country, lived merely to extract every possible rupee from his rack-rented people. It is hardly a stretch of imagination to conceive him deliberately blackening the British character by the use he made of their name in revenge for his wrongs, real and supposed. Mr. Maddock has recorded, that "His temper was soured by the perpetual opposition (thus) engendered, and his rule, though vigorous and efficient, was disfigured by cruelty and rapacity."

Such is the present misrule of Oude that, odious as was the revenue system of Saadut Ali, it is now remembered with considerable respect. Doctor Butter repeatedly refers to his reign as the period when there was some law in the land, "but since his death, no court of justice has been held by the Nawabs, and the Chuckledars attend to nothing but finance."

Further on he says, "During the reign of Saadut Ali, a single cannon-shot could not be fired by a Chuckledar without being followed by immediate enquiry from Lucknow as to its cause: now a Chuckledar may continue firing for a month without question." Again, "Since the death of Nawab Saadut Ali, in 1814, no lease has been granted for more than one year." Thus the period which, not only the Resident of the day, but the Military Officers employed in Oude designated as a reign of terror, is now remembered as one of comparative mercy and tranquillity. Saadut Ali, being a man of ability, plundered for himself; his imbecile successors suffer their minions to devastate the land. Under Saadut Ali there was one tyrant; now there are at least as many as there are local officers. Saadut Ali left his dungeons full of his ex-amils, and fourteen millions of money and jewels in his coffers.

Sir John Malcolm somewhere remarks that the quality of a Native Government may be estimated by the character of its district officers, and the infrequency of change among them. He might have offered a more brief and even a better criterion in "the revenue system." Throughout India, the land is the source of Revenue. Under almost every Native Government, the collections are farmed, and in no part of India are these vicious arrangements so viciously carried out as in Oude. On one occasion we were personally witness to a defaulting village being carried by storm; seven or eight of the inhabitants were killed and wounded, and all the rest were taken captive by the amil. Such occurrences are frequent.* While we write we observe in the daily

* The injury done to British border districts by these affrays may be estimated from the fact that, on the occasion alluded to, seeing a number of armed British subjects flocking around the village, after the aumil's *army* had retired, we taxed them with participation in the fight. This they at first denied, but on taking a matchlock from one of the men, we ob-

papers, a detailed account of the death in battle of the amil of Baraitch, and of the victorious Talookdar having, in consequence, taken to the bush, to be a felon probably for life, or at least until he pay the blood-money at Court. Year by year several of the largest landholders are thus temporarily outlawed. No man owing a fortalice thinks of paying the public revenue, until a force, large or small, is brought against him. Rarely indeed is the sum demanded conformable to the agreement made. The demand almost invariably depends on the nature of the crop, and on the Zemindar's means, real or supposed, to pay or to withhold payment.

The present income of Oude may be estimated at a million and a half sterling, and it arises almost entirely from the land revenue. The fiscal divisions are arbitrary. Mr. Maddock in 1831 showed twenty-four. Doctor Butter in 1837, twelve; and we have before us a list of twenty-five, large and small districts, obtaining during the present year. The charge of each chukla, or district, is generally sold by the Minister and his favourites to the highest bidder, or is given to a creature of his own. Lucknow bankers sometimes engage for large districts and appoint their own agents. These are by no means the worst cases, for low persons, who have risen to notice by the vilest arts, are often appointed amils. They have not only their own fortune to make, but to pay the Court bribes, while their friends remain in office; a change of Ministry turns the majority of them adrift.

The revenue contractors have all the powers of Judge and Magistrate; they are, in short, unshackled, un-

served that it had been just discharged. The parties then allowed that they had come to join in the defence of the village, but were too late, it having been surrounded during the night and the assault made at daylight. Thus are our subjects taught club and matchlock law.

checked governors of their chuklas. Five of the present twenty-five divisions are under what is called amaunee management; that is, of salaried officers, who collect the Government rents; but this system only obtains in districts so deteriorated that no one will bid for farming them, and in such cases the Ameens are under so little check that the cultivators are at their mercy nearly as much as under the farming system. Mr. (now Sir Herbert) Maddock, in an able memorandum, shows the modes by which the situations of amils are procured, and the sort of people who in his time filled the office, including, for instance, "Nawab Ameer-ood-dowlah," who has been raised to the dignity of an amil from the "very humble duties of a fiddler. His sister, formerly a concubine, or nautch girl, having gained the royal favour, is now one of the King's wives, designated by the title of 'Tauj Mahal,' and receives a Jageer, for the support of her dignity, of which her brother, the 'Nawab Ameer-ood-dowlah,' is the manager. In like manner, the individual placed in charge of Annow, &c., was formerly the humble attendant upon nautch girls, but has lately been advanced to the title of 'Nawab Allee Bux,' through female influence in the palace." Sir Herbert Maddock furnishes a detailed list of nuzerana received by one Minister (Mohumud-ood-dowlah) amounting to more than seventeen lakhs of rupees, and estimated that the amils share among them nearly fifty lakhs of rupees yearly.

Matters are far from improved since Sir Herbert Maddock wrote. The weak are still squeezed, while those who "are secured by forts and backed by troops" continue to pay pretty much as they choose. The picture drawn by Sir Herbert of the career of an amil in the year 1830 stands good for the same official of to-day. Rules and rates, justice and mercy, are disregarded now, as they were then, and in his words it may still be truly said that, "a few seasons of extortion such as this lays waste the fields and throws a multitude upon the world, now almost deprived of honest means to gain subsistence. These, driven from their homes, betake themselves to crime, and goaded by poverty, become thieves and robbers, infesting the country on every side." "The amil or his officers, finding a yearly decrease of revenue, are naturally urged to further exactions, until, at length, the kingdom has arrived at such a crisis that hundreds of villages have gone to ruin, the former cultivation is now a waste, and the hamlets once occupied are now deserted." The foregoing brief quotation is as applicable to the state of the police, and of the revenue, at the present day, as it was when Sir H. Maddock wrote. In the year 1806, when several gentlemen were examined before Parliament on the Oude question, Major Ouseley, an Aide-de-Camp, and personal friend of the reigning Nawab, Saadut Ali, testified to the infamous state of the police. The evidence of all others was to the same effect.

Sir H. Maddock, Dr. Butter, and all modern writers, show that the condition of the police is now, to the full, as bad as it was half a century ago. The latter gentleman states "that nothing is said about a murder or a robbery; and, consequently, crime of all kinds has become much more frequent, especially within the last sixteen years, and in the smaller towns and villages. Gang-robbery, of both houses and travellers, by bands of 200 and 300 men, has become very common. In most parts of Oude, disputes about land, and murders thence originating, are of very frequent occurrence; feuds are thus kept up, and all opportunities of vengeance laid hold of." Again, "Pipar, five miles

N. N. E. of Gonda in Amethi, contains a population of 4000 ch'hatris, who are robbers by profession and inheritance; every bullock and horse stolen in this part of Oude, finds its way to Pipar." Also, "Sarangpur, ten miles south of Tanda, has a population of 9000 Hindu thieves, dakoits (gang-robbers), and t'hugs, whose depredations extend as far as Lak'hnau, Gorak'hpur, and Benares." In the same page, it is stated that "In November, 1834, Tanda and its neighbourhood were plundered by the notorious freebooter Fatteh Bahadoor of Doarka, who surprised and defeated the Faujdar, and a toman of 100 men stationed there, and carried off about 100 of the principal inhabitants, who, on pain of death, were compelled to procure their own ransom, at sums varying from 50 to 400 rupees. Of this outrage no notice was taken by the Government."

The army is in much the same condition as it was when Sir James Craig declared that it would be useful only to the enemy. It is dangerous to the well-being of the State; utterly useless for war, most mischievous during peace. In round numbers the army may now be estimated at fifty-two thousand men, and its expense at thirty-two lakhs of rupees yearly.* Doctor Butter's account, written in 1837, describes its present condition with sufficient accuracy.

"The Army of Oude, excluding the brigade raised by Local Colonel Roberts, is an ill-paid, undisciplined rabble, employed generally in coercing, under the Chuckledar's orders, the 'refractory' Zemindars of his districts; in conveying to Lak'hnau, under the exclusively military orders of their own officers, the revenue when

* There are, also, not less than a hundred thousand armed men employed by the Talookdars and Zemindars, to defend their forts and fight *against* the Government.

levied; and occasionally, in opposing the armies of plunderers, who harass the eastern districts of Oude." And, again, "The nominal pay of the Sipahi is four rupees, but he receives only three, issued once in every three or four months, and kept much in arrears; he has also to find his own arms and ammunition. He gets no regular leave to his home, but takes it occasionally for ten or fifteen days at a time; and little notice is taken of his delinquency by the tumandar. There is a muster, once in every five or six months; and the man who is absent from it gets no pay."

"This army has no fixed cantonments, no parades, no drill, and no tactical arrangement: when one pultan is fighting, another may be cooking. Encounters hand to hand are thought disreputable, and distant cannonading preferred, or a desultory match-lock fire, when no artillery is available. There is no pension or other provision for the severely wounded, who, *de facto*, are out of the service, and return to their homes as they can." * * * "They have no tents; but when they make a halt, if only for two days, they build huts for themselves, covering them with roofs torn from the next villages."

We refer to Colonel Sleeman's little volume "On the Spirit of Military Discipline," pages 10 and 11, for a very striking anecdote, exemplifying at once the Oude Revenue system and the value of its present military force.

Having thus, from sources sufficiently independent, set forth the past and present condition of the finance, police, and military system of Oude, we shall now offer a brief historical sketch of the progressive causes of this condition.

Saadut Khan, the founder of the Oude dynasty, was one of the many bold spirits that came from the westward to seek their fortunes in Hindoostan. He combined with the usual qualities of a good soldier, the rarer talents required for an able administrator. Mr. Elphinstone has fallen into the error of earlier historians in calling him a merchant; he was, in reality, of noble birth, and his original name was Mahommed Ameen. In the year 1705, while still but a lad, he arrived at Patna, to join his father and elder brother, who had preceded him thither. On his arrival, finding the former dead, he and his brother proceeded to push their fortunes at Delhi. His first service was with Nawab Sirbulund Khan, whom, however, he soon quitted, resenting a taunt uttered by his master on occasion of some trifling neglect. The youth took his way to Court, where he soon acquired favour; and having materially assisted his imbecile sovereign in getting rid of Hosein Ali (the younger of the Syuds of Bara, who were at that time dragooning the King), Mahommed Ameen was rapidly promoted to the viceroyalty of Oude, with the title of Saadut Khan. He found the province in great disorder, but soon reduced the refractory spirits and greatly increased the revenue. He protected the husbandmen, but crushed the petty chiefs who aimed at independence.

Modern historians question the fact of Saadut Khan having, in concert with Nizam-ool-Moolk, invited Nadir Shah's invasion. We have not room to detail the evidence on which our opinion rests, but a careful comparison of authorities leads us to believe that he was guilty of this treacherous deed. The atrocities committed by Nadir are familiar matters of history. The traitor chiefs did not escape, and Nizam-ool-Moolk and Saadut Khan were especially vexed with requisitions. They were not only themselves plundered, but were made the instruments of extorting treasure from the distant provinces. Nizam-ool-Moolk, jealous of the power and ability of Saadut, took advantage of the persecutions of Nadir Shah to execute a plan for getting rid of his rival. He affected to confide to him his own determination of suicide, and agreed with Saadut Khan that each should take poison. The latter drank his cupfull, and left the hoary schemer without a rival in the empire.*

Saadut Khan, who had but a few years before been a needy adventurer, and had now been plundered by Nadir Shah, was still enabled to leave his successor a large treasure, estimated by some at nine millions of money. Though he accumulated so much wealth, he has not left behind him the character of an oppressor. On the contrary, he seems rather to have respected the poor, and to have restricted his exactions to the rich. He overthrew many lordlings, and established in their stead one stronger, and therefore better, rule. No qualms of conscience stood in his way. The aggrandizement of his own family was his one object, in furtherance of which he was regardless alike of gratitude, loyalty, or patriotism. So long as his own territory escaped, he cared not that Persian or Mahratta should ravage the empire, and humble the monarch, in whose weakness he found his own strength. He reaped much as he had sown; his ability and management established a sovereignty; his faithlessness brought him to a premature and ignominious end. He proved no exception to the rule, that they who are busiest in entrapping others are themselves the easiest deluded.

On the death of Saadut Khan, his two nephews,

* Mr. Elphinstone, noticing the current story of Saadut Khan's death, and of his and Asoph Jah's (Nizam-ool-Moolk) having called in Nadir, observes, "these fictions, like many others which are believed in times of agitation, disappear when full light is thrown on the period." We regret to say that this "full light" has yet to appear.

Sher Jung and Sufder Jung, each applied to the all-powerful Nadir Shah for the investiture of Oude: the petition of the latter, who had married Saadut Khan's daughter, being backed by the Hindoo vakeel of the late Viceroy, with an offer of a nuzzur of two millions sterling, he was of course invested with the Government.* Nawab Sufder Jung was accounted an able ruler; for a time he sustained the tottering authority of the King of Delhi. In the year 1743 his son Shoojah-oo-dowlah was married to the Bhow Begum, who, in after days, became so conspicuous in Anglo-Oude annals. On Nadir Shah's death, Ahmed Shah Abdalli seized the throne of Affghanistan, invaded India, and killed the Vizier Kumer-ood-deen Khan at Sirhind. At this juncture Sufder Jung distinguished himself by his zeal and ability. Mahommed Shah the emperor of Delhi dying shortly after, his son Ahmed Shah appointed Sufder Jung to the post of Vizier; that nobleman also retaining his viceroyalty of Oude. The first design of the new Vizier was, in 1746, against the Rohillahs, who were troublesome neighbours to his Oude viceroyalty. The period was favourable to his views; for Ali Mahommed, the founder of the Rohillah family, was dead, and Sufder Jung induced Kaim Khan † Bungush, the Affghan chief of Furruckabad, to conduct the war against his countrymen. Kaim Khan fell in the cause of his ally, who, in return, plundered his widow and seized the family jagheer, giving a pension to Ahmed Khan, the brother of the deceased chief. The Vizier made over his new acquisition, with the province of Oude, to his deputy Rajah Newul Roy, and himself proceeded to Delhi.

* Indian historians generally call these two millions cash taken from Saadut Khan, but, after comparing many authorities, we believe ours to be the correct version.

† The fine village, or rather town, of Kaimgunje, in Furruckabad, is called after the old chief.

It was not long before Sufder Jung tasted the bitter fruits of his own tyranny and ingratitude: the train of disaffection was laid, and a spark soon kindled it.

An Affghan woman of the Afredi tribe, who gained her livelihood by spinning thread, was maltreated by a Hindoo soldier of Newul Roy. She went direct to Ahmed Khan, the Vizier's pensioner, and crying for justice, exclaimed, "Cursed be thy turban, Ahmed Khan, who permittest an Afredi woman to be thus treated by a Kaffir. It had been better that God had given thy father a daughter than such a son as thou." Ahmed Khan was roused; in concert with bolder spirits, he plundered a rich merchant, and with the funds thus procured, raised an army, killed the Kotwal of Furruckabad, seized the city, and, within a month, was in possession of that whole district. Rajah Newul Roy, who was a brave man, came to the rescue from Lucknow, was met near the Kalinuddy, by the Affghan army, defeated, and slain. The victors crossed the Ganges and were soon in possession of the whole viceroyalty of Oude. Sufder Jung, on hearing of the disaster that had befallen his lieutenant, assembled a large army, estimated in the chronicles of the day at 250,000 men, and, accompanied by Sooruj Mul, the Jaut chief of Bhurtpoor, moved against Ahmed Khan, who came out to meet him, at the head of a very inferior force, but, by a sudden attack on the wing of the army commanded by the Vizier himself, wounded him and drove him from the field. His troops, observing that their commander's elephant had left the field, fled in confusion, and left Ahmed Khan undisputed master of the provinces of Oude and Allahabad. The Affghans had fought bravely, but they could not agree among themselves. Dissensions arose in Oude, and after a brief struggle the late conquerors were expelled the country.

Sufder Jung, as unscrupulous as the other leaders of the day, called in the Mahrattas to his support, and with an immense force again marched against Ahmed Khan, who, alarmed at the formidable aspect of affairs, forgave the Rohillah chiefs the death of his brother, and entered into a treaty of mutual defence with them. Unable to meet the Vizier in the field, Ahmed Khan crossed the Ganges, and fell back on his Rohillah confederates, who, giving way to their fears, abandoned the open country, and allowed themselves to be hemmed in under the Kumaon mountains. There they were reduced to such straits that a pound of flesh was sold for a pound sterling. Terms were at length granted, and the Mahrattas returned to their country loaded with the plunder of Rohilcund, and their leaders enriched by two and a half millions of subsidy. Sufder Jung was so far a gainer that he not only humbled, but crippled his Affghan opponents.

Factions soon arose at Delhi, and the Vizier was often sore pressed, and put to many shifts to retain his authority. The Queen mother was enamoured of an eunuch, of the name of Jawid, who, supported by the King as well as his mother, sought to supplant the Vizier during his absence in Rohilcund. Sufder Jung, on his return to Delhi, settled the dispute by inviting the eunuch to a feast, and there causing him to be assassinated. The King was enraged at this act, and employed Ghazi-ood-deen to avenge it. This youth was the grandson of Nizam-ool-Moolk, and had been brought forward by the Vizier himself. After some intriguing and bullying with varied result, the Vizier withdrew to his viceroyalty, and his rival assumed the functions of the vizarut. No sooner had Sufder Jung retired, than the pageant King found that in his new minister Ghazee-ood-deen he had saddled himself with a hard master. Hoping to escape from this yoke, he wrote to recall his late Vizier; but the letter found Sufder Jung dying; and Ghazee-ood-deen, on hearing of the effort thus made to supplant him, caused both the King and his mother to be blinded, and raised one of the Princes of the blood to the throne, under the title of Alumgeer the Second.

Shoojah-oo-dowlah, the son of Sufder Jung, had been brought forward during his father's lifetime, and on his death was placed on the musnud of Oude, now become hereditary in the family of Saadut Khan. A rival to Shoojah-oo-dowlah, however, arose in the person of his cousin, Mahommed Kooli Khan, the Governor of Allahabad, whose pretensions were unsuccessfully supported by Ishmael Khan Kaboolee, the chief military adherent of the late Viceroy.

Ahmed Shah Abdallee on his third invasion of India in 1756, after capturing Delhi, sent Ghazee-ood-deen, the Vizier of the so-called Great Mogul, to raise a contribution on Oude. No sooner had the Abdallee retired, than the Vizier called in the Mahrattas, upset all the arrangements made by Ahmed Shah, and, in concert with his new allies, who had not only captured the imperial city of Delhi, but had overrun a great portion of the Punjab, planned the reduction of Oude. Alarmed at the threatened danger, Shoojah-oo-dowlah entered into a confederacy with the hereditary enemies of his family, the Rohillahs, and when the Mahrattas invaded Rohilcund, carrying desolation in their path, and destroying thirteen hundred villages in little more than a month, Shoojah-oo-dowlah came to the rescue, surprised the camp of Sindea, the Mahratta commander, and drove him across the Ganges. Ahmed Shah was at this time making his fourth descent on Hindoostan, and called on the Mahommedan chiefs to join his standard against the Mahrattas. The Rohillahs did so, but Shoojah-oo-dowlah hesitated between the two evils of Affghan and Mahratta enmity. A move on Anopshuhur, on the Oude frontier, made by the Abdali, determined the choice of Shoojah, who, however, while he professedly joined the Affghan, kept up close communication with the Mahrattas. Throughout the battle of Panneput, which took place in January, 1761, the Oude ruler continued to temporize, holding his ground, but taking as little part in the action as possible. The entire success of either party was contrary to his views. He desired a balance of power, which would check a universal monarchy, either Hindoo or Affghan.

We must here retrace our steps. In the year 1758, when the wretched Emperor, Alumgeer the Second, was in daily danger of death from his own Vizier, Ghazee-ood-deen, he connived at the escape from Delhi of his heir, Prince Alee-gohur (afterwards Shah Alum), who, after seeking an asylum in various quarters, was honourably received by Shoojah-oo-dowlah and by the kinsman of the latter, Mahommed Kooli Khan, the Governor of Allahabad. Thus supported, and having received from his own father the investiture of the government of Bengal, Behar, and Orissa, Prince Alee-gohur crossed the Caramnassa river, with a design of expelling the English and their puppet, Nawab Jaffier Ali. At the head of a motley band of adventurers, the Prince appeared before Patna; and, so ill was that place supplied, that he might have taken it, had not his principal officer, Mahommed Kooli Khan, suddenly left him, in the hope of recovering the fort of Allahabad, which had been treacherously seized by his kinsman Shoojah. Alee-gohur was now obliged to relinquish his attempt; but, two years after (in 1760), though driven, in the interval, to the greatest distress for the very necessaries of life, he was again contemplating an attempt on Bengal, when his father was put to death,—another victim to the sanguinary Ghazee-ood-deen. The Prince, assuming the vacant title of emperor, appointed Shoojah-oo-dowlah his Vizier, with a view of securing the support of that noble; and now appeared again as Shah Alum, before Patna, cut off a small British detachment, and might have got possession of that city had he acted vigorously. It would be foreign to our subject to detail the circumstances by which the English were victorious, and Shah Alum was compelled to confirm their creature Cossim Ali in his *viceroyalty* of Bengal. The crest-fallen Emperor prepared, as soon as possible, for his return to Delhi, on the guarantee of his new Vizier, of Nujeeb-oo-dowlah, and other chiefs. He was anxious also to obtain the protection of a British escort, but though there was much desire to grant one, he was only escorted, by Major Carnac, to the border of Behar.

In 1763, Cossim Ali was driven by the oppressions of the English, and their disregard of all decency in the matter of the inland trade, to abolish all duties on the internal commerce of the country. This measure, which should have been warmly encouraged by the British authorities, was the main cause of the hostilities that followed. One outrage brought on another. Mr. Ellis, the most violent and injudicious of the many violent men then in authority, precipitated matters at Patna. The result was, that Cossim Ali was removed, and Jaffier Ali restored to the musnud. Cossim Ali could still muster some troops, with which he met the British, was defeated, and, on his flight, perpetrated that massacre of his English prisoners which will brand his name, as long as it is remembered. After this act of butchery, he fled for refuge to Shoojah-oo-dowlah, taking with him three hundred and eighty-five elephants loaded with treasure. The exile offered Shoojah a lakh of rupees for every day's march, and half that sum for every halt, as long as the war might last, with three millions sterling, and the cession of the Patna district, on the recovery of Bengal, if he would join him against the English. But Cossim Ali, desiring to have two strings to his bow, offered at the same time a large bribe to the Emperor for his own appointment to the viceroyship of Oude, in supercession of Shoojah-oo-dowlah. The latter intercepted Cossim Ali's letter and forthwith placed him under restraint, after gaining over Sumroo and other military officers with their troops. A mutiny in the English camp cramped, for a time, the British commander, but on the 22nd October, 1764, the battle of Buxar decided the fate not only of Bengal and Behar, but of Oude.

The immediate result of the battle was the surrender of the unhappy Emperor, who, instead of having been re-instated at Delhi, had been detained prisoner by his Vizier. The latter also begged for terms, and offered fifty-eight lakhs to the English Government and army. The victors refused to make any terms until Cossim Ali and Sumroo had been surrendered. The Vizier had plundered and arrested the former, but hesitated to surrender him: he offered, however, to connive at his escape, and to cause the assassination of Sumroo. As the British commander would not accede to this proposal, the negotiation with the Vizier failed; and arrangements were made with the Emperor, stipulating that he should be placed in possession of Shoojah-oo-dowlah's dominions, including Allahabad, and should in return grant Benares and Ghazeepoor to the British. Hostilities were accordingly recommenced against the Vizier; the British troops entered Oude, and took possession of Lucknow, the capital; while Shoojah-oodowlah, sending his family for refuge to Bareilly, sought for allies in every quarter. But when the news of the proposed arrangements reached England, the Court of Directors were exceedingly alarmed. They sent out positive orders against any such *demented* scheme of enlarging the British territory, and forbade all meddling with Delhi politics. The despatch arrived just in time to save the Vizier, who had been defeated in a skirmish at Korah, on the 3rd May, 1765. Deserted by his Rohillah and Mahratta allies, he came into General Carnac's camp on the 19th of the same month, and threw himself on British mercy. Not being behind the scenes, the Vizier was astonished and delighted at the moderation of the terms granted to him, which were that he should pay fifty lakhs of rupees to the British: that he should pledge himself not to molest Bulwunt Singh, the Zemindar of Benares, and that he should cede Allahabad and Korah to the Emperor. It is a curious feature in this case, and a damning proof how iniquitous had been our proceedings in Bengal, that the Vizier, now at the mercy of his conquerors and ready to cede all, or any portion, of his territory, yet demurred against admitting the English to trade, free of all duties. Government probably felt the justice of his apprehensions, for in the words of Mills, "Clive agreed, in the terms of the treaty, to omit the very names of trade and factories."

Next year (1766), Lord Clive had an interview with the Emperor and the Vizier at Chupra. The latter again expressed his satisfaction at the terms of peace, and paid up the fifty lakhs of rupees; and the Emperor again, vainly, requested an escort to Delhi. This first treaty did not involve any right of internal interference on the part of the British; yet little time elapsed before very stringent terms were dictated. They relinquished Oude because they would not, or, it was supposed in England, *could* not, keep it. They did not give it to the Emperor, because they considered that such a gift would imply future protection, and involve them in the wars of Upper India, a dilemma from which Government believed itself to have escaped by restoring the Vizier. On the conclusion of these arrangements, a brigade of British troops remained in the Allahabad district for the support of the King and the Vizier against the Mahrattas, without any provision for the payment of the brigade by those who benefited by its services. In the year 1766, however, the Court of Directors wrote, "As all our views and expectations are confined within the Caramnassa, we are impatient to hear that our troops are recalled from Allahabad." During the same year the Bengal Government became alarmed at the military schemes of the Vizier, at his "amazing improvement in making small arms," and at the large levies of troops entertained by him. In consequence of these suspicions, a deputation was sent to meet the Vizier at Benares, towards the end of 1768, when, after a warm discussion and much opposition on his part, he agreed to reduce his army to 35,000 men, of whom 10,000 were to be cavalry and only ten battalions were to be trained sepoys.

About this time Shoojah seized one of his principal officers, Rajah Benee Bahadoor, and caused his eyes to be put out. An attempt was made to procure British interference in his favour, but the reply given was, "that the Vizier was master within his own dominions." The occasion was an ill-chosen one for announcing the fact; but it would have been well had the law continued. In the year 1769, three of the Oude battalions mutinied; they were promptly put down; but their conduct somewhat reconciled the Vizier to the late compulsory reduction of his troops. In 1771, the Emperor left Allahabad and threw himself into the arms of the Mahrattas, after having made some secret terms with the Vizier for the cession of Allahabad. The next year the Mahrattas threatened Rohilcund and thereby Oude. Upon this the Vizier entered into terms with the Rohillah chiefs, and induced the Calcutta Council to allow Sir Robert Barker to accompany him with a British brigade. The combined force, however, did not prevent the Mahrattas from penetrating to the very heart of Rohilcund and even threatening Oude. It was during this campaign that the Vizier made the arrangement with the Rohillah chiefs, to relieve them of their Mahratta scourge, in return for which they were to pay him a subsidy of forty lakhs of rupees. The failure of payment was the excuse for the famous, or rather infamous, Rohillah war. In the year 1773 the district of Korah was included within the line of British defensive operations; but Colonel Champion, the commander of the advanced brigade, was instructed that, "not a single sepoy was to pass the frontiers of the Vizier's territories." The measure was induced by the forced grant of Korah and Allahabad by the Emperor to his jailors, the Mahrattas, which cession the British authorities determined to oppose, and to reserve its ultimate destination to themselves.

Up to this time, the diplomatic relations between the two Governments appear to have been conducted by a Captain Harper who commanded a regiment of sepoys in attendance on the Vizier. Mr. Hastings, however, desired to have a person in his own confidence at Lucknow, and therefore recalled Captain Harper. The order was opposed by Sir Robert Barker the commander-in-chief, who, on his own authority, sent the Captain back to the Vizier. The Governor-General was not a man to be so bearded; he carried his point after some angry correspondence, the commencement of that acrimony which prevailed in the discussion of Oude affairs during Mr. Hastings's administration, and which has been so prominent a feature in most of the discussions that have since occurred regarding that province. In September, 1773, Mr. Hastings meet Shoojah-oo-dowlah with a view of revising the treaty, "as the latter might call upon the Company for assistance, and yet was under no defined obligation to defray the additional charge thrown upon them by affording such assistance." On the 19th of the same month the new treaty was concluded, making over the districts of Allahabad and Korah to the Vizier, on condition of his paying to the Company the sum of fifty lakhs of rupees, and stipulating that he should defray the charges of such portion of the British troops as he might require; which were fixed at two lakhs and ten thousand rupees per month for each brigade. At this meeting the Vizier felt the Governor-General's pulse as to the support he was likely to receive in his project, already contemplated, against the Rohillahs.

Mr. Hastings took the opportunity to arrange for the reception of a permanent British Resident at Lucknow, telling the Vizier at a private conference that, "he desired it himself; but unless it was equally the Vizier's wish, he would neither propose nor consent to it." Shoojah declared he would be delighted, and Mr. Middleton was accordingly appointed. Scarcely had the Governor joined his Council when the Vizier wrote that he understood Hafiz Ruhmut and the other Rohillah sirdars were about to take possession of Etawah and the rest of the middle Doab, which he would never allow, especially "as they had not made good a daum of the forty lakhs of rupees, according to their agreement." The Vizier added, "On condition of the entire expulsion of the Rohillahs, I will pay to the Company the sum of forty lakhs of rupees in ready money, whenever I shall discharge the English troops; and until the expulsion of the Rohillahs shall be effected, I will pay the expenses of the English troops; that is to say, I will pay the sum of rupees 2,10,000 monthly." The Council affected some squeamishness about the Doab, which, however, they did not prevent the Vizier from seizing. Respecting the operations against Rohilcund, they gave a half-and-half sort of answer, *but held* a brigade in readiness to await the requisition of the Vizier.

The tale of the Rohilcund campaign has been often told; we shall not add to the number of narratives. Suffice it to say that the brunt of the battle of Kuttera fell on the British detachment; Colonel Champion reporting that the Vizier had evinced the most "shameful pusillanimity." The English commander was however not an unprejudiced judge. Shoojah-oo-dowlah, whatever were his faults, was never before accused of cowardice, and on several occasions, especially at Buxar, evinced great courage. It is to the credit of Colonel Champion that he did not like the work in which he was employed; and looking with abhorrence at the desolation caused by the Oude troops, who had ill supported him in the fight, he was not chary of his remarks on them or on their Prince. But it is no proof that a Native chief is a coward because he does not fight. He often looks on to await the result of the day. The British brigade were Shoojah's mercenaries; they were hired to fight his battles. He let them do so, and we are by no means certain that if the battle of Kuttera had gone against the British, and Colonel Champion had fallen instead of Hafiz Ruhmat, that the isolated English brigade would not have found a foe instead of friend in Shoojah-oo-dowlah. This campaign, with all its concomitant circumstances, forms the darkest spot in Indo-British history. Little can be said in behalf of the Vizier, and no sophistry can extenuate the conduct of a Governor and his Council, who hired out their troops for butcher work, openly avowing that they did so because they required the offered subsidy to meet the pressure on the local finances and to answer the demands of the home Government. Having given this unqualified opinion, it is just to add that report greatly exaggerated the virtues of the Rohillahs as well as the atrocities of their destroyers. Warren Hastings' conduct was made a party question both in India and England, and his deeds were accordingly misrepresented by enemies and slurred over by friends.

The Rohillah war was scarcely concluded, when the new arrangements for the Government of India gave Mr. Hastings' opponents a majority in Council. They lost no time in pronouncing their disapproval of his measures; they recalled Mr. Middleton, the Resident he had placed at Lucknow, and gave the appointment to a Mr. Bristow, notwithstanding his being personally obnoxious to the Governor-General. The men, however, who thus stigmatized Hastings' measures carried their zeal for reform no further than words. They scrupled not to receive the wages of iniquity. They not only pressed the Vizier for payment of the subsidy, but took advantage of the critical state of his affairs to raise their demand on him. The earthly career, however, of Shoojah-oo-dowlah drew near its close. He obtained Mr. Hastings' sanction for his return to Fyzabad, that he might make arrangements for liquidating his engagements to Government. On reaching his capital, he was seized with a violent illness which terminated his life. He expired on the 26th January, 1775, and was succeeded by his eldest son, Mirza Amanee, who assumed the name of Asoph-ood-dowlah.

No public man, not Cromwell himself, has ever been painted in more opposite colours than Shoojah-oo-dowlah. Taking Colonel Duff's version, the Vizier was "the infamous son of a still more infamous Persian pedlar," * * "cruel, treacherous, unprincipled, deceitful; possessing not one virtue except personal courage." Yet the same writer shows that when danger gathered round, Shoojah had sufficient resolution to relinquish the pleasures of the harem, and the field sports to which he was addicted, that he might set himself to reform the discipline of his troops, and retrieve the embarrassments of his finance. On the other hand, Francklin describes the Vizier as "an excellent Magistrate, a lover of justice, and anxiously desirous of the prosperity of his country." Still stronger is the praise bestowed by Jonathan Scott. He says of Shoojah-oo-dowlah that, "as a prince he was wise and dignified in character, as a private man, affable, humane, and generous." * * * "Sincerely beloved by his own subjects, even the sons of Hafiz Rhamat wept at his death." From these discordant materials, and the fact that after having virtually lost his sovereignty at Buxar, he not only recovered his position, but left to his son an inheritance nearly double what he had received from his own father; it may be inferred that Shoojah-oo-dowlah was an able, energetic, and intelligent prince, and that he possessed at least the ordinary virtues of Eastern rulers.

Asoph-ood-dowlah lost no time in sending a peshcush, or offering, to the Emperor, with five thousand men;

they arrived just in time to relieve the unfortunate monarch from the hands of Zabita Khan, and the opportune aid secured for their sender the post of Vizier, in succession to his father. The province of Oude had now descended to the fourth generation, and the office of Vizier to the third. On the accession of Asoph-ood-dowlah, the Calcutta Council affected to consider that the treaty with his father died with his death. After much discussion, the new Resident, Mr. Bristow, negotiated fresh terms, on the 21st May, 1775, the chief clauses of which were, that the Vizier should cede Benares and Ghazepoor, worth 23 lakhs annually, to the Company; raise the monthly subsidy from rupees 2,10,000 to 2,60,000 for the service of a British brigade, and agree to dismiss all foreigners from his service, and to deliver up Cossim Ali and Sumroo, if they should ever fall into his hands. He further consented to pay up all arrears due by his father. In return for these advantages, the English undertook to defend Oude, including Corah and Allahabad, as also the late conquests in Rohilcund and the Doab. The services of a second brigade, entitled "the temporary brigade" were, at the same time, placed at the disposal of the Vizier.

Another affair was now transacted, important at the time, and pregnant with future evil. The British Agent, supported by the anti-Hastings majority at the Council table, made over the treasures of the late Vizier to his widow, the Baho (Bhow) Begum, who was likewise put in possession of a princely jageer. To her this wealth proved a fatal possession, leading to the atrocities afterwards practised on herself and her servants. On the part of our Government the bestowal of it was both unreasonable and unprecedented. Shoojah had died largely their debtor, and the sum now made over to his widow effectually barred the settlement of their claims. The Begum, it is true, claimed the money as a legacy from her husband; but it is almost needless to say that under no native Government would such a bequest, even if effectually made, have been carried into effect. Uninterfered with, Asoph-ood-dowlah would have assumed possession of his father's wealth as naturally as of his place, and his mother would have been satisfied with whatever jageer or pension he assigned her. But party spirit in Calcutta divided the house of Oude against itself, and involved the ruler in difficulties which issued in crimes perpetrated by him against his mother, at the instigation of a British Governor-General.

The first year of the new Nawab's authority had not passed before he was surrounded by perplexities. The arrears of subsidy not coming in, tunkhwas or orders on the revenue, were obtained for four lakhs per annum, and the Baho Begum was induced, at the intercession of the Resident, to assist the necessities of the State with fifty-six lakhs of rupees, on condition however of Mr. Bristow's ratifying her son's engagement not to molest her with further demands. The Nawab had at length leisure to attend to the state of his army. Desiring to introduce discipline among his troops, he applied for, and obtained, the services of several European officers. They were not ill received by the soldiery, but soon after, on the discharge of some Irregulars, a mutiny broke out. An engagement took place between the Regulars and the Matchlockmen; 2,500 of the latter supported an engagement for some time with great spirit against 15,000 regulars, repeatedly repulsing them. The fight was only brought to an end by the explosion of a tumbrel. The mutineers lost six hundred men and the Nawab's Sepoys three hundred.

While such was the condition of the army, the Nawab gave himself up to drunkenness and dissipation. All authority fell into the hands of the minister, Moortaza Khan, whose rule was, however, brief. Kwajah Busunt, a eunuch, but the bravest soldier in the service, took advantage of the general dissatisfaction to encourage a party in favour of Saadut Ali, the second and favourite son of the late Vizier. Kwajah Busunt invited the minister to a banquet. In the midst of the feast, making some excuse for quitting the guest-chamber, he gave the signal for the slaughter of the unwary Moortaza Khan in the midst of the nautch girls and singers. Asoph-ood-dowlah himself had been invited to the entertainment, probably that he too might be got rid of; the murderer, however, reeling from the effects of the debauch in which he had participated, came boldly into the presence, and boasted of the deed he had performed. The Nawab ordered him to be executed on the spot. Saadut Ali, hearing of what had occurred, and alarmed for his own safety, immediately took horse and fled beyond the frontier. Thus, in one day, the Vizier lost his Minister, his General, and his Brother.

The troops were still in a very unsettled state, and discontent regarding the new arrangements and the introduction of British officers daily increased. Some of the European officers were so maltreated by their own men that they fled to the nearest English camp; others braved the storm, but it was only by the timely arrival of two of the Company's battalions that the mutineers were reduced or disbanded.

Such was the state of the army. The finances were in scarcely less disorder. The regular subsidy was originally $25\frac{1}{5}$ lakhs, the Francis junto raised it to $31\frac{2}{5}$, but what with the expense of the temporary brigade, extra troops, and numerous officers employed with the Oude army, as well as various miscellaneous accounts, the demands during seven years of Mr. Hastings' administration averaged 100 lakhs annually, while, in spite of constant screwing, the receipts only averaged 70 lakhs; leaving in 1781 a deficit of $2\frac{1}{10}$* crores of rupees. To meet this frightful item, there was a materially-decreased revenue.

Another point here requires remark. We have said that Mr. Middleton was recalled by the majority in Council, as one of their first measures. Mr. Hastings no sooner recovered his ascendancy by the death of Colonel Monson in 1776, than he removed Bristow and reinstated Middleton. The former was restored in 1780, in obedience to repeated and positive orders from the Court of Directors, which, however, were only obeyed on a compromise with Mr. Francis. Mr. Bristow was displaced a second time in 1781, by the Governor-General, who said that he required to have a confidential Agent at Lucknow. To complete the story of the bandying about of Agents, we may here mention that Mr. Bristow was again restored by orders from home in 1782, and, finally, again ousted by Mr. Hastings in

* On Oude financial questions Mr. Mill is both ambiguous and contradictory. At page 629, vol. ii. (4to edition), he states "the debt with which he (the 'Nawab') stood charged in 1780, amounted to the sum of £1,400,000," but at page 650 remarks that although when the treaty of Chunar was concluded (in 1781), "the balance appeared to stand at forty-four lakhs," the demand next year (1782) "by claims of unknown balances, exceeded considerably two crores and a half, that is, were at least equal to twice the annual revenue of the whole country." In the text we have shown that the current demand having been from 70 to 130 lakhs, and the receipts having averaged only seventy lakhs, there needed no "claims of unknown balances" to swell the amount of deficit. The last portion, moreover, of the quotation making the total revenue to be only one and a quarter crore, dovetails ill with Mr. Mill's own showing at page 493, vol. iii., that the revenue in 1801 was about Rs. 2,30,12,929. An increase of more than a million of money during twenty years of progressive deterioration! Mr. Mill quotes Middleton for his first statement, and "Papers" for the second, but appears to have overlooked their discrepancy.

1783. The Governor-General affected to have acted only for the public good in these several transfers. He declared he had no personal dislike for the man he so repeatedly removed, and much respect for his conduct; but "the creature Bristow" (as on one occasion Mr. Hastings registered him) was odious in his eyes, inasmuch as that gentleman's appointment to Lucknow was a standing proof of his own discomfiture in Council. The Governor-General hated him accordingly, and few men loved or hated as did Warren Hastings.

This double explanation is requisite as a clue to the proceedings we have next to record. In the year 1780–1, the finances of the Company were in a most disastrous condition. The authorities had reckoned on certain sums from the Vizier, and were disappointed. Mr. Hastings, therefore, determined, himself to proceed to Lucknow. In August, 1781, the Governor-General reached Benares when the outbreak occurred, provoked by his arbitrary proceedings against Rajah Cheyt Sing. During these transactions, Mr. Hastings, as usual, evinced great courage, the Nawab great fidelity. The latter joined Mr. Hastings in September at Chunar, when he contrived to convert the Governor-General from a violent and imperious taskmaster into a warm advocate. For two years the Nawab's remonstrances and entreaties had been treated with contempt or indifference: they were now listened to and complied with, and for a brief space he was treated with respect. An arrangement was effected that led to the withdraval of the temporary brigade and three regiments of cavalry, leaving only one brigade and one regiment to be paid by the Vizier. He was also *allowed* to resume all jageers, giving cash for certain estates guaranteed by the Company; all British officers were also withdrawn; and sanction was given to *plunder* the two Begums, the wife and mother of Shoojah-oo-dowlah, though, as already observed, one of them had been previously guaranteed by Mr. Bristow. The result of the several "arrangements was, an immediate supply of fifty-five lakhs of ready money to the Company, and a stipulation for the payment of an additional twenty lakhs, to complete the liquidation of his debt to them."

Approving entirely of the decrease of the Nawab's permanent burthen thus effected, we cannot too strongly reprobate the mode by which he was authorized, and indeed eventually urged, to raise present funds. Mr. Hastings' defenders vindicate his proceedings towards the Begums, on the ground that these ladies abetted Cheyt Singh's rebellion, and that they had no right to the treasure they possessed. The latter statement is true. One wrong, however, does not justify another! What had been granted and guaranteed, even wrongfully, should have been respected. The falsity of the first plea has been frequently shown. We need not, therefore, here repeat the evidence. If any justification for the Governor-General is to be found in the fact, it is true that he was at this time put to his wits' end for cash. As the Court of Directors importuned him, so he pressed the Oude Government. Such was his anxiety on the subject that in May, 1782, he deputed his secretary, Major Palmer, to Lucknow, with the express object of realizing the arrears of subsidy. The mission gave such offence to Mr. Middleton that he resigned his appointment; and to add to the Governor-General's difficulties, his own special Agent allowed himself to be talked over and stultified by the Oude Officials.

Large as was the balance due, the Major was persuaded into believing that the sheet was clear; and instead of enforcing old claims he listened to offers of a loan. Mr. Hastings was much provoked both at the gullibility of Major Palmer and at Mr. Middleton's abandonment of his post in his (the Governor-General's) difficulty. He wrote to Mr. M. in severe terms; and on the 10th August, 1782, addressed Hyder Beg, the Oude Minister, under his own hand, in a most extraordinary letter, considering it to be addressed to the minister of a sovereign possessing a shadow of independence. After telling Hyder Beg that he owed his position to him (the Governor-General) and that he had been disappointed in him, he added, "I now plainly tell you that you are answerable for every misfortune and defect of the Nawab Vizier's Government." He then demanded that the balance due to the Company should be liquidated by the end of the year, or threatened that Hyder Beg should be made over to the tender mercies of his master, for the examination of his conduct. Hyder Beg understood full well the process by which the examination of the conduct of disgraced ministers was conducted in Oude as elsewhere. Stringent, however, as were the measures taken, they did not realize the subsidy. They did not effect Mr. Hastings' wishes, but they did much to upset the authority of the Nawab in his own territory.

Mr. Hastings had very correct *abstract* notions on the subject of interference. His practice and theory were, however, sadly at variance. When money was wanted for the Company, he stuck at nothing. His two nominees, Middleton and Palmer, had failed him; and he now, in despair, re-appointed the Company's protégé, Mr. Bristow, arming him with the most extensive authority. The new Agent was informed that "The Resident must be the slave and vassal of the Minister, or the Minister at the absolute devotion of the Resident * * it will be necessary to declare to him (the minister) in the plainest terms, the footing and conditions on which he shall be permitted to retain his place; with the alternative of dismission, and a scrutiny into his past conduct, if he refuses." Mr. Bristow was further told that he was to "control the appointment of officers, nay, peremptorily to oppose it," when he (the Resident) considered opposition in any case advisable. In the face, however, of such instructions, Mr. Hastings was not ashamed, in October, 1783, to thus characterize the Resident's conduct:—"Mr. Bristow, after an ineffectual attempt to draw the minister Hyder Beg into a confederacy with him to usurp all the powers of the Government, proceeded to an open assumption of them to himself." And, on the strength of this shameless allegation, Mr. Bristow was, for the third time, removed.

Unable to realize his views by proxy, Mr. Hastings, in March, 1784, again visited Lucknow, where he remained five months, during which time he effected the liquidation of a further portion of the Vizier's debt, removed another detachment of troops, restored a portion of the confiscated jageers, and endeavoured to put the Oude affairs into some sort of order. At Benares, on his return, he addressed the home Government in these prophetic words:—"If new demands are raised on the Vizier, and accounts overcharged on one side, with a wide latitude taken on the other to swell his debts beyond the means of payment: if political dangers are portended, on which to ground the plea of burthening his country with unnecessary defences and enormous subsidies, the results would be fatal." Mr. Hastings knew how wide a latitude he had himself taken, "to swell the Nawab's" debts beyond the means of payment, and judging of the future by the past, he concluded that another Governor-General might arise who, portending political dangers, would make them "the plea of burthening his (viz. the Vizier's) country with unnecessary defences and enormous subsidies." In short, Warren Hastings foretold, in 1784, exactly what occurred in 1801.

We have entered somewhat fully into the occurrences of Mr. Hastings' administration, as they gave their colouring to the British connection with Oude.

When Lord Cornwallis assumed the government of India, the Oude minister, Hyder Beg, was sent to wait on his Lordship. The negotiations that ensued were concluded on the 21st July, 1787, by a treaty, relieving the Vizier from certain balances still due; and declaring him in all respects independent within his own territory. The letter of the Governor-General contained the following remarkable paragraph:—"It is my firm intention not to embarrass you with further expense than that incurred by the Company from their connection with your Excellency, and for the protection of your country, which, by the accounts, I find amounts to fifty lakhs of Fyzabad rupees per year. It is my intention, from the date of this agreement, that your Excellency shall not be charged with any excess on this sum, and that no further demand shall be made; any additional aid by the Company is to be supplied on a fair estimate."

The abuses of the Oude Government repeatedly attracted the attention of Lord Cornwallis and Sir John Shore. Both were anxious to effect some reform, but were deterred by the difficulty of interfering with any good effect. At length the Vizier's extravagance and debauchery brought affairs into such terrific disorder that, in the year 1797, Sir John Shore proceeded to Lucknow. His visit, however, had a double purpose. The ostensible, and we hope chief design, was to give the Nawab good advice, but his Highness was also to be supplied with a minister, and another pull was to be made at his purse-strings. The Company had resolved to strengthen their cavalry, and, in the face of Lord Cornwallis's treaty, it was thought convenient to make the Nawab bear a portion of the increased expenses attendant on this augmentation. The helpless Vizier consented, stipulating that the charge should not exceed five and a half lakhs per annum, to pay the expenses of two regiments. The Governor-General took some credit to himself, that in this transaction he had talked and not dragooned the Nawab into concession. There was more difficulty in effecting a change of ministry. The Governor-General consented that the eunuch Almas should be appointed, but just as he had given his sanction, he discovered an order by Lord Cornwallis against the employment of that person. The Nawab, debarred from the selection of his own favourites, at length consented to receive Tufuzzel Hoosein, a learned, able, and we believe respectable, man, who then held the office of Oude Vakeel in Calcutta. It was, however, a sore trial of the honesty of that minister to be thus brought from Calcutta, and forced upon his Sovereign by the Lord paramount. Had Sir John Shore been as experienced in human nature as he was in revenue details, and in Indian politics, he would not have thus introduced the new minister to the Nawab directly as the creature of the British Government.

Scarcely had the Governor-General left Lucknow, when the Vizier died, and the disposal of the viceroyalty of Oude was in the hands of a simple English gentleman. As in another paper * we have fully considered the claims of Vizier Ali, and described the process by which he was put up and put down, we

* "Calcutta Review," No. 1;—Article "Lord Teignmouth."

need not here repeat the story. But we are bound to record even more emphatically than before, our opinion that Vizier Ali was unjustly treated. The plea of his spurious birth would not, by Mahommedan law, have interfered with his succession; and never would have weighed with the English authorities had he not rendered himself obnoxious to them by desiring to degrade Tufuzzel Hoosein the minister, who was considered "as the representative of the English influence." Tufuzzel Hoosein met Sir John Shore on his way to Lucknow with all sorts of stories about the violence and debauchery of the Lord Vizier Ali, but the Governor-General seemed to forget that this report might be biassed by personal motives; perhaps, too, he was unaware that Tufuzzel Hoosein had been the tutor of Saadut Ali, and even during Asoph-ood-dowlah's life was suspected of intriguing in favour of the Vizier's brother. But enough; Vizier Ali was degraded after a few weeks' enjoyment of authority, and Saadut Ali was raised to the musnud. New terms were of course dictated to the new Prince. It was no time for making objections. The treaty was signed; and protected by British bayonets, the new Nawab entered his capital. The ex-ruler, similarly guarded, was removed to Benares.

The treaty thus made was signed on the 21st Feb., 1798. It raised the subsidy from fifty-six to seventy-six lakhs, and provided for the discharge of all arrears. The fortress of Allahabad was ceded, and the sum of eight lakhs of rupees made over for its repairs. Three lakhs were likewise given for the repairs of Futtyghur, and twelve lakhs more were to be paid for the expenses incurred in the late revolution. The Nawab, moreover, agreed to reduce his establishments, and to consult, as to the manner of doing so, with the

British Government. No Europeans were to be allowed to settle in Oude, and no political relations were to exist without the knowledge of the British Government. In return for all this, the British guaranteed Oude, and agreed to maintain for its defence not less than ten thousand men. If it should at any time be necessary to increase the number of troops beyond thirteen thousand, the Nawab was to pay the expense; if they could be reduced below eight thousand, a suitable reduction of the subsidy was to be allowed.

The advantages accruing to the Company from this arrangement are manifest; it not only gave them possession of Allahabad, but it increased the subsidy twenty lakhs, and defined, though not distinctly, to what extent the subsidy might be lightened or increased. Unfortunately it left the time quite undetermined, and on this omission were based the unwarrantable demands made by the next Governor-General in 1801. What will perhaps most strike the English reader of Sir John Shore's treaty is, the entire omission of the slightest provision for the good government of Oude. The people seemed as it were sold to the highest bidder. Vizier Ali was young, dissolute, and needy: Saadut Ali was middle-aged, known to be prudent, and believed to be rich. Being of penurious habits, he had, even on his petty allowances as a younger son, amassed several lakhs of rupees; and, in short, was a more promising sponge to squeeze than his nephew. From the general tenor of Sir John Shore's life, we believe that his heart was in the right place, though this his last diplomatic transaction, might, if taken alone, lead us to a different conclusion. Wherever his heart was, his head at least must have been wool-gathering. He set a bad precedent. He made the musnud of Oude a mere transferable property in the hands of the British

Governor, and he left the people of Oude at the mercy of a shackled and guaranteed ruler. This may have been liberality, but it was liberality of a very spurious sort. Much as we admire Lord Teignmouth's domestic character, we are obliged entirely to condemn the whole tenor of his Oude negotiations. Historians have hitherto let him down lightly, but his Lordship must be judged by the same standard as other public officers; by the right or by the wrong that he committed, and not by his supposed motives, or his private character.

A Governor-General of far different calibre succeeded. One of the first objects of the Marquis Wellesley, on his assumption of the Government of India, was the reformation, or rather the reduction of the Oude Army, and the substitution in their stead of a British force. The Nawab set his face against the measure. The Governor-General was not to be thus baffled. Early in 1799, he applied for the services of the Adjutant-General of the army, Colonel Scott, an able and respectable, but austere man. In the first instance he was placed at the service of Mr. Lumsden, the Resident, but the latter gentleman was shortly after recalled, and the appointment bestowed on Colonel Scott. So stringent were the measures now taken, that Saadut Ali threatened to resign the musnud. It was but a threat, and intended to alarm or to mollify his persecutors. The Governor-General, however, seized upon the words, and putting his own constructions on them, insisted on their literal fulfilment; adding a proviso, which, at any rate, the Nawab had never contemplated, that on his abdication, the East India Company should inherit the principality of Oude, to the injury of his own children. Much disgraceful altercation ensued. The Governor-General returned the Nawab's remonstrances with angry and threatening remarks; insisted on the immediate execution of his orders, and finally marched the British troops into Oude without sanction of the nominal ruler. The Resident issued orders to the district officers to receive and provide for the English battalions, and was obeyed. Saadut Ali now felt himself within the iron grasp of a power that could crush him, and made the most abject appeals for mercy. The Governor-General, however, seized this opportunity for carrying out his own views. Referring to the Nawab's previous statements regarding the inefficiency of his army and their danger to himself rather than to an enemy, Lord Wellesley insisted on its reduction, and the reception, in its stead, of a force of twelve battalions of British infantry, and four regiments of Cavalry. A large portion of the Oude troops were accordingly disbanded, and so judiciously was this reduction managed by Colonel Scott, that not a single disturbance ensued.

The Nawab finding himself once more secure on his uneasy throne, had time to reflect how he was to bear the increased burthen laid upon him. His predecessor had been put to continued shifts to discharge the subsidy of fifty lakhs: he had, himself, by better economy, contrived to pay seventy-six lakhs, but how was he now to meet the further demand of fifty-four lakhs, to set against which there was only a diminished expenditure of sixteen and a half lakhs caused by the reduction of a portion of his army? He accordingly declared his entire inability to pay the required sum. The Governor-General wanted just such a declaration. He made it an excuse for the dismemberment of the Principality, and proceeded to carry out the finance arrangements with as little delicacy as had been shewn in effecting the military alterations. Mr. Henry Wellesley was deputed as Commissioner to Lucknow, and in concert with the Resident, dictated the cessions that were to be made when the former, in virtue of his office as Lieutenant-Governor of the ceded districts, made the primary arrangements for their management. The lands thus extorted were, at the time, estimated to be worth 1,35,23,474 rupees per annum. We have had occasion at the commencement of these remarks to show that they must now yield double that sum.

Lord Wellesley's conduct in this transaction was most despotic. As a wise statesman he judged rightly that the subsidy to his Government was better secured by a territorial cession than by a bond for cash payment; but, in extorting the former, literally at the point of the bayonet, and at the same time nearly doubling the subsidy, he shut his eyes to the most obvious rules of justice.

This treaty, which was signed on the 10th September, 1801, left the Nawab shorn of the best half of his territory; we may easily judge in what spirit he prepared to introduce "an improved system of administration *with the advice and assistance of the British Government,*" into the remainder. Such were the vague terms of the only stipulation contained in the present treaty, for the benefit of the people. We need hardly add that it remained a dead letter. This may have been only a negative evil; but a similar looseness of expression in Sir John Shore's treaty admitted of more positive perversion. We allude to the provision, that when it should be necessary to increase the contingent beyond 13,000 men, the Nawab should pay the expense. Sir John Malcolm more shrewdly than honestly observes, that if there was any meaning in the provision, it left the British Government to judge *when* the necessity should arise, and how long it should continue. The Marquis Wellesley did not hesitate to consider *that* time to be when Oude had just *escaped* invasion by Zeman Shah, and the period to last *for ever.*

There *was* danger from Zeman Shah; no one who reads the history of those times attentively can deny the fact. The state of the Oude army, the position of Sindea, and the advance of Zeman Shah called for arrangements for the defence of Oude. But the truth is, that almost as soon as the tidings of Shah Zeman's approach reached the British authorities, the danger had passed away. Sir James Craig stated before Parliament: "The first certain accounts we had were, I believe, in September or October—I rather think October (1798);" and again, "The accounts of the Shah returning from Lahore, which may be considered as his abandonment of his enterprise, reached Anopshere in January 1799." Thus the knowledge of the danger lasted, at the farthest, five months. Arrangements were made as quickly as possible to meet the invasion; and extra troops were kept in Oude from November, 1798, until November, 1799, being *ten months* after the Shah's retirement, and a special charge of more than thirty-eight lakhs of rupees was made to cover their expenses. This was all fair and proper. It was right that the sum expended should be charged; but surely there is no excuse for adding to the above contingent charge a fixed annual demand of fifty-four lakhs to cover a danger that no longer existed, and which, from that day to the present, now forty-five years, has never arisen. The claim was clearly opposed to the spirit of Sir John Shore's treaty, and to both the spirit and letter of that of Lord Cornwallis.

One of the earliest evils resulting from Lord Wellesley's arbitrary measures was, that the Resident became personally obnoxious to the Nawab. Colonel Scott was a man whose character passed unscathed through an ordeal of the strictest inquiry, both in and out of Parliament; but Saadut Ali could only be expected to see in him the instrument of disbanding a large portion of his own army—that chief symbol of Oriental sovereignty—the agent who had arranged the forced cession of the best half of his territory. Thus circumstanced, Colonel Scott could hardly be an acceptable ambassador, and in fact, was rather deemed a hard taskmaster. Unfortunately his manner had in it nothing to compensate for the matter of the invidious duties imposed on him. Habituated to military details, and late in life called on to negotiate delicate questions of diplomacy and civil administration, Colonel Scott performed his disagreeable task rather with the bluffness of the military martinet, than with the suavity of the accomplished diplomatist. He carried out his orders honestly, but harshly. He effected the views of Government regarding the Oude army, as well as, perhaps better than, any other officer of the day could have done; but there his services ended. He did nothing for the improvement of the country. He was rather an obstacle in its way. The Nawab having a reduced field of action, secure from personal danger, and hemmed in by British bayonets, screwed his wretched people. The Resident was not only unable to prevent these oppressions, but by the provisions of the treaty was compelled to be the instrument in their execution. Year after year were British troops seen throughout Oude realizing the revenues, enforcing the most obnoxious orders, and rendering nugatory to the oppressed their last refuge, military opposition. Great as was the interference in Asoph-ood-dowlah's time, it was now much greater. In former times the pressure of the Resident's authority was occasional, and on specific questions, and was chiefly felt at Lucknow; the incubus was now a dead weight bearing down the provinces, as well as the capital. The Nawab was also as much vexed and irritated as ever by the presence and conduct of the Resident, by his interference in favour of, or in opposition to, persons and things in the very capital.

Such conduct, however, at this time tended less than formerly to weaken the ruler's power. The British army was now believed to be at the beck of the Oude Government to support its revenue arrangements. The Nawab was thus, though degraded in character, strengthened in position. The previous (authorized) interference had told rather *against* the Oude Court; it was now in its favour. The powerful were now supported against the weak. This system went on for years, and under several Residents. It was brought prominently to notice when Colonel Baillie was in office. A long, vexatious, and fruitless correspondence took place between the Nawab and the Government. Colonel Baillie was anxious to promote improvements, the Nawab liked neither the matter nor the manner of the suggestions offered. He cared for his cash, and for nothing else. No person however can read his replies to Colonel Baillie's demands without being satisfied that, under kindlier treatment at the outset, much might have been done with such a prince. We are specially struck at his being in advance of the Bengal Government of the day on Revenue arrangements. Colonel Baillie proposed that ameens should be sent into the districts to collect statistical information, that they should visit every village, and procure the revenue papers of former years.—"Those papers, after the minutest investigation which may be practicable, to be transmitted, under the signature of the revenue officers, to the presence, when your Excellency and I shall consider them, and be enabled to form an accurate judgment of the real resources and assets of every district in your dominions."* The Nawab replied, "I shall issue my orders to the ameens, agreeably to what you have suggested; but I recommend that this measure be carried into effect by actual measurement of the cultivated and waste lands, and of lands capable of being cultivated; in which case the exact measurement of the lands, as well as the amount of the jumma, will be ascertained, and the boundaries of villages will also be fixed, so as to preclude future claims or disputes among the Zemindars on questions of unsettled boundary."* The following reply to another suggestion shows how much better the Nawab understood his people, and how much better he was able to manage Oude than was the Resident:—

> "You suggest, that such ameens as perform their duties properly shall hereafter be appointed tehsildars; but in this case, if the ameens be previously informed, that after ascertaining the jumma of their elakas (districts), and transmitting the revenue papers for ten years with the Wasilbunkee accounts of the revenue, they will be appointed to the office of tehsildar, it is probable that, for their own future advantage, they will knowingly lower the jumma, and state less than the real amount. I therefore think it would be more advisable to separate the two offices entirely; or, at all events, that no ameen should be appointed tehsildar in the Zillah in which he may have acted as ameen. In this latter mode, the ameens who are found to be deserving may still be rewarded, and the opportunity for fraud may be prevented."*

The readers who have accompanied us through this hasty sketch of Saadut Ali's career, will perhaps concur in the opinion we gave at the commencement of this article, that his malgovernment was mainly attributable to English interference, to the resentment he felt for his own wrongs, and the bitterness of soul with which he must have received all advice from his oppressors, no less than to the impunity with which they enabled him to play the tyrant.

Lord Minto at length checked the Resident's interference against the people; he did not thoroughly

* Minutes of Evidence. Appendix No. 26, page 383.

understand the nature and extent of that at Court, and therefore disturbed not Colonel Baillie's domestic ascendancy. The Marquis of Hastings looked more into the matter and prohibited it entirely.

Saadut Ali died in July, 1816, and was succeeded by his eldest son Rufsat-ood-dowlah, under the designation of Ghazee-ood-deen Hyder. His accession delighted Colonel Baillie, and scarcely pleased the Calcutta Government less. The new Nawab, of course, agreed to every proposition of the Resident, whom he addressed as "My Uncle," and who reported that his advice was not only acceptable to Ghazee-ood-deen, but was urgently requested by him. The very spirit of credulity seems, at this period, to have possessed our countrymen. Not only does Colonel Baillie appear to have swallowed the sugared words of the Nawab, but the authorities in Calcutta adopted his views; and, taking advantage of what was deemed the amiable spirit of the grateful Nawab, authorized the several measures of reform, which, to say the least, Colonel Baillie was little competent to carry through.

A new light however soon broke in on the Governor-General, and he ascertained that Ghazee-ood-deen loved reform as little as his father had done. It was discovered that both Nawab and Resident had been puppets in the hands of the Residency Moonshee, who, by threatening Ghazee-ood-deen with the fate of Vizier Ali, contrived to bend him to what were called British views, while he found his account in allowing the Resident to fancy himself the friend and counsellor of the Nawab. The discovery of these intrigues induced a peremptory order from the Governor-General forbidding all interference, and the affair ended in the removal of Colonel Baillie, who, however, had in the interim negotiated a loan of two crores of rupees. The friends of Lord Hastings have asserted that these loans were voluntary, but Colonel Baillie has shown the transaction in a very different light. The money was extorted from the Nawab by the importunity of the Resident, who acted on repeated and urgent instructions from the Governor-General. During the Burmese war, and under another administration, a third crore was borrowed, we know not exactly by what process, but, as the greater part of the interest was settled on the minister of the day, Motumed-ood-dowlah (more generally known in India as Aga Meer), and his life, honour, and property were guaranteed, it may be inferred that he managed the matter.

Loans of this sort are generally discreditable to the borrowers; in Oude they have been doubly prejudicial. Most of them have been compulsory, and they have been the means of perpetuating, and immeasurably extending the guarantee system. The interest of each loan, whether from Nawab, King, or Begum, has been settled on the connections and servants of the several parties lending the money, with provision in each case that the pensioner was to be protected by the British Government. Thus, for the sake of temporary pecuniary relief, have we established and fostered a system which must vitiate any Government, and is doubly destructive to a Native State. At Lucknow, for years, the Residents held public durbars, where the guaranteed attended, and pleaded against their own Sovereign or his servants. Thus were the Monarch and his subjects arrayed against each other: thus was the Sovereign degraded in his own capital.

This abuse has been checked; but a still greater evil exists to the present day. The guaranteed are hundreds: the *privileged* are thousands. Every British sepoy from the Oude dominions can, through his commanding officer, refer a fiscal or judicial case to the Resident. This at first sight appears a valuable privilege to our Native soldiery, of whom, (as already stated,) the greater proportion are raised in Oude; but the plan works badly. Zemindars throughout the country will buy, beg, borrow, or steal the name of a British sepoy, in the hope of thus gaining attention to their petty claims. The consequence is, that the just appeals of real sepoys are frequently neglected, while a false claim is now and then forwarded. We are, indeed, of opinion that, much as the Oude Government is molested and degraded by sepoys' claims, true and false, the men themselves are rarely benefited by the Resident's interference. Litigation is promoted, hopes are excited, and eventually the party who would, if left to his own resources and the practices of the country, have arranged or compromised his quarrel, is led on to his ruin. But we have been drawn from the thread of our narrative.

In the year 1819, the Nawab Ghazee-ood-deen Hyder was encouraged to assume the title of King. Lord Hastings calculated on thus exciting a rivalry between the Oude and Delhi families; the Nawabs having hitherto paid the descendants of the Mogul all outward homage, and affecting still to consider themselves only as lieutenants of the Emperor. This arrangement was somewhat akin to some of the masquerades with which the Company commenced their career. While ruling Bengal and the Carnatic they were entitled Dewans; and now, while lording it over Oude, the puppet Nawab must, forsooth, be encouraged to assume a royal title, in order to act as a counterpoise to *the Great Mogul!*

Death will not, however, spare a King any more than a Nawab vizier. Ghazee-ood-deen died, and was succeeded by his son, Nuseer-ood-deen Hyder, who more than perpetuated the worst practices of his predecessors. Engaged in every species of debauchery, and surrounded by wretches, English, Eurasian, and Native, of the lowest description, his whole reign was one continued satire upon the subsidiary and protected system. Bred in a palace, nurtured by women and eunuchs, he added the natural fruits of a vicious education to those resulting from his protected position. His Majesty might one hour be seen in a state of drunken nudity with his boon companions; at another he would parade the streets of Lucknow driving one of his own elephants. In his time all decency, all propriety, was banished from the Court. Such was more than once his conduct that Colonel Low, the Resident, refused to see him, or to transact business with his minions.

In 1831 Lord William Bentinck visited Oude. He had received a frightful report of its misrule from Mr. Maddock, the Resident; but questioned the reality of the picture laid before him. He now traversed the country and judged for himself; he saw every proof of misgovernment, and was at length convinced that the existing system could not, and ought not to, last. He had one hope for Oude. Momtuzim-ood-dowlah, better known as Hakeem Mehndy Alee Khan Bahadoor, was then minister, and his energy and ability might, if unshackled, save the sinking State. To encourage his efforts, Lord William studiously manifested his regard for the minister, and forbade all further interference of any kind on the part of the Resident, who was prohibited from even advising unless his opinion was asked. The Governor-General warned the King of the consequences of continued misrule; he gave him and his minister a fair chance of recovering their common country; and resolved that, if it failed, the most stringent measures should be adopted, involving the entire management of Oude by British officers. His Lordship writes on 31st July, 1831—"But I am sanguine in my hope of a great present amelioration from my belief in the capacity and willingness of the present minister to effect it; and from the entire possession he has of the confidence of the King." * * * Sad proof how incompetent is the wisest European to read an Asiatic heart. The Governor-General left Lucknow fully impressed with the opinions above quoted. Hakeem Mehndy *had* effected much good, *had* reduced the public expenses, and *had* brought some order into the management of affairs. The subordinate officials feared him; the talookdars and village chiefs respected him. Under his strong administration the country at length tasted peace. In August, 1834, however, just three years after Lord William Bentinck's visit, the minister found himself, without the slightest warning, deprived of office, and threatened with dishonour, if not with death. The charges brought against him were, disrespect to the Royal relatives, and even to the Queen Mother. This was all fudge. At Lucknow, as throughout the East generally, the King is everything; his nearest relatives are nothing. An affront to the lowest minion about the Court would more probably have been resented, than one to a connection of the King. The pretext, however, was plausible; the minister was degraded, and nothing but the strong arm of the Resident saved his wealth, life, and honour. His real crimes were his ability, energy, and fidelity;* had he been more subservient and less faithful, he might have

* We are quite aware that the Hakeem has been differently painted. In the *Calcutta India Gazette*, he was depicted, in 1833, as "one of the most intriguing, avaricious, and rapacious men that ever breathed," but any acquainted with the paternity of those remarks would at once perceive how little dependence could be placed on them.—H. M. L.

escaped his exile to Furruckabad, where he lingered for some years, constantly affecting preparations for a pilgrimage to Mecca, but really longing and watching for a return to power. His wishes were at length fulfilled, and under a more virtuous ruler he died as Minister of Oude. But, during the interval, Hakeem Mehndy's head and hand had become feebler, while the flood of abuse had swelled. Unable to stem the current, he died at the helm, in the bold attempt. Often during his exile, we have heard the old man dilate upon the evils that ruined Oude, and declare that with fair play and a fair field he could yet recover the country. We then considered his day gone by, and little contemplated his having another opportunity of treading the slippery path of politics. The Hakeem's merits must be judged of by comparison with other ministers; and he will appear just, firm, and sagacious. It is therefore to be lamented that such a man was lost to Oude while his energies were still vigorous. On the accession of Mahommed Ali, Hakeem Mehndy was recalled to power, but his health was then declining, and his life was near its close.

His nephew and heir Munowur-ood-dowlah Ahmed Ali, a respectable but unenergetic man, has since been twice at the head of affairs: he is a better sportsman than a cabinet minister, and is altogether too honest and unpractised in court affairs to cope with the Ameen-ood-dowlahs and Shureef-ood-dowlahs of the day.

Lord William Bentinck, in his report of 11th July, 1831, entering into many details of past circumstances, and explaining his proposals for the future, added, "I thought it right to declare to his Majesty beforehand, that the opinion I should offer to the home authorities would be, that unless a decided reform in the administration should take place, there would be no remedy left except in the direct assumption of the management of the Oude territories by the British Government."* His Lordship with propriety adds, "I consider it unmanly to look for minor facts in justification of this measure, but, if I wanted them, the amount of military force kept up by his Majesty is a direct infraction of the treaty." The Minute continues in the following honest and disinterested strain:—

"It may be asked of me—and when you have assumed the management, how is it to be conducted, and how long retained? I should answer, that acting in the character of guardian and trustee, we ought to frame an administration entirely native; an administration so composed as to individuals, and so established upon the best principles, revenue and judicial, as should best serve for immediate improvement, and as a model for future imitation; the only European part of it should be the functionary by whom it should be superintended, and it should only be retained till a complete reform might be brought about, and a guarantee for its continuance obtained, either in the improved character of the reigning Prince, or, if incorrigible, in the substitution of his immediate heir, or in default of such substitute from nonage or incapacity, by the nomination of one of the family as regent, the whole of the revenue being paid into the Oude treasury."*

In reply to his suggestions to the home Government, Lord William Bentinck received instructions in the year 1833, at once to assume charge of Oude, unless, in the meantime his advice had been followed, and decided improvement had ensued. Averse to so strong a measure, and ascertaining that affairs *were* slightly amended, his Lordship postponed the measure, again warning his Majesty as to the inevitable result of continued misrule.

Nuseer-ood-deen Hyder, however, encouraged by long-continued impunity, persevered in his mal-practices. The treasures of his grandfather, Saadut Ali, were now drained to the last rupee, and every device was invented to recruit the finances of the State, or rather to supply the privy purse of the King. A low menial was his chief confidant; any man who would drink with him was his friend. In 1837 he became ill, and for some

* Minutes of Evidence. Appendix No. 27, page 404.

weeks was confined to his palace, but he was not considered in danger, when, suddenly at midnight of the 7th July, 1837, the Resident was informed that his Majesty was no more.

When describing the Fureed Buksh palace, we touched upon the occurrences of which it was the theatre on that eventful night. If space permitted, we should now gladly detail those brilliant operations. It was a sudden crisis, an unforeseen emergency, that tested the stuff of which our officers were made. Not only Colonel Low himself, but his assistants, Captain Patton and Captain Shakespeare, shewed admirable courage and coolness. A moment's indecision on the part of the Resident, or a failure on the part of either of the assistants in the duties assigned to them, would have deluged the city of Lucknow with blood, and cost the Residency party their lives; as it was, they were in great danger, especially Captain Patton, and were only rescued from the hands of the rebels by the speedy arrival of the 35th regiment. The conduct of the gallant Noke-ka-pultun that night was a good augury of the laurels they were so soon to earn in the more trying field of Affghanistan.

The case of the boy Moona Jan was dissimilar from that of Vizier Ali: the latter was acknowledged, the former disowned by his reputed father.

The new King, Mahommed Ali, was a cripple, a respectable old man, who had never dreamt of royalty, and whose very insignificance and previous seclusion saved his life during the emeute of the soldiery on the 7th of July. Grateful for his elevation, which he attributed to the British Government, he was willing to acquiesce in any reasonable terms that might be dictated to him, consistent with what he deemed his *inzut*.* He

* Honour.

fell into good hands; never was there a Resident more kind and considerate than Colonel Low. He understood his own position, and had sense to perceive that he gained more credit in fulfilling its duties than by stepping out of his sphere. Contented with exercising the legitimate authority of his station, he had no ambition to be "Mayor of the Palace" at Lucknow, or to maintain the balance of power between the rival factions around the throne. He was satisfied to look on in small matters—ready to advise in great ones. He was a plain soldierly man, who, having served an apprenticeship to politics under Malcolm, fought at Mehidpoor, and afterwards trod the intricate paths of Indian diplomacy at Jeypore, and with Bajee Rao, was well adapted for the Lucknow Court: doubly so as being in his own character the very antithesis of everything there; straightforward integrity, opposed to crooked chicanery. Colonel Low had seen enough of native courts to understand and fathom them, while he had escaped their corruptions. Inaccessible alike to bribes, threats, and cajoling, he was feared by the vile Nuseer-ood-deen Hyder, and respected by the amiable Mahommed Ali.

The new King had soon a new treaty laid before him; the document bears internal evidence of not being Colonel Low's work; indeed some of the clauses were entirely opposed to his views. Its two prominent features were, first, the introduction into Oude of an auxiliary force of two regiments of Cavalry, five of Infantry, and two companies of Golundauze at an annual expense of sixteen lakhs of rupees, to be defrayed by the local Government. The other was a stipulation for the management by British officers of such districts of Oude as should be notoriously oppressed by the local agents. Colonel Low was, we know, averse to saddling the King with more troops; but his views were overruled, and a portion of the regiments were raised. The measure was, however, very properly disapproved of by the Court of Directors, and the enrolment of the new levy prohibited, as being an exaction on the Oude State.

Mahommed Ali was evidently so much in earnest in his efforts for the improvement of his kingdom, that Government overlooked the glaring mismanagement still existing in parts of Oude, and did not act on the permission given by the new treaty.* The King's intentions were good, and the character of the Court rose very much during his short reign. He was unfortunate in the death of his two able ministers, Moomtuzim-ood-dowlah (Mehndy Ali Khan) and Zaheer-oo-dowlah. The nephew of the former, as already mentioned, then succeeded, and held office for two years: on his resignation a young nobleman, by name Shurreef-oo-dowlah, the nephew of Zaheer-oo-dowlah, assumed the reins of government, and retained them until the old King's death. Shurreef-oo-dowlah is a man of good ability; of considerable firmness and activity. His manners are pleasing; he possesses habits of business; on the whole he is considered the ablest and most respectable candidate for the ministry. He is however personally disliked by the present King.

On the death of his father in May, 1842, Mahommed Amjud Ali, the present King, ascended the throne. His conduct towards his minister was such as to cause his resignation within two months. He then appointed a personal favourite, one Imdad Hooseen, entitling him Ameen-oo-dowlah. After a trial of five months he was found wanting, and removed, and Munowur-oo-dowlah having returned from pilgrimage was reinstated. The new minister, unable to stem the current of Lucknow intrigue, held the office scarcely

* The whole treaty was disallowed by the home Government.—ED.

seven months, when Ameen-oo-dowlah was recalled to his master's councils. The favourite is generally supposed quite incompetent for the duties of his office, and indeed is said to trouble himself very little about them. He takes the profits and leaves the labours to his deputy, Syud-ood-dowlah, a low person who has rapidly risen from penury to power by the prostitution of his own sister. Not long since this man was an omedwar for the office of moonshee to one of Col. Roberts's regiments. So goes round the wheel! The King pays no attention to business, will abide by no warnings, will attend to no advice, and, it is rumoured, has secretly confirmed his imbecile ministers in their places for four years, in spite of the remonstrances of the Resident.

Let us briefly recapitulate. The condition of Oude is yearly becoming worse. The revenue is yearly lessening. There are not less than 100,000 soldiers in the service of Zemindars. The revenue is collected by half that number in the King's pay. In more than half the districts of Oude are strong forts, most of them surrounded with dense jungle, carefully rendered as inaccessible as possible. Originally the effect of a weak or tyrannical Government, such fortresses perpetuate anarchy. The amils and other public officers, are men of no character who obtain and retain their position by Court bribery. Only the weak pay their revenue; those who have forts, or who, by combinations, can withstand the amil, make their own revenue arrangements. Throughout the country nothing exists deserving the name of a judicial or Magisterial Court. The newswriters are in the pay of the amils, generally their servants; nevertheless, not less than a hundred dacoities, or other acts of violence attended with loss of life, are annually reported; how many hundreds then pass unnoticed! Within the last six months, the Government dawk has been robbed: within the last three, an amil has been slain. While we write (1845), the British cantonment of Cawnpoor has been insulted; and month after month, the local press tells of new atrocities. In short, the Government of the country is utterly palsied; its constitution is altogether destroyed; no hope remains. Were any vitality left in Oude, the country has, during the last twelve years, had a fair opportunity of recovering. If the system of a King, a Minister, a Resident, and a protecting army could subsist without ruin to the country so ruled, it has had a trial. The scheme cannot be said to have failed for lack of good instruments. The Oude rulers have been no worse than monarchs so situated usually are; indeed they have been better than might have been expected. Weak, vicious, and dissolute they were, but they have seldom been cruel, and have never been false. In the storms of the last half century, Oude is the one single Native State that has invariably been true to the British Government; that has neither intrigued against us nor seemed to desire our injury. It may have been weakness, it may have been apathy, but it is at least fact, that the Oude Government has ever been faithful, and therefore it is that we would not only advocate liberality towards the descendants of Saadut Khan, but the utmost consideration that can be shown them, *consistent* with the duty we owe to the people of Oude. Among her ministers have been as able individuals as are usually to be found in the East; and there have not been wanting good men and true as Residents. It is the system that is defective, not the tools with which it has been worked. We have tried every variety of interference. We have interfered directly, and we have interfered indirectly; by omission as well as by commission; but it has invariably failed.

One great error has been our interference in trifles, while we stood aloof when important questions were at issue. Another crying evil has been, the want of any recognised system of policy in our negotiations with the Lucknow Court. Everything seems to have been mere guess-work and experiment. One Governor-General or one Resident has adopted one plan; the next has tried something wholly different. The Nawab, or the King, the Minister, and the Resident, have each had their turn. One or other has alternately been everything and nothing. If an able minister was appointed or encouraged by the British Government, he was, as a matter of course, suspected and thwarted by his master; if the King did happen to employ an honest servant, the power of the latter was null, unless he had the Resident's support. The amils neglected him, the zemindars despised him. There could be no neutrality in the case: the British agent must be friend or foe; he must be for or against the minister. Thus could each member of the triumvirate vitiate the exertions of one or both the others; any individual of the three could do incalculable evil; but the three souls must be in one body to effect any good. Such a phenomenon never occurred; there never was an approach to it, unless perhaps for a few months in Colonel Low's time.

On reverting to the past, it will be found that we have interfered in the city, and have held aloof in the country; that at another time, while we spared the palace, we have entered the villages with our tunkhwas (revenue orders). Again, for a time, we have left both Court and country unmolested. Such sullen silence was always construed into the most *direct* interference; for, the King being guaranteed, it was believed that he was then at liberty to work his will without fear of consequences, since British bayonets would appease whatever tumult might arise. Our troops have carried the fortresses of the oppressed by storm, and put the brave defenders to the sword. On one occasion a terrible example was made, and not a man escaped. Our cavalry surrounded the fort, the infantry entered; and of the doomed defenders, not a soul survived.* At that period we not only guaranteed the Ruler, but were made the executioners of his will. A revulsion came: such acts were shown in all their naked deformity; and both Court and country were again for a while left to themselves. Fraud was then substituted for force, and occasionally large bands of ill-paid and licentious soldiery were sent to devastate the country they could not subdue. The British troops did their work of destruction speedily, and therefore with comparative mercy. The royal rabble spread, like locusts, over the land, and killed by famine what they could not destroy by the sword.

From this mass of mischief, who is the gainer? It may be supposed that the amils at least gain; not they. There may perhaps be twenty families in all Oude, that had profited by Government employ; but all others have been simply sponges. The officials have sucked others to be themselves squeezed in turn. Is it to remain thus for ever? Is the fairest province of India always to be harried and rackrented for the benefit of one family, or rather, to support in idle luxury *one* individual of *one* family? Forbid it justice, forbid it mercy! Had any one of the many Governors-General who spoiled Oude remained a few years longer in office,

* The fort of Puther Serai, in the year 1808.

he might have righted her wrongs. But, unhappily, while several have been in authority long enough to wound, not one has yet had time to bind up and heal. Hastings began the "stand and deliver" system with the Nawabs. More moderate governors succeeded, who felt ashamed to persecute a family that had already been so pillaged. They pitied the monarch, but they forgot that misdirected mercy to him was cruelty to his subject-millions.

For this culpable indifference, our Government had a standing excuse,—their hands were tied by the treaties of their predecessors, and their interference, even if justifiable, would do more harm than good. Poor casuistry! The truth is, that where a question admits of doubt, there can be little danger if, *with clean hands*, we take the weaker side; if, foregoing all thought of personal or political profit, we arbitrate in favor of the mass. There was no treaty for Warren Hastings' acts, or for half the acts of half his successors. A hole was, however, generally found for creeping out of every dilemma which affected our own interests. At the very worst, when a vacancy occurred on the musnud, a new negotiation soon set all to rights. On each occasion we dictated our own terms; on each of these opportunities we might as readily have made arrangements for securing good government as for securing our own subsidy: we were explicit enough on the one point; all else was left indefinite, the stronger party being, of course, the interpreters of the law. The Oude Government therefore suffered by diplomatic quibbles; the Oude subjects by revenue ones. In each case the weakest have gone to the wall. The result is before our eyes; the remedy is also in our hands. No one can deny that we are now authorized by treaty to assume the management of the distracted portions of the kingdom.—*All* are more or less distracted and misgoverned. Let the management of all be assumed under some such rules as those which were laid down by Lord W. Bentinck. Let the administration of the country, as far as possible, be native. *Let not a rupee come into the Company's coffers.* Let Oude be at last governed, not for one man, the King, but for him and his people.

We must be brief in the explanation of the plan we would recommend.

The King has made himself a cypher; he has let go the reins of Government; let us take them up. He should be prevented from marring what he cannot or will not manage. In every eastern court the Sovereign is *everything* or nothing. Mahommed Amjud Ali has given unequivocal proof that he is of the second class; there can, therefore, be no sort of injustice in confirming his own decree against himself, and setting him aside. He should be treated with respect, but restricted to his palace and its precincts. The Resident should be minister, not only in fact, but in name. Let it not be said that he works in the dark; but give him the responsible charge of the country, and make him answerable to the British Government for its good or ill management. While his personal demeanour to the King must be deferential, he should be no more under his authority than the commissioner of Delhi is under the Great Mogul. Divide the country into five districts; in each, place a British officer, as superintendent, who shall receive appeals against the Native officers. Abolish, *in toto*, the farming system. Give as quickly as possible a light assessment for five years, fixed as far as possible by the people themselves; that is, let the one-and-a-quarter million (or thereabouts), the country may be supposed able to bear, be subdivided in a great assembly of the people among the five districts; and then let the district, pergunnah, and village quotas be similarly told off, under the eye of British superintendents.

Due consideration must be given to the circumstances of all, and to the privileges that may have arisen from long exemption; and it must be remembered that one village may be ruined by paying half what another, in apparently similar circumstances, can easily afford; let the rich and powerful pay as well as the poor and weak. Reference must be had, and some consideration granted to past payments and past privileges as well as to present condition. Perfect equalization cannot be expected at once.

While the first arrangements are in progress, a strong military force should be at hand; and the first act of recusancy should be severely punished. The dismissal of the rural armies should be effected, and all forts belonging to notorious persons should be dismantled. Where possible, an amnesty should be given for the past. No individual, whom it may be possible to reclaim, should be branded. The motives that had driven men to the bush should be considered, and penalty bonds having been taken, they should be received and treated as reformed members of society. Under firm but liberal treatment, many a supposed desperado would retrieve his reputation. Speedy and severe examples should be made of amils and others convicted of fraud, extortion, or other oppression; and it should be early and distinctly understood that no position will screen malefactors or defaulters. The rule will disgust a few, but will delight the many.

The revenue settlement is the first great question in all eastern countries; when it is well effected, all remaining work is comparatively easy. At the risk then of being set down by men who deal in forms, rather than in realities, as a very unsound lawgiver, we say, first settle the revenue question satisfactorily, and the path of amendment will be smooth. Let men's minds be relieved as to the past and the future, and they will readily settle down for the present. Three months, at the utmost, should suffice to make the summary settlement we propose; no niceties need be entered into. Let the assessment be light, and let every man, high and low, who has to pay, have his quota *distinctly* registered, whether it be in cash or in kind; and let prompt and severe punishment follow the earliest instances of infringement of recorded agreements.

Let a date be fixed, anterior to which no Government claims for revenue shall be advanced. Let it also be at once promulgated that no civil case will be attended to of more than twelve, or at the utmost of twenty years' date; and no police case of more than three; and that all claims must be filed within one year of the date of the introduction of the British rule. All these cases should be made over to punchayets, *superintended* by the best men in the land. Brief reasons of decision in each case should be entered in a book, and copies of the same sent weekly to the superintendent. For ordinary civil, fiscal, and police duties, courts should be established or old ones confirmed in the several zillahs: punchayets should be encouraged; honest members* of such assemblies should be honoured and favoured, and dishonest ones discountenanced and disgraced.

What a change would such a system, honestly and ably worked out, effect within a single twelvemonth! It is

* In every community there are individuals whom disputants will readily receive as arbitrators: such men are usually elected *sur-punch*, or president, by the members chosen. —H. M. L.

delightful to think of it. We see the difficulties in the way, but difficulties are not impossibilities. No plan is all smooth, no measure of amelioration is without obstacles. Our main difficulty would be to select superintendents of sufficient experience, possessing at the same time energy and ability, strength of body and of mind, to face the chaos that would at first be presented them. Such men are, however, to be found. They must be paid, and liberally too, not in the Scinde and Saugor fashion. It would be the worst of all economy to employ men who would not remain at least five years to work out the primary scheme.

Our plan involves the employment of every present Oude official, *willing to remain, and able to perform the duties* that would be required of him. The majority of the present amils would resign, as would most of the officers about the Court. All valid tenures of land would of course be upheld, and all superannuated officials having claims to pension, would be considered. It would be desirable to retain the services of one or two respectable men, to assist the Resident and form with him a court of appeal from the superintendent's decrees.

When matters were thus put in train, village boundaries should be defined; a revenue survey, and a settlement for thirty, or even fifty, years should follow.

We do not anticipate the necessity of any permanent increase of establishment. If Mr. Maddock's estimate is correct, half the sum now plundered by the amils and the ministers would amply remunerate all the requisite officials.

The primary arrangements would probably require cash; but as the improvement of the country would be secured, an Oude loan of a crore of rupees might be raised, which the increase of cultivation and general amelioration of the State would enable us easily to pay off in ten or fifteen years. We repeat that the assessment should be light. The people as well as the Court should benefit by improvement, if they are expected to further it. There should be a liberal allowance for the King—twenty, thirty, or even fifty lakhs per annum might, as the revenues increased, be allowed. He should be furnished, to his heart's content, with silver-sticks, but very scantily with matchlocks. The King would be dissatisfied, let him remain so. He is not particularly well pleased just now, and, so long as we act honestly, the state of his temper is not of much consequence. In whatever spirit he might meet our proposed radical reform he would find few to sympathize in his dissatisfaction. His brothers, uncles, and cousins would be delighted with the change.

The guaranteed would be in ecstacies. Almost all others would rejoice at the reformation. The people of Oude—the men who recruit our "beautiful regiments"—would bless John Company.

The scheme we have here indicated, rather than detailed, is not for a day, nor for any specific number of years. It is refined cruelty to raise the cup to the lip and then to dash it away.. Let us not deal with Oude as we have done with Hyderabad and Nagpore. The kings of Oude, generally, have, as rulers, been weighed and found wanting. His present Majesty has habitually disregarded the spirit and letter of the terms concluded between his father and the British Government. The family must be placed beyond the power of doing further mischief. We have not been guiltless; in repenting of the past, let us look honestly to the future; for once let us remember the people, the gentles, the nobles, the royal family, and not legislate merely for the King.

If the Oude Residency could, with honour, be withdrawn, or if we believed that there was a possibility of the Government of the King holding together for a month, when abandoned by the British Government, we should at once advocate giving his Majesty the opportunity of trying to stand on his own legs; but knowing the thing to be impossible, we have offered the only practicable remedy for the ills that afflict the country, and shall be delighted to see it, or some such scheme, speedily carried out. This scheme is given in the rough. We have not even attempted to round it off; the principle is all we advocate. The details may be indefinitely improved, but whatever outcry or opposition our sentiments may elicit, we sit down satisfied with the reflection that we have suggested no breach of faith, but have promulgated a plan which the most conscientious servant of the State might be proud to work out.

MAHRATTA HISTORY AND EMPIRE.

[WRITTEN IN 1845.]

MAHARASHTRA, or the country of the Mahrattas, is, according to Hindoo geographers, one of the five principal divisions of the Deccan,* or, country south of the Narbadda and Mahanaddi rivers. The limits of Maharashtra are variously given; Mahommedans seldom troubled themselves about geographical questions, and it was long after they had overrun the different provinces of India, before they inquired respecting their original divisions. Mahrattas, indeed, are seldom mentioned by Mahommedan writers until the deeds of Shahjee, and his son Sivajee, brought their countrymen prominently to notice. When the historian Ferishtah alludes to the Mahrattas he calls them "the Hindoos," "the Bergis," meaning, by the first appellation, the population generally, in contradistinction to their Moslem conquerors; by the second, designating them marauders.†

* The Deccan of the Hindus comprised the whole peninsula south of the Narbadda and Mahanaddi, but Europeans have adopted the Mahommedan definition, and limit it to Telingana, Gondwana, and that portion of Maharashtra above the Western Ghats, being generally the country between the Narbadda and Kistna rivers.—H. M. L.

† Mr. Elphinstone states, at page 457, vol. ii. of his History of India, "The word Mahrattas first occurs in Ferishta, in the transactions of the year A.D. 1485, and is not then applied in a general sense." This is an error. It strikes us we have repeatedly seen them mentioned at earlier dates. By a hasty reference we have now found three such references: A.D. 1342, Ferishtah, as translated by Dow, says, "He at the same time conferred the Government of Doulutabad and of the country of the *Mahrattors* upon Cuttulech, his preceptor."—Page 289, vol. i. Again, at

Two points of the Mahratta history have, however, been recovered from the mazes of antiquity. Ptolemy tells us that, in the second century, there was a large city called Tagara, one of the principal marts of the Deccan, or country of the south; well known to the Greeks, and frequented by Egyptian merchants, 250 years before Christ. Its exact position has been the subject of controversy. Mr. Elphinstone considers that the site has yet to be ascertained, while Grant Duff places it on the Godavery, about fifty miles below Pyetan,—supposed to have been the Paithana of Ptolemy. Learned natives recognise the name of Tagara, and Grant Duff alludes to ancient deeds of grants of land engraved on copper plates, styling its monarch "the Chief of the Chiefs of Tagara." The second fact is, that a conquering sovereign, by the name Salivahan, whose era begins A.D. 77, and is the one now ordinarily used in the Deccan, ruled in the Mahratta country. He is said to have subdued the famous Vikramaditya, king of Malva; but this could not have been the case, as there are 135 years between their eras. The capital of Salivahan is recorded to have been at Pyetan on the Godavery.

The foregoing seem to be the only facts that can be gleaned from the mass of legendary accounts regarding Maharashtra, and its many petty independent States, antecedent to the inroad of the Mahommedans under Alla-ud-deen, in the year of our Lord, 1294. At this time, Jadow Ram-deo Rao was king, rajah, or mayhap, only "chief of the chiefs." He was at least sovereign of an extensive country, though there were at the time several

two places, in page 320 of the same volume, "Sirvadon, Chief of the Mahrattors," is mentioned. In Scott's translation of Ferishtah's History of the Deccan, among other inmates of "Feroze Shaw's" zenana, in A.D. 1398, are noted "Rajpootnees, Bengalees, Guzratees, Telingances, *Maharattins*."—H. M. L.

other chiefs in Maharashtra independent of his authority. Jadow Ram-deo Rao ruled at Deogurh, the modern Doulutabad. His conquerors, astonished at his wealth and power, styled him King of the Deccan. The plunder of his capital supplied Alla-ud-deen with the wealth which enabled him to usurp the throne of Delhi.

To make our subsequent historical details intelligible, it will be requisite briefly to describe the position and features of the Mahratta country. Mr. Elphinstone's History of India gives the following boundaries of Maharashtra. On the north, the Sautpoora range of hills, from Naundode, near Baroach, on the western coast, to the source of the Wurda river. On the east, the Wurda river, which, taking a south-easterly course, joins the Wyne Gunga, south-west of Chanda. On the south, the boundary is a waving line, running past Beder and Kolapoor to Goa; while the western limit is the line of coast from Goa to Damaun, and thence inland to Naundode.

The trapezium enclosed within this outline covers about one hundred thousand square miles, and is estimated to contain between six and seven millions of inhabitants. Some portions of the country are thickly inhabited; but large tracts are desolate, or very thinly peopled, giving as the average of the whole, scarcely above sixty to the square mile.* The most marked feature of the country, whose boundaries we have defined, is the Syhadree range of mountains, commonly

* Mr. Tone, who was an officer in the service of the Peishwa, says, "I believe it may be safely asserted that through the whole country (Bengal and Behar excepted) one acre in fifty is not cultivated." He wrote in 1818, and doubtless alluded to the country around Poona, where he had served; but even there, and distracted as the Peishwa's territory had been, we consider his statement to be above the mark. The Satara and Poona lands now bear a far different aspect; indeed, wherever British influence extends, and common care and intelligence is exerted, the change is soon extraordinary. We have, in more than one quarter, seen cultivation doubled, nay trebled, in a single year.—H. M. L.

called the Ghats. They run along the western coast of India, at an average distance of thirty-seven miles from the sea: their summits are from three to five thousand feet in height, rising abruptly from the west, and supporting a table-land, which averages three thousand feet above the sea and slopes gradually towards the east. This range divides Maharashtra into three great tracts, the Concan, the Concan-Ghat-Mahta, and the Desh (Des), or country to the eastward of the high lands. The Concan is that portion of the country which lies between the Syhadree mountains and the sea, and extends in a long narrow strip from the river Taptee, at Surat, to the Portuguese town of Goa. This division varies in breadth from twenty-five to fifty miles, and contains about twenty thousand square miles, or one-fifth of all Maharashtra. The Concan is a very rugged country, "interspersed with huge mountains and thick jungles; intersected by rivers and numberless rivulets." Some portions, however, especially near the coast, are remarkably fertile. Towards the Ghats the country is wild and picturesque in the extreme, the jungle verdure is there perpetual, and vegetation most luxuriant.

The table land above the passes is called the Concan-Ghat-Mahta, or Concan above the Ghats. The highest part of the Syhadree range is that which immediately faces the Concan. The breadth of this chain of mountains is about twenty or twenty-five miles, including the space from the summit of the ridge facing the Concan to the termination of the branches on the east side; the whole intervening space being designated Concan-Ghat-Mahta.* The area will thus be equal to rather more

* The general elevation of the Bombay sanatarium in that portion of the Syhadree range called the Muhabaleshwur hills is 4500 feet above the sea: the highest summit is 4700; the height above the subjacent country in the Concan is 4000 feet, and above the general level of the Deccan, at its eastern base, 2300 feet. The average breadth of the

than half that of the Concan. The whole tract from Joonere to Kolapoor is fairly populated, and the valleys are well cultivated. The people are hardy and patient, and under Sivajee made excellent soldiers. The Mawulees (or Mahratta inhabitants of a portion of the table land and valleys called the Mawuls) were the main instruments of his rise. North of Joonere, the valleys are less cultivated, and are occupied by Bheels and Coolies who were all plunderers, but many of whom have been reclaimed. The summits of the hills are frequently crowned with huge basaltic rocks, forming natural fortresses of great strength. Many of them have been improved by art, and from the earliest times these mountain fortresses have been considered among the strongest in India. Mr. Tone says, "I have counted, in a day's march through Candeish, nearly twenty fortresses, all in sight, in different directions." Often as the majority of these places have changed hands, they have seldom been taken by main force. Many contain springs of pure water; all have reservoirs, and, in native warfare, their weak garrisons could defy powerful armies. Gold or stratagem, treachery, famine or a *coup-de-main* usually gained them; it was reserved for the British to carry by storm in open day such places as Panalla, Samungurh, and Manogurh. The third great division of Maharashtra is the Desh, or Des, being the open country eastward from the foot of the Ghat-Mahta. The Desh is by no means an unvaried level, but becomes less broken as it recedes easterly. It is intersected by four chains of mountains, running east and west,—the Sautpoora, Chandore, Ahmednuggur, and Mahdeo hills; the first being the northern boundary of Maharashtra, the last lying to the north of Satara.

table land on which the settlement has been established is eleven miles and a half, and the average length eleven miles.—H. M. L.

The general aspect therefore of the Mahratta country, is hilly. The valleys are well watered, but indifferently cultivated. Five great rivers—the Narbadda, the Taptee, the Godavery, the Deema, and the Kistna—permeate the country.

The mass of the inhabitants are Hindus,* separated, as elsewhere in India, into the four great classes; but, as usual, innumerably sub-divided. The Brahmans have long almost monopolized all civil and military offices; though, while thus secularly employed, they forfeit the veneration evinced towards those who devote their lives to spiritual concerns. They commenced as servants; they now command in almost every Mahratta durbar. The name of Mahratta is applicable to all the inhabitants; but Grant Duff states, that "amongst themselves a Mahratta Brahman will carefully distinguish himself from a Mahratta. That term, though extended to the Koonbees, or cultivators, is, in strictness, confined to the military families of the country, many of whom claim a doubtful, but not improbable descent from the Rajputs." He might have added that, all over India, the Mahratta chiefs are considered to be Soodras of the three great divisions, husbandmen, shepherds, and cowherds. Mahratta women are well treated; those of rank are generally veiled, but it is little, if any, disgrace for them to appear uncovered. Scott Waring witnessed the wife of the Peishwa, Bajee Rao, practising her horse; and Mr. Tone says, at page 9, "I can affirm having seen the daughter of a prince making bread with her own hands, and otherwise employed in the

* "The Hindus" are too generally considered, or rather talked and written of, as one race, much as half-enlightened Indians believe all Feringhis (Franks) to be one people: their ignorance may be excused, but Englishmen should understand that between the Hindu of Tanjore, Mysore, Bengal, Oude, Maharashtra, and Rajputana there is quite as much difference in language, customs, forms, and features as obtains between Russians, Germans, French, Spaniards, Italians, and Englishmen.—H. M. L.

ordinary business of domestic housewifery." Widows usually perform suttee with the bodies of their husbands, unless when they have infant children, or are themselves called to govern, which has so often happened of late at every Mahratta court. In such cases the veil is, in a great measure, relinquished. The widow having then to counsel with men, and even to go into battle, forgets that she is a woman. Within an area of 100,000 square miles, there must doubtless be great variety of form and feature, but the Mahrattas generally may be considered small, active, well-made men. For Hindus their features are coarse. They are hardy, persevering, and abstemious. The cultivators and shepherds are frugal, patient, and industrious, and possess as many good qualities as can be expected from a people whose country has for centuries been a battle-field. They have the cunning incidental to their condition; to a race who have long lived on the defensive, who have been accustomed to be squeezed, and who have learnt to pay nothing that could not be enforced. The notions of Mahratta chiefs and soldiers are, for Indians, peculiar. They have none of the pride and dignity of the Rajput, Sikh, Jat, or Patan, and little of their apathy or want of worldly wisdom. The Mahratta considers plunder and profit to be the object of war; for this he will undergo fatigue, privation, and danger; but he has no notion of endangering or sacrificing his life on a mere punctilio. Mr. Elphinstone, after strikingly showing the points of difference between the sentiments of the Mahratta and the Rajput, affecting even the outward appearance of the two nations, remarks, "there is something noble in the carriage even of an ordinary Rajput; and something vulgar in that of the most distinguished Mahratta. The Rajput is the most worthy antagonist, the Mahratta the most formidable enemy; for he will not fail in boldness and enterprize when they are indispensable, and will always support them, or supply their place by stratagem, activity, and perseverance."

The village system prevailed in great purity in Maharashtra; all the accessible land in the country was portioned off into villages, the boundaries of which were defined. The arable land was divided into fields, and every field was *named* and registered. The majority of the cultivators were hereditary occupants (meerasdars), who could not be ejected as long as they regularly paid the assessment on their fields. The Government servants in charge of circles of villages were called Deshmukhs, and their accountants, Deshpandyas; the first answering to the Talukdar or Zemindar, the second to the Canungo of Hindoostan. There were also a class of farmers of the revenue called Khotes. One or other of the above would occasionally take advantage of circumstances, and usurp the lands over which they had been appointed mere collectors. During a period of anarchy, and under native rule, such persons effected in Maharashtra what, in a time of peace, and under a British Government, was deliberately accomplished in Bengal; showing that hasty, though well-intentioned, legislation may affect the rights and welfare of a people even as much as the worst tyranny. Every village was a miniature commonwealth. Each had its establishment of officials. The Patail, or head man, was usually a Sudra; he held an office nearly corresponding to the Punch, Mokudum, or Lumberdar of the N. W. Provinces. He superintended the cultivation, and managed the police. Disputes that he could not adjust were referred to a punchayet of "the inhabitants best acquainted with the circumstances." The Patail's clerk was termed Koolkurnee; he was usually a Brahman, though occasionally, as in Hindoostan, of any other caste. His office corresponded with that of Patwaree, or record keeper.* There was likewise the Mhar, or Dher, being the Goreit, Bolahar, or Dowaha, that is, the scout, guide, and watchman of the village. Then there were the handicraftsmen, and others, few of whom are now found as public servants in villages under British administration, but who are all over India recognised as remnants of the primitive village system, and used to be paid by assignments of land. Though in the Concan, as in Bengal, the Khotes, or farmers of the revenue, and the Pergunnah chiefs have generally transmitted their office to their sons, and superseded the village maliks; in the Ghat-Mahta, each village has still its Patail and Koolkurnees.

Ten years ago Colonel Sutherland pronounced the Berar (Nagpore) and Satara Governments the best native administrations in India, implying that their demands were the lightest on the cultivator. The injunction of the Shaster, that the Prince should only take one-sixth of the crop, is everywhere disregarded; where payments are in kind, three times that amount, or half the crop, is more usually exacted; it is a lenient administration that demands only one-third from irrigated and good lands, and one-fourth from dry and poor soils. As elsewhere, there are other petty but vexatious cesses, and the Customs system among the Mahrattas, as in other parts of India, is a fruitful source of annoyance to traders, yielding little corresponding profit to the rulers. The cultivators are divided into two great classes, Meerasdars, or hereditary occupants, with certain proprietary rights, and

* The Patail and Koolkurnee are terms introduced by the Mussulmans. The original Hindoo appellation of the former was Gaora, or, if the village manager, Gramadekaree; the Kalkarni was designated Gramlekak.—H. M. L.

Ooprees or tenants at will. "All property, or shares of hereditary right in land, or in the district and village establishments, termed under the ancient Hindoo Governments, *writtee*, is now best known throughout the Mahratta country, by the name of *wutun*, and the holder of any such enjoys, what is considered very respectable, the appellation of wutundar."—*Grant Duff*, vol. i. p. 43. So much are rural honours valued, that the fractional portions of the office of Patail were often sold at high prices; each holder of a portion designating himself Patail. When the monarch of an empire, Sindhia clung to what he called his hereditary Patailship.

Of the nine existing Mahratta States,* none, except Sawunt-waree, a petty chiefship, can claim any antiquity. Satara ranks from 1664; Kolapoor, from a younger branch of Sivajee's family that separated in the year 1720. The rest are formed from later acquisitions granted to military commanders, chiefly by the Peishwa, to be held in subordination to the empire, but which never paid allegiance to Satara, and a very brief one to Poona. All the principalities, except Satara, Kolapoor, and Sawunt-waree, are beyond the limits of Maharashtra; and except about Nagpore, where there are a few Mahrattas, the ruling classes in

* They are—

1. Gwalior, or Sindhia's Country.
2. Indore, or Holkar's ditto.
3. Berar, or Bhonsla of Nagpore.
4. Baroda, or Ghaekwar.
5. Satara, or the lineal descendants of Sivajee's son, Sambagee.
6. Kolapoor, or the lineal descendant of Sivajee's second son, Rajah Ram.
7. { Dhar,
8. { Dewas, are petty chiefships held by two of the oldest of the Mahratta families, "the Powars."
9. Sawunt-waree, properly Waree, a small State dependent on Beejapoor, the chiefs of which are called Desaee, Deshmukh, or Sawunt, *hence* Sawunt-waree.

There are also many Jaghirdars, more or less powerful, some holding direct from the British Government, others depending on Satara, Kolapoor, &c.

Absorbed into the British Territory:—

1. Poona, or the Peishwa's Principality.
2. Tanjore, or the Territory of Venkajee, brother of Sivajee.—H. M. L.

those countries are as much foreigners as are the Mahommedans in Oude, or the English in Calcutta.

With this brief general sketch we now proceed to our historical notice. In the year 1294 Alla-ud-deen, the governor of Oude and nephew of the Khiljee king of Delhi, Jelal-ud-deen, without asking the sanction of his uncle, moved across the mountains and forests of the Vindhya range, and, after a toilsome and dangerous march of 700 miles through hostile countries, reached the El Dorado of Deogurh. His force consisted only of 8000 men, a small army for so formidable an undertaking, but as large a one as its bold leader could have fed on such a route. Ramdeo Rao Jadow, the Mahratta prince of Deogurh, negotiated terms, but his son broke the treaty, and drew on his country doubly severe terms. Large cessions of territory were made, and the victor carried back with him the accumulated treasuries of centuries. Thus enriched, Alla-ud-deen returned to Delhi, only to assassinate his uncle, and seize the imperial throne. During the reign of Alla-ud-deen almost all Maharashtra was subdued; but on his death the Mahrattas recovered the greater part of their territory, and endeavoured to regain Deogurh. Its Mussulman garrison was, however, relieved by the Emperor Mubarik, who took the Mahratta leader Hirpal Deo, prisoner, and caused him to be flayed alive. Several insurrections occurred. The Emperor Mahommed Tughluk, among other wild schemes, endeavoured to remove all the inhabitants of Delhi to Deogurh, the name of which place he changed to Doulutabad, intending to make it the seat of empire. He had partially executed his merciless design when the Deccan fell from his hands, to be recovered after nearly four hundred years by Aurungzebe, only to remain a nominal appendage of the Mogul Empire for less than the term of a single life, and then to be for ever rent from the Delhi throne.*

The rebellion of the fugitive nobles,—who, in the year 1344, fearing the royal treachery, rose on their guards, slew them, fled to Doulutabad, and there, electing one of their own number, a simple commander of a thousand horse, as their king, raised the standard of rebellion,—belongs to the record of the Mahommedan empire in the South; but without a brief notice of the circumstance the Mahratta history would be unintelligible. The rebels agreed on a plan of warfare which has ever been the favourite one in the Mahratta country. A portion of the allied force under the new King, Nazir-ud-deen, defended Doulutabad, while the other chiefs acted on the communications and supplies of the besiegers. The Emperor divided his force accordingly, and himself prosecuting the siege, he sent a strong force against the field detachments.

The Delhi Empire never was at peace. It was especially troubled during Mahommed Tughluk's reign; and now, when he had nearly reduced Doulutabad, he was urgently called away by an insurrection in the North. The confederates, emboldened by his departure, gained courage; they were joined by many Mahratta chiefs, and, under Zuffir Khan, one of their own ablest leaders, gave the Imperial general battle, slew him, and gained a great victory. Nazir-ud-deen came out from Doulutabad to meet his victorious army, but, observing the influence that Zuffir Khan had obtained, wisely resigned the throne in his favour. Zuffir Khan had originally been the slave of a Brahman, who treated him kindly

* Aurungzebe only completed the conquest of the Deccan in the year 1687, and Nizam-ul-mulk became independent in 1723. Thus the Moguls had a troubled and exhausting occupancy of thirty-six years, in reward for centuries of exertion and incalculable expenditure of life and treasure.—H. M. L.

and foretold his future rise. The new king changed his own name to Alla-ud-deen Husein Kangoh Brahmani, in gratitude to his old master, whom he appointed his treasurer. Thus originated the name of the Brahmani dynasty.

Alla-ud-deen commenced his reign in the year 1347. His rise was mainly caused by the succours afforded by the native (Mahratta) chiefs, to whom he was not ungrateful. His dynasty lasted about 150 years. Maharashtra was, at his accession, divided into petty principalities. Every holder of an inaccessible hill or deep jungle was a polygar, literally a rebel. The new sovereign subdued the weak among those in the plains, and conciliated others by grants of lands, or by the confirmation of their possessions. By such means he made himself master of almost all Maharashtra, except part of the Concan-Ghat-Mahta, which his successors did not succeed in conquering until a century later. During this period there were several insurrections, but chiefly induced by Mahommedan officers. The Mahratta chiefs were generally faithful.

In 1396 the terrible famine designated "the Durga Dewee" commenced, and lasted for twelve years, depopulating large tracts, and leaving traces of its effects for forty years after. The inhabitants of whole districts were swept away; village land-marks were lost; their boundaries were forgotten, and, when the periodical rains returned, and endeavours were made to restore cultivation, the whole country was discovered to be in one mass of disorder. The polygars had increased in all directions; the hill forts formerly reduced by the Mahommedans, and abandoned in the great dearth, were now held by banditti, who infested the country and destroyed the returning hopes of those who had escaped nature's terrible calamity. Great efforts were made during successive years to repeople the villages and to reduce the hill forts. No rent was demanded for lands during the first year of fresh occupation, and only a tobra (horsebag) full of grain for each bigah during the second year. But little was effected until, by a systematic plan, the robber forts were reduced throughout the Syhadree range. An able commander, by name Mullik-ul-tijar, had great success. He subdued the whole Ghat-Mahta, and carried his arms into the still unconquered part of the Concan. He besieged and obliged a rajah, whose surname was Sirkay, to surrender, insisting on his embracing Islamism. The Mahratta consented, but deluded the Moslem into a previous expedition against the Rajah of Kondan, whom he designated his hereditary enemy. A detachment of 7000 Mahommedans started under the immediate orders of their commander, and guided by Sirkay, as to an assured victory, were led into an ambuscade, and every man massacred. The Deccanees, Hindoo and Moslem, have always been noted for such wiles of warfare.

Mahommed Shah, the second Brahmani monarch, divided his kingdom into four turufs (or quarters), to each of which he appointed a governor, or Turufdar; but as the empire extended by conquests from the rajahs of Telingana, Beejaungur, Orissa, and the Concan, it was found necessary further to subdivide the management of the country, separating each of the former divisions into two. Several arrangements were also made with a view of securing the fidelity of the local governors; but they all failed. Mahommedans can conquer, they cannot retain. There seems to be something in their creed and customs opposed to permanency and to good government. The subdivision into eight governments took place in the year 1478, and only eleven years afterwards, Adil Khan, the governor of Beejapoor, the founder of the Adil Shahee dynasty, declared his independence: soon after, four other Chiefs assumed the purple. Only three of these States,* formed from the extinction of the Brahmani dynasty, were in existence when the Mahrattas rose into notice. The revolutions in the several Mahommedan States of the Deccan all aided the eventual emancipation of the original inhabitants. The majority of the forts, especially in unhealthy parts of the country, were held by Mahrattas, sometimes as hired soldiers of the Mahommedan Government, but more frequently as Jaghirdars and hereditary defenders of the soil. In all times of weakness or of tumult these garrisons, called Gurhkuris, made their own terms; they either throw off the yoke altogether, or joined the party or pretender that offered the best terms. Deshmukhs, Dessaees, and other rural chiefs also, whether they acquired authority by birth, or as Collectors of revenue, or as military leaders holding lands in wild and secluded quarters, all made their harvest of Mahommedan dissensions and of Moslem pride and ignorance. From these Chiefs are descended the present "Mankurees," literally great men, many of whom, though reduced to poverty, claim superiority to the present mushroom monarchs of their race, and pay them very unwilling homage.

Except the Sawunt-waree family and the Powars of Dhar and Dewas, the princes of the present day are men of yesterday, descended at best from petty village officers. The Holkars were shepherds, and Mulhar Rao, the first leader of the name, for years grazed his uncle's sheep in Candeish. The Sindhias were of a higher, though broken family, so that Ranoojee, the modern

* The Beejapoor, or Adil Shahee; the Ahmednuggur, or Nizam Shahee; the Golcondah, or Kootub Shahee.—H. M. L.

head of the clan, served the second Peishwa as a common bargir, and report says, even carried his slippers. Damajee Ghaekwar and Pursojee Bhonslay were stirring leaders who rose from the ranks and occupied and bequeathed to their descendants the countries they were sent to plunder or to manage. Ballajee Wishwannah Bhutt, the first Peishwa, was hereditary accountant of a village in the Concan, and was originally employed as a common revenue karkoon or clerk. The family of Powar were Deshmukhs of Phultun in the sixteenth century; and the Sawunts were, even earlier, Dessaees or Deshmukhs of their present country of Waree, near Goa, and rose into importance under the kings of Beejapoor during the war with the Portuguese.* Bhonslah was the original name not only of the Waree family, but of the respective founders of the Berar, (Nagpore,) Satara, and Kolapoor houses, though only the two latter were related to each other. We will now briefly trace the history of their common ancestors.

Babjee Bhonslah was hereditary patail of several villages near Doulutabad. He had two sons, the elder named Mallojee, the younger Wittojee. Mallojee Bhonslah was an active, stirring soldier, and was employed under the banner of Lookhjee Jadow Rao, a Mahratta chief of rank in the Beejapoor service. Mallojee, having been for several years childless, engaged the services of a celebrated Mahommedan saint in his favour. A fine boy was in due time born, and, in gratitude to the Saint, was called after him, "Shah," with the adjunct of respect, "jee." Thus in the year 1593 was born Shahjee, the father of Sivajee. Mallojee, by an act of extraordinary impudence, took advantage of a jocose speech of his leader Jadow Rao on the occasion of the Hooli

* Hamilton erroneously dates their origin from the time of Sambajee, the son of Sivajee.—H. M. L.

saturnalia, and procured the unwilling acquiescence of that Chief to his daughter Jeejee's betrothal to his son Shahjee. Mallojee's opportune discovery of a large quantity of treasure reconciled Jadow Rao, and enabled him to purchase the rank of Commander of 5000 horse, with the title of Rajah, from the weak and venal court of Ahmednuggur, upon which the nuptials between the young couple were celebrated. Mallojee's good fortune was attributed to the auspices of the goddess Bhowanee, who prophesied that one of Mallojee's race should become a king, re-establish Maharashtra, protect Brahmans, and the temples of the gods; and that his posterity should reign for twenty-seven generations. With his new title, Mallojee received charge of the forts of Sewneree and Chakun, and of the pergunnahs of Poona and Sopa.

The Deccan monarchies were at this time constantly assailed by the Moguls. The Mahratta chiefs played their own game during these contentions. As a specimen of the times and of the value that was attached to their alliance, we may mention that Shahjee's father-in-law, Jadow Rao, having deserted the Ahmednuggur standard in the year 1621, was rewarded by the Emperor Jehangir with the rank and authority of Commander of 15,000 horse. He did not long enjoy his honours. Nine years afterwards he desired to return to his allegiance, was inveigled into a conference within the walls of Doulutabad, and there murdered. On this, his widow, a woman of masculine habits, with her followers and many of her connections, for ever abandoned the cause of the Nizam-shahee monarchs.

Shahjee, who had now succeeded his father and was recognised as a bold and able leader, followed the example of his mother-in-law, and received the rank of a commander of 5000 horse with a suitable jaghir. He was, however, soon disgusted, and offered his services to the Beejapoor Government to act against the Moguls, who were then effecting the conquest of the Ahmednuggur State. His offer was accepted, and he soon obtained the distinction of being considered the most activo and dangerous enemy of the Imperial arms. Doulutabad however fell to the Moguls; its minister became a pensioner, and its monarch a prisoner. Shahjee did not lose courage. He proclaimed another prince, assumed the management of the remaining Ahmednuggur territory, and soon recovered a great portion of what had been lost. In the year 1635, Shah Jehan was at length excited by the audacity of Shahjee to make a great effort to reduce both him and his supporters. An overwhelming force, in four divisions, moved against them, and the Deccanees were beaten at all points. The Beejapoor king then agreed to pay a tribute of twenty lakhs of pagodas; and, the forts of Shahjee being captured, he petitioned for re-admittance into the Imperial service. This was refused, but he was told that he might enter that of Beejapoor.

In the year 1627 Sivajee had been born in the fort of Sewneree, close to the town of Joonere, fifty miles north of Poona. Three years afterwards, to the great displeasure of Jeejee Bye and her friends, Shahjee married a second wife, Tuka Bye Mohitey, by whom he had a son called Venkajee. He had a third son, Suntajee, whose mother was a dancing girl.

In the year 1637, the Beejapoor Government entrusted Shahjee with the post of the second-in-command of an expedition into the Carnatic. On his departure, he left his family and his Poona jaghir in charge of a Brahman named Dadajee Konedeo. The agent was an able revenue officer and a faithful servant. He recovered the broken districts, encouraged agriculture, and, by good management, greatly increased the prosperity of his charge. Shahjee's services in the Carnatic obtained for him a grant of several of the valleys called the Mawuls of Concan-Ghat-Mahta in the neighbourhood of Poona; these he likewise placed under the Brahman's care. Dadajee found their hardy and simple inhabitants in the utmost penury, scarcely clothed, and barely able to defend their wretched huts from the wild beasts of the forest which daily increased on them. He took many of the Mawulees into his service, gave advances of seed grain to others, and by demanding no rents for nine years, and then establishing very light assessments, recovered a considerable portion of country. It is pleasant to find in the dark catalogue of Indian Rulers an occasional Dadajee Konedeo. Would that there were more such as he among our own ranks! Men who live for their duty, for the improvement of their respective charges, and not simply for the accumulation (even though it be honestly) of so many thousand rupees to take with them to Europe.

The men of business in Maharashtra were Brahmans. It was no part of the duty of a soldier to bend to the work of a scribe. Dadajee gave his master's son a good education, according to the notions of the times and the country. Sivajee could never sign his name, but he was an excellent horseman and marksman. He could use the matchlock as well as the bow, and was master of the different kinds of swords and dagger used in the Deccan. He was also instructed in the rules and observances of his caste, and in the popular parts of Hindoo mythology. He loved to hear the "Kuthas," or tales, in verse or prose, of the gods and heroes of antiquity; he delighted in martial exercises, and he hated the Mahommedans, as Hannibal hated the Romans. While a mere boy he joined some plundering bands in the

Concan-Ghat-Mahta; and, taking a fancy to the rude Mawulees, was often absent for whole days with parties of them, on plundering and hunting excursions. He thus became familiar with the defiles and paths of the rugged country around Poona, and attached to himself the most daring of the wild inhabitants. He marked the positions of the strongholds in his neighbourhood, and early determined to seize one of them. As peace now existed with the Moguls, and the Beejapoor army was employed in the Carnatic, the hill forts, generally neglected, were guarded even more slenderly than usual. Sivajee took advantage of this neglect: he bribed the Killadar of Torna, near Poona, to yield the place to him, and then wrote to the Beejapoor court, offering increased rent for the surrounding district, and protesting that he had nothing in view but his sovereign's advantage. His statement being backed by liberal bribes to the courtiers, he was allowed for several years to pursue his own schemes unmolested. Treasure was found at Torna; and its discovery of course attributed to Bhowanee, the tutelar goddess of Sivajee's family. Arms and ammunition were purchased, and within three miles of Torna he erected, on the mountain of Morbudh, the fortress of Rajgurh.

Sivajee now advanced step by step; one stronghold after another fell into his hands, and with them the command of the circumjacent territory. These continued successes at length alarmed the weak Beejapoor monarch, who could however hit upon no better expedient for reducing the rebel son, than to decoy and imprison the loyal father, then usefully employed in the Deccan. Bajee Ghorepuray, another jaghirdar, was the tool chosen for this act of treachery: he invited Shahjee to his house, and then had him seized. It was sufficiently well known that he was guiltless of any connection with Sivajee; but it was believed that the son, whom the royal arms could not reduce, might be brought to yield, if the torture and imprisonment of his father was the alternative. Shahjee was accordingly confined in a stone dungeon, the door of which was built up, and he was informed that the single remaining aperture should be closed if his son did not submit within a certain period. For four years, Shahjee remained a prisoner, and eventually owed his release to disturbances in the Carnatic and to the king's fear that Sivajee, who had opened communications with the Emperor Shah-Jehan, would offer his allegiance to the Moguls. On releasing his prisoner, the king permitted him to return to the Carnatic, first binding him not to avenge himself on Bajee Ghorepuray. Shahjee agreed to the terms. He verbally complied with all the demands made on him, but he did not forget that his brother of the faith had invited him to his house, and there seized his guest, and delivered him to Moslem bonds. He was therefore no sooner clear of the toils than he wrote to Sivajee, "If you are my son, punish Bajee Ghorepuray of Moodhole." This is the only record of communication between the father and son during many years. Well did Sivajee execute the vindictive order. He watched Ghorepuray's movements until the year 1661, when, finding a fitting opportunity, he pounced upon his victim, slew him and many of his family, and plundered and burnt their village. Shahjee was loud in acknowledgment of the pious deed, and soon after, came from the Carnatic to visit his son, and thank him in person for his filial conduct.

During his father's incarceration, Sivajee had been comparatively quiet, but no sooner was Shahjee released, than his son successfully resumed his unscrupulous efforts for effecting the conquest of the entire Ghat-

Mahta and Concan. At this time (1656), Prince Aurungzebe was his father's viceroy in the Deccan, and was entering on those intrigues with the celebrated Meer Joomleh, the minister of Golcondah, which led to the direct interference of the Moguls in that State; and which ended in the entire reduction of Golcondah, and the admittance of Meer Joomleh into the Mogul service. The Mahommedan power in the Deccan was fast approaching its close, but the wily, and occasionally sagacious Aurungzebe little thought that, while undermining and gradually absorbing the Mussulman principalities there, he was only clearing the field for a more powerful rival,—that he was preparing the way for "a people of fierce countenance," whose banner, within thirty years of his own death, should wave over the walls of Delhi, and whose leaders should soon after be levying contributions from Lahore to Tanjore.

Beejapoor was at this juncture in the throes of dissolution; it had lately very narrowly escaped the clutches of Aurungzebe, and was distracted by a factious and treacherous nobility, under the weak administration of an infant king. An effort was, however, now made to put down the insurrection of Sivajee; a large force was collected, and Afzool Khan, an officer of high rank, appointed to the command. He was a bold but arrogant man, and boasted, at taking leave, that he would bring back the rebel in chains to the footstool of the throne. Afzool Khan, however, knew the strength of the country in which he was employed and gladly listened to the humble messages of Sivajee, who, affecting only to desire peace, disclaimed all thought of opposing so great a personage as the Khan. The Moslem was deluded, and sent Puntojee Gopinat, a Brahman in his employ, to arrange with Sivajee the terms of the Mahratta's submission. The envoy was received with all honour, and Sivajee conducted himself during the first interview with great humility. During the ensuing night, the rebel leader secretly visited his guest's quarters, and, addressing him as his spiritual superior, appealed to him as a Brahman, in favour of his own cause, which he stated to be that of the Hindus generally. Sivajee urged that he had been called on by the goddess Bhowanee herself, to protect Brahmans and kine, to punish the violators of temples, and to resist the enemies of religion. These arguments were seconded by large promises, and the interview ended in Puntojee's entering into a scheme for assassinating his master. Accordingly, the Brahman returned to the Mogul camp to report that Sivajee was in great alarm and ready to surrender, if he could only receive a guarantee of his personal safety from the mouth of the Beejapoor commander. The deluded Khan fell into the snare. The place appointed for the meeting was a space, cleared for the occasion, at the foot of the fort of Pertabgurh. *One* road through the jungle was cleared; all other avenues were closed. A force was told off to attack the Beejapoor main army, when the death of Afzool Khan should be announced, by a signal of five guns from Pertabgurh. Parties were also so disposed as to cut off whatever escort might accompany the victim. Two persons only were let into the secret of the dark deed about to be perpetrated.

Sivajee prepared for the death-grapple, as for a religious though desperate deed. Having performed his ablutions, he placed his head at his mother's feet and besought her blessing. Then, attiring himself with a steel chain cap and hauberk under his turban and cotton gown, he concealed a bichwa, or crooked dagger, under his right sleeve, and placing on the fingers of his left hand a wagnuk,* he leisurely proceeded down the hill to the interview. Fifteen hundred troops escorted Afzool Khan; but he was requested by the traitor Puntojee to halt them, when within a few hundred yards of the base of the hill, lest Sivajee should be alarmed and decline the interview. The Khan accordingly advanced, armed simply with his sword, and attended only by a single soldier. Sivajee, too, was accompanied by one attendant, and as he approached the place of interview, repeatedly halted as if in alarm. To give him confidence, the traitor Brahman begged that Afzool Khan's follower might fall back. The chiefs then advanced and being introduced by Puntojee, gave each other the usual oriental embrace.† Sivajee, while his right arm was round the Khan's neck, with the left struck the wagnuk into his bowels. Afzool Khan, feeling himself wounded, pushed the assassin from him, and attacked him sword in hand. The chain armour of Sivajee resisted the blow, and, before the Khan's single attendant could step up to his support, the chief was slain, and his brave servant, refusing quarter, shared his fate. The signal was forthwith given; the ambuscades rushed out, few of the escort escaped, and it was only through especial orders, sent by Sivajee, that the slaughter of the main body of the enemy ceased.

The success of this abominable scheme established Sivajee's power; the plunder of the Beejapoor army

* A steel instrument with three crooked blades, like tiger's claws, made to fit on the fore and little finger.—H. M. L.

† How unchanged are Asiatics! Nearly three thousand years ago "Joab said to Amasa, 'Art thou in health, my brother?' and Joab took Amasa by the beard, with the right hand, to kiss him; but Amasa took no heed to the sword that was in Joab's hand; so he smote him therewith in the fifth rib, and shed out his bowels to the ground."—2 Sam. xx. 9, 10. Joab's weapon must have been something like a wagnuk.—H. M. L.

provided him with military equipments as well as with treasure; and the fame of the exploit encouraged his friends and terrified his foes. He fulfilled his promise to the traitor Puntojee Gopinat, who received the stipulated reward and afterwards rose to high rank in the Mahratta service. A hundred years afterwards the descendant of Puntojee paid the penalty of his ancestor's perfidy on the very spot where the traitor Brahman had betrayed the confiding Beejapoori.

Another effort was, however, soon made against Sivajee. A force, twice the strength of that lately sent under Afzool Khan, was employed under Seedee Johur. Sivajee's light troops devastated the enemy's country, while he threw himself into the fort of Panalla. The Seedee prosecuted the siege for four months, during the worst season of the year. The post was still tenable, but all the approaches to it were occupied, and Sivajee felt the error he had committed in thus allowing himself to be encaged. But, treacherous himself, he knew whom he could trust. He asked for terms and proceeded, slightly attended, to one of the enemy's batteries to negotiate a surrender. He thus threw the Seedee off his guard, and during the ensuing night, descended the hill, at the head of a chosen band of Mawulees, passed the besieger's posts, and was well on his march to the fort of Rangna before his flight was observed. When the fact was ascertained, he was sharply pursued, and was overtaken at a defile within six miles of the fortress. He left a party of his Mawuls under command of Bajee Purvoe, who had formerly been his enemy, with orders to hold the pass until a signal from the fort of Rangna announced his own safety. The orders were obeyed, the post was held, but at the cost of the life of the generous Purvoe. Sivajee himself thus escaped, but many of his forts were captured, and the Mahrattas would have suffered more severely, but for the court intrigues that caused the removal of the brave Seedee from the command of the invading army. This was, however, an expiring effort on the part of the Beejapoor Government; the revulsion expedited its own fall; while Sivajee, bending to the storm he could not brave, quickly recovered his temporary losses and was soon again in the field with fresh strength.

At this time (1662), the Sawunts, or lords, of Waree offered, if supported by the Court, to reduce the rebel, but they were soon abandoned by their weak paramount, and the whole of their own territory was subdued by Sivajee, who, however, restored their Deshmukhee rights, and by his judicious treatment soon attached them warmly to his cause. He occupied Sawunt-waree with his own troops, and drew their infantry to fight his battles in distant quarters. Sivajee was now master of a long line of sea-coast. He built ships and commanded an advantageous treaty from the already degenerate Portuguese of Goa, who supplied him with guns and naval stores. The successful rebel had now become a powerful Prince. Through his father's timely mediation, he was admitted to treat with the Beejapoor minister, and was recognised as master of a tract of country more than 250 miles in length, averaging 50 miles in breadth and in parts extending 100 miles eastward from the sea. He also had at command a devoted army of not less than 50,000 foot and 7000 horse.

Being at peace with Beejapoor, Sivajee next turned his arms against the Moguls. For a time the Mahrattas were unsuccessful; many forts fell into the hands of the enemy, who established their camp at Poona. Sivajee was not slow to take advantage of their position, and to use his own knowledge of its localities. Understanding that the Mogul commander, Shaisteh

Khan, occupied the very house in which he had himself passed his boyhood, Sivajee determined to cut him off in the midst of his guards. Accordingly, with twenty-five favourite Mawulees, the Mahratta Chief entered Poona at night; passed through the Mogul troops, wounded Shaisteh Khan, slew his son and many of his personal attendants, and then leisurely retreated, lighting his torches in defiance as he ascended the hill of Singurh, in the face of his pursuers.

In the year 1664, Shahjee was killed by a fall from his horse. He died in possession of large jaghirs, including the whole territory of Tanjore, to all which his younger son Venkajee, who was on the spot, succeeded; Sivajee reserving the assertion of his own right until a favourable opportunity should offer. In January of that year, having effected the requisite arrangements and gained perfect information as to localities, he made a feint of attacking the Portuguese settlements at Bassein, and then, at the head of four thousand horse, made a dash on the rich city of Surat, systematically plundered it for six days, and leisurely carried off his booty to the fort of Rajgurh. The Dutch and English factories only escaped. Their small garrisons stood on the defensive, and by their gallant bearing, created a very favourable impression on the minds of the Moguls as well as of the Mahrattas. Shaisteh Khan had been recalled, and the great Jey Sing in conjunction with Dilere Khan was now employed against Sivajee, and carried on the war with unusual energy. Sivajee incautiously threw himself into the strong fortress of Poorundhur, which was reduced to extremity, and the Mahratta was induced to trust to Jey Sing's guarantee and surrender himself. Sivajee's conduct seems unaccountable. At no time had he been so strong, and dissension was rife in the Mogul camp. Poorundhur might have fallen, but Sivajee would not have been himself if he could not have effected his own escape. Raja Golab Sing's conduct at the present day in the Punjab seems much akin to this; unscrupulously cutting off all who trust him, he is constantly trusting himself in his enemy's hands. Man is everywhere unaccountable; but he who has to deal with Asiatics can least calculate, with certainty, on the future by the past. He must be prepared for every vagary, for the violation of the plainest dictates of prudence during peace, for the neglect or breach of all the rules of strategy during war. He may reasonably expect *that* to be done which should not be done, *that* to be neglected which should be effected. No European diplomatist or soldier is so likely to be ensnared as he who, having taken the usual precautions, feels himself secure. The treaty signed, the picquets doubled, neither can be regarded as a guarantee of safety. Certain eventual destruction may await the enemy's move; he may be assured of it on *all* rational calculations, but the goddess Bhowanee or some other deity or demon may have promised success—the day of the Feringees may have passed, and the infatuated wretches rush on destruction. Their desperation then *is* dangerous. Rashness, nay madness, has succeeded in striking a blow where the best plans have failed. Indian officials should ever be on the alert.

Sivajee at once surrendered twenty forts, with the territories attached to them, and trusted to the fidelity of Jey Sing to be secured in possession of the remainder of his conquests as a Mogul fief, as well as for sanction to spoil the Beejapoor territory. Aurungzebe generally confirmed Jey Sing's arrangement and invited Sivajee to court. He accepted the invitation; but previously assembling his officers, gave them strict orders as to their conduct during his absence, warned them not to obey any order sent by himself, unless it was brought by certain messengers, and then, at the head of 500 choice horse and 1000 Mawulees, proceeded with his son Sambajee to Delhi. Aurungzebe, though possessing considerable ability, was a very short-sighted politician. It was foreign to his character to keep his word, or even to break it in a straightforward manner. He might have at once put Sivajee to death; he preferred to degrade him, probably with the intention of eventually taking his life, or, when sufficiently humbled, of employing him, like Jeswunt and Jey Sing, as a tool of his own policy. Sivajee was accordingly received contemptuously, and when his bold spirit revolted, he was placed under surveillance and made to expect the worst. He soon decided on the course he should pursue, and found an ally in Ram Sing, the son of Jey Sing, under whose charge he was placed. Indignant that his father's engagement should have been violated, he aided the prisoner's flight. The circumstances of Sivajee's escape, concealed in a basket, are not among the least romantic of his actions. He returned to the Deccan, and soon recovered all his lately-ceded possessions.

The first exploit now performed was the recovery by escalade of the strong fortress of Singurh, which among others had fallen into the enemy's hands. The fort is situated on the eastern side of the great Syhadree range, and is nearly isolated, being connected only by narrow ridges with the Poorundhur hills, while north and south it has a continued acclivity, often almost perpendicular, of half a mile. The summit is capped by a huge black rock, forming a craggy precipice, more than forty feet high and two miles in circumference. This rock was girdled by a stone wall, with towers at intervals, and was strongly garrisoned by a select body of Rajputs under a leader of renown. Having ascertained that, in the confidence of their own prowess, and of the strength of their fastness, the garrison had become negligent, Sivajee consulted Tannajee Maloosray, one of his bravest officers, as to the best plan of surprizing the place. Tannajee replied that, if permitted to take his own younger brother and 1000 selected Mawulees, he would engage to seize the fortress. His offer was accepted. A dark night was selected for the assault. Having received their orders at Rajgurh, the Mawulees separated, and by different paths, known only to themselves, proceeded to the rendezvous in the vicinity of Singurh. Tannajee then divided his men into two parties, one to storm, the other to support. He selected the most precipitous point of the rock, and by means of rope-ladders, led his advanced party, one by one, up the precipice. Scarcely three hundred had ascended when the garrison were alarmed. The challenge of the foremost sentinel was answered by an arrow, and the bowmen then plied their weapons in the direction where they perceived, by the lights, that the garrison were collecting. A desperate conflict ensued, and the Mawulees were gaining ground, when their leader was slain. They then fell back, and were on the point of retreating by the fearful path they had ascended, when Tannajee's brother, Sooryajee, with the relief, appeared, rallied the fugitives, and upbraided them for deserting their Chief, saying, "Will you leave your father's corpse to be tossed into a pit by Mhars?" He added that the rope-ladders were destroyed, and that now was their time to prove themselves Sivajee's Mawulees. In an instant the tide was turned, and, with a deafening shout of their battle cry, "Hur Hur Mahadeo," they returned to the charge and were soon in possession of the fort. Of the Mawulees, nearly one-third were killed or wounded, and five hundred of the Rajputs, with their commander, were found dead or wounded.

Sivajee was hardly consoled for the loss of his gallant officer by the capture of the important post. When congratulated on the success of his arms he sorrowfully replied, "The den* is taken, but the lion is slain; we have gained a fort, but alas! I have lost Tannajee Maloosray!" Sivajee, who, as he paid his soldiers regularly, was chary of gifts, on this occasion gave every surviving Mawulee a pair of silver bangles, and rewarded the officers proportionally.

A new tide of conquest had now opened on Sivajee; again, fort after fort fell before his arms or his finesse. The city of Surat (October, 1670) was again plundered; and for three days, at the head of 15,000 men, he leisurely squeezed all who had anything to yield. The English factory, as before, defended themselves. Hearing of the approach of a Mogul army, Sivajee suddenly decamped, leaving behind him a letter for the inhabitants in which he demanded a tribute of 12 lakhs of rupees as the price of exemption from future plunder. Such was often, with the Mahrattas as with the Sikhs, the origin of their territorial acquisitions. They plundered the weak, and gradually assumed a proprietary right in all they had the power to destroy or molest. Their visits were commuted for *chouth*, or a fourth of the produce, to be paid as protection, or rather exemption money; gradually the stronger party appointed their own collectors, and, step by step, assumed the government of the lands they had originally wasted. This year, we first hear the word *Chouth*. The large town of Kurinja being plundered, a regular agreement

* Singurh—*i. e.* the Lion's dwelling.

was taken from the local authorities to pay one-fourth of the yearly revenue; in consideration of which they were not only to be exempted from plunder but protected.

Sivajee's attention was now turned to the sea as well as the land, and his exertions were unremitting on both elements. He sought either to expel the Portuguese from the coast or to reduce them to the condition of tributaries. His troops, who had hitherto rather harassed than attacked the Moguls and had been formidable chiefly in forests and fastnesses, began to meet the Emperor's troops boldly in the plain and daily with increased success. His usual tactics were to affect retreat; to draw on the Mogul horse in their usual tumultuous disorder, and then, either to lead them into an ambuscade, or, suddenly rallying his apparently broken parties, to return to the offensive, and, by repeated attacks on the broken squadrons, to sweep all before him. The Mahratta and also the Sikh horsemen were long famous for such manœuvres; and so prevalent is this Parthian policy, not only among the Mahrattas, but throughout Indian warfare, that it is not unusual, as at the battle of Assaye, for gunners, when ridden over by cavalry, to lie quietly down till the torrent has passed, and then to rise and turn their guns on the squadrons that have overwhelmed them.

In 1673, Sivajee, after a siege of several months, captured the fort of Satara. The place had been long used as a state prison: its captor little anticipated that it would be the dungeon of his successors, whence they would be released and reinstated by the English traders, with whom, in their merely mercantile character, he now first became acquainted. Sivajee, who had long struck coins and styled himself Maharaja, was in June of this year formally enthroned. He was weighed against gold, the whole of which being then given to the Brahmans, sharpened their wits for the discovery that the donor was of high Rajput descent.

Aurungzebe's attention had been for some time withdrawn from the Deccan by the disturbances arising from his revival of the jezia or Hindoo capitation tax, a measure which transformed the Rajputs from faithful dependants and followers into stout rebels. Raja Jeswunt Sing had died at Kabul, fighting the Mogul battles. He was rewarded by an attempt to convert his children by force, but this outrage on his family, together with the jezia, drove the Rajputs into a hostile confederation which occupied the Emperor for two years. In the year 1676, he again felt at liberty to turn his attention towards the Deccan, and at this time he seems to have believed that his schemes for weakening the several kingdoms in that quarter had taken effect.

The Mogul influence had for some time been paramount at Golcondah; there was, what was called, a close alliance with Rajapoor; and even Sivajee now found it his interest to pay temporary tribute. Having determined to proceed to the Carnatic and oblige his brother to yield (according to Hindoo law) half their father's inheritance, he came to an understanding with the King of Golcondah, and took the politic step of offering a sop to the Mogul commander to spare his possessions during his absence; jocosely comparing his paying tribute to giving oil-cake to his milch cow, by which "she would produce the more milk." In 1676–7 he proceeded on his expedition at the head of 30,000 horse and 40,000 foot, but Venkajee soon found the inutility of opposition, and agreed to divide the revenues of Tanjore and his other districts; on which peace was concluded between the brothers. After an absence of eighteen months, Sivajee returned to Maharashtra and was soon again in hot hostility with the Emperor.

The Moguls, having now thrown off the mask towards both Golcondah and Beejapoor, appeared before the latter place. The Regent called urgently on Sivajee for aid. He gave it effectually, cut off the Mogul's supplies, and obliged them to raise the siege. His reward was the abrogation of the Beejapoor rights of sovereignty over all the conquests he had at different times made. During this campaign Sivajee's son, Sambajee, fled in discontent from his father to the Mogul commander Dilere Khan, who proposed to Aurungzebe to set him up as a counterpoise to Sivajee, but the Emperor declined to take a step that would virtually recognise, and thereby strengthen, the predatory system. Dilere Khan being soon after displaced, avenged himself by conniving at Sambajee's escape. The latter returned to his father and received partial forgiveness, but was detained at large in the fort of Panalla.

Scarcely were the terms of the engagement with Beejapoor concluded, when Sivajee's earthly career closed. His last illness was caused by a swelling in the knee-joint, ending in fever that carried him off on the 5th April, 1680, in his 53rd year. Few conquerors have effected so much with equal means. Long disowned by his father, and unaided by the local chiefs, until by his own stripling arm he had rendered himself independent, he died the recognised ruler of a territory fifty thousand square miles in area; his name was dreaded from Surat to Tanjore, and in every quarter between those remote points, his bands had levied contributions and tribute. The Mahommedan yoke was now for ever broken in Maharashtra. The long-dormant military spirit of the people was roused, to be quelled only in the entire disruption of that system on which it had risen. The genius of Sivajee emancipated the Mahrattas: succeeding chiefs, by neglecting the policy which had aggrandized their founder, and adopting an organization which they could never perfectly master, precipitated the State to a second downfall.

Our brief sketch will have shown the line of tactics that Sivajee pursued. Personally brave, he never fought when he could fly, or when stratagem or treachery could effect his object: but whatever was his design, he weighed it deliberately, gained the most accurate information on all necessary points, and then, when least expected, pounced upon his prey. The heavy and slow-moving Moguls must have been sadly puzzled at encountering such a foe. Many stories are told of the terror his very name inspired. He was equally feared as a soldier, a marauder, and an assassin. His own dagger, or those of his emissaries, could reach where his troops could not penetrate; no distance or precaution could keep his prey from him. The old Jaghir system, under which the Mahratta chief served the Deccan kings, was a good foundation for the regenerator of his country to work upon; but it must be remembered that it was not with the chiefs that Sivajee commenced operations, but with the despised and half-starving peasantry of the Ghat-Mahta and Sawunt-waree. It was when Sivajee had gained a name, and had himself become a *chief*, that chiefs joined his standard. It is ever so in India. There is always ample material abroad to feed the wildest flame of insurrection; but not until it has assumed a head, will those who have a stake in the land join it. They will talk, they will write, they will plot; but seldom, unless in instances of great infatuation, when misled by false prophets, will the chiefs of the land join an insurrectionary move, so long as their own *izzut* has not been touched.

During Sivajee's whole career, he cannot be said to have enjoyed, or rather suffered, one single year of peace. He seems from the outset to have declared perpetual hostility against all who had anything to lose. His pacifications, or rather truces, were but breathing spaces, to enable him to recruit or collect his means, or to leave him unshackled to direct his whole force in another quarter. Aurungzebe played into Sivajee's hands by his timid and suspicious policy. The Emperor was incessantly changing his commanders, and feared to entrust any one of his sons or generals with means sufficient to quell the Deccan insurrections, lest the power so deputed should be used, as he himself had used it, to the usurpation of the throne. Thus distrusted, his children and officers managed the war with Sivajee, as with Beejapoor and Golcondah, for their own aggrandizement. They fought as little as they could, while they plundered and received bribes as much as possible.

There was thus much in the times, and there was still more in the condition and *feeling* of the country, favourable to Sivajee. His cause was, or appeared to be, that of the people. They had long groaned beneath a Mahommedan yoke, and some openly, all secretly, hailed a liberator of their own blood, caste, and country. It was this strong feeling in his favour that enabled him to procure the excellent intelligence for which he was noted; his spies were in every quarter, in the very zenanas and durbars of his enemies, and always gave timely warning of all designs, and full information of the weak points against which to direct his enterprizes. With all these advantages it may seem more surprising that Sivajee's rise was not quicker, than that it made the progress we have shown; but it must be remembered that the Mahratta chiefs were never unanimous, that few ever joined the founder of their empire, that Sivajee's officers and soldiers were the creatures of his own genius, and that for many years the majority of his troops were infantry, excellent in their own strong country, but ill adapted for foreign conquest. Above all, there was the prestige of antiquity and of power around the Mahommedan thrones, and especially around that of the Great Mogul. In no quarter of the world does so much respectful fear attach to long-established authority as in India. If there is little veneration for sovereignty, there is abundance of awe. Loyalty and patriotism we put out of the question; but in every case of insurrection the majority of chiefs and men of war, of all castes, will first offer their services to the established power to fight either for or against their own kindred and country; and it is only when refused employment that they flock to the newly-displayed banner. The middle and lower classes act differently; their sympathies will be with their fellows, but they will naturally be cautious to conceal their feelings until the progress of events and the conduct of the contending parties afford some clue to the probable result of the struggle. Thus Aurungzebe might originally have commanded the services of all that were then considered the fighting classes of Maharashtra; but his suspicious temper, fearing to admit Hindus into his ranks, and even refusing the services of the Deccan Mussulmans, drove them into the ranks of his enemy. The Mahommedan Government in India had, in short, lost its tact, elasticity, and vigour: luxury had sapped the Moslem strength, and deadened their one solitary virtue. Their hardihood declined, and with it their empire fell. Sivajee was the first to take advantage of the imperial decay, and his example was soon followed in every quarter of India.

Sivajee early established a strict military system. His infantry, as already stated, were originally recruited chiefly from the Concan and Ghat-Mahta. The Hetkurees of the former were good marksmen, but his chief dependence was on the Mawulees, or inhabitants of the mountain valleys. He employed the latter on all undertakings requiring cool courage and hand-to-hand work. They never failed him. The usual arms of both were a sword, shield, and matchlock; but a bow was substituted for the matchlock of every tenth man, as being useful in ambuscades and night attacks. The cavalry were of two classes, Sillidars, or men bringing their own cattle, and Bargeers, who were mounted on horses of the State. A select body of the latter, forming a third and very important class, were designated the Pagah, or household troops. Individuals of this body were mingled with the sillidars and ordinary bargeers to overawe them, and act as spies on their conduct. Horse and foot of all ranks were hardy, active, and abstemious. Camp equipage was unknown among them, a single blanket, in addition to their light coarse vestments, completed their wardrobe; and a small bag of parched grain sufficed for their commissariat supplies. Thus furnished, the infantry would for days and days thread the defiles and jungles of their wild country, and, by paths known only to themselves, appear where least expected; while the cavalry, supplied with small saddle-bags to hold such grain or plunder as they might pick up, swept the country at the rate of fifty, sixty, and even eighty miles within twenty-four hours. The grand secret of Mahratta hardihood was, that chiefs and officers shared equally in the privations of their men. A picture was once taken of the Peishwa Bajee Rao by order of his enemy, the great Nizam-ul-Mulk, as he chewed his dinner of parched grain, sitting on his horse with all his baggage under him, and his long Mahratta spear stuck in the ground by his side, while he thus took his repast.

Plunder and profit formed the object of all expeditions, the test, and in Mahratta eyes the only proof, of victory. During Sivajee's life, all plunder was public property. It was brought at stated periods to his durbar, where the man who had taken it was praised, rewarded, or promoted.

> "Then lands were fairly portioned;
> Then spoils were fairly sold:
> The *Bergees* were like brothers
> In the brave days of old."

Sivajee had sense enough to perceive how much he should personally gain by the punctual payment of his army. The pay of the infantry varied from three to ten rupees per month, that of bargeers from seven to eighteen, and of sillidars from twenty to forty. All accounts were closed annually: assignments were given for balances on collectors, but *never* on villages. Cows, cultivators, and women were exempt from plunder. Rich Mahommedans and Hindus in their service, were favourite game. Towns and villages were systematically sacked, and where money or valuables were not forthcoming, Sivajee would take promissory notes from the local authorities. He shed no *unnecessary* blood; he was not cruel for cruelty's sake, but on these occasions of plunder he mercilessly slaughtered and tortured all who were supposed to have concealed treasure. An Englishman, captured by Sivajee at Surat, reported that he found the marauder, surrounded by executioners, cutting off heads and limbs.

The mountain fortresses were the key-stones of his power. His treasure, plunder, and family safe, he could freely move wherever an opening offered. His garrisons were under strict discipline, and were composed of mixed classes as mutual checks. All were told off to such duties as were respectively suited to their habits. Brahmans, Mahrattas, Ramoosees, Mhars and Mangs were in every fort. The whole were called Gurhkurees, and were maintained by hereditary assignments of rent-free land in the neighbourhood. The Ramoosees, Mhars, and Mangs were the scouts and intelligencers; the Mahrattas formed the garrison. All relied for their daily bread on the charge of their post; it was, in Grant Duff's words, "the mother that fed them."

The rainy season was usually the holiday of the Mahrattas; the infantry took their ease, the cavalry horses grazed at will on the rich pasture lands,—and, as often as possible, on those of the enemy. This was, however, a busy time for Sivajee and his confidants. They now made their inquiries, and spied out the land for the ensuing campaign. At the autumnal dussera, the scattered bands were collected; the Bhugwa Jenda, or national flag, was unfurled, and the wild marauders poured like a torrent over the country. Under penalty of death, not a woman was taken into camp,* and, unfettered and unencumbered, Sivajee's bands struck the severest blows at points most distant from the places where they were expected.

It is only justice to state that this extraordinary man, while devastating other lands, was not unmindful of the duty he owed to his own subjects. In his conquered territory, and where the inhabitants had compounded for security, he was kind, considerate, and consequently popular. He usually took two-fifths of the crop, and protected the ryot in the enjoyment of the remainder. He set his face altogether against the farming and

* In this, and in some other matters, the English might with advantage take a leaf out of Sivajee's book. Endless trains of cattle and camp-followers constitute *a very* weak point in our military system.—H. M. L.

assignment system, now, as formerly, so prevalent throughout the Mahratta and other native States. In civil cases he employed punchayets, the best, if not the only resource in countries where official honesty is uncertain. Punchayets may decree wrongfully; but, under efficient superintendence and such checks as are easily applied, they will administer quicker and more substantial justice, among a rude and simple people, than the most strait-laced courts. The truth or falsehood of nine out of ten cases that are tried in cutcheries, and that may long enough puzzle the wits of strangers, is well known in the adjoining villages. It needs, therefore, only that interested parties be prevented from being members of punchayets, that such courts be open, and, as far as possible, that suits be decided by them at a single sitting, which may be effected in ninety-nine cases out of a hundred.

To assist in the management of affairs, Sivajee appointed eight principal officers, the chief of whom, or Prime Minister, he designated Peishwa, an ominous name for his descendants. Among his countrymen and admirers, Sivajee is still spoken of as an incarnation of the Deity, to which opinion his deeds of blood and treachery are no drawback. Mahrattas consider that political assassination is wise and proper, and that necessity justifies murder.

Sivajee was small of stature, and of dark complexion. His countenance was intelligent and animated, his eyes piercing, his frame active rather than powerful, and, as already mentioned, he was master of all the weapons commonly used in his country. Scott Waring calls him a good son to a bad father, but he does not show that there was ever any intercourse between them; and, as we have shown, the only proof he gave of dutiful regard was in the destruction of his father's enemy; unless, indeed, it be considered an act of filial piety that he seized his parent's jaghir in his absence, and by his rebellion against Beejapoor occasioned Shahjee's long and cruel imprisonment. On the whole, we may pronounce the founder of the Mahratta empire to have been *the* man of his day in India: greater than any of the Mahratta chiefs who succeeded him, and unrivalled since, even by Hyder Ally or Runjeet Sing. Sivajee could not only conquer and destroy, but he could legislate and build up. There is the germ of civil organization in his arrangements; and had he lived the ordinary period of man's life, he might have left to his successors a united and well-established principality. He died suddenly, and with him his empire may be said to have expired.

Sivajee left immense treasure. The amount has been variously estimated; but always in millions of pounds sterling. Heaped together in his coffers at Rajgurh were the dollars of Spain, the sequins of Venice, the pagodas of the Carnatic, and all the various gold mohurs of the different quarters of India, with innumerable kinds of rupees of every shape and stamp. But all his spoil, the harvest of more than thirty years of crime and blood, of restless nights, of ceaseless and unseasonable marches, did not bring peace to the owner, nor save his son from a fearful death; it did not preserve his successors from the prison his own hands had prepared, nor his people from being split into factions that soon sealed their own destruction.

Sivajee had four wives; two survived him, of whom one performed suttee; the other, having intrigued to raise her own son, Raja Ram, to the *guddee*, was put to a cruel death by her step-son, Sambajee, who executed all the parties concerned in this scheme for his supercession.

Once established in power, Sambajee showed, indeed, a soldierly spirit in the field; but his government was lax, cruel, and corrupt. His troops plundered the husbandman with impunity; and this relaxation of discipline, though it attracted a large accession of daring and dissolute adventurers to the Mahratta standard, yet proved a bad preparation for meeting the formidable power that was coming against them. Aurungzebe was now employed in the final conquest of Golcondah and Beejapoor. When the absorption of those two kingdoms had been effected, he pushed the Mahrattas more closely, and, after some desultory operations, at length by a bold stroke, such as Sivajee had so often struck against the Moguls themselves, seized Sambajee, while in a state of intoxication, at an outpost slenderly guarded. Aurungzebe offered his captive life on condition of his becoming a Mahommedan. "Not if you give me your daughter," was the bold answer of Sambajee. Stung by the insult, the Emperor caused him to be cruelly mutilated, and then beheaded.

Sambajee's *life* might have injured the cause of his people: his cruel death, in the words of Grant Duff, "aroused their vengeance without alarming their fears." Raja Ram, the surviving son of Sivajee, was now dedeclared regent, during the minority of his brother Sambajee's son. The boy was, however, soon after taken prisoner by the Moguls, and was kindly treated by the daughter of Aurungzebe, who familiarly called him Sahoo, or Shao,* his name being Sivajee. For a time

* Among the elegant English misnomers of Indian words was that of Shao Raja, whom the Bombay factors of his day designated "the Sow Roger." The ignorance as to all that concerns India to this day in England is great, but some light has broken on our countrymen since, in the year 1764, Guthrie, the Malte Brun of his day, thus described the Mahrattas and their country, "Mahrattas are a kind of mercenaries inhabiting the mountains *between* India and Persia." Malte Brun, following Tone, is generally correct.—H. M. L.

the tide continued against the Mahrattas, but, far from being disheartened, their energies were rather thus drawn out. Raja Ram, after making arrangements for Maharashtra, and for the re-assemblage of his friends around the "Bhugwa Jenda," or national flag, when fortune should be more propitious, took refuge in the Carnatic. On the plea of his nephew's captivity, he assumed the government in his own name, was enthroned, distributed the usual presents, and made extensive grants of lands, including much that was not in the actual possession of the Moguls, but more that had never belonged to his predecessors.

After a brief but eventful career, Raja Ram died of fatigue, caused by long exposure when escaping from Zoolfikar Khan, the ablest, though one of the most venal, of the Mogul officers employed in the Deccan. He had besieged Raja Ram for seven years in the fort of Ginjee, and when *obliged* to take the place, gave the Raja due notice to escape. On other occasions Zoolfikar acted with sufficient energy: within one period of six months he is said to have marched, in pursuit of the Mahrattas, 5000 miles, and, in this space of time, to have engaged them nineteen times. In the year 1700, one month after Raja Ram's death, Satara was captured by Aurungzebe. Raja Ram left two sons, Sivajee and Sambajee, the former being the elder was, though an an imbecile, placed on the *guddee*. He was only ten years old; but his mother, Tara Bye, was a woman of energy and the virtual ruler. She moved from fort to fort, encouraging her son's adherents, while, in five different directions, his troops kept the field under able officers.

Aurungzebe was now at the head of his own army; and successively captured the principal strongholds of the Mahrattas. Torna was carried by escalade, sword in hand, during the night: all the others were won by gold. Several were retaken within the year, and the Emperor's hold on any of them lasted only while a strong force remained in the neighbourhood. The climate, the difficulty of bringing up convoys, the feeling of the people, all were against the Moguls. But while the Mahratta fortresses were thus temporarily yielding, and their country falling a prey to the Mogul, their own predatory bands were daily extending the influence of the Mahratta name. For a third time they levied contributions on the city of Surat, and plundered Burhanpoor, while their squadrons simultaneously ravaged Malwa, Candeish, Berar, and Guzerat.

The Mogul system, with all its pageantry, was rotten at the core. The royal presence, or the occasional effort of an able and honest officer, might gain a brief success; but what could one old man, bowed down with the weight of ninety years, with centuries of care and crime on his brow, perform? One who, though he had long exceeded the usual span of life, now felt he was approaching the hour of his own long account. Nor could the empire be upheld by chiefs and generals, who had never been cordially trusted, and whose success on behalf of their master would, in his eyes, be little less than treason, entailing on the victors disgrace, if not death. Most of them, therefore, were in the pay of the Mahrattas. They allowed convoys to pass into the fortresses they besieged, and occasionally even fed the garrisons themselves. So far from protecting the royal districts from plunder, the Mogul army connived at, if they did not aid in, their devastation; and the more-far-seeing chiefs collected and husbanded their resources, and quietly awaited the struggle they perceived must follow the Emperor's death. Worn out with disease, and vexed by the ill success of his measures, Aurungzebe now allowed himself to be almost persuaded by his favourite son Kaum Buksh, to recognize Mahratta independence and to pay the surdeshmukhee (ten per cent.) on the revenues of the six Soobahs of the Deccan. Their insolence and daily-increasing demands alone prevented the fulfilment of the compact. Feeling his end approach, Aurungzebe moved on Ahmednuggur; his army was attacked and defeated on the way, and the aged and dying Emperor narrowly escaped falling into the hands of his enemies.

Aurungzebe's last march was made. He died at Ahmednuggur, on the 21st February, 1707, and left the heritage of his manifold crimes to his three sons. To the measure of their respective ability, they followed his example. Two soon fell in civil conflict, and the eldest, Sultan Mauzum, succeeded to the distracted and already dismembered sovereignty, under the name of Shah Alum.

The release of Shao, the son of Sambajee, had been more than once proposed as a counterpoise to the party of Raja Ram's family; but although, as a preparatory measure, Aurungzebe had caused the youth to be united in marriage to two influential families, he had always hesitated to carry out the scheme. On the death of the Emperor, Shao fell into the hands of Prince Azim Shah, who released him, when he was immediately joined by many influential persons, and early next year (1708) seized Satara. Daood Khan, the Mogul deputy in the Deccan, also supported him. Thus countenanced, Shao's cause was on the ascendant; but young Sivajee, or rather his mother, Tara Bye, had still a strong party. During the monsoon of 1709, their partizans cantoned at Kolapoor, and the next year Sivajee determined to make that town and the neighbouring fort of Panalla, the residence of his court. In the year 1712, the young Prince died of small-pox, when Ramchundur Punt, the ablest supporter of the Kolapoor party, removed Tara Bye from the administration, placed her and her son's widow in confinement, and seated Sambajee, the son of Rajis Bye, the younger widow of Raja Ram, on the *guddee*. Next year, Shirzee Rao Ghatgay of Kagul, a name infamously notorious in modern Mahratta history, joined the party of Sambajee, and henceforward acted as a partizan of Kolapoor, or under the banner of Cheyn Kulik Khan, better known as the great Nizam-ul-Mulk, who was now Mogul viceroy of the Deccan, and who, wishing to weaken the Mahrattas by internal dissension, favoured the Kolapoor party.

In the year 1714, Balajee Wishwanath, the ancestor of the rulers of Poona, was appointed Peishwa, and received a grant of the pergunnah of Poona, and the fort of Poorundhur. Raja Shao was already a cypher, and his minister the real ruler of the Mahrattas. The latter now took the first step towards the dismemberment of the empire, by encouraging every chief at the head of an army to administer the country he occupied or commanded. The Peishwa thus gained temporary partizans; but the Satara Raja soon lost dependants. Unlike his father and grandfather, Raja Shao acknowledged himself a vassal of Delhi; and, while in the actual receipt of tribute from the Mogul officers, he affected, in his transactions with them, to consider himself merely as a head zemindar or deshmukh of the empire.

During all this time, the distractions at Delhi were clearing the way for Mahratta aggrandizement. Ten thousand of them, under Ballajee, accompanied Syud Hoossein Ally, the viceroy of the Deccan, to take part in a struggle against the Emperor. Ferokhsere lost his life in the contest, and the Mahrattas remained at Delhi till they had obtained from his successor, Mahommed Shah, grants of * revenue and privilege, which not only confirmed them in their own possessions, but authorized their inquisitorial interference in every province of the Deccan. The minute intermixture of territory, and the coparcenery system that divided districts and even villages between rival authorities, was a sufficient curse to the people as well as loss to the Mogul; but this legalization of the Mahratta demands on the reserved territory was a virtual cession of the whole. It subjected the country to the double tyranny of two sets of tax-gatherers—"that which the locust left, the cankerworm devoured."

Bajee Rao succeeded his father Balajee Wishwanath as Peishwa. As able an administrator as his father, he was a better soldier. Against the opinion and advice of more timid counsellors, he advocated the extension of Mahratta conquest into Hindoostan. Under his banner, in Malwa, in the year 1724, we first hear of Ranoojee Sindhia, Mulhar Rao Holkar, and Oodajee Powar: the two first, the fotnders of their families; and the last, the regenerator of his, and the founder of the Dhar principality. Already did the ambitious Peishwa look to a universal Mahratta empire. He promised the Raja that his flag should wave from the Kistna to the Attock; and alluding to the Moguls, "Let us strike," said he, "at the trunk of the withering tree; the branches must fall of themselves." All the

* The year of Mahommed Shah's accession, in 1720, forms an important era in Mahratta history. The imperial grants they then obtained acknowledged their claim, first to the *chouth*, or fourth of the revenue of the six Soobahs—Aurungabad, Berar, Beder, Hyderabad, Beejapoor, and Candeish; second, to the *sur-desh-mukhee*, or tenth in excess of the chouth; and thirdly, to the *su-raj*, or sovereignty of the sixteen districts possessed by Sivajee at the time of his death. Thus was the Mahratta aim of years gratified.—H. M. L.

ability and experience, however, of old Nizam-ul-mulk, now again the Mogul viceroy in the south, were employed to baffle the Mahrattas and evade their claims. This he perceived was to be best effected by fanning the flame between the rival cousins of Kolapoor and Satara, and throwing his weight into the scale of the weaker—Sambajee. In the year 1727 he stopped all payments, pending, as he said, a settlement of the Mahratta sovereignty. The usually pacific Shao was roused to action. The Nizam endeavoured to excuse himself by declaring that he only meant to relieve the Raja of his overbearing minister, the Peishwa. Shao would listen to no terms; hostilities ensued, and the Kolapoor troops were subsidized by Nizam-ul-mulk. The Satara party, whose cause was managed by the Peishwa, gained the day, which will appear the less surprising when it is known that Sambajee and his ministers each sought to obtain the handling of the Nizam's subsidies, not to enable them to meet the enemy, but to employ the cash for their own private debaucheries.

Nizam-ul-mulk was not the person to continue a losing game; he, therefore, patched up an arrangement and abandoned the cause of Kolapoor. Sambajee, left to his own resources, was, in the year 1729, so utterly defeated as to be obliged to yield his claim to the Mahratta sovereignty to Shao, and to accept a principality, comprehending, with certain reservations, the tract of country between the Wurna and Kistna rivers on the north, and the Toongbuddra on the south. The treaty now made was offensive and defensive, and provided for the division between the parties of such conquests as might conjointly be made to the south of the Toongbuddra. But there never has since been any cordiality between the Kolapoor and Satara chiefs, or rather between the former and the usurpers of the authority of the latter; for, within two years of the above-mentioned compact, the Peishwa Bajee Rao completely defeated the Ghaekwar, and his other rivals, in a decisive battle near Baroda, which left him the virtual head of the Mahratta sovereignty.

From this year (1729) we date the separation of the Kolapoor principality from that of the elder and Satara branch. The lieutenants of the latter, or rather of the Peishwa, proceeded in a bright but brief career, while the Kolapoor chiefs, holding aloof from the upstart servants of their family, proceeded in a course of piracies and petty warfare with the Dessaees of Waree and the jaghirdars around them. The last time the armies of the Mahratta empire acted together was in the year 1795, at Kurdla, where Nana Furnuvees, the clever but timid minister of the Peishwa, induced Sindhia and Holkar, the Ghaekwar, the Nagpoor Raja, and almost all the jaghirdars to combine against the Nizam. On this occasion the Mahrattas brought into the field 140,000 men, horse and foot.

The Peishwa had long been the mayors of the Satara palace. They received their khillats (dresses) of investiture from the imprisoned deseendants of Sivajee; but they were virtually monarchs of the Mahratta confederacy. The submission obtained from the founders of the several rival principalities was certainly loose enough from the beginning; but they *did* allow, in theory, the same superiority to the Peishwa as he conceded to his puppet of Satara. A double government, an *imperium in imperio*, has long been the fashion of India; prejudices and old associations are thus sought to be soothed, and the fact is overlooked, or forgotten, that a rallying point is thereby left to their enemies by those in power. The good sense of more than one of the Peishwas led them to think of ending the farce;

but a timid policy prevailed. The ruler of Poona continued to call himself the servant of the Raja of Satara, whom he kept a prisoner; and the chiefs of Gwalior and Indore, retaliating on the former, plundered and insulted him at will, while styling themselves his lieutenants. A decree could have been obtained from the effete King of Delhi in favour either of Sindhia or the Peishwa, and would have carried as much weight in India as did Pope Zachary's in Christendom, when the second Pepin obtained his sanction to place Childeric in a monastery, and add the title of King to his mayorial designation.

Henceforward we follow the fortunes of Kolapoor and Sawunt-waree. In December, 1760, Sambajee, the last lineal descendant of Sivajee, died without issue, when his widow adopted a boy called Sivajee, and conducted the government in his name. The Kolapoorians were, at this time, not content with plundering and levying *chouth* on shore, but they engaged in piratical expeditions along the western coast. In the year 1765, the British Government sent an expedition against them, and reduced the ports of Malwan and Rairee—the former place belonging to Kolapoor, the latter to Waree. The connection of Kolapoor with the Nizam was generally maintained, and, in the time of the Peishwa Mudhoo Rao Bullal, caused the loss of several districts, which were, however, recovered by the Raja taking part with Rugonath Rao during the period of his authority.

In the year 1766, Malwan and Rairee were restored, on condition that the Kolapoor Raja should indemnify the British Government for all losses and expenses, and that the Dessaee of Waree should enter into a new treaty. The piracies of these petty States were then for a few years suspended, only to break out more violently than ever. In the year 1789, fresh operations were contemplated against them, and only suspended out of consideration to the Court of Poona, whose dependant the Raja of Kolapoor was erroneously supposed to be. The Mysore war then occupied all the attention of the British, and the pirates worked their will until the year 1792, when an armament was fitted out against them. A humble apology was, however, accepted, and a treaty concluded, by which permission was obtained for the establishment of factories at Malwan and Kolapoor. None of these measures, however, were of any avail to check the system of piracy, which continued until the year 1812.

The petty States at Kolapoor and Waree were at war, during nearly twenty-three years, on a foolish quarrel regarding some royal privileges obtained for her husband, Kem Sawunt, by Luximee Bye, a niece of Mahdajee Sindhia. Lord Minto, then Governor-General, was solicited to aid Kolapoor, but he declined interfering. The Peishwa was less scrupulous, and sought to take advantage of the contest to subjugate both States. Acting under his orders, one of his officers, Appa Dessaee, obtained possession of Chickooree and Menowlee, and endeavoured to establish his own authority over Sawunt-waree. The infant Sawunt was strangled; but Phoond Sawunt, the next heir, taking advantage of the temporary weakness of the Poona commander, expelled him from the country, and seized the government.

During the first Mahratta war with the English, the Kolapoor troops were not found in the ranks of their countrymen; but their system of piracy and petty plunder continued. In the year 1812, therefore, when the British Government was settling the affairs of the Mahratta country, it was determined at length to put down the long-permitted piracies of Kolapoor and

Sawunt-waree. Stringent measures were adopted, the Raja at once yielded, consented to a new treaty, and was, in return, guaranteed against the aggressions of all foreign Powers. Phoond Sawunt was, at the same time, obliged to cede Vingorla, and engaged to suppress piracy, under the penalty of being also deprived of the forts of Rairee and Newtee. Some mercantile engagements were at the same time concluded.

Soon after the ratification of these arrangements, Phoond Sawunt died, and Doorga Bye became regent. Regardless of the British guarantee, she immediately attacked Kolapoor, and seized the fort of Burratgurh, which had formerly belonged to Waree. The old lady would listen to no remonstrances, and withdrew only on the advance of a detachment of the Madras army. She still, however, continued refractory, and though no retaliation was permitted on the part of the Kolapoor troops, the British were at length obliged to enter the Waree territory; and in the year 1819 completely reduced it. Certain cessions were then exacted as security against future misconduct, when the British troops were withdrawn, and Sawunt-waree, in its reduced limits, left independent.

During the last Mahratta war, the Kolapoor Raja heartily espoused the British cause, and was rewarded by the restoration of the two districts of Chickooree and Menowlee, already referred to, yielding an annual revenue of three lakhs of rupees. In July, 1821, the Raja was murdered in his palace by a chief, whose jaghir he had resumed. During the disturbances at Kittoor in 1824, the conduct of the Kolapoor authorities was very suspicious, and in a matter of dispute with Sawunt-waree, the young Raja infringed the treaty, and refused to abide by British arbitration. In this affair he was decidedly wrong, and he ought to have been punished. In our dealings with native States, it is as unfair to overlook palpable breaches of engagement as it is cruel to stretch or twist dubious questions. The homely adage "get an inch and take an ell" nowhere better applies than among Indian rulers. The first encroachment is the precedent for succeeding ones. The smallest infraction of a treaty should be promptly noticed; timely reproof may stop a career of ruin. We are quite aware that it is from no ungenerous motive that such admonition is often withheld; but we are not the less satisfied that a little trouble at the outset, where differences arise, might often avert broils, and eventual absorption. Most native chiefs are mere children in mind, and in the ways of the world; and as children they should be treated, with affectionate sympathy, but with systematic firmness. Grant them the most liberal construction of their respective treaties; but whatever that construction be, explain it clearly, and enforce it strictly. Slips should not pass unnoticed; but severity ought to be reserved for cases of obstinate contumacy. Such policy would convince all concerned, that their amendment and not their destruction, was the desire of the lord paramount. After a certain career of vice or contumacy, the offender should be set aside, and replaced by the nearest of kin who gives better promise. One man should not be permitted to ruin a State; nor in any case should the paramount benefit by the error of the dependant. Were some such principles as these steadily acted on, less would be heard of the bankruptcies and distractions of tributary and subject States.

In the year 1825, the Raja was, more questionably, interfered with, when desiring to resume Kaghal, the jaghir of Hindoo Rao, the son of the notorious Shirzee Rao Ghatgay. Both the father and son had long abandoned the Kolapoor service for that of Gwalior. Our right of interference referred only to *externals*, and we had no *right* to meddle, even by remonstrance, in domestic matters. Such slippery handling of engagements on our part, irritates native princes and affords them pretext for bad faith. In December, 1825, the Raja's misconduct obliged Government to march a force into his country, when a new arrangement was negotiated, stipulating for the reduction of the Kolapoor army, *attention to the advice of the British Government*, and the non-molestation of Hindoo Rao and certain other jaghirdars. Such a treaty could hardly have been expected to stand, nor did it. Princes do not relish unsought advice, any more than any other individuals, especially if it be such as they are pledged to take. It was, we believe, Colonel Sutherland who rightly called the obligation to take counsel "a withering clause;" its very nature, indeed, is to provoke irritation and opposition, and *to entail* eventual coercion. At any rate, it is useless to provide that advice should be taken, without specifically entering on the face of the engagement the penalty for neglect. The matter then becomes plain, and all parties can calculate their game. The treaty under notice was scarcely signed before the Raja broke through all its provisions. Instead of reducing his troops, he increased them, and seized the possessions of the guaranteed jaghirdars. Twice during the year 1827, a British force was assembled for the purpose of bringing the Raja to reason. In the month of October the troops moved on Kolapoor, when that fortified town, though occupied by between 2000 and 3000 Arabs and Sindhians, immediately surrendered. New terms were then dictated, restricting the Kolapoor army to 400 horse and 800 foot, exclusive of garrisons. Chickooree and Menowlee were resumed, and certain jaghirdars, whom the Raja had molested, received perpetual instead of life guarantees. The forts of Kolapoor and Panalla were occupied by British garrisons at the Raja's expense. He was also mulcted 1,47,948 rupees for damage done to his neighbours; and territory yielding 50,000 rupees was retained until the amount should be liquidated. A minister was also nominated by the British Government, which retained to itself the power of removing him and appointing another. This last measure was as inefficacious at Kolapoor as it has been everywhere else.

In the year 1829, the Governor of Bombay visited Kolapoor, and then proposed to withdraw the garrisons from that town and Panalla; but the measure was deferred, because the management of affairs had at that time fallen into the hands of an inimical Dewan. This person was removed, and his sovereign was warned, that if it should again be found necessary to send troops to Kolapoor, they would be permanently saddled on him. The Raja was a man of considerable, though misdirected, energy and ability. He quickly threw off the shackles of the British Government, and systematically disregarded every provision of the treaty. His army was increased to nearly ten thousand men; and, having no funds to pay them, having lost his best districts, having no field of plunder or piracy open to him, his finances fell into the most deplorable disorder. The troops were seldom mustered more than once a year; the men lived where they liked, and, being always a twelvemonth or more in arrears, were permitted great license, and became, as might have been expected, a mere mass of marauders, dangerous only to their own Government. In the Civil department there was the same reckless improvidence as in the Military. All the ancient titles and offices were kept up, and the same state affected as when the Kolapoor family had arrogated Mahratta sovereignty. Centralization was the order of the day. Every chief, every official of any rank resided in the city of Kolapoor. There were not less than twenty-one mamlutdars to manage the revenue of a tract of country not exceeding 2500 square miles, and scarcely yielding a clear income of five lakhs of rupees. All these mamlutdars constantly remained at Kolapoor, and acted by deputy. The durbar was, therefore, a scene of perpetual intrigue and chicanery, varied only by the lowest debauchery. Every Indian city is more or less a sink of iniquity; among them Kolapoor became a bye-word for foulness, for corruption and ill faith. Forgery and fawning were the steps to favour. Almost every chief and officer was, like the sovereign, loaded with debt: their estates and villages were mortgaged to money-lenders, and the Raja himself subsisted from day to day only by squeezing his officials and by anticipating the revenues of the State. We have said that the Raja had ability; we may add that his mind seems to have been tinged with insanity. In his saner moments, he was intelligent and energetic; occasionally, even just. He daily held open durbar, where all had admittance. Petitions were received, summarily discussed, and disposed of without appeal. The mamlutdars and courtiers were thus checked, and their illicit gains generally reverted to his own coffers. The highest officers were to be seen in chains one day, and the next raised to greater honours: allowed their full swing for a time, and then imprisoned, tortured, and fined. Strange as it may appear, such practices do not prevent scrambles for place now in India, any more than they did in olden times in Europe. Mahrattas, indeed, seem to enjoy such a troubled sea of politics. It offers a fair field for their peculiar abilities. They prefer, even more than other Indians, a mere nominal salary with the dim prospect of perquisites, to a fair and limited remuneration. It is astonishing how men become accustomed to live with their heads in their hands. It is now in India, as it was centuries ago in Greece and Rome. The Kolapoor system, however, had peculiarities of its own. So desperate had become the fortunes of the Chief, and of the court myrmidons, that the great majority were reduced to depend for their daily bread on the palace bounty; nearly a thousand of these minions fed daily at the durbar, and were reduced to the condition of mere personal retainers. Stranger still is the fact, that with such a head and such instruments, the condition of the country was not wretched. The secret lay in the Raja's vigorous despotism. An open court, with summary cruel punishments, kept down crime. While the city and the palace were filled with iniquities, the villages flourished; few, if any, fell into disorder, and, when the Raja's career ended, little waste land was to be found within his principality. His offences thus lay in prodigality, in personal debauchery, and in expending double or treble his income, rather than in unduly squeezing his cultivators. His last act was that of a desperate gamester. Shortly before his death, in the year 1839, he affected to proceed on a pilgrimage to Pundepoor; but the whole was a mere scheme to plunder certain wealthy parties on the Kistna. For this purpose, his ragged army was nearly doubled; every effort was made to raise immediate funds, and even the family jewels were pledged with this unholy object. Death cut short the project; and then cannon and other munitions of war were found concealed in the carts that were to accompany his train. On the Raja's death, his eldest son, the present chief, then a minor, was placed on the *guddee*, and a regency was formed by order of the British Government, consisting of his mother, his maternal aunt, and four Karbarees. The two ladies, of course, quarrelled. The British political agent, on paying a hasty visit to Kolapoor from Belgaum, finding them in warm contention, judged it politic to leave them so, considering that he should most effectually hold the durbar in check by countenancing both. Within six months of the agent's departure, the aunt, who went by the title of Dewan Sahib, being the most energetic and most unscrupulous of the two, got the better of her kinswoman and assumed the whole powers of government. Her supremacy, thus acquired, was acknowledged by the British authorities, though the step excluded the mother of the minor sovereign from all authority.

We return to our sketch of Sawunt-waree affairs. The measures taken in 1819 were soon found ineffectual to protect the British frontier from plunder. The Waree Government was unable to subdue or restrain its own turbulent chiefs; and the British authorities were constantly annoyed by the distractions of this petty chiefship. In the year 1822, the Dessaee, then in his twentieth year, was ousted from all authority by his Ranees, supported by an influential minister. So great, at length, became the disorganization of the country that, in the year 1836–37, the British Government was obliged to interfere, and to send a force to occupy the forts of Mahdogurh and Naraingurh, and the town of Waree. The Dessaee, thus relieved from his domestic persecutors, was delivered over to a *guaranteed* minister. He, of course, soon quarrelled with his monitor; but his complaints being attributed to the influence of disreputable favourites, he vainly appealed to the British agent (the collector of Rutnagirry). A formidable rebellion ensued, which it required a British detachment to quell.

In 1838, troops were again called out, being the fourth time that armed interference had been employed in Sawunt-waree within nine years. Phoond Sawunt, who has within the last twelve months* again given so much trouble, was then in arms, plundering the Waree villages and threatening the British frontier. The Dessaee thwarted all the efforts of this rough-riding minister to put down the rebellion, and accused him of being in league with the rebels. The British Government, tired at length of fighting the Dessaee's battles, assumed the direct management of the country, until such time as there should be a probability of his governing it well. Mr. Spooner, a Bombay civil servant, was placed in charge of the territory; but had a very up-hill game to play. The country, one of the very strongest in all India, and in many parts believed to be inaccessible to regular troops, teemed with malcontents. While many had real grievances, some feared the indispensable reductions incidental on the new arrangements; and others dreaded the substitution of a strong Government for their old system of misrule. All could plot, and even fight confidently, having their friendly jungles to fly to—a sure refuge in the sympathizing neutrality of the border State of Goa. On one occasion, the rebels acquired temporary possession of Waree; another time, they captured the fort of Humuntghar, blockaded the passes, plundered travellers, and attempted to levy the Government revenue. They were not only recruited from the Goa territory, but one of the leaders at the capture of Aumuntghar was a Goa Dessaee. A Sawunt-waree local corps was, at length, raised; and a new governor having arrived at Goa, who was less friendly to the malcontents, they were finally put down. Nine of the leaders were condemned to death; but their sen-

* That is, about 1844–45.

tences were commuted to banishment for life. The execution of a number of prisoners also took place, under the orders of Lieutenant Gibbard, the adjutant of the local corps. He pleaded the orders of the political agent; but was made to answer for the deed before a military tribunal. Sawunt-waree was thus, as the phrase runs, *settled;* but the flame was only smothered; and no sooner did disturbances break out in Kolapoor, than the Waree people were again up, and the son of the Dessaee was himself in arms.

We have now brought our sketch down to the period of the late disturbances in Kolapoor and Sawunt-waree. The united area of these two States does not exceed four thousand square miles, and their joint nett revenue, after deducting jaghirs and rent-free lands, scarcely amounts to seven lakhs of rupees. But, as already observed, the whole tract, especially Sawunt-waree, is a remarkably strong country, combining within a small area all the strong points of mountain and jungle fastnesses. The inhabitants, moreover, though poor, are hardy and lawless, and still bear in mind the exploits of Sivajee's favourite Mawulees and Hetkurees.

Predatory habits, formed during centuries of anarchy, are not to be changed in a day. British supremacy, has, throughout India, restricted the field of plunder and of warfare; but sufficient time has not yet elapsed materially to alter the feelings and associations of the marauding times. We have taken from the lawless their hunting grounds; we have prohibited their spoiling their neighbours; but we have neither given them an equivalent, nor allowed them an outlet for their energies. We have not even rendered their own homes secure. The guaranteed princes, who can no longer array their followers for foreign raids, must turn their hungry energies against those very followers. Money they *must* have to feed their own luxurious lusts. If they cannot plunder strangers, they must harry their own people. The rule holds good throughout India. The instances among native States, where the cultivator is certain of reaping what he has sown, and of being called on to pay only what has been previously agreed, are most rare. Indeed, they are to be found only in some few States of very limited extent, where the reigning chief, being a man of probity as well as of ability, sees with his own eyes, hears with his own ears, and, setting aside ministers and agents, looks after his own affairs.

The southern Mahratta States afford a good illustration of our argument. They have experienced all the inconveniences of a strong supremacy, without participating in its advantages. The British ægis has been thrown over the rulers and ministers of Kolapoor and Sawunt-waree, while no effectual measures have been taken to enforce their doing their duty to the governed. It cannot, indeed, be denied that these territories have been most egregiously mismanaged. Countries that have been repeatedly in arms within a short term of years *must* have grievances. Half-armed, hungry men do not give their throats to the sword for mere amusement. Men do not, for ever, love to struggle in a hopeless cause. We may then fairly infer that there *has been* abuse; and as both Kolapoor and Sawunt-waree have, during several years, been in a manner directly governed by British agents, we are obliged to attribute the maladministration which has entailed so much expense of blood and treasure, to our own ill-digested schemes; to the affectation of holding aloof, while we were daily and hourly interfering in the most essential manner, through native agents, by placing in the hands of native underlings, powers that no native of the present generation has head or heart to bear. With a British superintendent in Sawunt-waree, and a native agent in Kolapoor, acting as minister, as regent, as factotum, under the political agent at Belgaum, neither of the disaffected States can be considered as having been under a domestic administration; but our Government is as distinctly responsible for their bad, as it would have been entitled to the credit of their good management.

Sawunt-waree offers a notable proof, that the sword alone cannot sustain an Anglo-Indian administration. Martial law had long prevailed; the country had been harried; some malcontents had been justly condemned, other unfortunate men had been butchered. The native Government was wholly suspended; the management was entirely in our own hands; and yet, no sooner had troubles arisen in Kolapoor than it became certain that Sawunt-waree would rise. The worst expectations were realized. With scarcely an exception, every chief in the country took up arms, and forty of them, with their personal followers, driven from their fastnesses, are now in the dungeons of Goa, rather than surrender to British clemency. There is something very lamentable in all this, and it calls for no ordinary inquiry.

The circumstances of the Kolapoor outbreak are different. We have already noticed the dissensions among the members of the regency. The supremacy of the Raja's aunt was not of long continuance, and more than one change preceded the late outbreak. At length, a few months before the insurrection commenced, Dajee Krishen Pundit, a Brahman, who had risen from a subordinate position in one of our civil offices, was placed at the head of the regency. Within a month of his accession to power, his two coadjutors were dismissed by the political agent for peculation; and the

Pundit monopolized the combined powers of minister and regent. Dajee could not have been a notoriously bad man; the probability is, he was both able and moderate. But unlimited power has turned wiser heads than are to be found among the underlings of an Anglo-Indian *cutchery*. We accordingly find that Dajee neither bore himself meekly, nor was content to follow those two golden maxims, to let well alone, and to endeavour to make the best of local, even though bad, materials. He seems to have forgotten that he was a foreigner among a wild and a proud people, who could only be managed peaceably by and through their own countrymen; that if he did not employ the natives, they must and would oppose him; and that they could not remain neutral, and indubitably would be either his coadjutors or his enemies. Nevertheless, Dajee *did* make many changes, and *did* provide for his Brahman kinsmen.* He, moreover, not only checked the abuses and illicit gains of the Mankurees and other chiefs, but by touching their dignity made himself personally offensive: there can, therefore, be little doubt that, though few of them openly engaged in the insurrection, the majority instigated and encouraged the acts of the rebel Gurhkurees and refractory Sebundees. The former, we have already explained, were the hereditary holders of

* We have no desire to run down Dajee; on the contrary, we look on him as a favourable specimen of an Anglo-Native agent. Had he been *better* or *worse*, matters would have turned out differently. Had he leagued with local oppressors, had he gone hand in hand with the plunderers and tyrants he found around him, his reign would at least have been longer. Had he been a "faultless monster" he might have saved the State. But in all such cases, the difficulties in the way of a native agent are immeasurably greater than what would face a European officer. An ordinary Englishman may do a hundred things that the best and purest native dare not attempt. The latter, too, has his peculiar advantages. Each has his fitting place; and the grand point of skilful Anglo-Indian administration turns on the judicious blending of the double agency. Europeans and natives may, conjointly, build up what either, acting singly, would mar.—H. M. L.

the Hill forts that dot the Kolapoor country. From father to son, they had lived and died at their posts, and were supported by certain lands dependant on their respective charges. To interfere with arrangements which had existed since the days of Sivajee, if not before his time, was anything but prudent; nor can we perceive the policy, any more than the justice, of irritating the hereditary soldiery of this wild country. The immediate cause of offence was the appointment of mamlutdars (revenue officers) to manage the Gurhkuree lands. Perhaps it would be more correct to say that the Gurhkurees resented the removal of their own immediate agents, and the doubling up of appointments by which the charge of their affairs was made over to mamlutdars who managed the adjoining districts. This measure, as they supposed, affected their honour, and placed them at the mercy of strangers. We are far from believing that the Bombay authorities had any design to mulct the Hill garrisons; there was, therefore, the less excuse for trifling with their feelings, it may be their prejudices, by appointing people to do for them what they preferred doing themselves. We need hardly add that no stranger mamlutdar *could* have been appointed, to whose fingers a portion of the proceeds of the Gurhkuree lands would not have adhered.

In July, 1844, the flame broke out; the garrisons of the strong forts of Bhoordurgurh and Samungurh refused to admit the mamlutdar appointed to manage their lands. Dajee Pundit for a long time endeavoured to cajole the recusants, and eventually sent two of the principal officers of the State to cajole them into submission. The Gurhkurees were firm, and refused not only to admit any mamlutdar except of their own selection, but required the guarantee of the naiks (chiefs) of the five regiments of Sebundees at Kolapoor as security for their future good treatment. The very positiveness of the poor creatures seems to bear testimony to their having experienced wrong, and their fear of further injury. Dajee Pundit was desirous of granting their demands; but the political agent forbad any concession to men with arms in their hands; and hearing, in September, that the malcontents had levied contributions in their neighbourhood, recommended that a force should be sent against them.

It is to be regretted that, before the British functionary counselled recourse to arms, he had not done something more than communicate with the malcontents through native agents; that, in short, he had not himself visited the scene of disorder. We have little doubt that he might have entered either Samungurh or Bhoordurgurh with perfect safety, the former being only a long morning's ride from Belgaum. Or, supposing that he could not have proceeded thither in person, why not have called in a deputation from the recusants to state their grievances? This question may rouse the yells of fire-and-faggot politicians. "Visit or receive men with arms in their hands?" they will say. We reply, yes, decidedly so, as long as no overt act of hostility has been committed, and while there is reason to believe that the disaffected are moved by real, or even supposed, wrongs. It is not the fashion, we know, to argue thus,—the more the pity,—and the greater the necessity that our voice, feeble though it be, should be raised in the cause of humanity and of truth. Unfortunately, British Indian history abounds with instances where the neglect of so simple an act of justice has cost us dear, both in blood and credit. Whether, we ask, is it more creditable to grant terms to men in arms *before* or after they have used those arms? The historical reader will be familiar with cases of civil and military revolt; and will have observed, that in the great majority of instances, all that was at first humbly craved, and forcibly demanded only when redress had been refused, was finally conceded *after* blood had been shed. Are we always to slay in order to prove our strength? Far better to relinquish so sanguinary a dominion! This is one view of the case,—that justice should *first* be fully done, and that we should enter on no quarrel with dirty hands. We may, however, meet the coercives on their own ground, and entirely deny the necessity, at the present day, of brute force to vindicate our honour. Whatever may have been the case fifty years ago, a preliminary fusilade is not now requisite to prove that our measures of mercy are voluntary. Who, in his senses, ever doubted that the British Government *could* coerce the Gurlıkurees and capture their forts? Who ever denied that the Barrackpoor division could annihilate the unhappy 47th Bengal N. I.? There *have* been instances where prompt and rigid austerity was perfectly justifiable; but, for one such emergency, a dozen have occurred where early moderation, combined with firmness, would have been the true course of policy.

Acting on the agent's recommendation, the Bombay Government issued instructions that a detachment, amply sufficient to effect the pacification of the disturbed districts, should move from Belgaum, the headquarters of the southern division of the Bombay army. With whom the selection and strength of the field force rested, we are not exactly aware. It consisted of 1200 men, including two companies of European Infantry, one company of Native Rifles, a few Irregular Horse; and sixty artillery-men with four mortars, two howitzers, and two nine-pounders. One hundred labourers also accompanied the engineer officer as pioneers. The whole were placed under command of Lieut.-Colonel Wallace, 20th Madras N. I. This small detachment, though in division orders on the 12th September, did did not march till the 16th, and arrived opposite the fort of Samungurh, thirty miles distant, on the 19th of the same month. The strength of the fort lay chiefly in its position on the summit of a scarped rock; its walls were found to be from twenty to sixty feet high, and between one and two miles in circuit. The hill on which the fort stands is, however, commanded by an adjoining rock; the place was wretchedly equipped, and garrisoned by only three hundred men, and might, probably, have been seized by *coup-de-main*, the first day. It is obvious, however, that if the fort was not thus to be captured by a sudden attack, there was not much hope of the success of a detachment scarcely exceeding 1000 bayonets, and unaccompanied by battering guns. Fifty mortars might have settled the matter in a few hours: the fire of four could only have afforded amusement to the garrison of so extensive a position. On the 20th, Colonel Wallace took possession of the hill, commanding the fort, and the next day commenced shelling, but with little or no effect. On the 24th, the pettah was carried by storm, and no effort was wanting, on the part of the British commander to reduce the fort; but he soon found himself helpless, and applied for reinforcements and battering guns. The distance from Belgaum does not exceed thirty miles, and yet the guns, being impeded by heavy rain, did not arrive for more than three weeks, by which time much of the moral effect of the military movement had been lost, and the Gurhkurees had received confidence and recruited their numbers.

On the 22nd September the garrison of Bhoordurgurh sallied out upon the Kolapoor troops sent against their fort, and drove them off with loss. Alarm now spread, and fears were expressed for Rutnagiry, Vingorla, and even for Belgaum itself; at which last place sudden and novel precautions were taken, sufficient to indicate alarm and to provoke attack. When shall we gain experience and learn to be always on the alert?—In the words of Washington, "to organize all our resources, and to put them in a state of preparation for prompt action" * * * "to endeavour by unanimity, vigilance, and exertion, under the blessing of Providence, to hold the scales of our destiny in our own hands." Reinforcements were now ordered from various quarters towards the disturbed districts; and on the 8th October, General Delamotte, by order of the Bombay Government, assumed command of the troops in the field. On the 11th, four battering guns reached Samungurh, and were placed in position, and by the evening of the next day a practicable breach was effected. When the guns arrived, Mr. Reeves, the commissioner, allowed the garrison the opportunity of a parley to state their grievances; but he soon found that the Gurhkurees only desired to gain time, in expectation of support from Kolapoor, where, in the interim, the Sebundees, encouraged by our supineness, had risen in open revolt, and seized and confined the minister Dajee Pundit; and where, in fact, their leader, Babajee Thirakar, had assumed the government. Affairs were, therefore, allowed to take their course, and shortly before daylight on the morning of the 13th, the place was stormed and carried with little opposition. During the day, Mr. Reeves and Colonel Outram accompanied a wing of the 5th Madras Cavalry under command of Captain Graham, and cut up a large body of malcontents who had collected in the neighbourhood with a view of supporting the garrison. Colonel Outram had joined General Delamotte's camp the day before the storm, in a political capacity, and henceforward, wherever employed, threw into all proceedings that moderation, energy, and ability, which have everywhere so strongly marked his career.

To save further bloodshed, the joint-commissioners, Mr. Reeves and Colonel Outram, now offered, with certain exceptions, an amnesty to all who would immediately return to their allegiance. Few, if any, accepted the terms; a strong presumptive proof that the unfortunate men had real grievances. The day after the capture of Samungurh, Colonel Outram, with Colonel Wallace and 500 men of his brigade, proceeded to Kaghal, one march from Kolapoor, with the view of procuring the release of the minister who was imprisoned in the fort of Panalla, as well as of supporting the Raja and well-affected chiefs against the disorderly troops and their disloyal leaders. The movements of the head-quarters under General Delamotte were more dilatory and less decided. He did not leave Samungurh until the 12th October, and then hesitated a long time whether to move on Kolapoor or Bhoordurgurh, the garrison of which last place had, on the 10th October, plundered the British pergunnah of Chickooree, and robbed the local treasury. Whatever was to be done should have been done quickly; expedition was everything; and had a second blow, such as that at Samungurh, been speedily struck, in *any* direction, the probability is, that the insurrection would have been subdued.

There seems at this time to have been disunion in the counsels of the authorities; but their exact nature has not transpired. Government, evidently, was very ill-informed as to the nature of the outbreak, or the means most likely to quell it. Like most other insurrections, it had in the first instance been mismanaged and trifled with; its dangers were then exaggerated; troops were poured into the country under hap-hazard commanders, and it was only at the last stage of proceedings that efficient means of tranquillization were adopted. On the 24th October, after much negotiation, and not until Colonel Wallace's detachment had been strengthened, Dajee Pundit was released, and the young Raja of Kolapoor, with his aunt and mother and the majority of his chiefs, left the city and joined the British camp. The movement had been strongly opposed by the Kolapoor troops, about 500 of whom under Babajee Thirakar, finding their wishes defeated, absconded and joined the Bhoordurgurh malcontents. Babajee may be regarded as the leader of the rebellion. He had imprisoned the minister, usurped the government, and instigated the raid on Chickooree. He and certain other principals were, therefore, excepted in an offer of amnesty, which was held out to such as should return to their allegiance; but, strange to say, when General Delamotte *did* at least appear before Bhoordurgurh, with every means of speedily capturing the place, he admitted the garrison to a surrender; and actually allowed himself, on the evening of the 10th, to be detained for several hours at one gate, while Babajee Thirakar with his party escaped from another. Thus was the flame spread, rather than extinguished; for Babajee immediately moved to the still stronger fortress of Panalla, where the Kolapoorians imagined that, as in olden time, a long, if not permanent, stand could be made against all comers.

On the 25th November, General Delamotte appeared before Panalla, where Colonel Ovans, the Resident at Satara, was now imprisoned. This officer, who had lately been appointed special commissioner in the Southern Mahratta country, to the supercession of both

Mr. Reeves and Colonel Outram, had been waylaid on the 17th November, while incautiously travelling dak with a very slight escort from Satara to Kolapoor, and carried prisoner to Panalla. We pretend not to know the reason of Colonel Ovans' appointment, but after carefully comparing all we have heard on the subject, it is our belief that the Bombay Government, already in no good humour at the long continuance of hostilities, were at this time irritated by Colonel Outram's refusing to accept the permanent charge of the Kolapoor country, and, therefore, at once accepted the resignation, which he volunteered only on the expiration of hostilities. This must have been the real motive that actuated, perhaps unwittingly, the authorities, though they may have likewise disapproved of some particular measures he had pursued. We see at least no other mode of accounting for the act. The rumours and assertions circulated by a portion of the Press at the time must have been erroneous regarding the man who was selected to go to Kolapoor when affairs *looked black*, was offered the permanent civil management *when they looked blacker;* was then employed as a military commander in putting an end to the war; and has since the termination of hostilities been nominated to the charge of the political and military relations at Satara.

Whatever may have been the cause of Colonel Ovans' deputation, his career was, thus summarily, cut short, and the political management in the field remained in the hands of Mr. Reeves and Colonel Outram. Strenuous endeavours were made by the commissioners to effect the release of Colonel Ovans, whom the malcontents vainly tried to make the means of ensuring their own safety. All their overtures were, however, disregarded; they were desired to release their prisoner and surrender at discretion, or stand the consequences.

They did release him, hoping thereby to obtain terms of surrender, but they soon discovered their error.

On the 27th the Pettah was captured; and on the morning of the 1st December the batteries opened. The same afternoon the breach, being reported practicable, was stormed and carried in gallant style. Some of the garrison endeavoured to escape into the adjoining fort of Pawungurh, but were so closely followed by the British troops, that this second fortress fell into our hands the same day. Babajee Thirakar and some other ringleaders fell in the storm, and *many* prisoners were captured by the parties of troops judiciously placed in the plain around.

On the 5th December, Colonel Wallace with a light force proceeded against Rangna, seventy miles distant. He reached it on the 9th, the same day carried the Pettah, and the following night placed two guns and two mortars in position: their play, during the next day, caused the enemy after dark to evacuate the fort, and fly into the Sawunt-waree jungles. The principal fortresses of Kolapoor having thus fallen, their Gurhkurees being slain, imprisoned, or dispersed, and the country being full of British troops, there was now a temporary lull; but it soon appeared that the theatre, only, of hostilities had changed, and that the war itself was as far as ever from a conclusion. Two thousand of the Waree people, under Phoond Sawunt, and Anna Sahib, the son of the Dessaee, who were at this time devastating the Concan and stopping the roads, were joined by the fugitive Kolapoorians. From the nature of the country the military operations now became more difficult. Wherever an enemy can be approached, there is little cause for alarm. The strongest fortress or best-intrenched position, if relied on, renders the occupiers the more certain prey. It is but a question of time;

the result is certain. In a rocky, jungle country, however, abounding in deep, damp ravines, and in forest-covered hills and dells, and occupied by an acclimated people, the case is very different. In all such miasmatic localities, as long as malcontents are satisfied to fly to-day, to starve to-morrow, and altogether to live or die as the beasts around them, they may long baffle the operations of regular troops under ordinary commanders. And thus it was that the Sawunt-waree people acted; and thereby created, even beyond their own immediate limits, more alarm than their wretched means should have been permitted to do; but the fact is, that our regulars are as little adapted for jungle fighting as were Aurungzebe's heavy Northmen to cope on their own ground, with Sivajee's light Mawulees and Hetkurees.

Troops employed in mountain and jungle warfare require something more than mere bull-dog bravery. Coolness, tact, activity, and a general acquaintance, at least, with similar localities are as necessary in the leader, as is some adaptation of his men to the enterprize. Soldiers that will fearlessly mount a breach, silently stand in array to be mown down by artillery, or unflinchingly hold their ranks to repel repeated charges of cavalry, will falter under a dropping fire from unseen foes. Men must be familiar with rock, ravine, and jungle, to fight well among them. It is curious how ill we generally make our selections from our ample and varied resources—employing grenadiers as bush-rangers, and keeping riflemen for garrison duty—pushing into the front of battle, men who are fit only for the invalids, and keeping the young and active soldiers of every rank comparatively in the background. We generally get so well out of our scrapes that the waste of blood and treasure is too little considered; and few lessons are gained from past experience.

Fortunately for Government, the man they wanted was at hand. Colonel Outram, who was now, about the end of December, at Bombay, with the intention of proceeding to Europe, at once forgot past neglect and past injuries, and came forward to rescue the Government from their difficulties. He volunteered to return to the seat of war, and there organize and lead a light corps. Nobly did he fulfil the large expectations that were now centred in him. Within a fortnight he was again in the field, the soul of all active measures; his very advanced guard driving before them the half-armed rabble that had kept three brigades at bay.

Never was the magic power of one man's presence more striking, than on Outram's return to the seat of war. It might seem invidious were we to dwell on the panic that then prevailed at Vingorla and Waree, but the slightest glance at the proceedings in those quarters will show that the insurgents had inspired a ridiculously-formidable idea of their own importance. All communications had long been cut off; the posts were brought *by long sea*, from Malwan to Vingorla, and many of the inhabitants of this latter place nightly took refuge in boats in the harbour. The troops were harassed with patrolling duty, yet the neighbourhood was rife with murders and robberies, the perpetrators of which sent insulting messages to the authorities. On one occasion a religious meeting was dispersed by a wag suddenly calling out that the enemy were upon them. Vingorla, be it remembered, stands in an open country.

At Waree, matters were, if possible, still worse; there the troops remained as in blockade, not a soul venturing beyond the lines. All outposts were called in and the malcontents permitted to consider themselves masters of the field. When the garrison was reinforced by the arrival of the 10th and a part of the Bombay Native Infantry, the authorities determined to occupy the gorge of the valley of Seevapoor, in which lay the villages of the insurgent Phoond Sawunt, and thus cut off this focus of rebellion from the less-disturbed districts. The scheme was a good one, but failed from the manner in which its execution was attempted. A detachment of two hundred sepoys set out; they were *sniped* at from the jungle and one man was wounded, when, instead of closing with the enemy, they took post in a sort of enclosure, and were soon beset by increased numbers. A reinforcement of two hundred men joined them, but the combined force, after losing twenty killed and wounded, retreated to Waree. This success, of course, increased the confidence of the insurgents, whose insolence was not restrained even by the arrival soon after of Her Majesty's 2nd Regiment. They gave out that they were tired of thrashing sepoys and wished to try the metal of the "*Lambs.*" They soon obtained an opportunity of proving their metal, but the sight of that fine corps was too much for their nerves. The Europeans were then kept idle, first at Waree, then at Dukhun-waree, and full scope was given to the activity of the enemy.

At this juncture, Outram landed at Vingorla, where, picking up two or three excellent officers, he pushed on to Waree, and thence towards Seevapoor. From this date, the 14th January, matters took a turn; hitherto the three brigades had been playing bo-peep with the enemy, and from the tops of the Ghats, examining through telescopes the stockades below, which the commanders did not think it prudent to attack. But now, at length, a decided movement was announced for hemming in the rebels in the valley of Seevapoor.

Twelve hundred men were placed under Outram, with orders to beat up the low ground from Waree towards the forts of Munohur and Munsuntosh; Colonel Carruthers, with a brigade, was to occupy the Seevapoor valley on the other side of the ridge on which those forts are situated; while Colonel Wallace was, on a given day, to descend the Ghats, and it was reckoned that his troops, dove-tailing with those under the immediate command of General Delamotte, would complete the encirclement of the rebels. This is not the time or place for commenting on Colonel Wallace's descent of the Elephant Rock, and premature attack on the open village of Seevapoor. That officer probably thought that he acted for the best, but we doubt whether disobedience to orders can ever be so viewed. Without any disparagement of his personal courage, we cannot help thinking that Colonel Wallace manifested a very contradictory estimate of the enemy's strength. If they had been as formidable as he considered them, then his descent of the rock, exposed to such a foe, was absolute infatuation. Nothing but their weakness and cowardice could justify the risk. But if the foe was so contemptible, he could have easily taken the route *he was desired*, driven them from stockade to stockade, *at the time ordered*, and thus, completing the chain of operation, have probably ensured the apprehension of every individual rebel chief. Much have the merits of Colonel Wallace's case been debated, but we cannot perceive how he could have expected to escape a court-martial, though he may have reckoned on ensuring an honourable acquittal, from the nature of his offence. There seems, however, to us, no more resemblance between his disobedience at the Elephant Rock and Nelson's at Copenhagen, than there is between the fame of the two offenders. Judgment having been already pronounced on Colonel Wallace by a military tribunal, we should have avoided referring to his case, could our narrative have been otherwise rendered intelligible.

To return to Colonel Outram. No communication was practicable between the troops above and below the Ghats, and he was left with his small band to his own resources, without definite orders, and with very scanty supplies, to carry out the most difficult operation of the campaign. Merrily and confidently he advanced through the wild sylvan scenes never before trod by European foot. The ears of his people were now daily saluted by the echo of the artillery on the overhanging Ghats; sounds which could only be supposed to indicate "the tug of war" above, and loss of ribbons and laurels to those below. But such fears were soon relieved by finding that the firing was only Colonel Wallace's long practice with extra charges from the summit of the Elephant Rock at the village Seevapoor, some three miles distant in the Concan below.

Each day Outram found points of his route stockaded by the enemy, but they never made a stand, the advanced guard and skirmishers being generally sufficient to disperse the wretched rabble. At length, on the 20th of January a combined movement was ordered upon the high peak to the west of Munsuntosh. The main attack was to be made by Colonel Carruthers, who, supported by a portion of Colonel Wallace's brigade, was to carry some stockades in his front, and then move up the Dukhun-waree or Sevapoor side of the ridge, while Colonel Outram was to make a diversion from the Shirsarjee or Gotia valley. This last detachment performed their part; but, on reaching the summit of the peak, from which an extensive view was commanded, no sign appeared of either brigade. They saw the stockades which Colonel Carruthers was to have attacked but which being now taken in flank were abandoned, the enemy flying to Munsuntosh, within eight hundred yards of which fort Outram established a post. Colonel Carruthers' brigade had been prevented by the nature of the country from taking their full share in the operations of the day. The next morning another combined movement was made on the village of Gotia, immediately below the forts; again the nature of the country favoured Outram, the advanced guard of whose detachment captured the village with all its stockades, though very strongly situated.

From these brief details we may infer how easily the war might have been terminated, months sooner, by more decided measures. The enemy had only to be reached, to be routed. The troops, both Bombay and Madras, were ready for their work, but a spirit of undue caution and delay prevailed at head-quarters.

We cannot understand how it happened, but Colonel Outram was now left, unsupported, to carry on operations against Munsuntosh. One of those accidents which no human foresight can obviate, frustrated his attempt to gain that fortress by a coup de main. He carried three stockades, below the fort, attempted to blow open a gate, failed, and was driven back with considerable loss. He held his ground, however, high upon the ridge, retained possession of the stockades, and was on the eve of again storming the fortress when the enemy evacuated not only Munsuntosh, but the adjoining fort of Munohur. Outram had skilfully thrown out parties, to command the debouches from the south and south-west faces of the forts, leaving the remaining portions of the cordon to be filled up by the brigades. Colonel Wallace, however, failed on his part, and thus suffered the rebel chiefs, who had all been engaged, to escape over the Sisadrug ridge, close to one of his posts, into the Goa territory. Outram followed hard upon their track, had several skirmishes, took many prisoners, and on one occasion, nearly captured the chiefs. Again he scoured the wild country beneath the Ghats, encouraging the loyal, and beating up the disaffected villages. The nature and value of his services during the operations we have glanced at, are not to be measured by the actual opposition experienced or loss sustained, but by the estimate formed by other commanders of the obstacles and enemy to be encountered, and by the fact that the rapid and skilful movements of his small detachment, terminated, in a few days, an organized opposition which had for six weeks kept at bay three brigades, differently handled. The total silence of Government, and the non-publication of any opinion regarding the Sawunt-waree operations, might, at first sight, lead to the inference that Outram's management gave as little satisfaction as did that of his fellow commanders. But, the promotion since bestowed on him, amply proves that Government took the same view of his conduct throughout the campaign as did General Delamotte, Colonels Brough and Wallace, and indeed all his comrades. Outram's is an almost isolated instance of a man receiving not only civil promotion but brevet rank, without his good fortune exciting jealousy; a remarkable exception, only to be explained by his rare qualities as a soldier, and his conciliatory demeanour as a man.

The tone of our remarks upon Colonel Outram may savour of partial panegyric, to those of our readers who have not followed out his career as we have done. No personal feelings however, can mingle in our praise of a man whom we have never seen, and whom we know only by his public acts. Those who have watched his course, will probably concur in our eulogiums; indeed, any unprejudiced man, reading the despatches published during the war, the proceedings of Colonel Wallace's court-martial, and the discussions which they elicited at the three Presidencies, must acknowledge that every affair in which Outram had a voice, was carried out with an energy and promptitude, very unlike the procrastinating indecision perceptible elsewhere. He arrived at Samungurh—the fortress was carried forthwith; and (what so rarely happens in Indian operations) the success was immediately followed up, by despatching Captain Graham to disperse the enemy's covering force; a work which that officer ably accomplished. Again, in the despatch published by the Bombay Government, we see Outram mentioned as "the man who volunteered his services, and was among the foremost who entered the fort of Panalla." The reader has only to contrast the whole conduct of his detachment, from the 16th of January to the conclusion of hostilities, with any other operations of the campaign, and he will bear us out in the opinion that he was the soul of every decided measure.

If our narrative has kept to Colonel Outram's detachment it is for the simple reason that they appear to have had all the fighting to themselves. No discredit thereby attaches to the troops under the other commanders, who were always ready for action, and who, when opportunity offered, as at Samungurh and Panalla, behaved with the accustomed gallantry of the Madras and Bombay armies.

We must wind up this hasty, though perhaps prolix sketch of Sawunt-waree affairs. By the capture of Munohur and Munsuntosh the strength of the insurrection was broken. The strongholds of the rebels were taken, their boldest leaders slain or captured, and all others, to the number, as already stated, of forty, fled for shelter to Goa. Outram was then again called on to act the diplomatist. His parties still followed up the remaining small marauding bands, while he, himself, proceeded to Goa, and by the union of firmness and conciliation induced the Portuguese authorities to remove their *sympathizers* from the frontier, and to substitute a cordon of such troops as would prevent the Goa territory being made the place of ambush from which the insurgents should at discretion devastate Sawunt-waree. And now we may be permitted to congratulate Government on their selection of such a man as Colonel Outram to the important duties of the Satara Residency. Our satisfaction would be increased could we persuade the authorities to give him such assistants as he can trust at Satara and Waree, and place him in authority at the central post of Kolapoor, with combined powers as Resident, Commissioner, and Military Commander.

Improved arrangements, we are aware, have already been made. The Anglo-native agent at Kolapoor has been replaced by an able British officer, and in Sawunt-waree there could not be a better local superintendent than the officer lately appointed. Captain Jacob is, like Colonel Outram, a good soldier as well as an able and conciliating civil officer. Such are the men required; men who, personally despising danger, are forward in the hour of action, and, reckless of their own blood, are chary of that of others. In no quarter of India are such men more appreciated than in the Southern Mahratta country, where their names alone are worth regiments. They will preserve peace if it is to be preserved, and if the sword must be drawn, will carry on war, so that it shall speedily end in permanent and prosperous tranquillity.

After more than six months of military operations,

and the employment of nearly ten thousand troops, in so insignificant a corner of India, peace has been secured, or, more correctly, war has ceased. Let us now, by honestly and carefully looking into past abuses and errors, and by not too rigorously judging those who have been driven or reduced to misconduct, secure the future tranquillity of the country. This can be effected only by a *permanent* system of good management *consonant to the spirit of the people.* We should remember that rude tribes are not ripe for refined institutions, and that it is better to work on quietly, slowly, and surely, than to risk new convulsions by sudden, even though beneficial changes. The people of Kolapoor and Sawunt-waree have, we believe, been partially disarmed and many of their fortresses have been dismantled. Both these measures should be completed. Broad military roads should also be constructed to intersect these territories in all directions, and the jungle cleared at least a hundred feet on either side. Such operations will involve present expense, but they will prevent future sacrifices. No country, such as that under notice, can be reckoned secure until those responsible for its peace have facilities for quickly reaching its most remote corners at all seasons of the year.

Half a dozen good officers under such a man as Colonel Outram might, in a few years, wipe away the reproach that is now attached to our name in the South Mahratta country. Under their supervision, all real rights and immunities would be clearly defined, and speedily established; and all imaginary claims dismissed. A revenue system would be organized calculated to protect cultivators from undue exaction, and a scheme of police might be enforced that would make the rock and the bush too hot for marauders. The Mankurees, Chiefs, and Jaghirdars, would settle down into their places. The Raja of Kolapoor and the Sin Dessaee of Sawunt-waree would each, also, find his level; they would respectively be the pageants that mild, meek sovereigns in the East, who have the good fortune to possess *wise and virtuous* Viziers, usually are. They would be treated with respect, and they would profit by the amelioration of their territories. The labour, the responsibility, and let us not forget, *the honour of all improvements*, would belong to the British officials, who, eschewing the fiction of a double government, putting aside all screens of dewans, ministers, or karbarees, would openly stand forward as the avowed managers of the country, on behalf of the ruling power.

The readers of these Essays will observe that we distinguish between the cases of these Mahratta States and that of Oude, where every measure short of superseding the King has been fruitlessly tried. Our relations with Kolapoor and Sawunt-waree stand in a different position. We have ourselves been for years the managers of these countries; the present disorganization has been matured before our own eyes, and in our own hands; we should therefore nurture our change until its health is thoroughly recruited, and restore full sovereignty to the legitimate princes, if we can then find among them any whose characters will justify that measure; otherwise we must continue to be the direct managers, and persevere in a course so manifestly advantageous to the hereditary chiefs themselves. No pains should be spared to explain to them the eventual intentions of Government in their favour, and they should be as clearly informed that intrigue or treachery will, at once and for ever, forfeit their thrones. Free personal communication on the part of the European superintendents with these princes, and constant, though not intrusive, endeavours to enlighten their minds may gradually effect much. But whatever be the result, the British Government will have done its duty, and the good administration of the country will have been secured, either in our own hands or in those of the hereditary rulers.

We are quite aware of the difficulties in the way of our scheme, and of the tact that will be required to carry it out, but we are not the less confident of the result, if the superintendence of affairs is entrusted to the hands we have suggested. Intrigue, nay rebellion, may at first arise; but it will not be repeated, if summarily and decidedly dealt with. As our scheme admits of no *just* cause being given for insurrection, and provides that determined malignancy shall receive no quarter, we can perceive no likelihood of the arrangement meeting with prolonged opposition. It is the spasmodic tyranny of weak rulers that invites continual attack. The Government that is one day oppressive, the next cowardly, and the third day frantically vengeful, may fairly calculate on insurrections on every emergency. The British administration of the present day happily acts in another spirit, and the East India Company has only, where legitimate openings offer, to carry among the ryots of its protected princes some portion of the benevolence that now influences its dealings towards its own subjects, and protected India will soon assume a new aspect. Blessings will, then, be poured out, in many a rich plain and fruitful valley, where curses are now plentifully showered on those who have, unwittingly, given over the husbandman, the strength and marrow of the land, bound hand and foot, to the tender mercies of his irresponsible tyrants.

NOTE.—The deliberate opinion we have formed of Colonel Outram, has in no respect been altered by the perusal of that florid romance, entitled, "The Conquest of Scinde," concocted by the Governor of Guernsey from facts and fictions furnished by the Governor of Scinde. The foregoing remarks were written before the appearance of Colonel Outram's letter to General Napier; a letter that was not needed to set "the Bayard of the Indian army" (as Sir Charles Napier in an inspired moment happily designated him) right in the eyes of the Indian public. Still less do they require a further vindication of his conduct, though they will welcome every item of information that he may feel justified in giving. We fearlessly assert that every right-minded man acquainted with the progress of events during the year 1842, not only acquits Colonel Outram of the absurd and contradictory charges alleged against him by the Napiers, but recognises in his conduct throughout Scinde transactions, both civil and military, the spirit of a soldier, a gentleman, and a Christian. We may hereafter have the gratification of sketching the career of this much-abused man, who, with a singularly conciliatory and kindly disposition, had the fortune to incur the hatred of two first-rate haters (Lord Keane and Sir Charles Napier), men too, who fully appreciated his good qualities, till his manliness and honesty thwarted their own views. In the year 1838, Outram carried to Affghanistan a character such as could not be paralleled by any officer of his standing in India. His services during the first Affghan campaign were second to those of no officer then and there employed. Had he remained in the Ghilzee country or at Khelat, many of our disasters might have been averted.

But it is by his civil management, first, of lower Scinde, and then of both the Upper and Lower Provinces and of all Belochistan, that Outram has won our highest admiration. When the European inhabitants of Calcutta trembled for our Indian empire; when, in the highest places, men grew pale at the evil tidings from Affghanistan, Outram held his frontier post with a firm hand, a brave heart, and cheerful tone, that *ought* to have been contagious. Vigilant, conciliatory, and courageous, he managed, with his handful of troops, not only to prevent the Ameers from taking advantage of our disasters, but to induce them to aid in furnishing supplies and carriage for the relieving, then considered the retreating, army. The merits of his exertions on that occasion are little understood. He obeyed, as was his duty; but he did not the less clearly perceive the ruinous tendency of the Government orders. He had the moral courage to sacrifice his own immediate interests by stemming the then prevalent tide of cowardly counsel. James Outram in one quarter, and George Clerk—a kindred spirit—in another, were the two who then stood in the breach; who *forced* the authorities to listen to the fact against which they tried to close their ears, that the proposed abandonment of the British prisoners in Affghanistan would be as dangerous to the State as it was base towards the captives. These counsels were successfully followed: the British nation thanked our Indian rulers, while, of the two men, without whose persevering remonstrances and exertions Nott and Pollock might have led back their armies, without being permitted to make an effort to retrieve our credit—Clerk was slighted, and Outram superseded. As cheerfully as he had stepped forward did Outram now retire, and again when his services were required was he ready to act in the field, in willing subordination to the officer who had benefited by his supercession.

The Napiers accuse Outram of jeopardizing the British army in Scinde: this is mere nonsense. His negotiations, followed up by Sir Charles Napier's acts, were sufficient to endanger his own life. They did so, and nothing but his own brilliant gallantry and that of his small escort rescued them from the toils. The British army was able to take care of itself. Had Outram, however, when deputed to Hydrabad, been permitted the *fair discretion* that his position demanded, had he been authorized definitely to promise any reasonable terms; his abilities and his character would have secured an honourable peace; but it was not in human nature that the Ameers should long continue to listen to an envoy sent to demand everything, and to offer nothing. This was not negotiating, it was dragooning. A British officer escorted by a single company was not the proper delegate for such a mission. Sir Charles Napier at the head of his army was the fitting ambassador.

Outram's chivalrous defence of his assistant Lieutenant Hammersly is one of the many instances in which he advocated the right at the peril of his own interests. Hammersly was as brave, as honest-hearted a young soldier as ever fell a victim to his duty. We knew him well, and no one who did so need be ashamed to shed a tear over his fate. He was literally sacrificed *for telling the truth*—a truth too that was of vital importance to the beleaguered Candahar army—nay, to the interests of British India.—Peace be to the memory of this noble fellow!

LORD HARDINGE'S INDIAN ADMINISTRATION.

[WRITTEN IN 1847.]

THE general diffusion among our countrymen in India of a spirit of fair and candid inquiry is a marked and gratifying sign of the progress of improvement. A course of enlightened and consistent policy in a ruler is now certain of being met with calm and dispassionate consideration, and, when shown to be characterized by integrity and honesty of purpose, of being received with cordial approval.

We may, therefore, safely predict that the administration of Lord Hardinge which has become, by his departure from India, matter of history, will be unanimously praised by all who make Indian affairs their study; and that the Eastern career of this soldier-statesman will commend itself to their judgment and approval as strongly as it evidently has done to that of the Court of Directors and both sides of both Houses of Parliament.

We proceed to detail those acts; prefacing them with a few words regarding the early and Peninsular career of Lord Hardinge, chiefly compiled from the Memoir of Lieutenant-General Sir Benjamin D'Urban.

Lord Hardinge is descended from an old Royalist family of King's Newton, county Derby; through which he traces his ancestry up to the Conquest. His immediate ancestor raised troops for Charles I., hazarded his life and lost his estates in the service of the Stuarts. Lord Hardinge's uncle, Richard Hardinge, of Bellisle, county Fermanagh, was created a Baronet in the year 1801, and was succeeded by his Lordship's elder brother, the Reverend Charles Hardinge, of Bounds Park, Kent, and Rector of Tunbridge. Lord Hardinge had three other brothers: of whom one died young; Col. Richard Hardinge of the Royal Artillery, still alive; and Captain Nicholas Hardinge, who, in his 27th year, when in command of the "*San Fiorenzo*," fell in the moment of victory at the close of a three days' action with "*La Piedmontaise*," an enemy's ship of far superior force. A monument in St. Paul's Cathedral records his achievements.

Before Henry Hardinge had attained his fifteenth year, he joined his regiment in Canada. At the peace of Amiens he returned to England, and, having studied at the Royal Military College, was selected for a situation on the Quartermaster-General's Staff with the expedition, in 1807, under Sir B. Spencer, to the coast of Spain. He was actively employed under Sir A. Wellesley in the campaign of 1808, was present at the battle of Roleia, and severely wounded at Vimiera. At the close of the war he conveyed despatches to Sir John Moore, with singular rapidity through many dangers. With the rear-guard at the side of his heroic chief, he shared in the many severe affairs of the retreat on Corunna, and was one of the officers near him when he fell. In March of the same year (1809) he was appointed Lieutenant-Colonel and Deputy Quartermaster-General of the Portuguese Army, under Sir B. D'Urban. He served at the passage of the Upper Douro, on the borders of Gallicia; afterwards in Castile; and at the battle of Busaco.

Highly distinguished in the campaign of 1811 under Lord Beresford in the Alemtijo and Spanish Estremadura, it was at Albuera that his brightest wreath was won. The fight had gone against the handful of British soldiers. Half of those under fire had fallen, when Colonel Hardinge, on his own responsibility pointed out to Major-General Sir Lowry Cole, that on his moving up his division depended the fortune of the day. These fresh troops were, on the instant, hurled against the enemy's left flank; while Colonel Hardinge caused the right to be simultaneously assailed by the re-inspirited brigade of Abercrombie. The heavy columns of the superb French Infantry were thus checked, rolled back and broken: the British guns, already limbered up and ready for retreat, were again brought into action, and the enemy driven from that fierce field.

This glorious turn in the tide of that fight, which itself turned the tide of the Peninsular War, was the achievement of Lieutenant-Colonel Hardinge, then only 25 years old; immortalized by Alison in his record of Albuera, as "the young soldier with the eye of a general and the soul of a hero."

Lieutenant-Colonel Hardinge served at the siege and capture of both Ciudad-Rodrigo and Badajoz; and especially distinguished himself at the storm of the strong outwork "La Picurina." During the operations which led to the battle of Salamanca, he officiated as Quartermaster-General of the Portuguese Army, and for his conduct received the Military Order of the Tower and Sword.

At Vittoria, Colonel Hardinge was severely wounded in the body, and while still suffering from a painful surgical operation, resumed his duties in the Pyrenees. He afterwards served at St. Sebastian, at the passage of the Bidassoa, and in the battles of the Nivelle and Nive.

In February, 1815, when in command of a Portuguese brigade of infantry, he, in conjunction with General Byng's brigade, gallantly carried with the bayonet some strongly-occupied heights near Pallas. He was then engaged at Orthes, and in the operations ending with the battle of Toulouse. For the battle of Orthes Colonel Hardinge received his ninth medal.

During the whole of the Peninsular War, Col. Hardinge was never absent from his duty except for very short periods after his wounds at Vimiera and Vittoria. At the peace, his signal services were rewarded by his Sovereign with a Company in the Guards, and by the distinction of Knight Commander of the Bath, an honour usually reserved for general officers.

Sir H. Hardinge accompanied Sir C. Stewart to the Congress of Vienna, and on the renewal of the war was attached by the Duke of Wellington in a political capacity, with the rank of Brigadier-General to the head-quarters of the Prussian army under Blucher. At the sanguinary battle of Ligny on the 16th June, Sir H. Hardinge again distinguished himself. About 4 P.M. his left hand was shattered by a common shot, but, refusing to dismount or leave the field, he placed a tourniquet on his arm and sat out the battle, retiring after night-fall with the Prussian army. At midnight, in a hut by rushlight, attended by a single servant, he had his hand amputated. Sir Henry had previously despatched his brother, who was his aide-de-camp, to report to the Duke the fate of the day, and to bring an English surgeon. At daylight the French beat-up the bivouac, when Sir Henry, determined not to fall into the enemy's hand, though faint from loss of blood, accompanied the retreating Prussians. At Wavre he rejoined the gallant Blucher, who, though still suffering from a fall, and from having been ridden over by a whole brigade of cavalry, got up and kissing his friend affectionately, begged he would excuse the garlic (with which he was perfumed), and condoled with him on Ligny, but characteristically added, "Never mind, my friend, if we outlive to-morrow, Wellington and I will lick the French."

After the battle of Waterloo, the Duke of Wellington devoted a separate gazette to the merits of Sir Henry Hardinge and to a notification of his own regret for his severe wound. From bad management in the first instance Sir Henry's arm had to be several times re-dressed, causing him extreme torture; yet within the fortnight he rejoined the army at Paris, where he was received with military honours by Blucher, in the palace of St. Cloud, and there placed in possession of the apartments of Marie Louise.

At the expiration of the occupation of Paris, the King of Prussia, in testimony of his high opinion of his political and military services, decorated him, at a grand review, with the Order of Merit, and of the Red Eagle; and the Duke of Wellington, personally, presented him with the sword from his own side.

During these eventful seven years Sir H. Hardinge had received four wounds, and had four horses killed under him; nor was he singular. Men long unaccustomed to warfare are frightened at such losses as those of Ferozeshah, Múdkí, and Sobraon; and forget, in these recent events, the casualties of Albuera, Talavera, and Waterloo. If, after a hard day's fight in India, all the "means and appliances" of a cantonment hospital are not found upon the field; if doolie-bearers, (who get no pensions!) run away and leave their wounded charge to be cut up by a straggling enemy; and every wound is not dressed and soothed with cerate on the instant; loud is the cry against the "culpable negligence of the authorities:" but let them talk over Wellington's campaigns with any of his veterans, and learn how men of the best families of the land, lay stiff and cold where they fell, unattended for hours and hours, or even for the whole night, as Ponsonby on the field of Waterloo; or (to take a still nearer example) as our own gallant old chief, Lord Gough, whose wound at Talavera remained undressed for two whole days, though a Lieutenant-Colonel commanding a regiment; and as Sir Henry Hardinge, who though attached to the Prussian army, in a high and honourable position, had to wait eight hours for a surgeon to amputate his hand.

Peace came at last, and with it peaceful duties. Sir Henry Hardinge now served for some years as a Captain in the Guards; he then entered Parliament, and for twenty years sat as Member for Durham and Launceston. During this period he was employed for a short time as Clerk of the Ordnance; on two occasions as Secretary-at-War, and twice for short periods as Secretary for Ireland. Sir Henry was early distinguished for his clear business-like statements, his matter-of-fact manner of transacting his official duties, and for the vigour which he threw into all his actions. It is as much the fashion to decry "Military Civilians," as to undervalue "Heaven-born" warriors. Such men as the Duke of Wellington, Sir H. Hardinge, and a host of others of all ages, should ere this have taught the folly of the first error, as Cromwell, Washington, Clive, and Blake, that of the other. When will the world perceive that wisdom, foresight, and courage, are the gifts of God, and not the mere results of social position?

The quickness of perception, the physical and mental energy and business habits which had been so often tried in the field, were now to be tested in the Cabinet, and in the Parliament of England—the noblest arena in the world. Here Sir Henry's temper is described by a candid political opponent as warm, but generous, kindling at the least imputation, but never "allowing the sun to go down upon his wrath." His adversaries described him as "really a kindly and generous man, warm in friendship, placable and scrupulous in hostility. Plain, sincere, straightforward, just, and considerate." They allowed him not only these personal qualities, but all the ordinary ones of a safe practical executor of the suggestions of others. They gave him credit for "understanding what he undertakes, and undertaking nothing but what he understands." Still, in reference to his nomination to the post of Governor-General of India, the same party observed that, "to consolidate our Indian empire by ameliorating its institutions; improve justice; remove remaining restrictions on industry; lighten taxes; to execute great public works; to extend education; and above all to raise the natives and give them a higher social position, a more elevated tone of feeling, and a greater share of political power, require a great and zealous man. But to achieve such results, or even to propose them, requires higher qualifications than we can give credit to Sir Henry for possessing."

That the writer erred in this estimate will, we doubt not, be acknowledged when the extent of what Lord Hardinge *has* done for education, for public works, for the reduction of taxes, and for the general amelioration of the people of India, is known to him. It is strange that the charge should ever have been made, for in the only departments in which Lord Hardinge had been tried, he had uniformly endeavoured to better the condition of those under him. The British soldier is indebted to him for many boons and liberal regulations, which add to his comfort during service, and improve his condition in old age; and thus he has justly earned the title of "*the soldier's friend.*" To him also we believe it is, that England owes the humane prohibition to the military and police against firing volleys on mobs. The instructions are now precise and positive as to when the soldier is to supersede the magistrate, and then instead of wholesale measures being at once resorted to, *only one file*, in the first instance, is allowed to fire; the remaining soldiers standing prepared to resist attack.

But the time was come when Sir H. Hardinge was to be called into a new and wider field of action. In May, 1844, his kinsman and friend, Lord Ellenborough, was removed from the Government of India by the indignant Court of Directors, whose authority he had defied; and the Ministry of the day, though disposed to defend their colleague, wisely acquiesced in a measure which they could not prevent. With equal wisdom, their selection for the vacant office fell on Sir H. Hardinge. The Court heartily and unanimously acquiesced, and the lovers of official scandal were disappointed at the sudden termination of what at one time bade fair to be a bitter controversy, nay a struggle for superiority between the Directors and the Ministry.

The new Governor-General was selected not as a brilliant orator or Parliamentary partizan, but as a tried soldier and straightforward practical statesman. Without, however, impugning the candour of either the Cabinet or the Court, we may believe that each had a motive for the choice they made. The former, perhaps, desired as much as possible to soothe the feelings of Lord Ellenborough; and the Court, in accepting his kinsman, doubtless considered that they gave the best possible proof that they had recalled his Lordship on public grounds alone, and with no factious motive. The appointment, in which the Ministers and the East India Company thus happily concurred, was equally popular with the public both in England and India. In the latter, the friends of Lord Ellenborough (and they were not a few, especially among the juniors of the army) looked with hope and confidence to a similarity of military feelings in the mind of his successor —at once his relative and a soldier; while all trusted to Sir H. Hardinge's acknowledged character for fairness, decision, and plain dealing.

Not long before, when the tidings of the Cabul disaster reached England, Sir Henry Hardinge had been offered the command of the army in India; which he declined. And now, for two whole days, he is understood to have resisted the temptation of £25,000 a year, with authority greater than that of the Autocrat of Russia, over a population inferior in number only to that of China. At the age of 60, to give up his family, his seat in the Cabinet, and the society of the greatest men of the times, for the sake of responding to the call of his country and proceeding to the far East, at the behest, and, in a measure, at the mercy of the Board of Officials, who had so summarily dismissed his relative and friend, required no little forgetfulness of self—no ordinary sense of public duty. A common mind would not have so confided. In this, as in many other passages of Lord Hardinge's Indian career, we recognise the prompt courage of the hero of Albuera.

The usual pledges were now given and taken; the usual dinners eaten, and the accustomed speeches enunciated, but with more than their accustomed interest derived from the past, and more, we believe, of sincerity with reference to the future. On this occasion at least the promises of peaceful policy were not forgotten, though doomed to be disappointed; and after-dinner visions of great works, and plans for the internal improvement of the Anglo-Indian empire, for once did not melt into air.

In his speech on the victories of Múdkí and Ferozeshah, delivered on the 2nd of March, 1846, Sir Robert Peel thus well described the circumstances under which Sir Henry Hardinge accepted his high office:—"I well know what was the object of my friend, Sir Henry Hardinge, in undertaking the Government of India. He made great sacrifices from a sense of public duty; my gallant friend held a prominent place in the Councils of Her Majesty: he was, I believe, without any reference to party divisions, held in general esteem in this House, as well by his political opponents as by his political friends. He was regarded by the army of this country as its friend, because he was the friend of justice to all ranks of that army. It was proposed to him at a time of life, when, perhaps, ambition is a less powerful stimulus than it might have been at an earlier period—it was proposed to him to relinquish his place in the Councils of his Sovereign—to forego the satisfaction he must have felt at what he could not fail to see, that he was an object of general respect and esteem. He separated himself from that family which constituted the chief happiness of his life, for the purpose of performing a public duty he owed to his Sovereign and his country, by taking the arduous and responsible situation of Chief Governor of our Indian possessions. He went out with a high military reputation, solicitous to establish his fame in connection with our Indian empire, not by means of conquest, or the exhibition of military skill and valour, but by obtaining for himself a name in the annals of India, as the friend of peace, and through the promotion of the social interests and welfare of the inhabitants."

Such we are told by the Premier of England, by him who best knew them, were the motives of Sir Henry Hardinge in accepting the vice-royalty of India: and when we glance over the parting address of the Chairman of the Court of Directors, to the new Governor-General, and apply it as a touchstone to that Governor's administration, we cannot fail to perceive how honestly and ably Lord Hardinge has acted up to both the Court's instructions and to his own pledges.

After assuring Sir Henry that he had the Court's "entire confidence—a confidence founded on the reputation he had established for himself not only as a soldier but as a statesman;" the Chairman slightly but distinctly alluded to the fact that the general administration of British India is the direct charge of the Court of Directors, "subject to the control of the Board of Commissioners for the affairs of India;" and, drawing thence the corollary that "the maintenance of respect for the authority of the Court is demanded by the existing sytem of the Indian Government," significantly added, "we are persuaded that you will impress this feeling upon our servants abroad, not merely by precept, but *by your example*."

The Civil and Military services, and (with some emphasis) the Governor-General's "constitutional advisers, the members of the Council of India," were then recommended to Sir Henry's attention; the Native soldier's good qualities were lauded; and lastly the Chairman thus urged upon Sir Henry's notice the questions of peace, conciliatory policy, and their results—consolidation and internal improvement:—"By our latest intelligence, we are induced to hope that peace prevails throughout India. I need not say it is our anxious desire that it should be preserved. You, sir, well know how great are the evils of war, and we feel confident that, whilst ever ready to maintain unimpaired the honour of our country, and the supremacy of our arms, your policy will be essentially pacific.

"To the Native States which still retain independence, you will extend the shield of British protection. It has hitherto been considered a wise and just policy to uphold and support those which are in alliance with us; and in dealing with those which are more immediately dependent upon our Government, we have, with a view to soothe the feelings, and conciliate the attachment, of both chiefs and people, permitted the former to retain the recognised emblems of authority, their titles, and other insignia of rank and station. Peace, apart from its other advantages, is desirable with a view to the prosperity of our finances and the development of the resources of the country.

"The strictest economy consistent with the efficiency of the service" was then enjoined.

The Chairman next touched on education; observing, it "has long been the desire of the Court to encourage education among the people of India, with a view of cultivating and enlarging their minds, of raising them in their own and our estimation, and of qualifying them for the more responsible offices under our Government. It is, however, necessary, with reference to the subject of education, to exercise great prudence and caution, in order to avoid even the appearance of any interference with their religious feelings and prejudices, and to maintain on such points the strictest neutrality.

"Finally, Sir Henry, I would earnestly recommend the whole body of the people of British India, and its dependencies, to your paternal care and protection. It has always been the earnest desire of the Court of

Directors that the government of the East India Company should be eminently just, moderate, and conciliatory. The supremacy of our power must be maintained, when necessary, by the irresistible force of our arms; but the empire of India cannot be upheld by the sword alone. The attachment of the people, their confidence in our sense of justice and in our desire to maintain the obligations of good faith, must ever be essential elements of our strength. I beseech you, therefore, to keep these sacred principles habitually and permanently in view. The Court has selected you for the high office of Governor-General with reference not less to the confidence which they entertain in your character for justice, moderation, and benevolence, than to your undoubted possession of a sound practical judgment, and a firm and indomitable spirit. You are already in possession of the highest renown as a soldier, and we feel assured that you will now rest your happiness and your fame on the furtherance of measures tending to promote the welfare and best interests of the Government, and of the people committed to your care, and it is our earnest prayer that after an extended career of useful and valuable service, you, may return to your native country, bearing with you as the best and most gratifying reward of your labours, the thanks and blessings of the people of India."

In a modest rejoinder Sir Henry promised *less than he has performed.*

Sir H. Hardinge reached Calcutta on 23rd July. The tremendous heat of the Red Sea at that season did not prevent him from minutely inspecting the works of Aden, and drawing up a memorandum in correction of the errors of the Bombay Engineers, and proving how unnecessary was the extravagant expenditure then going on upon the rock. Afterwards in India full information was called for, and the Governor-General recorded in another very able paper, that works to an extent sufficient for 1200 men in peace, and 1500 in war and proportionate artillery, would make good the post against all probable comers; since a European enemy must either drag his guns by land, 1500 miles, or be master of the sea.

It is in similar adaptations of ways and means that the officers in every department of the Government of India have found Lord Hardinge's strength to lie; his practical intellect sees and seizes at once upon the strong and weak points of a question; and above all a military fallacy stands no chance with him. Thus in the instance before us he justly ridiculed the inconsistency of making Aden a Gibraltar, while Singapore, Hong Kong, &c., are left comparatively defenceless. The Aden papers have generally transpired; and are justly considered as among the very ablest that have emanated from Lord Hardinge's pen.

One of the first acts of the new Governor-General in India was to appoint the late private secretary of Lord Ellenborough to the important commissionership of Tennasserim and Moulmein. Captain Durand has since been removed; but, when appointed, no man in India, of his standing, bore a higher character for talent, application, and business habits; and even those who have since condemned him, find him guilty mainly of errors of judgment. A more honourable man than Captain Durand of the Bengal Engineers does not exist. By his appointment to Tennasserim, the Governor-General was enabled to call up Major Broadfoot, who had for two years held that commissionership to the north-west frontier, where Lord Ellenborough had contemplated employing him. These two selections, and a general adherence to his predecessor's policy, satisfied men's minds, that, however, in personal demeanour to the Court of Directors, and in some domestic questions, Sir Henry Hardinge might act on his own special views, yet there would be no systematic repeal of Lord Ellenborough's acts—no running down of his opinions because they were those of his predecessor; a practice too often prevalent in India in places both high and low; so much so, indeed, as often to lead natives to suppose that there is no stability in our institutions; and that one official comes after another only to reverse his orders. Sir Henry Hardinge came to India "forewarned, fore-armed" against this restless error. He had visited Mount-Stuart Elphinstone in England and asked his advice. The veteran statesman warned him against *meddling with civil details*. The advice was wise; and, what is rare, has been as wisely acted on. The advantage of letting things alone where there is no certainty of mending them, is here too little understood, especially by the half-informed. William Fraser, who was murdered at Delhi, was once consulted by one of his subordinates, who in despair declared that he had tried every means he could devise to bring the people of a certain district into order, but without avail. "Did you ever try what could be done by letting them alone?" was the reply. We recommend the anecdote to every magistrate in India, who has got a little leisure, and is thinking what to do with it!

We would not be understood to imply that Lord Hardinge neglected civil affairs; but when it can be truly said that the most industrious magistrate in India may let "well alone," and yet find ample occupation for *all* his time, how much truer is it in regard to a Governor-General! As he cannot possibly have leisure for fiscal and judicial details, there is real wisdom in his leaving them to such men as are usually found in the position of Lieutenant-Governor of Agra, or Deputy-Governor of Bengal.

We shall be delighted to hear that Lord Hardinge has recommended the permanent appointment of a Deputy-Governor at Calcutta. The system works admirably at Agra. The Governor-General cannot, and, in our opinion, ought not to, enter into all the minutiæ of civil *details;* but it is most important that the man who has to do so should not only be up to his work, but be a fixture for at least a moderate term. By some such arrangement alone can he be enabled to turn his experience to proper account, or encouraged to sow with any reasonable prospect of seeing some portion of the fruit of his labours. The improvement of the North-West Provinces under Mr. Thomason's four years' administration has been most marked; but what possible amelioration can be expected under a system that, in ten years, has given us nine Deputy-Governors over a province containing thirty millions of inhabitants, and paying a revenue of nine millions? Fortunately for Bengal, it has had an able secretary in Mr. Halliday. But, however excellent the ministerial officers, and however worthy and efficient the Deputy-Governor, if the latter is to be annually relieved, he can at best only keep matters straight for the day. It is morally impossible he can do more. He would indeed be unwise to hazard his own reputation in the projection of schemes which his successor might mow down in the bud.

The Punjab has been called *the* difficulty of recent administrations; but the Government of Oude has been the difficulty of *all.* A fortnight had scarcely passed over the head of the new Governor-General before his attention was drawn to Lucknow affairs. The King, a poor vacillating creature, who had only a twelvemonth before rejected from his counsel the upstart Ameen-oo-dowlah, now again desired to place him at the head of the Ministry to the exclusion of the Vizier Munowur-oo-dowlah, who was giving satisfaction to the Envoy. Strong measures were advised: no less than enforcing the article of the treaty, which authorizes the assumption by the British Government of the direct control of all districts whose mismanagement endangers the public tranquillity. The Governor-General did not consider the case to require such an extreme measure; but, addressing the King, as a friend and well-wisher, solemnly warned him of the consequences of a systematic disregard of the Envoy's representations and advice.

In the same manner, mixing firmness with friendliness, and respect for individual treaties with determination to maintain the general peace, Sir Henry Hardinge endeavoured to persuade the foolish Nepal Rajah, the equally foolish Nizam, and the whole host of petty princes, to look to their own concerns; to conduct themselves with moderation and good faith; and not to fear British encroachment.

As little communication as possible was kept up with Lahore; and the British Administration of the day, after years of war and its baneful consequences, sat down in earnest hope of peace, improvement, and retrenchment.

Sir Henry Hardinge lost no time in redeeming one of the most important of his pledges to the Court of Directors. On the 10th of October, 1844, was passed that memorable education resolution, by which employment under Government was secured to native youths, whether educated in private * or Government schools,

* It is to be regretted that, from the benefits of this truly liberal measure, *private* Institutions were wholly shut out, owing to the narrow and exclusive test of examination which had been adopted See 5th Miscellaneous Notice of No. IX. of the *Calcutta Review* for a full explanation of this important subject.

on proof shown of qualification, ability, studious habits, and integrity. The effect of this noble resolution was immense; and the Calcutta Baboos, especially, lost no time in responding to the call of Government. Early in December they called a meeting, and voted an address of thanks, which was signed by more than 500 native gentlemen, presented to the Governor-General, and by him most graciously received and answered. He told the deputation that he advocated education as mutually beneficial to the governors and the governed: that he felt the advantages to Government of the services of natives of superior intelligence and integrity; but added that he patronized learning on the far higher principle that it increased the happiness and prosperity of society. His speech concluded with these words: "Rely upon it, gentlemen, you cannot perform a more patriotic service to your countrymen than by encouraging and promoting education among the native population."

The Governor-General on another occasion distributed the prize medals at the Hindoo College, and in reference to the speech he then made, a respectable Baboo declared, "Never did words more convince me of the ardent sincerity of the speaker than did the unaffected but stirring language of Sir Henry Hardinge."

Having thus patronized the Hindus, the Governor-General, early in March, 1845, attended the distribution of prizes and scholarships at the Mahommedan College in Calcutta, where an address was delivered by the students, and received with the same encouraging kindness which had been shown to the disciples of the rival creed. In his reply, Sir Henry Hardinge called the attention of his youthful audience to the exciting and wondrous facts of steam and railroads, and the magic power conferred on man by the discovery of electromagnetic telegraphs; showing how deeply even at that early day the mind of the Governor-General was impressed with the value of such means of communication in an empire so vast as that over which he ruled. Sir Henry concluded by holding out the encouraging example of a distinguished pupil of the college named Syud Hossein, who had recently been made a deputy-magistrate, and among whose qualifications was a knowledge of English as well as of several Oriental languages.

The education minute affected the middle and reading classes of the Natives; and much about the same time (30th October, 1844), was issued a notification scarcely less interesting to the lowest and poorest. It involved a considerable reduction in the price of foreign salt. This measure, which had been contemplated during Mr. Bird's Deputy-Governorship, seemed to be called for not less by motives of humanity than by the soundest maxims of policy. Nevertheless, the measure was regarded by many as a bold one; since it was expected to affect the revenue to the extent of not less than 12 lakhs of rupees; and that at a time of great pecuniary pressure, at the close of a five years' war, and the opening of a new administration. There is, however, at least as much of wisdom as of mercy in all such reductions of duties; for by them smuggling is starved, and revenue ultimately augmented.

We come next to a question which has been much canvassed both in England and India;—corporal punishment in the army. A large majority of experienced Indian officers were agreed that Lord Wm. Bentinck's well-meant abolition of flogging in the Native army had entirely failed as an experiment of discipline. Insubordination had increased. Evil doers were under no restraint; and a sepoy had actually on one occasion stepped out of the ranks and dared his commanding officer; telling him that the worst punishment he could inflict was dismissal. It was proved, that, while on the old system the average instances of corporal punishment had not exceeded one in 700 per annum, the number sentenced, under the new system, to labour in irons on the roads had been not less than one in a hundred and fifty—amounting to as many as ten thousand in ten years,—a frightful catalogue, and one, that the benevolent heart of Lord Wm. Bentinck could never have dreamt of. Abstractedly considered, corporal punishment is odious; but it is nevertheless true that many men in the Native, as well as in the European ranks, have gained and honoured commissions, whose backs have been scored at the halberds; we much doubt, however, whether any have recovered the moral searing of labouring with robbers and pickpockets on the public roads. The number alone of men punished by the new code, was sufficient proof of its inefficiency. The punishment brought misery and dishonour into hundreds of innocent families; while, at the same time, from its being generally inflicted far from the scene of the offence, it was no example to the comrades of the offender, of the consequences of insubordination and neglect of duty.

But a cry had been raised in England against "the lash." With some right feeling, much sickly sentimentalism had been expended on it in Parliament, and by the Press. In India also there was opposition to the idea of restoring flogging to the list of military penalties; and Sir James Lumley, the respected Adjutant-General of the Bengal army, declared it not only unnecessary, but highly dangerous.

Sir Henry Hardinge calmly heard all that was to be said on both sides; and, having given the opposing arguments the consideration of an experienced soldier, decided upon repealing Lord Wm. Bentinck's abolition. In a masterly record of his own views, he exposed the error of the prevailing system, miscalled *humane*, by exhibiting the statistics of its convictions and punishments; and then, separating *flogging* from *dismissal*, and showing that one was not a necessary consequence of the other, he stripped the bugbear of half its ignominy, and all its worldly ruin.

Let us not be mistaken. We are no more advocates for flagellation than the softest-hearted of our readers, but we know that the purposes of discipline, especially in camp and on service, often require instant and summary punishment for offences not in themselves involving moral degradation; and that, therefore, as one great object of all punishment is, or should be, the prevention of crime, it was not only justifiable, but absolutely necessary that the law should be altered and discipline restored, by a return to a *modified and closely-checked* system of corporal punishment. God forbid that any right-minded man should advocate flogging, except as the *effectual* substitute for the *ineffectual* punishments of imprisonment and death! Moreover, we would fence in the penalty with every possible restriction, and never inflict a lash more than the particular case required. The purposes of discipline are as likely to be effected by 50 lashes as by 500, and in no case would we have them inflicted except under the orders of the chief military authority on the spot. Prompt punishment is required for mutiny and insubordination—crimes, which, unless on the instant put down, soon convert obedient armies into ruffianly mobs. Neglectful compliance with orders soon engenders jeers and abuse, then blows, and lastly bayonet thrusts or bullets. Twenty lashes within a few hours of the offence may suppress the spirit, which, unchecked, requires the infliction of death.* On the other hand there is much detriment to the service, and no possible good to any party, in marching men as prisoners, as has been the case, from Affghanistan to the British provinces, or from Saugor to Arcot and Madras.

Some such thoughts as these must have been passing through the Governor-General's mind, when he summoned Lieut.-Col. Birch the able Judge Advocate General of the Bengal army, down from Simla to Calcutta; caused the whole of the Articles of War to be revised; and, in the face of a still strong opposition, and at a time when he was told that a dangerous feeling of discontent was prevalent in the Native army, had the new code quietly introduced. We can recollect that it was not without some misgivings that the first case of corporal punishment was enforced in our own neighbourhood; but neither then, nor since, have any murmurs been heard against the law. The quiet and well-disposed Native soldiers know that the punishment will never be their fate; and the dissolute and unruly have no voice or discretion in the matter; indeed, it is merciful to themselves to have a punishment which they dread.

We have said that the late Adjutant-General was strongly opposed to the re-introduction of flogging in the Native army; but we are happy to add that he lived to correct his error, and *acknowledge* it. We have still

* Within the year 1847 there have been fully fifty convictions of European soldiers for gross insubordination. Almost all the offenders have been either imprisoned or transported: three were shot, but only three or four men were flogged. They received fifty lashes each, but we are inclined to believe that their convictions were not generally known when the crimes were committed that entailed corporal punishment.

The law, or rather its practice, still requires amendment. "An eye for an eye" is the law of retributive justice, and surely flogging is a more suitable punishment for the soldier who strikes his officer than transportation *which he desires.* We are satisfied, that, if the first ten of the culprits above noticed had, each within twenty-four hours of his offence, received fifty lashes, and then been imprisoned, on the silent system, with hard labour for a year or so, the three executions as well as the expense and loss of all the transportations would have been avoided.—H. M. L.

greater satisfaction in recording that the returns of the army in the three Presidencies show that the punishment is *so rarely enforced, as to be almost a dead letter.*

We have enlarged on this topic, because we consider the restoration of corporal punishment as the boldest act of Lord Hardinge's Indian career. He found more than one regiment in mutiny, and a feeling prevalent that a spark was all that was wanted to light a flame. A large proportion of the Native army was on, or near the frontier, subject to the temptations and seductions of the rioting Sikh troops, whose emissaries were leaving no means untried to spread defection in our ranks. The Governor-General had before his eyes the fate of Sir John Craddock and Lord Wm. Bentinck, at Madras; and, little as was said when the event turned out happily and all went well, he must have foreseen as it were already in type, and only waiting for the printer's ink, the columns of invective and reprobation which would have assailed him had a single *file* demurred upon a punishment parade, much more if the new order had caused general disaffection among the sepoys. An Aliwal is trumpeted even to nausea; but the bold spirit of legislation, the *moral* victory, whose loss would have been revolution, passes by unnoticed in the calm of its own success.

It was during the autumn of this year (1844) that the little war of Kolapoor and Sawunt-waree took place. We have already (in a previous essay), pretty fully detailed its rise, progress, and termination, and have little to add to that account. The Governor-General is understood to have urged on the Bombay Government prompt and energetic measures, nor did he disguise his disapprobation of the dilatory proceedings of General Delamotte and his colleagues; and though a member of the Cabinet which had approved, or at least shielded, the appropriation of Sindh, might well have been expected to be prejudiced against the sturdy advocate of the unfortunate Amirs, Sir Henry at once approved of the nomination of Lieut.-Colonel Outram to the command of a light field force; and that able and gallant officer, as we have already shown, justified the confidence reposed in him by bringing hostilities to a speedy close.*

The war concluded, able officers were nominated to conduct the civil management of the lately-disturbed tract, where—much in the manner recommended in the preceding essay—the whole authority was left in the hands of the British agents; in Kolapoor during the minority of the Prince; in Sawunt-waree apparently for ever. All has since remained perfectly tranquil in that quarter, mainly owing to the same means that have more recently tranquillized the Punjab. The forts were dismantled, or occupied for the Government: the hereditary militia honestly disposed of, paid up and discharged; or such as had claims retained and usefully employed in police and other duties. There is a favourite and true saying in the East that without "siyasut" there can be no "riyasut;" or, to be intelligible at home—that severity is inseparable from good government. And on this principle the Governor-General acted in the case before us. He insisted on the punishment of the leaders of the insurrection; but forgave all others.

Immersed in these high duties of a civil ruler; patronizing literature, encouraging education, cheapening the poor man's food, drawing tight the bands of military discipline, maintaining peace, and repudiating aggression,—the charge has been brought against Lord Hardinge that he descried not the cloud which was

* In reference to Colonel Outram's services on this occasion, we understand Lord Hardinge to have said, that he was just the sort of fellow he would wish to have in the field at the head of a Light Brigade.—H. M. L.

rising over the North-West frontier; that he permitted the Sikh invasion to take him by surprise and thus jeopardized the empire, and sacrificed many valuable lives. Strange to say, the most forward of these accusers has been the *Quarterly Review*,* the political organ of his Lordship's party. We are prepared to prove that the assertions which it contains are as groundless as they are injurious to Lord Hardinge's reputation; and because the explanation afterwards offered by the *Quarterly** was tantamount to no explanation at all.

The mail which first bore to England the news of the Sikh invasion, carried, we believe, only a hasty and exaggerated account of the battle of Múdki; and in a time of profound peace the country was aroused with the intelligence that nearly 100,000 Sikhs † were encamped upon British territory and threatening a British outpost. Public confidence and common sense fled at the announcement; and without reflecting that the beleagured post was held by the best general officer in the Bengal army, at the head of 10,472 men; that this force which had the advantage of holding a walled town and a partly-intrenched cantonment was more than double that which won the battle of Assaye, and four times that which stemmed the whole torrent of Holkar's army at Delhi; ‡ and above all that those most qualified to judge (Sir Hugh Gough, Sir John Littler, and Brigadier Wheeler), were perfectly satisfied not only of the safety of Ferozepore but also of Loodiana;—without giving a moment's consideration to any of these things,

* No. 155, June, 1846; and No. 157, December, 1846.

† We do not estimate the Sikh *Army* which crossed the Sutlej at more than 60,000; but the crowds of armed plunderers, who flocked in the train of the camp to what they deemed certain victory, swelled the invading force to at least 100,000.—H. M. L.

‡ Burn and Ochterlony had 2½ regiments and some trustworthy irregulars. Holkar mustered 70,000 men!—H. M. L.

the Press assumed defeat, in the interval between the two mails, and a portion of it *yelled* for the recall of an "imbecile" Governor, and an "incapable" Commander-in-Chief. Other mails arrived; and with them the tidings of the glorious victories of Ferozeshah, Aliwal, and Sobraon. And when Sir Robert Peel, in Parliament, in that clear and convincing manner for which his statements are remarkable, detailed the policy which had been observed by the Governor-General towards the Lahore durbar—although the Right Honourable Baronet, in avoiding exaggeration, very largely understated the strength of the frontier posts at the time of the Sikh irruption,—yet the House and the country generally, went with him when in concluding that part of his speech he declared,—"*It is quite clear that my gallant friend the Governor-General did take every precaution to ensure the safety of the British dominions in India, in case of sudden and unprovoked attack.*"

The *Quarterly Review* undertook for "the incapable Commander-in-Chief," the same friendly office which the Premier had performed for "the imbecile Governor-General:" and zealously did it execute the task. But it was not content with eloquently advocating the claims which that undaunted leader had upon his country's admiration. In the warmth of biography it forgot history; and taking for its model those warlike medals in which the erect figure of the victor is made to appear gigantic by the corses prostrate at his feet, it elevated the subject of its memoir *by denying* all merit, all sagacity, all military forethought, to his friend and superior, the Governor-General, beyond the bold-heartedness that is common to every British soldier.

The words of the reviewer are as follows:—"If there had been urgent arguments addressed to Lord Ellenborough in favour of a peaceful reign, the wish both of the Directors and of the Cabinet on that head; was expressed with increased earnestness to Sir Henry Hardinge. It is necessary to state all this clearly, in order that the true causes of our seeming unpreparedness to encounter the danger of a Sikh invasion, when it came, may be understood. Sir Henry entered upon the duties of his office more anxious than perhaps any other Governor-General had ever been before him to signalize the entire term of his residence in India by the useful labours of peace. At the same time *he did not consider himself bound either to censure or to retrace the steps which his predecessor might have taken in an opposite direction.* He found that the attention of Lord Ellenborough had been turned seriously towards the North-Western frontier; THAT ALL THE TOWNS FROM DELHI TO KURNAUL WERE FILLED WITH TROOPS; that the Commander-in-Chief had already surveyed the whole extent of the protected States with a view to make choice of military positions; and that the advanced posts of Loodiana and Ferozepore were garrisoned. *Sir Henry Hardinge neither undid anything of all this, nor found fault with it; but he carefully abstained from the discussion in Council or elsewhere of topics which might turn men's thoughts to war;* and, without neglecting any necessary preparations, bent himself to the arrangement of plans for the better education of the people of India," &c.—Pp. 187, 188, No. 155 *Quarterly Review*, June, 1846.

"Sir Henry Hardinge, continued during the winter of 1844 and the early spring of 1845, to prosecute his plans for the general improvement of India. That he kept his eye upon the Punjab, and was neither regardless of the confusion into which its affairs were falling, nor of the consequences to which this might probably lead, is most certain. He had already directed that the works both at Loodiana and Ferozepore should be strengthened; and raised the garrison of the latter place from four thousand to seven thousand men. The former was held by about six thousand; and at Umballa, where Gough's head-quarters were established, and among the cantonments in its rear, lay about seven thousand five hundred, of all arms. *But as Sir Henry certainly did not anticipate that the whole power of the Punjab would be thrown across the Sutlej, he naturally concluded that there was force enough at hand to meet and repel whatever invasion might be hazarded."—Page* 189, *No.* 155 *Quarterly Review, June,* 1846.

Such entire ignorance of localities, and of what, in reality, had been done on the frontier is displayed throughout the article on which we are commenting, that if we were writing for India alone, the *reviewer* might safely be left to his own meditations; but, as an air of authority pervades his essay, it may be necessary to remark, for the benefit of readers in Europe, that not only "all the towns from Delhi to Kurnaul were" *not* "filled with troops," but that not a single soldier was stationed in any one of them at the period referred to; moreover, that Kurnaul itself had been abolished as a military station, a twelvemonth before Lord Hardinge arrived in India.

If the English language conveys any meaning at all, the extracts we have quoted imply that Lord Ellenborough had prepared everything on the frontier for war; that Lord Hardinge refrained out of delicacy from countermanding those preparations, which he, however, considered unnecessary; but that he as carefully refrained from adding to them a single man or a gun, except at the post of Ferozepore; satisfied that the force which his predecessor had collected between Meerut and the Sutlej was "enough to meet and repel whatever invasion might be hazarded."

The table below will show how the case really stands:*

Post.	Strength as left by Lord Ellenborough.	Do. at first breaking out of war.	Increased preparation made by Lord Hardinge.
Ferozepore	4,596 men. 12 guns.	10,472 men. 24 guns.	5,876 men. 12 guns.
Loodiana	3,030 men. 12 guns.	7,235 men. 12 guns.	4,205 men.
Umballa	4,113 men. 24 guns.	12,972 men. 32 guns.	8,859 men. 8 guns.
Meerut	5,783 men. 18 guns.	9,844 men. 26 guns.	3,971 men. 8 guns.
Whole frontier, exclusive of hill stations which remained the same	17,612 men. 66 guns.	40,523 men. 94 guns.	22,911 men. 28 guns.

Yes; as the *Quarterly Review* in self-correction says in its "note," two numbers later, "The state of prepara-

* We have taken these figures chiefly from a "Note" which we can scarcely say *appeared*, but which *is to be found* in the 157th number of the *Quarterly Review*, of December, 1846. The materials of this "Note" the editor says he received "from India;" and that he advances them "on authority which it is impossible to controvert;" yet it will scarcely be credited that after having, six months previously, in a widely-circulated article on the War, disseminated the belief that the military Governor-General of India had been so absorbed in peaceful occupations as to forget his frontier and endanger the empire; when in process of time he received "from India" and "on authority" the completest refutation *in figures and facts;* the only *amende* which he makes as *an historian* and instructor of the public mind, is to smuggle the contradiction into his 157th number, at the bottom of a page and the tail end of an article on "the state of Ireland"!!! This, too, without any announcement in the Table of Contents, either on the cover or fly-leaf, that such a "Note" was to be found by any one anxious to know the *truth* about the war in India. We wish not to be uncharitable, but it is apparent that if there had been as much desire to make known the corrections, as to blazon the errors, some more conspicuous place would have been found for the "Note," and the *usual* means have been adopted of attracting the attention of the reader by including it in the Table of Contents. That we are not imagining a grievance is proved by the fact that the Indian papers which copied the entire original article of nearly forty pages, took no notice, so far as we know, of the *Note* of scarcely more than three. This can only be attributed to their being unaware of its existence. Certainly they could not have found it devoid of interest.—H. M. L.

tion with reference to the Sikhs, at the time of his arrival in India (July, 1844), *did not satisfy him* (Lord Hardinge) *at all.* On the contrary, within three weeks of his arrival in Calcutta,—as soon, that is, as he had received from the Commander-in-Chief a correct state of the distribution of the force in advance, *he came to the conclusion that it would by no means suffice, even for defensive purposes; and that it was wholly inadequate to carry on an offensive war, should such be forced upon him.* In like manner the answers to his inquiries relative to the state of the magazines and means of transport, declared that to assemble 36,000 men—the total amount of troops stationed within a circuit of some hundreds of miles—would require two months after the order to concentrate should have reached Benares. Sir H. Hardinge saw that this state of things would never do; *and he began forthwith to reinforce every post in advance* —yet did it so quietly, that even in our own provinces the operation passed unnoticed."—*Note in No.* 157.

The result was that before he had been three months in India, Sir Henry Hardinge had several corps marching from the farthest confines of the Bengal Presidency towards the North-Western frontier; apparently in the usual course of relief; but "giving orders that not a man should withdraw from his position till the relief arrived; upon one pretext or another he kept the whole together; thus doubling without the smallest appearance of care on that head, his disposable force."—*Note in Quarterly Review, No.* 157.

With a similar prescience of their coming necessity, the Governor-General in September, 1844, only two months after his arrival in India, gave orders for European barracks to be built at Ferozepore, and they were completed in April, 1845. In January, 1845, Sir Henry wrote *privately* to the Governors of Madras and Bombay for remount horses; and borrowed 600 from the former and 500 from the latter, for his artillery; 968 of which reached Muttra in November, 1845, *before the war broke out.*

From Bombay also the Governor-General summoned H. M.'s 14th Light Dragoons, foreseeing that if there was a war the British cavalry on the frontier would have warm work of it.

Equal preparation was made in the Ordnance department. In January, 1845, the horses of light field batteries were increased from 98 to 130; four bullock batteries got horses; and two batteries of iron 12-pounder batteries were prepared with elephants.

"It was not, however, by providing men and guns alone that the Governor-General put matters in a train against every emergency. Fifty-six large boats prepared by Lord Ellenborough were brought up from the Indus, and reached Ferozepore in September, 1845. The flooring, grappling, cables, &c., arrived likewise complete; and a pontoon train was borrowed from Sindh, and rendered available. It was this forethought which enabled the engineers to lay down the bridge below Ferozepore in the course of one night and one day; and to do their work so securely, that the whole of the invading force—24,000 strong, with 40 pieces of siege-cannon, 100,000 camp followers, and 68,000 animals—passed without the occurrence of a single accident."—*Quarterly Review, note in No.* 157.

To quote still further from the ungracious recantation of the *Quarterly;* "it appears in a word, that the new Governor-General judged it necessary to re-arrange with the concurrence of the C. C. the whole plan of distribution; and the result of his arrangements was that no less than 14,000 British soldiers fought at Múdki five days after the declaration of war; and after leaving a strong detachment with the baggage, 17,727 men, including seven English regiments and 69 guns at Ferozshah three days later." These figured statements are a sufficient answer to the charge against the Governor-General of being unprepared; for no one who has seen a single regiment, much less a brigade or division move, can be ignorant that the rapidity with which this force was concentrated was unprecedented in Indian warfare, —that not a tithe of the amount was ever before assembled in an equally brief period—and that, without long-continued previous preparation, not one-half of it could possibly have been brought to bear within any reasonable time.

To assist, however, a just estimate of what Lord Hardinge did in the way of preparation, let us reduce our speculation to one simple question; viz. If, out of 32,479 men including the European regiments in the Hills at and above Umballa in December, 1845, only 17,727 men could be brought into action after junction with the Loodiana and Ferozepore forces; and if that number but just sufficed to beat back the most formidable enemy and win one of the most bloody battles which British India has ever witnessed; what sort of an army could the Commander-in-Chief have assembled and brought into the field, and what would have been the position of the empire, had the strength of the frontier at and above Umballa remained as Lord Ellenborough left it in July, 1844, at 13,538?

Thus far we have only compared Lord Hardinge's military preparations on the North-Western frontier, with those of his immediate predecessor, who contemplated not merely *defensive*, but *offensive* operations, because the narrow limits of a review forbid us to extend the retrospect. But should the historian, in his search after materials, ever glance his eye over these pages, we call upon him to go farther back and bring the light of former times and former administrations to bear upon the one before us. Let him tell the mole-eyed critics of one war, how other wars came upon British India; how the Indian army was *prepared* when the Government had virtually broken the treaty with Mysore; when Hyder Ali's invasion burst upon our defenceless frontier; when his hordes swept the country around Madras; and, having destroyed one army, and paralyzed the only other in the field, his nightly watch-fires illumined the senators of the "benighted Presidency!" *How prepared*, when the Burmans broke through treaties, invaded our territories and for six months sat down in front of our hastily-assembled army; and how prepared, when the Nepalese murdered our police officers, occupied our lands, and one after the other destroyed our detachments! or, as more akin to what might have been expected from the Sikhs, what was the extent of our preparation when, on two occasions, the Mahrattas confederated against us, or even when the Pindarri bands burst upon our borders and devastated our districts? When all shall have been fairly told, it will be, we think, unnecessary to add that in no one of these instances were we in a tenth degree as well prepared for war as in 1845, though in all we had at least as much reason to expect it.

The retrospect may be further pursued. Was there less cause, antecedently, to dread the Mysore troops, the Burmans, the Mahrattas, and the Nepalese, than the Sikhs? Which of all these enemies had the best military reputation; and which was considered in India most formidable to the British Empire? Was it the warlike banded force of Mysore, led by French officers under their able, unscrupulous, and powerful chief, in the first flush and tide of his conquests, and in the hour of our greatest weakness; the disciplined and veteran battalions of Perron and De Boigne, backed by a formidable artillery and by bands of hardy cavalry; the undaunted and energetic Gúrkhas, proud of a hundred victories; the lusty Burmans, scarce rested from a long career of unchecked success;—or, was it the *supposed* rabble of dissolute and mutinous Sikhs, with weapons scarce cleansed from the murder of their sovereign, and the massacre of their best and bravest leaders? Anarchy doubtless has its strength. Its wild impulsive throes may overthrow whatever is immediately within its reach, and by a mad assault may even surprise and conquer kingdoms; but it was left for the Sikh soldiery to prove that the centurion and the sentinel may be training themselves for offensive war, while apparently busied in murdering their consuls and their tribunes;—France herself cannot show such an example. The French were invaded; the Sikhs were invaders.

And let not the historian, who begins the parallel we have suggested, stop here. Let him, after showing how former wars came upon British India, set forth how they were *carried on* by the administrations of the day; let him recount the dangers and destitution of Rangoon, the six months' delay at Chittagong, the constant famine-stricken state of the Arracan division, and the little better condition, and still worse results of General Shouldham's column, during the Burman war; the disasters of the two Woods, the defeat and death of the gallant Gillespie, the fruitlessness of the whole first Nepal campaign, and the all but failure of the second, saved only by Ochterlony's happy rashness; the starving state of the army at Kandahar and Ghuzni, and lastly the battles of Meaní and Dubba, fought just after a British regiment had been sent by one route out of Sindh, and the Bengal column by another;—and then, let him compare these blunderings into victory with the noiseless combinations of Lord Hardinge, who, in nine days after the invasion, brought no less than 17,500 men (among whom were no less than seven* British regiments) into action at Ferozeshah, and six weeks later finished the campaign with an addition to his European force of two regiments of infantry and two of cavalry at Sobraon; so that the most terrible war which has ever threatened our empire was gloriously concluded in sixty days, at which period Sir Charles Napier, with a reinforcement of 16,500 fresh men and 50 guns, was close at hand! We have thrown out these last suggestions to those who read, or may one day add to, the history of India. We must leave the campaign to stand upon its own merits, unrelieved by the contrast of others less successful; and feel sure that after a calm perusal of the facts we have adduced, and the *figures* we have given—those obstinate and indelible proofs—it will seem astonishing to our readers that the cry of want of preparation should ever have been raised against Lord Hardinge; and that 22,911 men and 28 guns should steal up so softly to the frontier as to be unnoticed even by the newspapers. In the end, however, according to the old motto, "truth will prevail" even in the teeth of a "*Quarterly Review;*" and whenever the time shall come (may it be distant!) for history calmly to review the closed list of Lord Hardinge's military deeds in India, we believe that this very quality of *foresight*, which, from ignorance of *facts concealed by himself*, he is now so strangely denied, will be accounted foremost among his claims to the title of an able general. It is true that his fire and vigour in action at sixty does no shame to the glories of his early fields; but his *main excellence* consists in prudence of preparation, and that

* There being at the time only eleven in the Bengal Presidency.

accurate calculation of time, place, necessity, and result, which in strategy is called combination. Seldom indeed in any country has been found a soldier, who so minutely entered into the economical details of his army, who so thoroughly understood those details, and as far as in him lay brought them to bear upon the work in hand. We wish too that he could have left behind him in India a little of that "mens æqua rebus in arduis," which is so happily perpetuated on his medal. Our countrymen in the prostrate East become enervated by long prosperity; and little fitted to meet even temporary trouble. Like the Romans of old, we have vitality enough to survive a Thrasymenus or a Cannæ, but we not only cannot forgive a Varro, but find it difficult to understand a Fabius. We are too loud in consternation at occasional disaster and unaccustomed loss; and in scanning the conduct of our leaders are too ready on half information, or no information at all, to register as dastards and imbeciles, men who—perhaps before we were born—had proved themselves in the field, and in the Cabinet, equally brave and wise.

Among the injurious insinuations of the "*Quarterly Review*" in chronicling events previous to the war, it was pretty broadly implied that not only did not the Governor-General make military preparation himself, but that he would not allow the Commander-in-Chief to do so for him. As an instance, the supposed marching and counter-marching of the Meerut division was quoted; and we now extract the same Reviewer's recantation "*upon authority which it is impossible to controvert.*"

For example, at page 190, Sir Henry Hardinge is described as arresting, in November, 1845, the advance of a force which Sir Hugh Gough had ordered up from Meerut, and declining to reinforce the garrison of Ferozepore with an additional European regiment. This turns out not to have been the case. No regiments were ordered to remove from Meerut, so early as the month of November, with the exception of H. M.'s 9th Lancers; and even that corps was subsequently halted at the Commander-in-Chief's suggestion. Other regiments were directed to *hold themselves in readiness*—and that they were in a condition to move so early as the 11th of December was owing entirely to the vigorous measures adopted by the Governor-General in his dealings with the Commissariat.

Not only, indeed, was the Governor-General no stop upon the Commander-in-Chief's proceedings, but the two veterans were united in opinion both as to the measure of danger, and the means of meeting it. Both believed that the frontier might be insulted, perhaps invaded, by desultory hordes of marauding horse, and loose bands of Akalís; but neither imagined that the threat which, since the death of Runjít Singh, had so often been idly made in our times of trouble and even of peril, would now be carried out at a period of perfect peace, when the undivided resources of the British Indian Empire were available to repel attack. And it should be remembered that they held this opinion in common with Major Broadfoot, Captain P. Nicolson,*

* A very erroneous idea was prevalent after the Sikh war with regard to its having been foreseen by some of the political officers on the frontier, and not by others. It has been said—chiefly, we believe, on the authority of private letters, some brief and hurried expressions of which might very easily be misconstrued by inexperienced readers at a distance—that Captain Nicolson was always of opinion that the Invasion would occur, but that Major Broadfoot scouted the idea; and this has been made a handle for exalting the sagacity of the former at the expense of the latter. Captain Nicolson was an able and zealous officer, and did his best at a difficult time: certainly his manly and upright character wants not the support of an untruth! We have seen copies of more than one of Captain Nicolson's letters written just before the Sikhs crossed. In one to Captain Mills, so late as the 2nd of December, 1845, he wrote, "I do not think the Sikh army will come on, but it is feverish." "The whole army with guns and commissariat to some ex-

Mr. Currie, Sir John Littler, Brigadier Wheeler, Captain C. Mills, and indeed all the ablest and best-informed officers on the frontier. Time has shown the error of the belief; and recorded it in the blood of the two first of the wise and gallant men we have enumerated; but even after this lapse of time, and familiar as we are with the actual result, their judgment seems to us sound and consistent with *human* reason and probability. For it was *not* credible that the Lahore *Government* would calmly sit down in the midst of its difficulties, and make the horrible calculations which it did of its inability to stand another month against the army—that the next revolution would be directed against the lives and properties of the few surviving Sirdars; and that the vengeance of a foreign army would be a lesser evil than the

tent is ready for a start, but I cannot help thinking it is taking up its position rather with a view to defence *in case of our advance** than with the idea of crossing the Sutlej *en potence.* Small bands of them we must look for," &c. &c.,—and again the very next day to Major Broadfoot —"If the Sikhs do cross the river *it will be for plunder; but I do not think they will cross. Small independent bodies may.*" Shortly after the war we saw some original letters of the same officer to Major Broadfoot, and though we cannot recall the exact words, we can positively state that up to the last moment they expressed a firm belief that the Sikh army, *as an army,* would never be mad enough to cross the Sutlej. We mention these facts, not to depreciate Captain Nicolson's real merits, but simply to vindicate the memory of Major Broadfoot, who had no equal on the frontier, and few perhaps in India. Captain Nicolson having been Major Broadfoot's assistant, could have had no other sources of information than those open to his official superior. By his position at Ferozepore he only saw and heard what was reported a few hours later to Broadfoot, and what the latter could corroborate or correct by Captain Mills' and his own immediate emissaries. We have quoted the opinions of all on the frontier that the enemy would not cross, *as an army.* To their testimony we may add that of Major Lawrence in Nepal and Captain Cunningham at Bahawulpúr, both of whom, it is understood, discredited the *fact* of the invasion *after* it had occurred. But we needlessly accumulate evidence on the subject. We very much doubt whether the Sikhs themselves knew their *own* intentions twenty-four hours before they carried them out. *They had prepared the means of a great military movement—Chance—accident—caprice determined the quarter against which it should be directed.*—H. M. L.

* The italics are the Essayist's.

fury of its own,—that, *therefore*, it was expedient to fling the soldiery upon British India, supplying them with every possible means of success, taking, if unsuccessful, the chance of clemency and forgiveness, and if victorious the merit and profit of repelling the English from Hindoostan. We repeat that this calculation was too monstrous to be altogether credible, though not too monstrous to be true. We have shown that Lord Hardinge did not credit its probability, but *was* prepared for its possibility.

A few words will not be misplaced here as to the bygone policy of our Government on the frontier in question.

It has ever been the wish of the British Government to assist in the maintenance of a strong Sikh Government in the Punjab. It is understood that those who had the best means of forming a judgment on the question, Colonel Richmond, Major Broadfoot, Colonel Lawrence, and Mr. Clerk—in whatever other points they may have differed, were all agreed in this, that no advantage that might be gained by annexation could equal that of having an independent and warlike but friendly people between us and the loose, wild Mahommedan hordes of Central Asia. Not that the latter are in themselves formidable, even in their own country; but that their unsettled government, or too often absence of all government, must ever render them unsatisfactory neighbours. Much, however, as the maintenance of a Sikh Government in the Punjab was desired, it was early perceived that the chances were against it. One after another the ablest men in that unhappy country were cut off; falling by each other's hands or plots; often the assassin with his victim.*

* Dr. MacGregor, in his History of the Sikhs, naïvely mentions the name of the Múnshí who now holds Raja Dhyan Singh's written order for the

The violent death of Jowar Singh, though for an instant it promised to prevent hostilities, in the end rather accelerated than postponed them. No man dared to seize the helm. Raja Lal Singh was not wanting in courage; and Maharaja Golab Singh has abundance; but neither coveted the viziership of the "Búrcha Raj,"* which involved responsibility to a thousand exacting masters. Intoxicated with success at home, where no man's honour was safe from their violence, where they had emptied the coffers of the State and plundered those of Jummú, the unsated soldiery now sought to help themselves from the bazaars and treasuries of Delhi. This madness of the Sikh army was the true cause of invasion, and not the acts of either the British Government or its agents.

Next to Runjít Singh, Maharaja Sher Singh was the truest friend in the Punjab to the British alliance. He was not a wise man, but in this at least he showed wisdom. Few, indeed, are the native chiefs, or natives of any rank, whose wisdom is consistent and complete. Many are clever in the extreme—acute, persevering, energetic, able to compete with the best of Europeans in ordinary matters, to surpass them in some; but the most accomplished character among them has its flaw. We never yet met one that was not an infant at some hour of the day, or on some question of life. Maharaja Sher Singh is an instance. Brave, frank, and shrewd, he might have been a strong, if not a great ruler, had

murder of Maharaja Sher Singh; and also the one written by Ajít Singh for that of the false vizier; but his believing in the existence of such documents only proves how little qualified the doctor is for the office of the historian. Asiatic ministers in general are much too prudent to give *written* orders for the assassination of their rivals or masters; Rajah Dhyan Singh was the last man in the world to have put on record such a document!—H. M. L.

* "Burcha," somewhat equivalent to our Butcher, was the designation applied to the Lahore Pretorians during their reign of terror.—H. M. L.

he not been the slave of sensuality, and shrunk from the exertion of opposing the Jummú brothers. He felt himself in their toils, but lacked the energy to snap the cords. He saw that they ruled, though he was king. He wanted the resolution to act as one.

It is as difficult for an administration to shape its conduct so as to please all parties as it is for an individual to do so. Great was the outcry against Lord Auckland for anticipating, what he believed, invasion; and as loud against Lord Hardinge, because he acted contrarily. It is now much the fashion, in some quarters little cognizant of facts, to declare that among the duties of the paramount Power is the obligation to interfere in the concerns of every State of India at all internally disturbed. The loudest setters-forth of such doctrines, however, shut their eyes to the fact that interference may possibly rather increase than prevent mischief; and that British troops once marching into any native State, the independence of that State then virtually ceases. In short, that unless we subdue and occupy for ourselves, which, under the circumstances here referred to, we have no right to do, the chances are that we inflict injury rather than confer benefit. Interference therefore must be made on pure motives, for the good of the people, and not for the improvement of the finances of India. The day has gone by for annexing principalities because they are rich and productive. The spirit of the age is against such benevolence. With so much of preliminary remark, we may observe that it is now no secret that in the spring of 1841 Maharaja Sher Singh *did* make overtures to the British Government, and was offered an armed interference in his favour. A force of 10,000 or 11,000 men was, moreover, actually told off, and under preparation at Kurnaul, to move into the Punjab under Major-General Sir James Lumley, and the vituperators of Lord Hardinge's preparations for the defence of the frontier will—or ought to be—"at a loss for words to express their indignation," when they hear that only four years previous to the Sikh invasion of British India it was calmly contemplated to march a force not exceeding that of Sir John Littler's at Ferozepore to Lahore, to put down the whole mutinous Sikh army.

In referring to this circumstance, however, we are far from desiring to make it the handle of an imputation against Lord Auckland's administration: we only give it its weight in judging of Lord Hardinge's military prudence. The intentions of Lord Auckland and of his advisers were most pure: his lordship was perfectly aware of the dangers of interference, but he believed that the benefits to all parties would outweigh the evils. He acted on the light of his day. He calculated on divisions in the Sikh camp, separation of interests in the Sikh durbar, and immediate junction of the Maharaja and his partizans with the British auxiliary force. And the event might certainly have justified the measure; but we doubt whether the military movement, much less the political scheme, would have succeeded. For if the Sikh soldiers could drag their chiefs and officers over the border which Runjít Singh had never crossed but to repent, and there induce them to lay down their lives for the Khalsa, how much greater must have been their influence, how infinitely more determined would have been their opposition, had *we* been the invaders of Umritsur and Lahore. Our own opinion is that a massacre of Sher Singh and his adherents would have closely followed the British passage of the Sutlej, and that the whole Khalsa army and the flower of the Jat population would have united to oppose us in one decisive action which would have destroyed our army, or have given us the keys of the Capital. Our British Indian readers—many, we trust, heroes of the Sutlej—are now in a position to judge as accurately as we can of what might have been the result; but let them in fairness remember, that their own knowledge is recent and dear-bought *experience*, and not prescience: perhaps at the opening of the war of 1845 they themselves (as the custom was in the British camp) both thought and talked contemptuously of the Sikh army. How then shall any man "throw a stone" at Lord Auckland, who only trod in the steps of those who went before him, and whose opinions were—in this respect at least—enthusiastically embraced by *his successor*.

Within a twelvemonth the Cabul catastrophe depressed our military reputation in India more than any disaster since the retreat of Monson. The necessity was recognised of making extraordinary efforts to recover our pre-eminence and our prestige. Yet General Pollock's avenging army never exceeded 10,000 men, until united with Sale, when, with Irregulars "of all sorts," it might have mustered 15,000 of all arms. It may be said, "Lord Ellenborough relied upon Sikh friendship and co-operation, or he would never have permitted so small a British force to carry on operations at the further extremity of the Punjab." On the contrary, Lord Ellenborough recorded on the 15th March, 1842, his opinion that no reliance was to be placed on the Sikh sirdars or soldiers co-operating with the General; and ordered accordingly that the army should not advance, unless General Pollock could "by his own strength overawe and overcome all who dispute the pass, and keep up at all times his communication with Peshawur and the Indus." Thus wrote the Governor-General, who was at heart a soldier; and, as the advance took place, we must presume the General, who was chosen from all India to the high office of avenging his country, felt himself equal to the task, and that the political officers (Mackeson, Lawrence, MacGregor, and Shakespeare) employed under his orders, saw no peculiar danger in the move. In short Lords Auckland and Ellenborough, backed by public opinion, based a mighty military operation on the belief that a British army no larger than Littler's at Ferozepore,* though watched by 30,000 disaffected Sikhs, could "by their own strength" force the formidable Khyber; and when reinforced by Sale, could "keep up their communications with the Indus."

When we remember Plassey, Buxar, and numberless other victories of early days; when we call to mind that the great Duke, in the face of Holkar, the most dangerous enemy we had encountered since the days of Hyder Ali, divided his scarce 10,000 men, and with less than half that number fought and won the glorious battle of Assaye; when, indeed, we review all our greatest battles in Burmah, Nepal, India, Affghanistan, and China, and see what handfuls were enough for victory; and, lastly, when we acknowledge the estimation in which, with very few exceptions, our officers held Sikh soldiers *till they tried them* in 1845; surely we need not too closely scrutinize either the intentions of Lord Auckland or the overt acts of Lord Ellenborough. But if we can—nay, if we must—exculpate those noblemen, how unjust to arraign Lord Hardinge! The armed interference contemplated by Lord Auckland was postponed by the vacillation of Sher Singh and the lateness of the season, until at last it was prevented altogether by the Cabul catastrophe. On the return of

* We refer the curious reader to the Affghan Blue Book, No. 89, for Sir Jasper Nicholl's own expression of his "extreme unwillingness" to part with his brigades. There is much food for reflection in the mode Colonel Wild was first sent up to Peshawur, and General Pollock, and then Colonel Bolton, successively followed.—H. M. L.

Generals Pollock and Nott from Affghanistan, Lord Ellenborough, at the head of 40,000 men and 101 guns, met them at Ferozepore. Early in 1843 the assembled thousands dispersed, and the frontier station was left with only 2500 men, and so remained until after the battles of Maharajpúr and Punniar, when it was strengthened by two regiments. Lord Ellenborough contemplated the erection of a strong fortress at Ferozepore, but the foundations were never laid; and the intrenchment that was substituted scarcely, if at all, strengthened the position.

We may take this opportunity of stating the opinion to which mature consideration, and the gradual disclosure of facts, has led us; that,—whereas the War Establishment of the Indian army, including 33,000 British soldiers, as also irregulars and contingents, did not exceed 300,000 men, and had to defend a frontier of 12,000 miles, and protect as well as coerce a population of not less than 100,000,000* souls, a large proportion being of warlike habits, and ill habituated to our yoke,—so far from Lord Hardinge having failed to bring up to the frontier in 1845 every soldier that was available, his error lay, if anywhere, in having denuded the provinces by *bringing up too many*. But the result justified the measure, and showed that the statesman had not been forgotten in the soldier. At Gwalior, by Lord Ellenborough's arrangements, a hostile army of 30,000 men had merged into a friendly contingent of 6000. Nepal was quiet, or at least engrossed in its own petty domestic broils; Burmah was somewhat similarly situated; Oude, the Deccan and Mysore preserved an obedient subordination; and from Rajpútana Colonel Sutherland is said to have written that 100,000 gallant Rajpúts were ready

* With a population of 34,000,000 the French army is 450,000, or more than four to one of the Indian, in reference to population.—H. M. L.

to march to the support of Government. There remained then only the chances of domestic insurrection, and of disaffection in our own army. How well the native soldiery resisted all appeals from the Lahore incendiaries; how true they were to their salt, when double pay with unlimited licence was offered them; is best shown by the fact that not above thirty men deserted from the Ferozepore garrison of 10,472; and that *after* hostilities commenced not an individual among them abandoned his colours; nor are we aware that twenty did so from the whole army during the war.

Domestic insurrection was a more probable contingency. There is no denying that much alarm was felt in Bengal, and in those parts of the Agra presidency which were farthest from the seat of war; but a crude conspiracy at Patna, which injured only the few desperate men concerned in it, was the only treason of which we ever heard.

If, however, partial commotions had been the consequence of the withdrawal of troops from the lower provinces; it was perhaps wise to hazard them for the great purpose of bringing the war to a rapid and glorious close. The rising of a mob, or even the tumultuous gathering of armed men without discipline, or means, is a small matter when compared with the approaching tide of a regular army of 60,000 men, well supplied with artillery, and daily swelled by numberless recruits of its own creed from the very country it invaded.

To combine the defence of the frontier with the defence of the provinces, one other alternative presented itself to Lord Hardinge. He might have increased the army. But he rejected the idea for reasons sufficiently obvious and cogent. Already the expenses of the State were more than a million above the income; already the Government was threatened with bankruptcy.

Let us do justice therefore to the all but overwhelming difficulty of the Governor-General's position; and honour to the firmness with which he met and overcame it. It was, we may rely upon it, no easy task—no light responsibility—to defend a wide frontier with a scanty army, await a war with an empty treasury, and so cautiously prepare for hostilities as not to give cause for offence. The latter was hardest of all. The threatening rupture with the Khalsa might not come in a day, or a year, or might even be staved off for the duration of Lord Hardinge's administration; but in all human probability it was nigh at hand, could not be avoided, and *yet in good faith could not be anticipated.*

Yes, it is our opinion that up to the date of the actual invasion we had no "casus belli;" and had we invaded the Punjab, because the mad Sikh soldiery, as they had often done before, threatened to invade *us*, the princes of India would have supposed that our long and patient forbearance had been merely an untiring ambush,—a lying in wait till dissension had thinned the ranks of the Sikhs, in order that when they were exhausted with intestine strife, we might come forth and spring upon the prey. The press of Europe too would have found in such a questionable policy another theme for calumniating "perfidious Albion," and in all probability that very portion of the Indian Press, which has systematically assailed Lord Hardinge's "want of preparation" might have then been loudest in vituperating his *aggression*.

Native States have, at any rate, appreciated the chivalrous good faith which marked his conduct. Character, we can assure our friends, is as useful, and "honesty" as "good policy" in Asia as in Europe. The Duke of Wellington, with reference to Gwalior, well said that he would prefer giving up any advantage to bringing by implication a stain upon our name. We would desire that our forbearance and good faith should ever prove to the millions who so closely watch our actions that we have come among them as messengers of peace, protection, and good-will; that we are slow to take offence, and abhor the subterfuges of the aggressor,—though when injured, we have the power and the spirit to avenge ourselves. This train of thought pervades Lord Hardinge's policy, and we honour him for it.

Having now fully discussed the Governor-General's preparations for defensive war upon the North-Western frontier, let us pass to the war itself,—first pausing a little to see what reason there was to expect invasion in 1845 more than in any other year since the death of Shere Singh, and next to add a few words as to how we had been prepared in former times to resist agression.

Mr. Metcalfe's veto, rather than Ochterlony's battalions, stopped Runjít Singh's southward career in 1808; and when the station of Loodiana was established and left, with three or four regiments, 150 miles in advance of all support, the British authorities must have either estimated the Sikhs very lightly or confided in them very implicitly. Thus Loodiana remained for thirty years, until strengthened by Lord Ellenborough. But more extraordinary still, Ferozepore, though the base of the grand movement of Affghanistan, was, after the first few months, left with a garrison of three, four, and sometimes of even two regiments.

How jealously Runjít Singh watched British movements in Affghanistan is well known; how he forbade the passage of the Punjab, obliging the army of the Indus to proceed by the wide circuit of Sindh and the Bolan Pass; how, after the Lion's death, Sir J. Keane's return to the provinces, during the cold weather of

1839–40, was only not opposed through the extraordinary personal influence of Mr. Clerk and the estimation in which he was held by the Sikhs,—is also no secret. Those who were with Sir John may remember, that when he arrived at Shahdurra with the mere skeleton of a brigade, and saluted the fort of Lahore, his compliment was not returned; and barely the commonest personal civilities paid to himself. Some at least of his companions may also remember that an official notice then reached him from Captain Nuthall, an intelligent commissariat officer, who had been for months employed in collecting supplies in the Punjab, that a treacherous attack on his camp was intended, and that simultaneously with it the Sikhs purposed to cross the river, burn Ferozepore, and march on Delhi. Whether there was any truth in the information is perhaps not now ascertainable; but one thing is certain, that, about the same time the British kafila for Affghanistan, on which our very existence in that country depended, was refused a passage; and not till after a month's delay, and *again* through Mr. Clerk's personal influence, was it permitted to pass.

The reader of the *Delhi Gazette* will also remember how, during the next year, 1840–41, Major Broadfoot's progress with Shah Sújah's family to Cabul was impeded as much by his own Sikh escort as by the mutinous soldiers on his way; and how, but for his own indomitable courage, he probably never would have reached his destination. It is also well known how *cordially*, in 1841–42, that ill-fated and ill-used officer Brigadier Wilde, was supported by his Sikh allies, and how, on General Pollock's arrival at Peshawur and during his two months' stay there, they were considered more as enemies than as friends; and yet, by entrusting them with the escort of our treasure and our supplies, the safety of the army was virtually placed in their hands.

But still more to the point are the little-remembered facts, that, in the year 1843, and again in 1844, the Sikh army *actually left Lahore* with the declared purpose of invading the British provinces: the frontier authorities considered it possible they *would* come, and General Vincent, commanding at Ferozepore a force scarcely half the strength of that of Sir John Littler, received his orders how to act *in case they should.* And yet, after all these threats, all these symptoms for years disregarded by two successive administrations, that of Lord Hardinge, *which alone took all the steps that could with propriety be taken, has been recklessly accused of neglect and supineness.*

We offer Sir Robert Peel's opinion in regard to the course pursued by Lord Hardinge as expressed in the admirable speech already referred to:—

"It is quite clear that my gallant friend the Governor-General did take every precaution to ensure the safety of the British dominions in India, in case of sudden and unprovoked attack. In the early part of the year, at the time when he was occupied with his functions as Governor-General, and when it was most material that he should perform them in conjunction with his Council at Calcutta; in a minute, dated on the 16th June, he submitted to the Council his opinion that our relations with the Court of Lahore became so doubtful, that, great as was the inconvenience of separating the Governor-General and his Council, it was desirable, with reference exclusively to Indian interests, that he should proceed to the left bank of the Sutlej, in order that on the spot he might be enabled to give such directions as appeared necessary, and which, if given at the distance of a thousand miles, might be inappropriate. The unanimous opinion of the members of the Council was, that it was for the public interest that the Governor-General should proceed to join the army; and, in conformity with this advice, in the month of October he took his departure for the left bank of the Sutlej. Up to an early period in December, the opinion of my gallant friend (Sir Henry Hardinge) was, that there would be no irruption from the right bank of the Sutlej into the British territory. He felt confident that the Sikhs must be convinced that such an attempt could only end in signal defeat, and, therefore, that it would not be made. So far as he could reason from experience, he had a right to arrive at this conclusion. In 1843, the army of Lahore left the capital and advanced to the Sutlej; but after remonstrance on our part it retired again and abandoned the enterprize. In 1844, exactly the same conduct was observed; the Punjab army, eager for pay, or for booty if pay could not be obtained, and, instigated by the Government and the chiefs, appeared to contemplate an irruption; but, in 1844, as in 1843, the army withdrew to the interior. Accounts, however, reached my gallant friend towards the end of November last, which led him to believe that an invasion of the British territory was seriously menaced. The House will find by the Papers recently presented by command of Her Majesty, that on the 20th November, Major Broadfoot addressed a letter to the Commander-in-Chief, and another to the Governor-General to this effect:—

"'Governor-General's Agency, Nov. 20, 1845.

"'Sir,—Since I had the honour of waiting on your Excellency to-day, I have received Lahore letters of the 18th instant (morning). During the night of the 17th, the chiefs had agreed on, and the durbar had ordered in writing, the following plan of operations. The army was to be divided into seven divisions, one to remain at Lahore, and the rest to proceed against Roopur and our hills, Loodiana, Hureekee, Ferozepore, and Sindh, while one was to proceed to Peshawur; and a force under Rajah Golab Singh was to be sent to Attock.'

"The decision then taken by the Lahore durbar was, that four divisions were to be employed in an attack upon the British territory, but they were not to make a concentrated or simultaneous movement; and the policy of the course adopted by the Governor-General was thus demonstrated. The Lahore army, in four divisions, was to make four separate attacks on different points along the river—the first division was to force the eastern extremity of the line; another to attack Loodiana; a third pass the river at Hureekee; and the fourth attack Ferozepore. Those divisions were to consist of about 8000 men each. The House will see by reference to the Papers laid before them how difficult it was for any person, even the most experienced, to speculate on the decision to which the governing powers at Lahore might arrive. They will see, too, that the Ministers, or those who held the reins of government, spent their days in such continuous drunkenness and debauchery, that no resolution of theirs could be depended on. An account written by the Agent at Lahore, to the Secretary to Government, dated Umballah, November 21st, founded on information received direct from Lahore, presents this picture of the councils of the Punjab:—'The Ranee (that is, the regent, the mother of the infant Maharajah) complained that whilst the troops were urging the march, they were still going home to their villages as fast as they got their pay; and Sirdar Sham Singh Attareewallah declared his belief that unless something was done to stop this, he would find himself on his way to Ferozepore with empty tents. The bait of money to be paid, and to accompany them was also offered, and at length the durbar broke up at 2, P.M. Great consultations took place in the afternoon; but I know only one result, that the Ranee had to give her lover his formal dismissal, and that he (Rajah Lal Singh) actually went into the camp of the Sawars he is to command, and pitched his tent. What the Ranee says is quite true of the sepoys dispersing to their houses; the whole affair has so suddenly reached its present height, that many of the men themselves think it will come to nothing, and still more who had taken their departure do not believe it serious enough to go back. On the day after this scene took place, *i. e.* the 19th, the usual stream of sepoys, natives of the protected States, who had got their pay, poured across the Sutlej, at Hureekee, on the way to their home.'

"There appears also an account of another conversation, in those papers, which took place between the Rajah Lal Singh, and Bhaee Ram Singh, one of the principal officers and advisers of the Lahore Government, and who seems to have been the only one of them in whom, from his character and wisdom, the slightest confidence could be placed. In a letter from Lahore, dated the 24th day of November, the following conversation was detailed: Bhaee Ram Singh, addressing Lal Singh, said—

"'The English have interfered in no affairs of the Khalsa; what is the wisdom of your making religious war at the bidding of the soldiery? None of the nobles have discovered the real intentions of the English. The Governor-General's agent, who is a steady friend, has written in the plainest terms, that the English Government desires only friendship like that of the late Maharajah Runjeet Singh; but that if anything wrong is done by the Sikh army, the rulers of the kingdom will be held responsible, for rulers must account for the acts of their troops and subjects. Be cautious how you march to Hureekee with the troops.' The Rajah said, 'Bhaee Sahib, what can I do? if I remain, the soldiery seize me by the throat.'

"*In a word, the councils of the durbar seem to have shifted from day to day, and no one could speculate with any degree of confidence on the probable result.**

"On the 9th of December, the Governor-General, thinking our relations with the Punjab very critical, and that it was desirable to take every precaution against any sudden irruption, gave orders that the division of troops at Umballah, consisting of 7500 men, should move towards the Sutlej. On December 11th, the very day on which the Lahore army crossed the Sutlej, the British and native troops of that division were on their march from Umballah to the frontier. The whole proceedings of the Governor-General and the Commander-in-Chief, subsequently to that day, as well as before it, were characterized by the greatest prudence, skill, and foresight. From Umballah the troops marched to a place called Busean, where, owing to the prudent precautions of the Governor-General, they found an ample supply of food and stores. It was resolved that a junction should be effected with the Loodiana division, and that it would be better to incur some risk at Loodiana, rather than forego the advantage of a junction with the Loodiana division of the army. Those troops advanced accordingly towards Ferozepore, and learned by the way that the army of Lahore, amounting to not less than 60,000 men, had crossed the river, and were prepared to attack the British army. The expectations of the Governor-General were entirely justified by the result."

Our extract is long, but to the purpose. Sir Robert Peel under-estimating the force at Ferozepore at only 7500, but over-estimating the number of heavy guns in position, correctly states that "the army of Lahore shrunk from the attack of so formidable a post," and moved down to give battle to the army advancing from Umballah. There is much in the extract quoted by Sir Robert Peel from Major Broadfoot's despatch to induce belief that, whatever were the insane intentions of some wild spirits among the Sikh army, there was still, even late in November, no general intention of invasion. "*On the 19th (of November) the usual stream of sepoys,*

* The Italics are ours.

natives of the protected States, who had got their pay, poured across the Sutlej, at Hureekee, on the way to their home." This in itself was justly considered a pacific symptom. These men were not emissaries sent to mislead our sepoys. Such did not come in *streams*, but stole over one by one, and were, without exception, Hindustanís, who had relatives in our ranks.

So late as during the month of October, 1845, the tenor of the Governor-General's conversation and correspondence was sanguine as to peace for another year at least; to the Commander-in-Chief alone did he urge preparation for a defensive war, and it was at this time that confidential orders were issued for two-thirds of the force at and above Meerut to be prepared by the 12th of November, with the means of moving on the shortest notice.

On the 22nd of November, the first *authentic* intelligence reached Major Broadfoot, and through him the Governor-General, that invasion was intended; and the very same day the report was contradicted. The greatest indecision prevailed at Lahore, in the Camp as well as in the Court. Both felt that they were on the brink of greater events than in their worst revolutions they had ever shared in—greater too than they felt able to direct and guide to their own profit. Astrology was now called in; as if the perpetual stars would shed down firmness upon such miserable mortals and be accomplices in their plots! But the soothsayers themselves declared that a fortunate day would not arrive before the 28th of November; and the soldiery who would have hailed "*To-morrow*" as an oracular response from Heaven, now called the interpreters of fate, impostors. The majority of voices was for an immediate march. The Ranee and her advisers, who felt that all authority was lost, urged them to be gone at once; but this very impatience roused the suspicions of the soldiers. Hesitation again fell upon them; and Lahore became like a sea without a tide, agitated by opposing winds. Thus doubtful did matters remain for more than twenty days: the whole Sikh army, it is true, at last left Lahore; but, as on former occasions, they still hesitated to "cross the Rubicon," and finally commit themselves. The great delay, however, was in persuading the sirdars. *They* had property to lose. The rabble had only property to gain. Sirdar Tej Sing, who ultimately was Commander-in-Chief of the invading force, consented only when openly and loudly taxed with cowardice, and even threatened with death.

In the "Calcutta Review," No. XI., September, 1846, appeared as truthful an account as could be given of the military events which followed; of the rapid march of the British army from Umballah and Loodiana; of the hard-contested and glorious battles of the Sutlej. We shall only now add what seems deficient in that account; or correct what we may have since discovered to be inaccurate; keeping in view more particularly, as we are bound in this memoir, those personal exertions of the Governor-General, which would have been out of place in a history of the war and its many heroes.

Her Majesty's 80th Foot marched from Umballah on the 11th December, for Ferozepore, or a day before the invasion took place; and so little did the military authorities expect that it was running into danger, that the families of the men actually moved with them. On the 2nd December, the Governor-General had dismissed the Lahore Vakeel because he had given no satisfactory answer to the Political Agent's demand for an explanation of the reason of the advance on the Sutlej. A week was allowed him to satisfy the Governor-General that hostility was not intended. That week was required to complete the commissariat arrangements. The Deputy Commissary-General had required six weeks for preparation, and received for answer that it must be done in as many days. The energetic Broadfoot volunteered to undertake the task, and was ready within the time. The army of the Sutlej is indebted to him for food.

On the 12th of December the Commander-in-Chief moved with his head-quarters from Umballah. On the evening of the same day the Sikhs commenced crossing the Sutlej. On the 13th the Governor-General proclaimed the Cis-Sutlej States at once invaded and incorporated with British India. Sir Henry, being some days' march in advance of the Commander-in-Chief, rode over to Loodiana, inspected the fort, and, deeming it secure, withdrew the Loodiana troops to Bussean, the great grain depôt on which the British army depended, and which was only sixty miles from the Nuggur Ghat, at which the Sikh army crossed.* The Sikhs might have easily made a forced march on that important place, reached, and burnt it on the evening of the 14th of December, had not the Governor-General, by that time, thus thrown in front of it the Loodiana force of 5000 men. The main column of the British army, under the Commander-in-Chief, from Umballah, did not reach Bussean till the 16th, and the importance of the Governor-General's combination will be better understood when we explain that if Bussean had been fired by the enemy, the advance of the whole British army

* Among other instances of ignorance of localities, the Quarterly Reviewer increases the distance from Loodiana to Ferozepore by one-fourth, and places Bussean between them. The commonest map would have shown his error, and considering that the *whole* army and *all* its supplies moved by way of Bussean, he *might* have taken thus much trouble.—H. M. L.

would have been delayed ten days at least, until food could have been brought from the rear; and Ferozepore would have been all that time without relief! On the 15th and 16th, as the Governor-General's camp passed Raí ke Kote, it was disencumbered of its heavy baggage, spare tents, &c., and the elephants and camels thus rendered available were forthwith employed in bringing up stores for the army. The elephants, in particular, were most useful on the 19th December, in bringing up the wearied men of the 1st European Regiment and Her Majesty's 29th Foot, who had made an extraordinary march from the Hills to join the army, but, after all, were too late for Múdkí. This provision and application of carriage was one of many instances which the war afforded of the Governor-General's happy management and attention to *details.*

On the 15th, the Sikhs crossed their heavy artillery. On the 16th they encamped at Lungiana, about three miles north of Ferozepore; and Sir John Littler gallantly marched out with two brigades, and offered them battle, which the boasting enemy declined. On the 17th the Sikhs advanced a division, and occupied the celebrated position of Ferozeshah, which they immediately entrenched. On the morning of the 18th, another strong division of upwards of 30,000 men, horse and foot, with 22 guns, was pushed on to within a few miles of Múdkí, where, concealed in the jungle, it awaited the arrival of the British Generals, whose destruction they looked forward to with confidence, from a belief that they were attended only by a small escort.

On that morning the British army had made a fatiguing march of twenty-one miles from Churruk to Múdkí, where a Sikh picquet was on the watch, and retired to inform Rajah Lal Singh and the troops in ambuscade that now was the time to make their spring.

The British picquets had hardly been planted; scarcely one of the soldiers had breakfasted; and officers were at their ablutions or snatching a little sleep upon the ground, when Major Broadfoot, who was sitting at luncheon with the Governor-General, received a scrap of paper. Looking at it, he rose with the exclamation, "The enemy is on us." He rode to the front, and passed the word along. Some mistrusted his information, and even when he showed the clouds of dust raised by the advancing enemy, his warning was not implicitly believed, and the dust attributed to skirmishers. "That dust," he energetically exclaimed, "covers thousands; it covers the Sikh army." The story is differently told in different quarters; but though, like Plutarch's biographies, the anecdotes of Broadfoot may not be all strictly true, yet they are all illustrative of his bold, energetic, and able character. While the British troops were yet forming, he returned from his reconnaissance, gallopped up to the Commander-in-Chief, and gracefully saluting him, pointed to the rising cloud of dust ahead, and said, "There, your Excellency, is the Sikh army!" It was the political agent making over the frontier to the soldier. The cannon shots that almost immediately began to lob in from the still unseen guns soon told their own tale.

The Commander-in-Chief at this time despatched an aide-de-camp to the rear to hasten on H. M.'s 29th and the 1st Europeans, still a march behind; and the Governor-General had previously sent back his active commissariat officer, Captain G. Johnston, with elephants, as before mentioned, carrying food and water to assist the movement.

The victory of Múdkí has been well chronicled by eye-witnesses; and its details need not here be repeated. Suffice it that, the battle won, every exertion was made to improve it. Expresses were sent in every direction with information; Sir J. Littler was, in the first instance, warned to be ready to move by his right to join head-quarters, and afterwards directed to combine with it by mid-day of the 21st near Ferozeshah. On the night of the 19th, H. M.'s 29th and the 1st Europeans, accompanied by the 11th and 41st N. I., arrived in camp, and at daylight of the 21st, after two full days of rest to the army, the whole force moved, without baggage, in light marching order, on Ferozeshah.

During this halt of two days, the wounded and sick were cared for, and secured in the fort of Múdkí, a regiment and a half being told off to protect them and the baggage of the army. Regarding the latter arrangement, we understand there was much difference of opinion, but the Governor-General insisted that none should be taken to the field. The decision was a wise and a humane one. It was better in every sense to place a strong detachment at Múdkí, than, leaving the wounded with a small one, to embarrass the column with the *care* of the baggage train; while the fort, defended by a regiment and a half, was safe for a time against the enemy's cavalry and loose plunderers, which alone could penetrate to the rear of our army. Much needless alarm, however, was caused by idle reports in the camp at Múdkí, which would have been more reasonable had it been left less protected.

Leaving 5000 men to hold his position, and watch Tej Singh, Sir John Littler prepared, early on the 21st, to join head-quarters, with 5500 men and 21 guns. Permitting his division to snatch a hasty meal, at 8 A.M. of the 21st he quietly moved off, by his right, leaving his camp and picquets standing, and at mid-day had effected his junction, without Tej Singh's being aware of his departure from Ferozepore—so ably was the movement conducted.* Sir John sent word of his approach to the Governor-General and Commander-in-Chief, who had arrived within a mile of, and opposite to, the intrenchment of Ferozeshah, when the ever-active Broadfoot, riding forward with a few horsemen, conducted the General to the Commander-in-Chief. Arrangements were now made for the struggle. A question has arisen—the combination having been completed by mid-day—why the attack was delayed till half-past three? Time was of the utmost importance: all the force expected having arrived, it was vitally important to strike the blow before Tej Singh could join: why, then, was there a delay of nearly four hours? We have never heard the question satisfactorily answered, and shall therefore leave it, with other points of this battle, and of the war generally, to be hereafter explained.

A few minutes before 4 P.M. the attack commenced, Sir Hugh Gough leading the right, Sir Henry Hardinge the centre, and Sir John Littler the left. The advance was made partly in line, partly in echellon, the Governor-General preferring the first formation, as less likely to create confusion, especially in difficult ground. The right and centre were successful; the left wing was repulsed. Daylight failed and prevented complete success. The loss on our side was severe: ten aides-de-camp fell by Lord Hardinge's side, five killed and as

* The intelligence department of the Sikhs, during the war, has been as unduly trumpeted as that of the British has been depreciated. Their information is proved on this as on many other occasions to have been very much worse than ours. Tej Singh's conduct on the 21st and again on the 22nd, though usually attributed to treachery, may much more safely be imputed to ignorance of what was passing around him and to incapacity as a General in chief; perhaps, also, in part to the conflicting orders of his many masters in his own ranks. Doubtless he, like many others, had little inclination for the war; but, once involved, he could not help himself: his life, then depended on his fidelity to the Khalsa.—H. M. L.

many wounded; among the latter was his nephew, Robert Wood. His two sons, though closely attending their father, escaped unscathed.

At the side of his chief, whom he refused to leave when wounded by a shot from the Sikh tents, fell the gallant and accomplished Broadfoot; here the chivalrous Somerset sank mortally wounded; the young and promising Munro was lost to his country; here the brave Saunders Abbott received his wounds, and lay uncomplaining by the side of the Governor-General, during the remainder of the night. The staff of the Commander-in-Chief almost equally suffered; his Adjutant-General, his Quartermaster-General, and most of his aides-de-camp being wounded, either here or at Múdkí. Providentially the two noble chiefs remained unharmed.

In his speech already referred to, Sir Robert Peel happily notices the night's events. We cannot do better than quote his words:—

"The night of the 21st December was one of the most memorable in the military annals of the British empire. The enemy were well defended within strongly-fortified entrenchments—their guns were served with the greatest precision, and told on our advancing columns with great effect. The right of the British army was led by the Commander-in-Chief, whilst the left centre was headed by Sir H. Hardinge. Our forces made an attack on the enemy's camp during the three hours which as yet remained of daylight; but they had not sufficient time to complete that victory, which was gloriously achieved on the following day. The British army, however, made good their attack, and occupied a part of the enemy's camp. In the middle of the night the camp took fire, and further conflict was for a time suspended in consequence; but as soon as it had ceased the army of Lahore brought forward their heavy artillery, and poured a most destructive fire upon our troops. The details of those occurrences have been given with admirable clearness in the despatches of both commanders; but there have been private letters received which speak of them with less of formality, and perhaps give truer and more faithful accounts of these actions than the official documents. Perhaps the House will excuse me if I read an extract from a private letter from the Governor-General to a member of his own family."

The right hon. Baronet then read as follows:—

"'The night of the 21st was the most extraordinary of my life. I bivouacked with the men, without food or covering, and our nights are bitter cold. A burning camp in our front, our brave fellows lying down under a heavy cannonade, which continued during the whole night, mixed with the wild cries of the Sikhs, our English hurrah, the tramp of men, and the groans of the dying. In this state, with a handful of men, who had carried the batteries the night before, I remained till morning, taking very short intervals of rest by lying down with various regiments in succession, to ascertain their temper, and revive their spirits.'

"My gallant friend, as you see, spent that eventful night passing from regiment to regiment, cheering the men by his own example of constancy and courage—doing all that human means could do to ensure victory to our arms. 'I found,' my gallant friend goes on to say—'I found myself again with my old friends of the 29th, 31st, 50th, and 9th, all in good heart' —regiments with which he had served in the Peninsula, and with them that regiment which has earned immortal fame in the annals of the British army—Her Majesty's 80th Regiment.—'My answer to all and every man was, that we must fight it out, attack the enemy vigorously at daybreak, beat him, or die honourably in the field. The gallant old general, kind-hearted and heroically brave, entirely coincided with me.'

"Let the House observe how anxious my gallant friend is to do justice to his companions in arms:—

"'During the night I occasionally called on our brave English soldiers to punish the Sikhs when they came too close and were impudent; and when morning broke we went at it in true English style. Gough was on the right. I placed myself, and dear little Arthur (his son) by my side, in the centre, about thirty yards in front of the men, to prevent their firing, and we drove the enemy without a halt from one extremity of the camp to the other, capturing thirty or forty guns as we went along, which fired at twenty paces from us, and were served obstinately. The brave men drew up in an excellent line, and cheered Gough and myself as we rode up the line, the regimental colours lowering to me as on parade. The mournful part is the heavy loss I have sustained in my officers. I have had ten aides-de-camp *hors de combat*, five killed and five wounded. The fire of grape was very heavy from 100 pieces of cannon; the Sikh army drilled by French officers, and the men the most warlike in India.'

"From my affectionate regard for this gallant man, I am proud to be enabled to exhibit him on such a night as that of the 21st of December—going through the camp—passing from regiment to regiment—keeping up the spirits of the men—encouraging them—animating their ardour—and having lost ten aides-de-camp out of twelve—placing his young son, a boy of seventeen or eighteen years of age, in the front of the line, in order that the British troops might be induced not to fire on the enemy, but drive them back by the force of the British bayonet. It was characteristic of the man to read these details. He had two sons present, one of whom was a civilian, and the other in the army. On the afternoon of the 21st, he sent the civilian to the rear of the army, saying that his presence disturbed him, and that, if he refused to retire, he would send him away in arrest as a prisoner; but the presence, he said, of his younger son, an officer, whose duty called him to the field, only made the father more desperately resolute in the discharge of his duty. On the 22nd, after the battle was over, he took his eldest son, when visiting the sepoys and the wounded, and he showed them a Governor-General of India who had lost his hand, and the son of a Governor-General who had lost his foot, and endeavoured to console them in their sufferings by proving to them that men in the highest rank were exposed to the same casualties as themselves."

The event of the night—that long, long night—was

doubtless the capture and spiking of the great gun, which, within 300 yards, had been pouring death on our harassed and recumbent ranks. But Her Majesty's 80th, supported by the 1st Europeans, at the Governor-General's word were in a moment up, and spiked it; and for the rest of the night the enemy was silent. In this attack, Sir Henry Hardinge's nephew and aide-de-camp, Colonel Wood, advancing with his own regiment, H. M.'s 80th, was severely wounded. It is pleasing, even still, to listen to the stories current regarding those eventful hours. "And sure he talked to us as to ladies in a drawing-room, so quiet and polite," is a frequent remark of the soldiers of the artillery, of H. M.'s 29th, 31st, 50th, 9th, and of the 1st Europeans, who, lying around the Governor-General, witnessed his composure during the night. It must be remembered that Lord Hardinge, during these perilous hours, not only personated the Soldier and the General, but the Father and the Viceroy. His thoughts then were not simply for the army, but for the mighty empire in his keeping—for his brave boys by his side; and yet the rude men around him could perceive no symptom of anxiety on his brow—nay more, their own stout hearts were encouraged and inspirited by his calm and cheerful bearing.

The "Quarterly Review" has disseminated much error regarding the events of this momentous period. No officer carried messages of retreat between the Governor-General and the Commander-in-Chief, though some few did take upon themselves to advise that course, and one officer, by his inquiries for the road to Ferozepore, showed what was passing in his own mind. The statement bears absurdity on its face: the two chiefs lay within a hundred yards of each other, and once or twice, during the night, consulted together. There is not, indeed, a doubt that neither for one moment hesitated what should be done—"to die at their posts rather than yield an inch to the enemy." It is not, however, to be denied that this *was a night of danger—of great danger.* Darkness had covered our ranks, while the scarcely-thinned foe, driven from his foremost entrenchments, and with his formidable artillery still almost intact, fell behind his second line, and strengthened it for the morning's fight. And where were our battalions? Nearly two whole divisions were absent. Sir John Littler had been repulsed, and Sir Harry Smith, in the darkness and confusion, after having actually occupied a portion of the village of Ferozeshah, in the heart of the Sikh intrenchment, retired two miles from the field; so that of 17,500 men, not more than 7000 can have lain that night before a foe still numbering 40,000 men and 60 guns—a situation such as might have daunted a Roman heart. Sir Henry Hardinge calmly prepared for the worst; he sent orders to his secretary, Mr. Currie, at Múdkí, to destroy his papers, in case of accident to himself; he positively ordered his wounded nephew into Ferozepore, as well as the gallant Prince Waldemar and his suite, who, with equal reluctance, left the field.

By daylight of the 22nd all arrangements for renewing the attack were made. Colonel Benson, accompanied by Captain A. Hardinge, the Governor-General's youngest son, had been despatched before dawn, to bring up Sir John Littler; but before they could reach, the Governor-General and Commander-in-Chief had advanced at the head of their line. On hearing the first shot, Captain Hardinge spurred on to his father, saying that as his aide-de-camp he must be in his place. Indeed this young soldier was the only member of the Governor-General's staff that remained unharmed. Colonel Birch,

Colonel Parsons, and the Hon. Captain West now officiated as aides; and taking them with him, Lord H. advanced at the head of the left, as Lord Gough did of the right, of the line, keeping thirty yards in front to prevent the troops from firing, and desiring the staff to tell them that if they fired, they fired on him. The opposition was slight, most of the guns were taken in reverse, and now wheeling to the right, past the village of Ferozeshah, the Commander-in-Chief and Governor-General swept down the whole left and rear of the enemy's position, halting when they had cleared the works at the opposite extremity.

Not till now did Smith's and Littler's division rejoin; but there still remained work to do. Sirdar Tej Singh had at length been roused to action, perhaps by some of the early fugitives from the combat of the night; and scarcely had the tired troops united, before his fresh battalions and squadrons, amounting to scarcely less than 30,000 men and 60 guns, came in view—showing how needful had been the dawn's attack, and how dangerous would have been a single hour's delay. Whether daunted by the defeat of the night, or suspicious of a stratagem, in the flank movement of the cavalry and part of the artillery, on Ferozepore, Tej Singh, after little more than several demonstrations and a distant though destructive cannonade, withdrew.

Thus was the Sikh invasion repelled. The Búrchas had found themselves overmatched; accompanied even as they were by thousands of their brothers, and of wild Akalís, eager for war, and to wet their swords in Feringi blood—for the savage soldiery and their kinsmen ruled not only the durbar of Lahore and the villages whence they came, but sought to have a share in the supposed certain plunder of Delhi. Few of these amateurs, however, were seen after Ferozeshah; nor were they much heard of again until after the terrific rout of Sobraon, when they lay in wait for their discomfited comrades, ready to cut down and rob all stragglers who might escape to the right bank of the Sutlej. Thousands of the Sikh soldiers are understood to have fallen by their hands.

But now that the first roll of the tide of invasion had been resisted, how did Sir Henry Hardinge occupy himself? His exertions seem to have redoubled. Night and day his active mind was at work. Collecting information, getting up supplies, urging on the indolent, encouraging and cheering the active and willing, now suggesting plans to the Commander-in-Chief and his lieutenants; now writing to Calcutta, to England, to Delhi, Umballah, and Kurnaul, and now riding out to army head-quarters to consult with the Commander-in-Chief in person.

On the death of Major Broadfoot, Major Lawrence was sent for from Nepal, although there were aspirants to the vacant office on the spot; and he proved his zeal by joining within a fortnight. In the interim Mr. Currie carried on the duties of the frontier; while Major Mackeson was entrusted with the charge of the Cis-Sutlej States.

A brief return to disputed points may be here excused. It is not easy within the limits of a single essay even to refer to all that has been said and written regarding Lord Hardinge's acts. Their bare enumeration would nearly occupy its entire space. Lord Hardinge is blamed for the "*defenceless state*" of the frontier; but we have shown by figures that he doubled and trebled the strength of posts. We may now add, that shortly after his arrival in India, he seriously contemplated altogether withdrawing the posts of Loodiana and Ferozepore, and was only prevented from doing so by the knowledge that the act would be misinterpreted. Retrogression is at all times difficult; never more so than in the face of a powerful and insolent enemy. No one at all acquainted with Lord Hardinge can doubt that he is the last man in the world who would have taken up those positions. No one knows better than himself that he who tries to defend everything defends nothing, and that, in Major Broadfoot's admirable words, "the defence of the frontier against aggression is the power of Government to punish the aggressive nation; and towards the exercise of that power the frontier force will contribute best by securing against all comers those important stations," viz., Loodiana and Ferozepore.

If it had originally devolved upon Lord Hardinge to have made provision for the defence of the frontier, he would doubtless have simply watched the fords, and kept in hand, in the neighbourhood of Sirhind, a strong field force ready to meet any enemy that might cross. It was idle to expect that two isolated posts could defend a hundred and fifty miles of river, fordable at twenty different points, and crowded with boats. Our readers may rely upon it that Major Broadfoot only expressed Lord Hardinge's conviction when he said that the Ferozepore force was meant for the protection of Ferozepore and the frontier *in peace*, and not for general war purposes.

On another point much discussion has arisen. On one side it is asked why Lord Hardinge fought the battle of Ferozeshah *so late* on the 21st December, and on the other why he fought *at all* on that day. But a fact which has been stated in previous accounts of the war must not be forgotten, viz., that on the 19th, Lord Hardinge had asked for and accepted the office of second in command of the army. We have never hesitated to approve of the arrangement under all the circumstances of the case, and we hold to our opinion. There are seasons when all secondary considerations must be waived—when the post must be abandoned, the detachment sacrificed, for the safety of the army. Once in the field *in this capacity*, though the Governor-General could suggest his wishes, he could not, without going to extremities, issue or enforce orders. It belongs not then necessarily to the province of Lord Hardinge's biographer to enter into the details of the different actions of the war, but we must remind those who would have counselled a halt at Ferozeshah that it could not have been made—neither supplies nor water being procurable. Strategy is good: excellent in its way; but *water* more than ground directs military movements in India, where no general can succeed who does not look minutely to this important point. The wells near Ferozeshah were at intervals of miles; *and by them* were the movements of the British army influenced.

The writer in the "Quarterly Review," however, reversing the real state of affairs, gives Lord Hardinge no credit for what he really did do in cases where he acted with energy, and leaves him, at least by implication, to bear the blame of defects in operations over which he had virtually little or no control. That writer's remarks, and the strictures of others, on the order of battle on the three different occasions, and on the want of information of the enemy's movements, are examples of the latter; while, with regard to the former, the reviewer, apparently ignorant that in India not a man or a gun can move without the sanction of the Governor-General, emphatically claims for the Commander-in-Chief alone all credit for the bringing up of troops and stores for the combinations which preceded Aliwal; and yet it was at Lord Hardinge's suggestion, and by his orders, that the troops engaged there were assembled from the four quarters and combined at Loodiana. Brigade after brigade was pushed on from army headquarters: Wheeler went after Smith, Taylor after Wheeler; Lawrence, at the last moment, to help on Taylor; all at the Governor-General's suggestion; while the Shekawatti brigade westward and H. M.'s 53rd from the southward were brought up by his direct orders. All this was known, or should have been known, by the historiographer of the war.

During the war, *precise* information was seldom procurable. Many able and good men were employed in procuring intelligence, but the Indian army, possessing no establishment trained in time of peace to procure the information required in war, can never be more than partially successful in this respect. The thing is not to be done in a day. A quartermaster-general or a political officer may in himself be all energy and ability, but, unaided, must inevitably fail to secure accurate and precise information. All this requires *known* and tried native agency—men who have a stake in the State. Serving against Asiatics we can never have our Colquhoun Grants, who will enter the enemy's lines and ascertain their state and preparation; but there is no possible reason why we should not have imitators of him in our Native army. To pay men, teach them, trust them in peace, and thus to have them ready for war, is the true policy. We shall then have men whom we can rely on, instead of chance-comers, who *may* be honest, but if energetic and able are too often rather serving the enemy than us. Thus has it ever been since Hyder Ali sent his shoals of Hurkaras to deceive and mislead our generals, down to the late war, when, as in all previous campaigns, the intelligence arrangements had to be made *after* hostilities had commenced. Lord

Hardinge, in a measure, has provided the nucleus of a remedy, and in the small guide corps raised on the north-west frontier under Colonel Lawrence's supervision, has given the means of acquiring information, and has prepared a body of men to meet future contingencies. We would have had him act on a larger scale, and even in peace time attach several officers to the corps to learn their duty and acquire information of roads and rivers, wells and tanks, supplies, means of carriage, and other milito-statistical details—so much required, so little attended to in India. The very formation, however, of this corps is a sufficient answer to those who charge Lord Hardinge with neglecting, during the war, so important a point as that of procuring intelligence of the enemy: while it proves equally that his lordship felt during the campaign the necessity of some such permanent establishment.

We entirely deny that during the Sikh campaign there was anything like *general ignorance* of the enemy's movements; or that the authorities were not kept at least as well informed of what went on around them as during any other war that was ever conducted in India. But supposing the fact to be otherwise, is it not too much to blame the head of a Government whose whole tenure of office has been three and a half years, and who was called into the field within less than half that time after his arrival, for evils which arise only from the defective institutions of an Asiatic system that has prevailed over our European notions—a system that has existed from the days of Clive and Hastings, and through every Administration down to the present day? If the Governor-General denied either the quartermaster-general or the political agent the means of supplying information, then, indeed, is he to blame; but because, with a thousand pressing matters before him, he did not, even before he could look around, reform and remodel an important branch of the public service, he is, forsooth, to be made the scape-goat for many imaginary and some* real defects in the system bequeathed to him by his predecessors!

But we digress, and should here rather detail how, personally, the Governor-General at this time exerted himself in all departments; how he urged the reinforcing of Sir Harry Smith, how he sent Lieut. Lake of the engineers, Lieut. Clifford of the artillery, and finally Major Lawrence, one after another to *see* to the munitions and reinforcements in support of the Loodiana movement. Nothing escaped his attention; not even the minutest commissariat or ordnance details. He thought of the brandy and beef for the European soldiers, as much as of the grape shot for the artillery, and the small arm ammunition for the infantry. All this time the heavy train was winding its weary way by the Bussean road from Delhi. The Governor-General was therefore intensely anxious that the seat of war should not be moved from the Ferozepore side eastward, and consequently strained every nerve to crush Runjore Singh, and prevent even his light troops moving southward. To effect this object, the force before Sobraon was greatly weakened, but the Commander-in-Chief as well as the Governor-General saw the advisa-

* Our approval of the scheme of training a guide corps, such as is here indicated and strongly recommended, may appear to be at variance with the opinions elsewhere expressed in this essay against natives of India proving useful in a double capacity. In a measure it is so: but the low castes of the northwest frontier are a bolder, and altogether a different race from those of Hindoostan. In India, sowars are notoriously blind guides, and we never heard that a sepoy was expected to know his way anywhere: if then Col. Lawrence can obtain faithful guides of ordinary courage he will do good service. One or two hundred would have been invaluable to have carried despatches between the different posts of the army during the war. Col. (General Sir George) Schovell's guides, though many of them French deserters, were often thus employed during the Peninsular war.—H. M. L.

bility of the measure. An excellent brigade under Colonel Taylor of H. M.'s 29th, which was detached to reinforce Sir Harry Smith, had reached Dhurmkote within 20 miles, and would have been up next day, when on the repeated and urgent suggestions of the Governor-General and Commander-in-Chief to attack, Sir H. Smith on the 28th January fought the battle of Aliwal. This action secured the communications, and the authorities could now await without anxiety the arrival of the siege train. Lord Hardinge had visited the army head-quarter camp on the 28th January, and, riding back, his horse fell under him and so severely bruised his leg that he was a cripple during the rest of the campaign. Suffering great pain, and for a month scarcely able to sit on horseback, he yet did not forego his labours, nor did he fail to sit out the whole action of Sobraon, though he went to the field in his carriage, and only mounted his horse when the batteries opened on both sides.

On the 8th February Sir H. Smith's division rejoined head-quarters; on the 9th the train reached camp; on the 10th the Sikhs were driven across the Sutlej. As far back as the middle of January, the Governor-General had in his home despatch contemplated the probability of coming to action by that day. We do not purpose again to fight the battle of Sobraon in these pages, but will offer a few briefs words on some hitherto unexplained points. The question has been often asked why were not the entrenchments at Sobraon and Ferozeshah turned; why attacked in the face of the formidable Sikh artillery? The same question might be asked of almost every Indian battle. The Duke of Wellington wisely *counselled* taking an Asiatic army in motion, but he himself with half his numbers attacked them at Assaye, in position and by a forward movement. At Mehidpúr, where perhaps the next most formidable display of cannon was encountered by an Anglo-Indian army, Hyslop and Malcolm,—the latter at least accustomed to Indian warfare, and trained in the school of Wellington, —not only attacked the long array in front, but crossed a deep river under fire. But the fact is that Ferozeshah was not to be outflanked; its oblong figure was nearly equally formidable in every direction, and had Sir Hugh Gough attacked on the northward face, he might have subjected himself to the double fire of Tej Singh in his rear and the works in his front; besides having abandoned the line of communication with his wounded and baggage at Múdkí.

As matters *turned out* at Sobraon, perhaps the cavalry and Grey's division, with some horse artillery, might have crossed the Sutlej simultaneously with the attack, and completed the destruction of the panic-striken Sikhs. We say *perhaps*, for even now we are not satisfied that the move would have been a safe one. The Nugger and Uttari fords are deep and uncertain; our troops on the other side must have been for at least two days without any certain supplies; and above all, with the experience of Ferozeshah before us, we did not know that every man's services might not be required on our own bank of the river. No man in camp, not even the Commander-in-Chief and Governor-General (and there were no two more sanguine of victory), expected such complete success as crowned our efforts on the 10th February.*

* Major General Sir Robert Dick's column, as one powerful wedge, was alone intended to attack; but by some mistake it was left weaker by a full brigade than was contemplated. Smith's and Gilbert's feints were converted into real attacks on Dick's repulse, and thus it was that a larger front was exposed and more loss incurred than otherwise would have been the case. This is to be lamented. Too much, however, has been said of the casualties during these battles, and we have only to look to the returns of the Peninsular war or to those of Assaye, Argaum, Laswari, Delhi, Mehidpúr, and Maharajpore, to find that the loss in

Here again the Governor-General was attended by both his sons, and his nephew; and the same calm collected demeanour was on this occasion observable by those around him, as under more trying circumstances at Ferozeshah. The artillery fire did much execution, and cleared the whole area except the immediate breastworks in their front; but as the Sikh gunners stood manfully to their guns, and rather than otherwise increased their fire, there was some hesitation whether the column of attack should be brought forward. About 9 o'clock the Commander-in-Chief and Governor-General held a few words of converse. Councils of war do not usually fight; but their's was not of such sort. The gallant Gough was all fire, and confidence; and the equally gallant Hardinge bade him by all means proceed to the assault, if he felt satisfied of success. He told him that loss must be expected, but should not prevent attack if it was likely to prove successful. It is well known how both chiefs simultaneously ordered up Smith's and Gilbert's divisions, how those generals as well as Dick, reeling before the shock of the Sikh batteries, retired; but only to re-form and again on all sides to renew the attack;—the best proof of discipline that soldiers could give; and one which the Portuguese, to whom Sir Henry Hardinge was often accustomed to liken the sepoys, seldom evinced. It has been narrated

former campaigns averaged at least as much as that of the Sikh battles, and generally — indeed, in India always—from the same cause, the enemy's artillery. It must ever be so. Assaults are not to be made on positions, bristling with heavy guns, without loss; and if more cautious measures, involving delay, might in the first instance save some lives, it must also be borne in mind that such delays tend to give confidence to the enemy, who, on the other hand, promptly confronted and well beaten in a hand-to-hand fight, seldom renews the conflict. We are far from advocating bull-dog measures or the neglect of science, but we would impress on our readers, that we hold India *at least* as much by the conviction of our prowess and our pluck as by our civil institutions, and, therefore, that deeds which at first sight may appear brutal and sanguinary, in the end may actually save life.—H. M. L.

elsewhere how the Governor-General, at the very commencement of the attack, had three troops of horse artillery brought up by their drivers and kept in reserve at Rodawala, until their gunners, employed with the heavy guns, had fired away all their ammunition and could retire to bring these field-pieces up to complete the destruction of the Sikh army. This may seem a small matter, but is in keeping with all Lord Hardinge's military conduct. Though an infantry officer himself he saw at once what no artilleryman appears to have perceived, and evinced his sense of its importance by despatching three several officers to bring them up. In this manner, with a view of ensuring the execution of his orders, he detached the officers of his staff so rapidly one after the other that he was repeatedly left almost alone during the heat of the action.

Our tale is of the Governor-General and our narrative must keep him constantly in sight; but we would not for a moment imply that the Commander-in-Chief did not throughout the day do all that a soldier could do. Never indeed, on India's fertile field of glory, fought a braver spirit than Lord Gough; and we believe that no British general in the East has ever won so many battles.

By 1 P.M. the battle and the campaign were over, and not a Sikh in arms remained south of the Sutlej. The moment was a proud one for both the Commander-in-Chief and Governor-General, but we doubt whether, in the mind of either, there was elation, and whether the first and saddest thought was not the heavy cost of victory: recollections of the noble soldiers who had fallen, the brave who had suffered, the widows and the orphans who survived. Such men as Lords Hardinge and Gough *can* appreciate peace, can separate the tinsel from the gold, and in the parade and panopoly of war picture also to their minds its horrors, with a force and vividness which can hardly be appreciated by an amateur soldier.

By half-past 1, Colonel Wood, the ever-active aide-de-camp, now military secretary, of the Governor-General, scarcely recovered from his wound received at Ferozeshah, was off with the tidings of victory to Ferozepore, which though twenty-five miles distant he reached in an hour and a half, and returned half way to meet the Governor-General at 5 P.M. That night the passage across the river commenced, and by the incredible exertions of Colonel Abbott and the engineers, the whole army was at Kussúr, one march in the enemy's territory, and thirty-five miles from the scene of action, on the 13th, the third day after the battle!

We *now* know that the Sikh power was completely broken by the repeated heavy blows of Múdkí, Ferozeshah, Aliwal and Sobraon; *but such was not then the general opinion;* and there were not wanting many, even in high places, to solemnly warn the Governor-General against crossing the Sutlej, as some of them said, "only to be driven back with disgrace." Better men declared, that we had not the means to lay siege to both Gobindgurh and Lahore, and that without such means it would be injudicious to cross. While thus pressed on the spot, there had been for some time *as* impressive suggestions from irresponsible persons elsewhere to advance and to hazard all in the Punjab *before* the enemy were broken and *before* our train and ammunition had come up. The Governor-General's practical common sense steered him safely between these extremes. He waited not an hour beyond the arrival of the siege train: he felt that all now depended on time, on closing the war before the hot season could set in on our European troops, entailing death in a hundred shapes on all ranks, and the expenses of another campaign on the Government.

Some have blamed Lord Hardinge for the partition of the Punjab, and above all for raising Rajah Golab Singh to a throne and independent principality. We will here add a few "last words," briefly commenting on the other courses which were open to the Governor-General.

It was out of the question to annex the Punjab. The lateness of the season, the weakness of our army, especially in what constitutes its pith and essence, the Europeans,—who, after four pitched battles and the skirmish at Búddawal, were reduced to barely 3000 men, forbade it. In this view the Governor-General was supported by the opinion of the best soldiers in India, among whom was Sir C. Napier. Our occupation of the country, even if successful, would have been expensive and dangerous. It would, for years and years, have interfered with useful projects in India; perhaps, like Scinde, have entailed another debt. Under any circumstances, it would have brought us into renewed contact with Affghanistan and its difficulties—our sepoys into collision with the fierce and hardy mountaineers of the north, with whom a struggle which can bring neither glory nor gain could not fail to be unpopular. This is the matter-of-fact view of the case.

The exaltation of Golab Singh is a part of the same question. Those most hostile to this act of the Governor-General have founded their chief objections on the badness of his character. He is represented as a monster, as an unholy ruffian who delights only in mischief. We admit that he is a bad man: we fear, however, that there are few princes in India who are much better,—few, who, with his provocation, have not committed equal atrocities. And let it not be forgotten by those who justly execrate his worst act, that the victims of his barbarity were also the victims of their own. They had not merely rebelled against his authority, but had cut in pieces his police officers and thrown their fragments to the dogs. We go as far as any of our readers in execrating Golab Singh's conduct even on such provocation: we but ask that it *be* remembered.

From this chief let us turn not only to almost any leading member of the Lahore durbar, but to any independent chief at present alive in India, or to any that have passed away during the last hundred years; and then let us decide if Golab Singh is a worse man than they were. Is he worse than his rival Sheikh Imam-úd-dín, who with no personal animosity, but simply out of zeal for the powers of the day, cut up, and removed in pots, the late Treasurer of Lahore and his brother? Is he more vile than Rajah Lal Singh, another rival, who was one of the chief parties to the murder of Hirah Singh, of Kashmera Singh, and of many others? Compare him with the Rajah or ex-rajah of Nepal and the present minister of that country, with their hands dyed deep with blood! If we go back to the Nawabs of Oude and to the Nizams of Hyderabad, to Tippoo or his father Hyder Ali, or to the deeds of our protégé, Amír Khan, is there a man among them all at whose hands not only blood, but innocent blood, could not be required, or who, taking him all in all, is morally preferable to Golab Singh? It is not so much what he *formerly* was, as what he has been *during the last eighteen months*, that ought, in fairness, to be considered. Has his new career been cruel and tyrannical, or otherwise? He certainly has not gained the ear of the press, and especially of the Lahore scribes. Watched as he is, by a hundred Argus-eyed enemies, what single atrocity has been brought home to him? The general tenor of the reports of the score of English travellers who have visited his country during the years 1846 and 1847, is, that though grasping and mercenary, he is mild, conciliatory, and even merciful; that he indulges in no sort of sensuality, and that he has permitted himself to be guided by the advice of the British political officers employed with him.

Golab Singh, then, is morally no whit inferior to other Native princes, and in intellect vastly the superior of all. We may, therefore, conclude that if a Sovereign was to be set up, it would not have been possible to have found a better; certainly not among the princes and ex-rajahs of the Hills, than whom a more dissolute and despicable race it would be difficult to lay hands on. Besides the re-enthroning them would have been returning to the system which took us to Affghanistan, and it must be always borne in mind that we gave, or rather confirmed, to Golab Singh *little that he did not either possess at the time, or over which he had not some authority*. The Blue Book proves that even Sheikh Imam-úd-dín and his father had been creatures of Golab Singh, and had held Cashmere by his influence. The Rajah's power and means, it is true, were overrated, but that again was not the fault of Lord Hardinge; who could but judge from the information before him. It was not then sufficiently understood how much Rajah Dhyan Singh's death, the exactions of the Sikhs during the past two years, and perhaps his own penuriousness, had weakened his military power. Had terms been refused to Golab Singh, and he had proved an Abdul Kadir, where would have been the end of the vituperations levelled against Lord Hardinge? Insurrection, however incurred, would have excited instant attention, while measures which ensure tranquillity are received with silence or treated with indifference and contempt.

One very inconsistent portion of the clamour against Lord Hardinge has been, that he has given up a Native population to a ruler alien to their own faith. The charge is an unreasonable one. As a tolerant Rajpút, Golab Singh must be more acceptable to his subjects than can be intolerant Sikhs. A large proportion of them are Rajpúts; there are few or no Sikhs in the Hills, and even of the majority who are Mahommedans, most are of Hindoo lineage, men whose ancestors in the proselytising days of Mahommedan power were *forced* to change their religion. Such races of Mahommedans are very different from those of pure descent.* They retain many of the feelings, prejudices, habits, and even superstitions of their Hindoo forefathers, and to them a Hindu, a Rajpút, and a mountaineer could not be objectionable simply on the score of faith. One of the first acts of Golab Singh was to proclaim freedom of worship through his dominions; while even to this day in the face of Colonel Lawrence and the British officers, the Mahommedan cry to prayer has been suffered rather than sanctioned at Lahore. But those who are loudest

* At one time there was something like an accusation of treachery put forth in reference to the promotion of Golab Singh; but the fact is, that Lord Hardinge's dealings with him may with advantage be contrasted with those of all and any Indian officials towards hostile princes and their dependents from the days of Clive and Jaffier Alli down to those of Marquis Hastings and Ummír Singh Thappa, or even with the more recent cases of Haji Khan Kakur in Affghanistan, and Morad Ali, in Scinde. Golab Singh, of his own accord, held aloof and was virtually an enemy to the Sikhs during the war:—he obtained them a favourable peace, the terms of which, if there had been any honesty or patriotism among the Chiefs, they could have fulfilled in a week, and thus have deprived *him* of Cashmere. His redemption of *their* bond corrected the only mistake that was made in the whole transaction; for after all that had passed it would have been cruel to have left him to be vizier of Lahore, to avenge the plunder of Jummú—the murder of his sons and brothers.

on this question appear to forget that this is not the first or the tenth time that a chief of one creed has been placed over a people of another. They forget the transfer of Khyragurh and the Nepal Terai to Oude, of Tonk to Ameer Khan; they are oblivious or unmindful of the partition treaty of Mysore, or of the offer, so late as the year 1842, of the Affghan province of Julalabad to the Sikhs. These are some of the instances in proof that Lord Hardinge acted in this matter, in conformity with the practice of some of his ablest predecessors. We are far from presuming that the errors of one administration palliate those of another, but it will be acknowledged by all practical men that, provided honesty and good faith are preserved intact, a wider latitude must of necessity be admitted in political measures than would be admissible in domestic matters. Public men have something more to do than simply to gratify their feelings. Lord Hardinge needed not to seek for the best or the most amiable man in private or in public life; what he wanted was the best ruler,—the man who could best secure tranquillity in a hitherto troubled tract. The chief who would have the ability and the courage to manage tribes which, in the memory of man, had never been managed. The task was not an easy one. Lord Minto and other Governor-Generals gave away many petty principalities, but as in the instances of Hansi, Kurnaul, &c., they were soon surrendered as uncontrollable.* When all these points are considered, it will, we doubt not, be conceded that, in this branch of the arrangement, Lord Hardinge acted wisely and well.

If then the Punjab could not become English, what

* Few chiefs of India would have refused the sovereignty of the Hill country, but we know no individual among them, except Golab Singh, who, circumstanced as it then was, could have managed it.—H. M. L.

should have become of it? Some—not many—would have given it back to Dhulíp Singh, or rather to the Búrchas, and thus allowed them another opportunity to try their arms against us. Strange as it may seem, we have heard respectable and intelligent men advocate such a course. Others would have had a Punjab, as well as a Cis-Sutlej protectorate,—perhaps the wildest of all schemes. Surely we have by this time had enough of such a system, to forbid again voluntarily shackling ourselves with such arrangements. A native principality is always more or less a source of care, the more so, indeed, the more that it is interfered with, unless managed altogether by our officers. But when we come to a hundred petty chiefships, each with its owner possessing full internal authority, we have all the vices, the absurdities and inconveniences of the Native system of Government on a large scale, without its advantages —incapable of resisting foreign aggression or of preserving domestic peace, and at feud with their surrounding neighbours, regarding every village boundary. The paramount Power has all the odium of being the protector of such petty rulers, and therefore the aider and abettor of their misrule. It has been our fortune for the last forty years to have borne with this system on the western frontier, and it would have been insanity had we enlarged it. We should have had all the expenses of defending these chieflings from foreign powers, from internal commotion, from mutual violence, and when the day of danger and trial arrived, many would have acted as the Ludwa Rajah did during the late campaign.

In a word, Lord Hardinge had not the means for annexation, had he desired it. It was necessary to punish and weaken the invader without, if possible, destroying his political vitality. To lessen his power for mischief by dividing his territory was the only alternative; nor, in doing so, would it have been practicable to have annexed the Hill provinces, adding the upper half of it to the British dominions. A position so isolated and difficult of access could only have been held by means of a chain of strong military posts. The ruinous expense of such a measure is the most conclusive argument against it. Would those, again, who clamour against handing over the Hill territory to Golab Singh have approved of annexing the Lower Provinces to the British dominions, thus fastening the more cruel and distasteful rule of the Sikhs upon the Mountain tribes? or would those who urge the danger of the neighbourhood of the Sikhs, even now that their army is dispersed, have listened with complacency to a proposition which would have given them so advantageous a position of annoyance as the possession of the Mountain ranges which bound the plains of the Punjab? It was necessary to provide for the management of the Hill portion of the Sikh territory, and now, nearly two years after the event, we deny that, politically or morally, a better practical arrangement could have been made.

We have perhaps said enough to prove that those on the spot and best qualified to judge were not of opinion that we were at the time in a condition to seize and annex the Punjab, had the Governor-General been so disposed. It is very easy to decide what should have been done twenty months before. The Sikhs *have* come to terms, and *have* settled down, because they have been well treated *by us,* and protected from their own army and chiefs *by us;* because scarcely a single jaghir in the country has been resumed, and because the rights and even prejudices of all classes have been respected. It is, however, by no means so certain that, had the country been occupied, all jaghirs summarily resumed as has been done elsewhere in India, and held until it might be the pleasure or convenience of Government to examine into the tenures—and had our system, even in its most moderate form, but with its necessary vexations to a loose wild people, been introduced, it is by no means so certain that the Sikh population would have sat down quietly under the yoke. They have lost little that they held under Runjít Singh; they are therefore patient and submissive, if not contented and happy; but had they been reduced to the level of our revenue-paying population, there cannot be a doubt that ere now there would have been a strike for freedom.* The Sikhs perhaps care as little for their Government as do other natives of India; but, like others, they care for themselves, their jaghirs, their patrimonial wells, gardens and fields—their immunities and their honour. And in all these respects, the Sikh and Jat population had much to lose. The Sikh position must not be mistaken. They are a privileged race; a large proportion have jaghirs and rent-free lands; all hold their fields on more favourable terms than the Mussulmans around them.

A guerilla war, the Sikh horsemen plundering the plain, Golab Singh acting the part of Abdul Kader in the Hills, would have given us at least one long year's warm work. Its expense may be calculated. Then let any one conversant with such matters estimate the expense of holding any equal extent of territory in India —of the North-West Provinces, of Bombay, or Madras. Let him calculate the cost of the military and civil establishments, and then consider how much of the single crore of rupees that comes into the Punjab treasury would reach the general exchequer of British India. We fear that for some years at least the deficit would be considerable. Besides the British garrison of Lahore

* Written before the annexation of the Punjab.

costing 30 lakhs per annum, 25 Infantry regiments, 12,000 Cavalry, and 18 or 20 batteries, are now kept up, irrespective of numerous Irregulars. For a long period not a man less could we maintain; with more than the usual proportion of Europeans, with batta to the sepoys, with a hundred *et ceteras* that always start up after an arrangement has been closed.*

These are substantial reasons for the Governor-General's moderation, and many others even as cogent might be found; but he acted on higher and nobler grounds than mere expediency. He desired to punish a gross violation of treaties—he did not desire to destroy an old and long-faithful ally. No one more than the Governor-General saw the chances of a break-down in the arrangement of March, 1846; but it is as idle as it is malicious therefore to blame him for its consequences. The question rested entirely on the honesty and patriotism of the Sikh cabinet. Were they or were they not disposed to sacrifice their own selfish desires to the hope of rescuing their country from internal anarchy and foreign domination? Because one good, one able man was not to be found in a whole people, was that a just reason for condemning the Governor-General's acts? He at least did his duty, nobly, wisely, and honestly. Carefully abstaining from such interference as would weaken the executive, he authorized remonstrance of the most decided kind to the durbar in behalf of the disbanded soldiery: as decidedly he supported the constituted authorities against the assumptions of Dewan Múlraj of Mooltan; he forbore on the strong provoca-

* When it is considered that the pay of the officers of a regiment of Native Infantry of 800 men exceeds that of the Native officers and soldiers, while the Sikh rates of pay are lower than those of our ranks, some idea may be formed of the expense that would be incurred by the substitution of British battalions and batteries for the Sikh troops now employed in the Punjab.—H. M. L.

tion given at Kangra, and forgave the offence of Cashmere—punishing, in the latter case, one individual, where a very slight stretch of privilege would have authorised a disseverance of the whole treaty.

We need not here repeat our arguments, but may satisfy ourselves with congratulating Lord Hardinge and the British public on the great success of his lordship's Punjab policy. The candid reader will remember how some of the bravest of the land, how Sir Charles Napier himself, expressed alarm at the first occupation of Lahore; how the cry of Caubul was in every man's mouth; and disaster was loudly predicated. We have heard that Sir Charles Napier so fully considered there was danger in the arrangement, that he volunteered to take command of the Lahore garrison. To hold the post of honour, as brave a man was found in Sir John Littler; and near two years have now passed over with less of outrage, less of crime in the hitherto blood-stained Punjab than in our most favoured provinces. Daily the newspapers have told of improvements or of contemplated ones, of favours and kindnesses showered on chiefs, people, or soldiers, so as to give all well-disposed among them reason to approve our rule.

The idle attempt, or rather thought, of a half-crazed Brahmin, supported by a score of as wretched and worthless creatures as himself, last February, has been, for their own purposes, trumpeted into something by designing Europeans, but silence and contempt is a sufficient answer for their malice. They would desire to mar, they would rejoice to break, the peace—the calm that they hate—which they prophesied would never be.

The effects of this honest policy of Lord Hardinge have extended far beyond the limits of the Five Waters. The princes of Central Asia have looked with wonder upon such acts of moderation—upon the twice-emancipated Punjab—on the twice-surrendered Cashmere. Dost Mahommed Khan has been quieted, the chiefs beyond his limits cease to look for the coming English squadrons. The princes of India, too, have evidence that we do not seize all that is fairly within our reach. Oude, Hyderabad, and Gwalior may still hope for prolonged existence.

It would be no unpleasant theme to dilate on the Cashmere campaign, on the extraordinary fact, never before witnessed, of half a dozen foreigners taking up a lately-subdued mutinous army through as difficult a country as there is in the world, to put the chief, formerly their commander, now in their minds a rebel, in possession of the brightest gem of their land. Roman history tells no such tales—shows no such instantaneous fellowship of the vanquished with the victors.

A still pleasanter tale would be that of the voice of a suppliant people, a unanimous nation, calling on their conquerors to remain for their protection—calling, as the Britons of old, to their masters not to abandon them; to remain and protect their infant sovereign and to save them, one and all, from themselves—from their mutual animosities. The best part of the continental Press, while giving Lord Hardinge credit for his moderation, could not credit that Mr. Currie and Colonel Lawrence had not brought about this happy event—this combination, in their opinion, so fortunate for both parties.

How it *was* brought about cannot be better explained than in Lord Hardinge's own despatches; and though our essay has already exceeded the usual limits, we give nearly in full Nos. 2 and 9 of the Blue Book papers; the first of which clearly lays down the principles of the Governor-General's policy; and the second tells how his agents carried out the preliminary arrangements after the deposition of Lal Singh. Little comment is required on either. They speak for themselves; and are as honourable to the head as to the heart of the writer.

In Despatch No. 2, dated "Simla, September 10, 1846," the Governor-General commences by informing the secret committee that the political agent had reported that, in conformity with his instructions, he had repeatedly declared to the durbar that the British garrison of Lahore would, in fulfilment of the agreement of 11th March, be withdrawn during the month of December. As directed, the agent separately informed each member of the durbar of this determination, in order that there might be no misunderstanding. With the exception of Dewan Dína Nath, they unanimously declared that the Administration could not stand if the British troops were withdrawn. Six months' respite was asked, but the agent, instructed of the Governor-General's strong objections to the subsidiary system, distinctly refused. We must, however, give his lordship's own words:—

"The avowal of the Vizier and his colleagues, on the 10th of September, has not been elicited by any suggestions offered to him by the officiating agent. That officer has treated the Vizier uniformly with respect, and his declarations have not originated in any attempt to excite his fears; but they appear to be the voluntary impressions of his own judgment, as shown in former conversations shortly after the officiating agent's arrival, when he expressed the danger, to which he was daily exposed, of being assassinated.

"I have no doubt the Vizier and the durbar are convinced of the sincerity of the British Government's purpose to promote the establishment of a permanent Hindoo Government in the Punjab, and that the British Government has no desire to interfere in their internal affairs.

"The durbar has profited by our advice and mediation in settling their differences with the Dewan of Mooltan. They know that the political agent has abstaining from enforcing the article of the treaty for the payment of the arrears to the disbanded soldiery, in order that the British authorities might not appear to court popularity at the expense of the Vizier's Government; that the greatest pains have been taken, and most successfully, to maintain a strict discipline amongst our troops; that the inhabitants of their great city can, for the first time during many years, sleep in safety; that the insolence and rapine of the Khalsa soldier have been repressed; and that, upon the whole, a most favourable change has been effected in the feelings of the Sikh people, and even soldiery, towards the British authorities, since the occupation of the capital in March last.

"There can be no doubt of the great improvement of our relations with the people of the Punjab, in this short space of time, which is corroborated by the satisfaction which has followed the assessment of lands made in the Julunder and the ceded territories.

"I notice this state of popular feeling, as far as it can be correctly ascertained, not only because its existence is a satisfactory proof that the occupation has been followed by desirable results, but because this disposition, on the part of the people, to confide in our justice and lenity, will be an essential means of carrying on a Government through a British minister, if such an expedient should be adopted. At any rate you will be enabled to form a correct judgment of the present state of our relations with the Punjab.

"In my despatch of the 3rd instant, I stated my impression that no permanent advantage to the Maharajah's interests, or to our own, would be derived by the continued presence, under existing circumstances, of our troops at Lahore. That opinion remains unaltered.

"*I do not think that the British Government would be justified in supporting a native Government in the Punjab, merely because it may conduce to the safety of a regent, and a minister obnoxious to the chiefs and people, and to whom the British Government owes no obligations. These are the very individuals who, for personal interests of their own, excited the Sikh soldiery to invade the British frontier; and considerations of humanity to individuals would be no plea for employing British bayonets in perpetuating the misrule of a native State, by enabling such a Government to oppress the people.*

"*Our interference, if it should ever be called in, must be founded on the broad principle of preserving the people from anarchy and ruin, and our own frontier from the inconvenience and insecurity of such a state of things as that which, it is assumed, will follow when the British troops retire.**

"To continue to hold Lahore, without reforming the evils so clearly existing under the Vizier's Government, would not only, if that Government is to remain as it is now constituted, be an infraction of the agreement entered into on the 11th of March, but would, in all probability, be an unsuccessful attempt. If the various classes who now justly complain of the misrule of the Regent and the Vizier find that a British force, in opposition to the terms of the treaty, continues to occupy Lahore in support of a bad Government, the confidence which we have inspired up to the present time will be changed into mistrust of our intentions; the Sikh troops remaining unpaid would refuse to serve at the distant stations; and, with a British garrison at Lahore, the whole of the country beyond the Ravee would not fail to be a scene of disorder and bloodshed. I, therefore, adhere to the opinions expressed in my last despatch, that the British garrison ought not to remain beyond the stipulated period, if a Native Government continues to administer the affairs of the Punjab.

"I have, since my arrival in India, constantly felt and expressed my aversion to what is termed the subsidiary system, and, although it was probably most useful and politic in the earlier period of British conquest in India, I have no doubt of its impolicy at the present time, but more especially on this, the most vulnerable, frontier of our empire.

"The period of the occupation of Lahore was expressly limited to the end of this year, for the purposes specified in the agreement of the 11th of March, namely, that the Sikh army having been disbanded by the VIth article of the treaty, a British force should be left to protect the person of the Maharajah and the inhabitants of the city, during the re-organization of the Sikh army. By the XVth article of the treaty it was stipulated that

* The Italics are the Essayist's.

the British Government would not exercise any interference in the internal affairs of the Lahore State.

"At that time, the entreaties of the Regent for our assistance appeared to me not only reasonable, but as imposing upon me a moral duty, exacting, as I was as that very time, from the Lahore Government, the disbandment of their mutinous army. It is true this assistance, and the whole measure of occupation, was no part of the original policy in framing the treaty, for you are aware that the application for our troops was made after the treaty had been signed. But it was evident I had no alternative, if I felt confident, as I then did, that the British garrison would be able to effect its declared objects without compromising the safety of the troops. I, therefore, did not hesitate to afford the aid solicited, although I did so with reluctance.

"On every occasion, the Lahore Government has been assured that the British Government deprecates interference in their affairs: they have been informed that our troops were ready to retire at any moment, if the re-organization of the Sikh army, and the improved state of the country, would admit of their being withdrawn.

"It may be further observed, that the occupation of Lahore could not be considered in the light of a subsidiary arrangement, because the instructions given to the General officer and to the Political Agent were, that the garrison was placed there to preserve the peace of the town, but was not to be employed in any expedition, even between the Ravee and the Sutlej.

"The force was expressly given as a loan of troops for a peculiar emergency, and to aid the Lahore Government in carrying out an essential article of the treaty, which required the disbandment of their army. No payment was demanded, except for certain extra allowances granted to the native troops, whilst serving beyond the Sutlej.

"*If therefore, the proposals of the Regent and the durbar are merely confined to a further loan of British troops for six months, on the plea that a Hindoo Government cannot be carried on unless supported by British bayonets, I am of opinion that the application must be refused.*

"There has been ample time for the re-organization of the Sikh army, and by proper management the durbar could have fulfilled the limited objects for which the British force was left at Lahore. The means of effecting these objects have been invariably neglected, in opposition to the friendly admonitions of the British Government. I have not failed to exhort the Vizier to pay the troops with regularity, as the only mode by which the Government and the army can be on good terms, and without which no efficient service, or correct discipline, can be expected. Two regiments have been recently driven into mutiny for want of pay—such a course being their only means of obtaining their just dues,—whilst estates of large value have been given to the brother of the Maharanee, at well as to the relations of the Vizier. It is surprising that, after the experience of the last five years, of a mutinous army controlling its own Government at Lahore, the durbar cannot understand, or will not practise, so simple a system to ensure obedience.

"It is not necessary that I should recapitulate the acts of impolicy and injustice which have marked the conduct of the durbar during the last five months. Having a right to interfere, by the terms of the treaty, in matters relating to the payment of the disbanded soldiery, I have frequently urged the durbar to do their duty; and this advice, given with moderation, had led the Sikh Government to make the confession of its own weakness, and to implore the Governor-General to prolong the period of occupation.

"It is impossible to place any confidence in the professions of the Maharanee or the Vizier, that the advice of a British agent would be followed, if the garrison were to be permitted to remain: the British Government would, in such case, be a party to the oppression of all classes of the people. Again, if the troops are withdrawn, we are warned that the country will be plunged into a state of anarchy, and the destruction of all government will ensue. Neither of these results would be consistent with the humanity, or the sincerity, of our policy, and they would be equally opposed to our best interests.

"The other course—which it may be open to the British Government to take, and which has constantly occupied my attention since the 3rd of September—would be, to carry on the government at Lahore in the name of the Maharajah during his minority (a period of about eight years), or for a more limited time, placing a British minister at the head of the Government, assisted by a Native Council, composed of the ablest and most influential chiefs.

"This course, however, could not be adopted, even if the offer to surrender the Regency were to be made by the Maharanee, unless Her Highness' solicitations were cordially and publicly assented to by the great majority of the chiefs.

"If, therefore, the chiefs should not join the Regent and the durbar in calling upon the British Government to act as the guardian of the young prince during his minority, and to conduct the Administration, no attempt would be made to carry such a measure into execution. I should, in that case, scrupulously adhere to the terms of the agreement. Those terms could not be suspended, even temporarily, without some such public act as that of assembling all the chiefs who have an interest in the State, through the lands they hold from the Maharajah; and in any such proceeding, the proposal must originate with the Lahore, and not with the British authorities.

"The marked difference between the system of having a British minister residing at Lahore, and conducting the government through native agency, and that which now prevails of a Native Government administering the affairs of the State, without any interference, foreign or domestic, excepting from the Regent, would amount to this—that, in the one case, our troops are made the instrument for supporting misrule, and giving countenance and strength to oppression; in the other, by British interposition, justice and moderation are secured by an Administration conducted by native executive agency, in accordance with the customs and feelings, and even prejudices, of the people. An efficient Administration, working satisfactorily, being fairly established, the British interposition might be withdrawn; or, if necessary, it might continue till the coming of age of the Maharajah, when, as may be hoped, his country would be made over to him in a much-improved and prosperous condition.

"The principal means of ensuring a successful government would consist in the strict administration of justice between the Government and the people, in the regular payment of the troops, and the guarantee to the chiefs, of the unmolested enjoyment of their estates, which should only be liable to forfeiture on a strong case of misconduct clearly proved.

"The native officers of the army would remain, as at present, generals and colonels at the head of their troops; and innovations, unless required for important purposes of government, would not be introduced.

"Such a system of British rule might not answer as a permanent one, but it might be adopted, if the durbar and chiefs are convinced that the Government, without such an alternative, would fall to pieces on the retirement of the British garrison.

"If, therefore, the proposal of the Regent and durbar should lead to an offer to carry on the Lahore government by a British Minister, during the minority of the Maharajah, and the proposal should be confirmed by the influental chiefs, publicly convoked for the deliberation of such a measure, I should be disposed to give to the experiment a favourable consideration.

* * * * * *

"If no such proposal leading to modifications of the treaty should be made, it is my intention to withdraw the British force from Lahore the latter end of December, in accordance with the agreement. I shall, in this case, have afforded the Lahore durbar every facility in my power to avert the misfortune which the Vizier and his colleagues anticipate on the retirement of the troops; and you may be assured that, in the transactions now pending, the conduct of the British Government shall be strictly regulated by principles of justice and good faith.

"With regard to the apprehended failure of the Vizier to establish a Sikh Government, I am satisfied it will not have been caused by any difficulties which might not have been obviated by a firmer minister. At the same time, it must be admitted, that he has been placed in a position of great difficulty, which might have baffled the skill of an abler and better man. It is due, however, to the Rajah, and must be admitted, that he has on all occasions cheerfully assented to every proposal for the comfort and accommodation of the British troops.

"If the hope, which I have expressed since last March, that a permanent Sikh Government might be formed, should be disappointed, the result will not prove that the measure could have been dispensed with at the time it was adopted.

"The force was left expressly for the purpose of protecting the inhabitants of a large city from spoliation by a disbanded army. The occupation has fulfilled that object, and has given to the Sikh Government the time to re-organize their army; it has given to the Lahore Government the opportunity of performing its duty to the State: and if, from causes beyond the control of the Governor-General, the attempt to establish a Sikh Government should fail, that result can in no respect reflect unfavourably on the policy of the attempt. It has not impaired the British character; on the contrary, it has caused it to be respected, not only by force of arms, but by the removal of national prejudices. At the time I consented to the occupation, the question then raised by the opponents of the measure was, not whether a Sikh Government would succeed or fail, but whether the British garrison could maintain its position in Lahore?

"The risk of occupying the capital, in my judgment, was not commensurate with the moral obligations imposed upon me, and the political advantages which have followed that act; and, at this moment, it will not be forgotten by reflecting men, that a great military object has been obtained, of giving to this admirable Indian army a salutary lesson, that, under the firm management of an able commander, there are no difficulties in occupying a large town, the capital of a foreign nation, which cannot by good discipline be overcome.

"I, therefore, never can regret a measure which, up to this hour, has secured the capital of a neighbouring State from ruin, and has maintained unimpaired the reputation of the British power throughout our Eastern Empire."

The above masterly document tells how honestly the Governor-General endeavoured to prop up the State that had been struck down by the hands of its own children: it does more—it emphatically lays down the somewhat novel, though happily-growing, doctrine that British protection ,when accorded, is not merely a shield for the native sovereign and his myrmidons, but that it covers the people also—that the country of an ally may be defended, but may not be harried, by British bayonets.

The other despatch with which we enrich our pages states that the culprit Vizier of Lahore was tried in open court in the presence of sixty-five of his Peers; *not by them, because they were his enemies;* but by five British officers, every individual of whom was more or less his friend and well-wisher. It then tells of the terms on which Lord Hardinge consented to carry on the Administration of Lahore for eight years. Even Lal Singh, though anxious for a Resident and a Contingent on the old system, preferred this scheme to being left to the mercies of the Sikhs and the fate of his predecessors. But without further preface we offer the extract nearly in full as published in the Blue Book:—

No. 9.

" *The Governor-General to the Secret Committee.*

" *Camp, Bhyrowal Ghat,*
(Extract.) "*December* 21, 1846. (No. 59.)

"In my last despatch, of the 5th instant, I informed you of the arrangements which had been made at Lahore, for conducting the inquiry into the allegations of Sheik Imamoddeen, relative to his proceedings in Cashmere.

"The collection of papers which accompanies this despatch will bring before you all the circumstances that have since occurred, and will show, that the course contemplated by me, in my communication to you of the 19th of September, in the event of the Lahore Government desiring the continuance of the British troops, has been acted upon.

"I have to request your attention to Mr. Currie's letter of the 5th of December, forwarding the minutes of evidence and abstract of the proceedings taken in the investigation of the Cashmere insurrection.

"*You will observe that the inquiry was conducted in the most open and public manner. All the leading chiefs of the most influential families, sixty-five in number, attended to witness the proceedings.*"

* * * * *

The Governor-General then enters into some details of the trial of Rajah Lal Singh; acknowledges the services of Mr. Currie and his colleagues, and thus proceeds :—

"In the subsequent transactions to which I am now about to draw your attention, and which refer to the terms on which alone I could consent to the continued occupation of Lahore by a British garrison, you will find that all the anticipations of my confidence in this valuable officer's ability have been realized.

"In the same letter (of the 7th of December) in which I confirmed Mr. Currie's proceedings, I instructed him to address the Maharajah, expressing the deep interest I took in His Highness's welfare, and stating that, as the time had nearly arrived when the British troops would, in observance of the agreement of the 11th of March, withdraw from Lahore, I was anxious, after the Vizier's deposition, that the Government should be so reconstructed as to afford the best prospect of preserving the Raj; that I was anxious the British Government should remain on terms of peace and amity with the Government of Lahore; but that I was determined, after the experience of the last nine months, and the recent misconduct of the Vizier, not to leave a British force in the city, beyond the stipulated period, for the sake of supporting a Native Government which can give no assurance of its power to govern justly, as regards its people, and no guarantee for the performance of its obligations to its neighbours.

"I stated, that it was the duty of His Highness's Government and the Chiefs, to decide upon the course which they might deem to be most expedient; but that in these arrangements I could exercise no interference, further than in giving to His Highness's Government the aid of my advice and good offices in promoting the interests of the State.

"These sentiments were conveyed to His Highness in Mr. Currie's letter of the 9th of December, and the answer is contained in a recapitulation of each paragraph by the durbar, concluding with the request that I would leave two regiments of infantry, one regiment of cavalry, and a field-battery, at Lahore, with Lieutenant-Colonel Lawrence as the Resident, for some months longer.

"Mr. Currie, in his reply to this letter of the Maharajah's, informed His Highness, that the application for the continuance of a British force at Lahore involved a departure from the conditions of the articles of agreement concluded on the 11th of March, and stated that it would, therefore, be advisable that the members of the durbar and the principal sirdars should assemble, in order that Mr. Currie might declare, in their presence, the only terms on which the Governor-General would consent to a modification of the arrangements, and to the continuance of a British force at Lahore, after the expiration of the stipulated period.

"The paper containing these conditions was carefully translated into Persian and Hindoostanee, and delivered by Mr. Currie to the chiefs, when they met on the 15th of December. For the purpose of avoiding all misunderstanding, the different articles were explained—the sirdars retired for consultation, and, after some discussion relating to the amount of the contribution for the expense of the British garrison, the terms were agreed to.

"In order to afford full time for further deliberation, it was resolved that the sirdars and chiefs should reassemble on the following day, when certain individuals should be selected by themselves to draw up articles of agreement, in conjunction with Mr. Currie and Lieutenant-Colonel Lawrence. The chiefs accordingly reassembled at Mr. Currie's durbar tent, at 3 o'clock of the 16th instant. Each article was discussed separately: the contribution was fixed at twenty-two lakhs; and every sirdar present signed and sealed the paper. All the chiefs, in number fifty-two, on the conclusion of the meeting expressed their satisfaction that the Maharajah would be under the protection of the British Government during his minority, which will continue until the 4th of September, 1854.

"At these meetings the chiefs unanimously concurred that a State necessity existed for excluding the Maharanee from exercising any authority in the administration of affairs, and the durbar and the chiefs have come to the decision that Her Highness shall receive an annuity of one lakh and a half.

"You will observe, that a British officer appointed by the Governor-General in Council, with an efficient establishment of subordinates, will remain at Lahore, to direct and control every department of the State.

"The feelings of the people, and the just rights of all classes, will be respected.

"*A Council of Regency, composed of leading chiefs, will act under the control and guidance of the British Resident.*

"*The Council will consist of eight sirdars, and the members will not be changed without the consent of the British Resident, acting under the orders of the Governor-General.*

"*The power of the Resident extends over every department, and to any extent.*

"*A military force may be placed in such forts and posts, and of such strength, within the Lahore territories, as the Governor-General may determine.*

"*These terms give the British Resident unlimited authority in all matters of internal administration, and external relations, during the Maharajah's minority.*

"*The concession of these powers will enable the British Government to secure the peace and good order of the country—the authority will be exercised for the most beneficial purposes: these terms are more extensive than have been heretofore required, when Native States have received the protection of a British contingent force. My motive in requiring such large powers has arisen from the experience of its necessity during the last nine months; and my reluctance on general principles to revert to the subsidiary system of using British troops to support a Native Government, while we have no means of correcting the abuses of the civil administration of a country ostensibly under British protection. A British force, acting as the instrument of a corrupt Native agency, is a system leading to mischievous consequences, and which ought, when it is possible, to be avoided.*

"The occupation of Lahore will afford the means of counteracting much of the disorder and anarchy which have disturbed the Punjab for the last five years, chiefly owing to a numerous Sikh army, kept up in the vicinity of the capital, in numbers greatly disproportioned to the revenues of the country, and by whose republican system of discipline, the soldiery had usurped all the functions of the State.

"The control which a British garrison can exercise in enforcing order amongst the disbanded soldiery, will, in conjunction with a British system of administration, protect all classes of the community. The immediate effect of depriving a numerous body of military adventurers of employment (there being still many to be disbanded to reduce the numbers to the limits of the Treaty of Lahore), may be troublesome, and a source of some uneasiness.* No policy can at once get rid of an evil which has been the growth of years. But the operation of a system of order introduced into the Punjab, will subdue the habits of this class, as has been the case in our own provinces since the Pindarree war, and, by gradually mitigating the turbulent spirit of the Sikh population, encourage the people to cultivate the arts of industry and peace.

"A strict adherence to the letter of the treaty, by the withdrawal of the British garrison at this moment from the Punjab, after the avowals made by the durbar, that the Government could not stand, would probably have led to measures of aggrandizement, and the extension of our territory, after scenes of confusion and anarchy. This danger was felt by the most able of the sirdars, and it reconciled them to the sacrifices which the terms inevitably required for the interest of the Lahore State. By the course which has been adopted, the modification of the terms of the agreement of last March, has been made with the free consent of the sirdars, publicly assembled, who were made fully aware of the extent of the power which, by the new articles, was to be transferred to the British Government.

"The confidence which the Sikh chiefs have reposed in British good faith must tend, by the unanimity of their decision, which partakes, as far as it is possible in an eastern country, of a national sanction, to promote the success of this measure.

"I have deemed it expedient, that the ratification of the new terms of agreement entered into for protecting the Maharajah during his minority should be made as public as possible. It has, therefore, been determined, in communication with the sirdars, that His Highness shall come to my camp on this side of the Beas on the 26th instant; and I propose afterwards, when the agreement will be formally ratified, to pay His Highness a friendly return visit at Lahore."

---

* In some quarters we understand that Lord Hardinge is reproached with allowing the arrears of a thousand or two of Sikh sowars to remain unpaid. The following facts therefore will be instructive:—The Sikh army has during the last twelve months been reduced not less than 20,000 men; and the finances thereby relieved by 30 lakhs. Not only have *all* these men been paid their arrears, but the army still kept up, which was found in arrears of from nine to sixteen months, is now paid nearly as regularly as our own. The infantry are two months in arrears, and the majority of the cavalry only five; and their not being paid up as well as the infantry is for the excellent reason that there is no money. When these facts have been digested, we would beg attention to the contrast afforded by the following. The Gwalior cavalry, remodelled and taken under our protection in January, 1844, was still owed in June, 1847 (3½ years after the treaty) the monstrous sum of 25 lakhs of rupees. If 10 lakhs of the marriage gift of the Bazee Bhaie have been appropriated to the payment of those arrears, as was suggested, we understand, by the local agents, there will still remain, four years after the treaty, a larger arrear to the Gwalior cavalry, than is owed to the whole Sikh army nine months after the treaty that transferred it with the rest of the Lahore State to British care. We attribute no sort of blame in this matter to Col. Sleeman, or Sir R. Shakspeare. The treaty of Gwalior did not give them the authority to act; that of Lahore *did* give Col. Lawrence. We only add one more example to the many on record of the evils of the *old* subsidiary system, and the advantages of the new.—H. M. L.

Compliments to Mr. Currie and Colonel Lawrence here follow, and the despatch thus concludes:—

"In every part of India the most perfect tranquillity prevails.

"No efforts on my part will be omitted to preserve this desirable state of things. My views and measures have been uniformly directed to maintain a system of peace, by consolidating the British power in India, and not by objects of aggrandizement, and I trust that the arrangements now about to be ratified will tend to this effect, and that the course which I have adopted will be found by you to be consistent with true policy, and conducive to the interests of British India."

The treaty of March, 1846, was no sooner signed than arrangements were made for the management of the valuable acquisitions obtained. Mr. John Lawrence, one of the most experienced officers in the civil service, was sent for from Delhi, in which neighbourhood he had served for many years with great credit. To his care, as Commissioner, was entrusted the Jullunder, with half a dozen assistants, while Major Mackeson, with a similar staff, superintended the Cis-Sutlej States, both acting under the agent of the Governor-General. The arrangement answered so well, that within the year almost all the complicated questions caused by the war were decided, and the Sikh chiefs put on a new and improved footing. Major Broadfoot had truly observed that these chiefs had long ceased to be the *protected*, and might latterly rather be called the *restrained*. They had ceased to *fear* the Punjab ruler: they now only feared our preventions from plunder. The police powers of many of these were withdrawn: the customs of all commuted or abolished. The disorderly and untrustworthy contingents on both sides the river were commuted for a money payment sufficient to pay several good regiments; the jaghirs of all examined, and possession allowed until so done; and, above all, a very light summary assessment was completed, within three months, in the Jullunder, and, during the year, elsewhere. The Governor-General's only instructions to the

Commissioners being to be moderate in their demands, and not to distress the people. Thus has order been brought out of anarchy, and a most fruitful and lovely district, already yielding fifty lakhs, been added to British India.

Simultaneously with these arrangements, retrenchments in a small way were commenced, but it was not until the treaty of December, 1846, was signed, that the Governor-General felt justified in reducing the military force. Now, however, that affairs were put on a more promising footing, the strength of every infantry corps in the service was reduced, as also of all the irregulars; the police battalions were one by one disbanded; and, without any apparent effort, more than 30,000 men were reduced from the Bengal army alone. There is no denying that while this bold measure saved much to the State, it curtailed establishments with less injury to public credit than ever was before accomplished.

There is one feature of this question which the future historian will dwell on with special satisfaction. Scarcely was the Punjab war over, when the party in the British Senate with which the Governor-General had always acted were ejected from power. They had honoured and rewarded him, and he might now have retired, or, when remaining at the request of his political adversaries—who seem to have treated him with as much consideration as if one of themselves—he might not unreasonably be expected to forward no financial arrangements that would affect his popularity during the brief remainder of his stay in India. An ordinary man would certainly thus have acted; but far otherwise was Lord Hardinge's practice. In the face of the clamour of a portion of the Press he as honestly and unflinchingly used the shears as Lord William Bentinck could have done—as effectively as if he himself were to have been the gainer. He had submitted his resignation to the home authorities. He had expressed his desire to be relieved in the winter of 1847; so that, without any apparent dereliction of duty, he might have left every invidious measure to be carried out—every reduction to be enforced by his successor.

We shall enter somewhat fully—we trust not tediously—into these reductions, premising that, since the year 1837, the Indian army had been increased by no less, in round numbers, than 120,000 men. More than half of these levies were discharged, and yet all vulnerable points were left as well guarded as they ever were; and the North-west frontier was placed on a footing of strength sufficient to satisfy the most clamorous alarmist.

With the exception of the cavalry, every branch of the Indian army had been increased since 1837; the officers by no less than 834; in the proportion of 656 to the infantry, 146 to the artillery, and 32 to the engineers. Above 50,000 men were reduced after the war, leaving the army still stronger by more than that number than it was in 1837. None of the officers, Native or European, were touched. Certain local corps were disbanded; while other "irregulars," more urgently required, were subsequenty raised. Among these are the Scinde and Sikh levies. The chief reduction was caused by bringing down the strength of corps from 1100 to 800 men.* This was effected by giving a bonus of from three to twelve months' pay to every man willing to take his discharge; and by permitting men to invalid in 1847 who, in the usual course, would not have been passed till 1848. No soldier, however, of the regulars was discharged against his will; and none of the irregular horse who had served seven years;

* They were permitted gradually to fall to 750.

while every individual of the latter, however short his service, discharged on the reduction, received a gratuity of twelve months' pay, being no less than £24 for a private horseman—a noble sum, a fortune to many.

Eight regiments of cavalry were raised during the war; and all of them for very good reasons were irregulars. First because a corps can be formed in a month or two, and costs only £19,000 per annum; while one of regulars costs £39,000; secondly, because they are more easily moved and provided for; requiring (including officers) only thirty-seven doolie bearers and twenty-two camels, while a corps of regular cavalry requires sixty and 200 respectively; lastly and above all, because, during the Sikh campaign, after every exertion, we never had 4500 sabres in the field opposed to not less than 30,000. We were deficient in *numbers*, not material. When Punjab affairs were settled, the strength of corps of irregular horse was reduced to 500, and it was subsequently designed to bring them down to 420, the strength of the regular cavalry; but, as in the infantry, the full number of corps as also their constitution was kept up, so as to enable officers on the shortest notice to fill up their ranks. The gratuity of a twelvemonths pay to the discharged men was a humane measure, because many had incurred debt to enable them to enter the service, and it then became clearly a man's own fault if he was unable to make a fresh start in life with a trifle in his pocket: it was a politic act, because it induced volunteers, when required, to crowd to our ranks.

Thus the reduction in the Native army was effected, with the least possible detriment to efficiency. The cavalry, the arm in which we were most deficient, was increased by eight regiments; and the number of sabres, even after reductions, by some hundreds. For the police battalions the more efficient Scinde and Sikh levies were substituted. The police corps did not give satisfaction. No man who has much worked with natives could have expected otherwise. The theory of a military police is excellent; but as a general rule natives of India will not take to a double trade. They will not both fight and write; they will not do menial work and head work. There are of course exceptions to this as to every other rule; but with some personal experience in these matters, we are decidedly of opinion, that the native of India who has been in the habit of doing one work well, will fail in a double duty. There are a dozen reasons for what we aver. Listlessness, cowardice, vanity, and the prejudices of the caste to which they belong, all interfere with such combination of duties. He who reckons on orientals by European rules will assuredly reap repentance. The Sikh and Scinde levies are more decidedly military bodies than the police battalions, and bring into our ranks men who have fought against us; and might, if not employed, do so again. This, indeed, is another reason for encouraging irregular cavalry, as it is chiefly formed of the most military portion of the Mahommedan population.

Though several European regiments were sent home after the war, it is quite a mistake to suppose that the European force in India was then decreased below the usual average. On the contrary, it very far exceeded what was considered sufficient to defend India during any period of the China, Gwalior, Scinde, and Affghanistan campaigns,—the fact being that though between the years 1837 and 1842, the force in Bengal was increased by no less than one dragoon and seven infantry regiments, an equal number were generally absent beyond the limits of India. During the years 1843–44, and '45, this branch of the army counted three regiments of dragoons and fourteen of infantry, being one of the former, and five of the latter, in excess of the establishment of 1837. In the year 1838, while the whole European force in the Bengal presidency was only two regiments of cavalry and nine of infantry, one of the first and two of the last were in Affghanistan; and in 1840, when the infantry establishment was increased to twelve regiments, not less than six were absent, viz. three in China, and three in Affghanistan. In the year 1846 the infantry regiments were again increased to sixteen by orders from home, but before the reinforcements could arrive peace was declared.*

It was, we understand, intended after the war to keep three regiments of dragoons and eleven of infantry on the Bengal establishment, being *one* of cavalry, and *two* of infantry in excess of the establishment of 1837, before Gwalior or the Punjab was subdued!

At Madras, in the year 1841, there were eight European regiments, but of these three were absent; viz. one in China, one at Aden, and one at Moulmein; leaving five. The establishment was reduced to eight!

At Bombay, the European force was

In 1837 ...... $4\frac{1}{2}$ regiments (a wing being at Aden).
" 1838 ...... $2\frac{1}{2}$ "
" 1839 ...... 3 "
" 1840 ...... 4 "
" 1841 ...... 4 "

One regiment went home, leaving seven; but a wing

* This was a very natural and proper caution on the part of the home authorities, but it was unadvisedly made a handle for the report that Lord Hardinge wrote to England, after Ferozeshah, for 12,000 troops. The fact, however, is, he did not write for a man. Lord Hardinge was not the person to wait till the middle of a war before he indented on England for all he considered necessary. No: his reinforcements were much nearer; Sir Charles Napier was in Scinde with 23,000 men. When the war ended in February, 1846, Napier was at hand with 16,000 men and fifty guns; while supports from England could hardly have reached before the spring of 1847, unless by Egypt, and there in April and May the soldiers would have suffered from heat.—H. M. L.

being at Aden, and two regiments in Scinde, the same number as in 1837 remained for the duties of the presidency.

Thus we have shown that the European force actually within the limits of India was left considerably stronger than at any former period—though for the first time since our sovereignty commenced there was no organized army (Nepal excepted, which has no cavalry) in India but our own. To make the matter still plainer to unprofessional readers, we may remark that, during profound peace, the European force in India, though 5000 men less than the war establishment of 1846, was 10,000 in excess of that of the year 1835, and 9000 stronger than that of 1837, when the hostile army of Gwalior was on our flank, the Sikhs in our front, and the expedition to Affghanistan was already on the tapis!

The increase to the army since 1837, in Bengal alone, exceeded 50,000 men; the reductions, including Queen's regiments sent home, exceeded 30,000 men, at a saving of £700,000. In Bombay, including a European regiment, 7000 men, at a saving of £300,000, and in Madras 10,000, at a saving of £160,000.

Thus the total reductions made by Lord Hardinge were £1,160,000, while with the Lahore subsidy of £220,000, and the Jullunder and Cis-Sutlej proceeds (after deducting expenses) of £500,000 more, we have a total improvement of the revenue during the year 1847 of £1,880,000 sterling;—so that, with reductions at Bombay and Madras, the relief to the finances of India could not have fallen short of two millions of money; giving, for the first time since 1838, a prospect of escape from bankruptcy.

The advocates of annexation, those who think the Indus or the Solemane range should be our border, may with advantage reflect on the above facts. Annexation that tends to insolvency can never be beneficial. Hitherto our debt has increased with our frontier; and we are satisfied that the Punjab would be no exception to the rule. Its revenues are *not* four millions, as influential journals in England consider; they are scarcely one-third of that sum; and of it nearly half is expended in jaghirs and the British subsidy. Could we with our present establishments safely hold the four Western Doabs, or the other half? We think not; and had we tried to do it, where would have been the reductions above displayed? Would those who feared to occupy Lahore, with 10,000 men, *at the earnest prayer* of the Sikh nation, have had no misgivings, when again in front of the formidable Khybur—when again confronted with the Murrís, the Bogtís, and the Vizerís, while the irritated Sikh population was in their rear? Each river of the Punjab would have been as dangerous, or at least as dreaded, as a Khúrd Cabul or a Khybur, and we must literally have kept up an army in each Doab, or India and Europe would have rung with forebodings of disaster—instead of a reduction of the army, then, there must have been an increase, and especially in the most expensive branches; the Europeans;—the artillery and the cavalry. Above all, instead of sending home Queen's regiments, we must have indented for six or eight more, and for years at least the country would have been a loss to us. The balance-sheet is the best answer against annexation!

In proof that the reductions we have noticed did not unduly affect our military strength, we proceed briefly to contrast our posture, in the most vulnerable quarters, before and after the war.

A European regiment was withdrawn from Moulmein—wisely, we think. The force there was not strong enough to make, though it might tempt, war. Our steamers enabled us to reinforce the Tenasserim coast, and to destroy Rangoon, at a few hours' notice.

The small fortified posts of Petoragurh and Lohú Ghat on the western Nepal frontier, inviting attack, were dismantled, and their garrisons withdrawn. The regiment of native infantry was recalled from Almorah, where it should never have been stationed, and the fort at that station was strengthened, and made tenable against all comers until it could be relieved.

An irregular cavalry corps was stationed at Gorukpúr, in communication with that at Segowlie; the best possible arm to employ in watching the Gúrkhas. By Lord Ellenborough's arrangements, Gwalior had become an armed friend, occupied by a British force more than double that which won "Meaní."

There remains only the North-Western frontier. We have already shown, but may repeat, that in July, 1844, when the Sikh army was in force at Lahore, the British troops at and above Meerut, amounted to 24,000 men and 66 guns, but were increased by Lord Hardinge by 1st of December, 1845, to 45,000 men and 98 guns. After the war, though there were not 3000 Sikh soldiers in the whole country around Lahore and Umritsur, and those under our orders, Lord Hardinge had 54,000 *men and* 120 *field guns as well as a battering train of equal strength at and above Meerut!* *

A comparison of these numbers should satisfy the most apprehensive mind, that, in making his well-considered reductions, Lord Hardinge never hazarded the safety of the empire. Not only during the whole of the year 1846 were moveable brigades, complete in carriage and equipment, kept up at Lahore, Ferozepore,

* We are indebted for much of the information contained in this portion of our article to some instructive, and apparently authoritative, letters signed Zeta and Omega, which appeared in the *Bombay Times*.—H. M. L.

and Jullunder, but in the midst of profound peace they were retained. Each consists of one European regiment and three of Native infantry, one of cavalry, and twelve guns. The former had also two companies of sappers and a second regiment of cavalry. These brigades were under two distinguished brigadiers, Campbell and Wheeler, both aides-de-camp to the Queen, and the whole commanded by Sir John Littler. These three brigades could be reinforced in ten days by four regiments of British infantry; while there were three of cavalry, with seventy guns and 20,000 Native infantry, in reserve.

Lord Hardinge's Ordnance arrangements ought alone to satisfy men's minds that, in all that concerned military matters, he was thoroughly at home. Not a man or a gun from the war establishment was reduced; 60 nine-pounder guns before drawn by bullocks were soon horsed, and there were siege and field artillery on and near the frontier sufficient to meet any contingency, and it cannot be his Lordship's fault if our Horse artillery ammunition ever again runs short in action, or if our siege trains are ill-supplied.*

We have entered at such length into the origin, conduct, and results of the war with the Sikhs, the great episode of Lord Hardinge's Administration, that we have space only to glance at some of the civil measures

* The old system did not allow sufficient ammunition to the field artillery. Lord Hardinge rectified the error. We would, however, correct an impression that prevails in some quarters, that, because the Governor-General expressed himself warmly regarding the deficiency of ammunition at the beginning of the campaign, he, therefore, thought ill of the Bengal Artillery. Far otherwise. He thought them, as all who have seen their practice must do, as good artillery as any in the world. Indeed, his Lordship was often heard to expatiate on the excellences of the men and of the captains, and we believe it to have been his opinion that the *chief want* of the artillery, as of the Bengal army, in all its branches, was a senior list. We may here mention, what is little known—we are not sure that it is so to Lord Hardinge—that the chief reason for the ammunition having run out at Ferozeshah was the extraordinary number of waggons that blew up. Of eighteen that went into action under Lt. Col. Geddes, no fewer than seven exploded.—H. M. L.

to which the restoration of peace enabled him to turn his attention.

The question of the great Ganges canal had met with cool advocacy and warm opposition. Mr. Thomason's views were opposed; Major Cautley, the able projector, was in England, and the war called away his excellent successor, Captain Baker, and his assistants. Doubts were raised as to the advisability of opening a new canal, when those, on a much smaller scale, now running past Delhi and Kurnaul, had rendered these towns and cantonments unhealthy. A sanatory committee was appointed and ordered to proceed to the canals; there to investigate the amount of sickness usually caused by them, and to draw up a full report embodying their own suggestions. The committee prepared a very curious table, demonstrating most clearly that the size of the spleens of children, in the tract irrigated by the Delhi canals, increased in proportion to their vicinity to the inundation. The fact was not ascertained from examination of bed-ridden patients, but from scores of boys and girls who were running about the villages. It was, however, also ascertained that these symptoms of disease were little thought of by the people themselves, and that sufferers from intermittent fever preferred to be subject to such trials rather than to lose the fertilizing waters of the canals. It was also shown that the course of the Jumna canals being through a low line of country, difficult of drainage, caused swamps and stagnant pools, at the most unhealthy season of the year, as around Kurnaul. Much if not all of this might be remedied, and it was believed that Delhi and Kurnaul might be restored to comparative salubrity.

By a judicious system of drainage, it was expected that malaria might be prevented, and with this view it was designed that the Ganges canal should follow the highest ridge of the Doab, at a prescribed safe distance from towns and cantonments. Thus, irrigation would be prevented in the vicinity of masses of people, and it might be hoped that care and attention would mitigate the existing canal evils to the rural population. Indeed we do not see why irrigation might not be prohibited within prescribed distances of village sites; but, as already remarked, the cultivators prefer good crops with miasma and visceral disease, to dearth, hunger, and starvation. Malaria doubtless does shorten life, but it is unquestionable that for hundreds whom it has destroyed in India famine has carried off its tens of thousands. Who can estimate the misery and mortality of the famine of 1837? the loss and expense of which alone, in a single year, cost the Government a million of money—much what the Ganges canal is estimated at! Only four years previously, in 1833, that of Guntoor cost sixty lakhs and the lives of a quarter of a million of people!

Another danger was prognosticated. It was feared that to divert from the Ganges seven-eighths of the main stream would endanger its navigation. As the proposed canal is to be navigable for boats, and as the river is now scarcely so, throughout the year,* this objection seems to us unimportant.

After a rigid calculation of the advantages to be gained and the risks to be encountered, the Governor-General, in March, 1846, visited the head of the canal and its most important feature the Solani aqueduct, and then authorized the vigorous prosecution of the work. We understand that the annual expenditure of a quarter

* We have ourselves, in an English wherry, been a dozen times aground, in the month of March, between Furrukabad and Allahabad. — H. M. L.

of a million sterling has since been sanctioned from home. Six years will probably open a canal of not less than 600 miles in length, to spread its fertilizing waters over 1,200,000 acres, to secure from famine several millions of people, and to remain a lasting monument of British architecture and of British benevolence in India.*

That Mr. Stephenson and his staff made their way to Calcutta, prepared to commence the grand Northern Railway, is mainly attributable to Lord Hardinge's sound advice and practical good sense. It must ever redound to his credit that when his colleagues, men supposed to be more cognizant of India's wants, doled out such a small modicum of Government assistance as would have smothered the project for ever, the Governor-General, taking an enlarged and statesman-like view of the question, declared, "I am of opinion that the assistance to be given ought not to be limited merely to the land;" and further on, "the value of the land is not commensurate with the advantages which the State would derive from rapid and daily communications between Calcutta and Delhi;" and again, "the calculation of the contribution to be given should be based on the political, military, and commercial advantages which would be derived from the completion and full operation of such a line." His Lordship's task was a peculiarly hard one. He had, at a time of great financial pressure, in the face of the combined opinion of his civil counsellors, to advocate a large outlay. He had his reward in seeing the foundation of that noble work laid, which it was Lord Dalhousie's privilege to see fairly in operation. In his Lordship's character and previous career, there was an earnest that he would not be found wanting in works of improvement: indeed in his speech at the dinner given

* It will be borne in mind that this was written in 1847.

to him by the Court of Directors, on the 4th of November, his Lordship declared that he would do all that prudence permitted in opening out communications between different parts of the land. The guarantee of five per cent. for twenty-five years made the investment an excellent one as a private speculation, while to Government the advantages of railroads are incalculable. With the means of rapidly transporting our munitions, our batteries, and our battalions from one end of the empire to the other, we may confidently defy all danger, and the strength of British India will be more than doubled. Famine can no more stalk in one quarter, while plenty smiles in others. The trains that convey provisions for our English soldiers to the fort of the Himalayas will return with the products of those mountains, whose dyes, herbs, and minerals will now find a market.

Lord Hardinge has added another to the number of sanataria, and has, we hope, prepared the way for all Europeans, henceforward invalided for India, to be sent to the mountains. We are satisfied that it is only misapprehension of the advantages to be gained that prevents the veterans of Chunar now, to a man, volunteering for the Hills. And who can deny, when masses of men can be transported from the sea to the frontier and back again within the week, that *every* European regiment in the service should have its chief hospital in the Hills, where at least half the period of service of every English soldier should be spent?*

While anxious to further the introduction of railroads, Lord Hardinge very far from neglected those communications to which we must still, for so many

* A few months ago ice was sanctioned for European hospitals, and we hear that it is now determined to allow punkahs, both day and night, in the barracks in the plains. This is indeed doing as we would be done by: the measure will save many lives.—H. M. L.

years, be indebted. On his arrival, finding the works on the Great Trunk road languishing, and the roads scarcely passable for want of bridges, &c., he gave every encouragement to the Executive officers, and placed the means of completing the whole line of road in three seasons in their hands. The war impeded this as well as many other measures, but more than fifty bridges were built on this road during two years and a half, no less than fifteen of them being in one march of fourteen miles. Many drain bridges were then also prepared, and much metalling work completed. In short, except the bridges over seven rivers, it was expected that ere June, 1848, the whole line of road from Calcutta to Meerut would be quite ready. As it is, travellers in carriages now (1847) go up and down for eight months of the year, easily reaching Delhi and Meerut from Calcutta in a fortnight.

During Lord Hardinge's Administration there was very much discussion, especially in the south of India, regarding interference with the religion of the natives. At an early date the Governor-General made his stand. By his own example encouraging the observance of the Christian religion, he not only discountenanced interference with the rites of the Natives, but prohibited Government officials from involving themselves directly in schemes of conversion. By all legitimate means, without interfering with the labour of the missionary, he encouraged general education and the enlightenment of the Native mind; the rest he appears to have left to God and to His appointed time.

The notification of October, 1846, prohibiting Sunday labour, is evidence of Lord Hardinge's sincerity, and will be long remembered to his honour. Viewed merely as a secular measure the good will be great. It will be a check to many who, having little to do during the week, from mere listlessness and carelessness, were wont to desecrate the sabbath, or permit it to be desecrated by their subordinates. The Moslem and the Hindoo, who worship after their own fashion, have now some proof that the Christian respects the faith he professes.

On several occasions we have discussed the subjects of infanticide and human sacrifice, and have now great pleasure in recording Lord Hardinge's efforts to put down these crimes as well as suttee and man-stealing.

During the year 1846–47 scarcely a month failed to record some act of prohibition of one or other of these crimes in the territories of protected chiefs, in Central or Northern India. Several princes having come forward and reported their desire to put an end to these atrocities, it now rests with the paramount power to see that these edicts be not infringed by present rulers themselves or by their heirs. Where a prince reports an edict of his own to the British Government, he virtually calls on it to witness the act, and where he swerves from such attested deed the least punishment that is his due is an expression of the severe displeasure of the Governor-General, which in most cases will have the desired effect. The great gain to humanity of recent measures will be better understood, when it is considered that at the death of a petty chief, such as the Raja of Mundí near Símla, who holds a country yielding scarcely £40,000 a-year, as many as a dozen women had been incremated;* and that throughout the Hindu States, up to the period of the recent prohibitions, the point of honour had been for every widow to immolate herself. The murder of Raja Híra Singh,

* We have heard an officer assert, who counted the figures on the sepulchres at Mundí of the last ten Rajas, that the average number of victims was 45 !—H. M. L.

at Lahore, involved the suttee of no less than twenty-four helpless women, of whom two were his own wives, and eight his slaves.*

The suppression of infanticide will be much more difficult than that of suttee. In different quarters of protected India, whole villages and tribes confess that they have no daughters—declaring that such is the will of God; but, even in our own oldest provinces, it is by no means certain that child-murder does not largely prevail. The right course seems now being pursued to eradicate this horrid system:—not by sweeping penalties (carelessly or not at all carried out), but by watching events, by instructing the people, and by discountenancing all who, having local influence, do not lend it in support of humanity. In the Jullunder Doab, the Bedís, descendants from Gúrú Nanuk, permitted no female child to live, and throughout the Punjab they shed blood almost with impunity. One of them, however, we observe, by the *Delhi Gazette*, has recently been hanged at Lahore, for murdering his mother and brothers, and from the day of the introduction of our rule into the Jullunder, the Bedís have been given to understand that they are subject to the law like other people. When the Bedí of Oona, the head of their "tribe of Levi," was told by the Commissioner that he must forbid the crime within his extensive jaghir; he replied he could not, but that he would himself, by a life of celibacy, support British views. Mr. Lawrence told him that he must take his choice of obeying or

* In Major Broadfoot's despatch, dated 26th September, 1845, published in the Punjab Blue Book, reporting the death of Sirdar Jowahir Singh and the burning of his four widows, it is stated, "Suttees are sacred, and receive worship; their last words are considered prophetic, their blessing eagerly sought for, and their curses dreaded. Dewan Dínanath, the Raní, the Maharaja, and others, prostrated themselves before them, and obtained their blessing. . . . The Suttees blessed them, but cursed the Sikh Punt."—H. M. L.

of surrendering his lands; he appears to have preferred the latter alternative.

Child-stealing, and the selling of men, women, and children, for purposes of slavery or prostitution, are crimes—though still practised in British India, and most common throughout Native States,—not sufficiently considered in their frightful consequences. By recent notifications we observe that child-stealing has been made penal in the Punjab, and that the very name of slave has been prohibited in the Gwalior territory. These are wholesome effects of interference; most holy fruits of protection.

Attention thus excited towards suttee, infanticide, and child-stealing, very slight efforts on the part of Government and its officials will surely tend to eradicate the crimes throughout the limits of Hindoostan. Some few Hindus may pervert, or disregard their own shasters; but the more sacred and authoritative of these writings in no way sanction suttee. We never heard a Hindu pretend to prove that they did, and not many months since a good Brahman emphatically told the writer of these remarks, that in prohibiting infanticide, we had compensated for permitting the crime of cow-killing. Be it remembered that the majority of Hindus consider a cow's life more sacred than that of a man!

During the administrations of Lords Hardinge, Ellenborough, and Auckland, much anxiety was displayed to put an end to the human sacrifices of the Khonds and other wild tribes south-west of Calcutta. It has been shown by the *Calcutta Review* that, among other recorded atrocities, as many as twenty-five full grown persons have been sacrificed at a single festival by the Khonds; that a caterer for such impious rites had pledged and actually delivered up his own two daughters, for want of purchased offerings; and that in some of the Khond districts, those who could not procure other victims gave up "their old and helpless fathers and mothers to be sacrificed."

The measures lately undertaken have been carried out under the orders of the Deputy-Governor of Bengal, under the general supervision of the Governor-General. In all his communications on the subject, Lord Hardinge advocated the combination of energy with forbearance. It has been clearly demonstrated that mere advice, or earnest remonstrances, or partial tokens of favour, would not alone effect the humane purposes of Government; but it does not therefore follow that hanging and destroying are to be advocated, or that we should carry our measures at the point of the sword. This would, in our opinion, rather retard civilization, would drive the wild tribes into their wildest fastnesses, and sooner extirpate the offenders than eradicate the offence. Of the nature and extent of Captain Macpherson, the Khond agent's, success, chiefly through his administration of justice, ample accounts have been furnished; but of Lord Hardinge's designs comparatively little is known. Perceiving the utter impossibility of a single agent, however zealous and able, effecting much over 60,000 square miles of wild mountain country, he suggested giving him six European officers as coadjutors, each armed with full powers to act, and each supported by three efficient native assistants. Thus at a stroke was the machinery to be increased eighteen-fold! These European and Native agents were to go among the Khonds as friends and benefactors. They were to be authorized to make them small presents, to advise and to consult with them, to administer justice, and to explain that a merciful God does not smile on murder, and that the blood of human victims does not fertilize their fields, but that valleys, happier and richer than their own, as free from famine and disease, are witnesses of no such detestable rites. Failing by such means, we understand it to have been Lord Hardinge's intention to have sanctioned all possible measures short of devastation and spoliation; and we have little doubt that when mild measures, such as those which have already been shown to have proved so far successful, are thus energetically enforced, there will be little need of recourse to the sword. But the evils of centuries cannot be eradicated in a day, especially in a country whose climate is so deadly, that for half the year few Indians, much less Europeans, can live.

If we have not yet (1847) obtained Post-Office reform, it is assuredly not Lord Hardinge's fault. All his acts prove him to be quite alive to the advantages of rapid and cheap communication and exchange of opinion. We understand that during the spring of 1847, he sent home the Post-Office papers with a strong recommendation that the suggestions of Mr. Riddell, the Agra Postmaster-General, should be sanctioned.

On the present system, there are two rates of postage for newspapers; two annas and three annas, according to distance. Letters all pay according to distance and weight; a quarter tola, or one-fourth of a rupee, being considered a single letter. These rules largely affect the prices of the presidency newspapers in the Mofussil, and enable all who wish to send small letters to club together, and thus transmit a dozen advices or letters by a single postage. It was soon ascertained that Natives did so, and that merchants employed collectors of these scraps of letters in different quarters, who on salaries of five or six pounds a year collected and transmitted letters at decimal rates, and in the same way received packets containing bundles, the contents of which they delivered according to their directions.

The new rules were proposed to meet these difficulties. A one-anna stamp was to pass newspapers from one end of India to the other, and, though lightly taxing Calcutta, Bombay, and Madras readers, would largely benefit all Mofussil ones. Proprietors must benefit, as the reduction would now induce many Mofussilites to take daily papers. In regard to letters, one rate of half an anna, or three farthings, was suggested for all distances, one-eighth of a tola (rupee) being, however, the weight of a single letter, so that there could be little, if any advantage, in an agency between the Government and letter-writers and receivers. At present the north-western provinces alone pay any postal revenue to Government. The present income, we believe, is about £10,000, but double that amount is swamped in the expenses of the other presidencies, leaving a deficit of a lakh of rupees on all India, which was expected to increase to five, as the first effects of the new scheme. The Post-Office revenue had, however, lately increased ten per cent. per annum, and under such an impulse as was proposed, letters and newspapers would vastly increase, so that it was not too much to expect that eventually a gain would be obtained instead of a loss incurred, by the new arrangement, independent of Government packets being carried free. Should, however, this hope be disappointed, it would still be the interest as well as the duty of Government to remodel the Post-Office establishment. The whole system, especially in Bengal, is discreditable to an enlightened Government. There is now little or no check on the delivery of letters, and while the post runs at the rate of ten miles an hour westward of Benares, the letter-bags are still carried around Calcutta on men's shoulders.

The inhabitants of Calcutta have reason long to remember Lord Hardinge's warm approval, in August,

1846, of the measures for the improvement of the Calcutta conservancy. All such reforms have everywhere obtained his support. But to a commercial people perhaps his removal of all restrictions on trade is his best recommendation. Throughout British India, trade is now free, and even in almost every Native state the worst restrictions have been removed. The town duties not only of such places as Loodiana and Umballah have been abolished, but those of Surat, yielding eleven lakhs of rupees, have been released.*

No sooner was the Jullunder Doab annexed than all transit and town duties were annulled, and those of the Cis-Sutlej States soon followed. In Central India the example has been followed, so that with exceptions, so few as to be scarce worth mentioning, trade in India is now taxed at single points on the great Customs line or on the seaboard. In the north-western provinces the said Customs line has been reduced from a double to a single one; would that the state of the exchequer permitted its being altogether removed! The Sutlej and the Indus are now, *in reality*, free of imposts, to the sea; and, under British influence, considerable reformation in Customs' arrangements has been effected in the Punjab. Cotton cultivation has not been neglected, and we understand that a full report on this important staple is now before Government.

Lord Hardinge took great interest in the endeavours for the cultivation of tea, and authorized its enthusiastic promoter, Dr. Jameson, to commence plantations in different quarters of the lower Himalayas. The present price that Indian tea fetches is an earnest that England will be independent of China for this essential of English

* It is only fair to say that the Salt Tax was simultaneously increased at Surat, but the loss to Government in that town alone by the new arrangement was estimated at four lakhs; the duty levied on salt being seven, while the town duties removed were eleven.—H. M. L.

life, at least as soon as the Chinese can grow their own opium.

Thus much has been done or laid in train during Lord Hardinge's Administration of forty-two months. His benefits to the Services have not been less real, though not so apparent as those to the State.

In the first place, by reducing the expenditure within the income, no retrenchment of salaries was made. And no rational man can, for a moment, suppose that England could continue to hold India at an annual loss of a million and a half. As, then, it is not likely to part with its brightest gem, sooner or later all servants of the State must pay the penalty of undue expenditure, be it on visionary schemes of war or of peace. In this, then, Lord Hardinge deserved gratitude, that he never wilfully allowed a rupee of public cash to be unnecessarily expended: he closely scanned and jealously scrutinized all attempts, however plausible, on the public pocket; and when he rewarded liberally, and freely abandoned present profits, it was because he had sense and far-sightedness enough to perceive that there is no reaping without sowing, and that, in the end, it is cheaper and better to pay well and to act liberally, than by stinted measures to cramp zeal and retard improvement.

But far more than in mere pecuniary matters are we indebted to his lordship. The spirit of consideration and kindliness that prevailed throughout his Administration, not only to those around him and enjoying his personal society, but to all officers of the State with whom he had occasion to communicate, was of a marked kind. Under Lord Hardinge there was no blackballing of classes nor undue encouragement of others. Men were judged by their own merits—due consideration being paid to just recommendations, especially in favour of sons of meritorious officers. Himself a thorough soldier, the Governor-General always upheld the civil authority as necessarily supreme, but he discouraged all jealousies between civilians and soldiers, and taught that each is most honoured in best fulfilling his duties.

All branches of the army, European and Native, were indebted to him for distinct acts of favour.

To his advocacy, when Secretary-at-War, several Company's officers are indebted for being aides-de-camp to the Queen. And it is believed that he strove earnestly to obtain for the army a senior list. The Company's regiments in the three Presidencies are indebted to his voice for their extra captains. Additional pensions have, at his recommendation, been allowed to widows of officers killed in action, and also to the heirs of native officers.*

Free quarters have been allowed to all ranks at Lahore; the families of European soldiers have been allowed to join them, both in Scinde and the Punjab, a measure that, considering Lord Hardinge's precise notions on military questions, can only have been caused by his strong desire to make the soldier as comfortable as possible, since none more than himself saw the objections to crowding Kurrachee and Lahore with European women and children.

On the close of the war of sixty days, while the treasury was still empty, a gratuity of twelve months' batta was granted, not only to those who had been actually under fire, but to all who had arrived at and above Bussean by a certain day. For months of exposure in Affghanistan and Burmah half this amount of batta was granted!

* We presume that the gallant Lord Gough referred to this boon, when, in a parting speech at his own hospitable table the night before Lord Hardinge left Simla, he observed, "The noble lord (Hardinge) had done much for the army; both for the living and the dead—he had made *both* more comfortable!"—H. M. L.

The European soldier's kit, by a general order of February, 1846, is now carried at the public expense: the sanatarium of Dugshae and the barracks for European artillery at Subathú are the work of Lord Hardinge, in continuation of the best act of Lord Ellenborough's Administration.

The boons peculiarly affecting the Native soldier are not fewer. The pension of sepoys disabled by wounds in action has been largely increased; in some cases from one rupee eleven annas to four rupees, in others from four to seven rupees per mensem. By an order of 12th February, 1846, the benefit of these pensions was extended to sepoys of local corps.*

By Government orders of 15th August, 1845, the long-vexed and dangerous question of Scinde pay was decided, and troops in that province were put on a footing with those in Arracan. In February, 1846, the same rates were granted in the Punjab.

Hutting money was allowed to the whole Native army by Government orders of August 15, 1845, and on the same date an order was issued authorizing sepoys to put in plaints in all the civil courts on unstamped paper.†

Sepoys wounded in the battles of the Sutlej received rations gratis while in hospital, and when scurvy broke

* Pity it is that these corps which, as in the cases of the Nusserí and Sirmur Battalion, were present at Bhurtpur and during the Sikh campaign, are not called "Irregulars," instead of being misnamed "Locals," and accordingly underpaid. They would to a man volunteer for general service, and having little fellow-feeling with our sepoys, and few prejudices, would be invaluable light troops. We feel satisfied that their case could never have been rightly brought before Lord Hardinge, or that he would have put them on a proper footing. We have heard that on an occasion of reviewing one of the Gúrkha Corps, Lord Hardinge asked a zealous Hibernian officer how it was the men were so small. "They get such small pay," was the answer. We presume he meant to say that higher rates would obtain finer men.—H. M. L.

† We should have preferred to have seen the sepoys hutted, or rather barracked, by Government. The present system of hutting is injurious to discipline, and might, without difficulty, be improved.—H. M. L.

out among the wounded Europeans, the Governor-General's own state tents were instantly pitched for the accommodation of a portion, and he constantly visited both Europeans and natives, talking to the former, and expressing his commiseration of the sufferings of all.

These are some among the many benefits conferred by Lord Hardinge on the army of India. As already observed, Sir Robert Peel gave testimony in Parliament that he was regarded by the army of England as its friend, "*because he was the friend of justice to all ranks of that army.*" He has, at least, equal claims on the army of India, where he was equally the friend of the sentinel, the subaltern, and the veteran. He equally sought the welfare, the happiness of all. Before he had put foot in the East, he had advocated the interests of its exiles; and when he had shared in their dangers, and partaken of their honours,—when his name was for ever connected with the glories of Múdki, Ferozeshah, and Sobraon, history delighted to designate him, like his illustrious Captain, a "Sepoy General." His interests and theirs became one; his honours had been won by the Indian army, and on a hundred occasions he bore testimony to the merits of that army, and he will doubtless always be esteemed among its warmest friends.*

Though thoroughly a utilitarian, Lord Hardinge was possessed of a fine taste, and was fully alive to the beauties of art. When in Paris he refused to touch a picture from among the master-pieces in St. Cloud, as he would not set an example of spoliation; but he carried to England purchased specimens of art and

* The essayist here added :—"We may venture to remind him that much is expected at his hands; and first and foremost it is confidently hoped that his voice will advocate the furlough memorial, if indeed he has not yet satisfied the home Government that, much as it is the interest of their servants to be permitted to visit England, it is immeasurably more that of their masters to induce them periodically to go there."

nature from every corner of India. During his residence, he encouraged the preservation and repair of the Eastern architecture around him. On the occasion of his visit to Agra in October, 1845, he frequently visited the Taj Mahal, the fort, and the palace. Finding that some of the large slabs of stone from the palace had been removed, and that the marble railing was lying ruined and unfixed, and the whole place much out of repair, he reprehended such desecration, ordered the pavement to be restored, and the injuries to be repaired. After causing every enquiry to be made to ascertain the original design of the Kútub Minar at Delhi, and finding that neither descriptions nor old drawings gave any authority for the grotesque ornament placed on its summit by Colonel Smith, Lord Hardinge directed its removal.

To the Archæological Society of Delhi, instituted mainly for the purpose of exploring the various ruins of India, Lord Hardinge afforded his encouragement and assistance, and placed at their disposal the services of any officer distinguished for his skill as a draughtsman.

The revenue survey of the Jullunder and Cis-Sutlej States was nearly completed in Lord Hardinge's time; others in Rajpútana and Central India being set on foot; and no sooner did Mr. Thomason, the able Lieutenant-Governor of Agra, project a college of instruction for civil engineers at Rúrki, near the head of the Ganges canal, than the scheme was sanctioned, and an excellent officer of the engineer corps, Lieutenant MacLagan, placed at his disposal as its principal. As sanctioned by the Governor-General, the grand trigonometrical survey will also soon be extending its operations into Cashmere and to the banks of the Indus.

Thus in no department are we aware that Lord Hardinge was found wanting to the extent of his opportunities and the means at his disposal. He carried on war in all its details, like a thorough soldier, and in all points encouraged the arts of peace, like a practised and far-sighted statesman.

His last public movement was a vice-regal visit to Lucknow. The public had been for months on tiptoe at the prospect of annexation, though the whole tenor of Lord Hardinge's career might have satisfied people, not only that he would not at the last stage of his career open a new and wide field of diplomacy, but that under *any* circumstances, and at *any* time, he would *not* annex Oude to India in the manner many desired to do. Our opinions regarding the great Indian "difficulty" are unchanged since, in a previous essay, we propounded what might honestly and with advantage to all parties be done for Oude.

Indian officials cannot be too careful to read treaties in their spirit as well as in their letter; lest it be thought that, like the Romans of old, we diplomatize only to deceive,—that our pacifications are only truces. We should not only disdain such practices, but prove to the world that we do so.

Premising thus much, we would ask those honest and able men who advocate the annexation of Oude if, in their opinion, the treaties with either Oude or Hyderabad contemplated our ever obtaining another rupee from those countries? If such be the case, on what possible plea can we take to ourselves territories, because they are mismanaged, more especially when there is no concealing from ourselves that much, if not all, of this mismanagement, has been caused by our own measures. No; if mistakes have been made, let them be honestly amended, as they would be with Burdwan or with Betteah, or with any other private estate. *Appropriation* is no more the remedy for the mischiefs of a principality than of a zemindary. We must abide by our treaties, public as well as private, whatever be the inconvenience. If Oude and Hyderabad affairs are really as disordered as they are declared to be, let us by all means temporarily, or, if need be, *permanently* assume the management of part or all, but justice and the faith of treaties forbid the appropriation of a rupee of their revenue to the general purposes of the Indian Government. It will be a reward, ample and sufficient, to recover large tracts from anarchy, and to bring under our influence a numerous population with whom our only connection can be that of paternal protection. Twenty or fifty lakhs of revenue will not increase our strength so much as may the love and gratitude of people thus rescued from oppression. Above all, we shall have preserved our reputation for justice and good faith—we shall still be recognized as the reverers of treaties.

As the time for delivering over his charge drew near, Lord Hardinge became restless and impatient. We have heard him likened to a schoolboy on the approach of holidays. He now counted the days till his release. And can it be wondered that, at his age, after an absence from his family approaching to four years, and borne down with such labour as at any period of life is scarcely endurable, his heart should have bounded at the prospect of release—of return to domestic happiness.

The bare perusal of our faint description of Lord Hardinge's Indian career may enable the reader to judge of a Governor-General's labours. Petitions and appeals; every measure military, political, or civil; every arrangement, medical, scientific, police, or revenue, with the hundred miscellaneous matters of the three Presidencies, are all liable to be referred for his decision. The responsibility and anxious thought, the amount of business and of office work which it entails, is almost beyond belief, and is to be surmounted only by ability, method, punctuality, and great industry.

In these attributes and in sound good sense, in quick perception, in judgment, in resource, and in calm prompt courage, we believe Lord Hardinge to have been excelled by few men. His memory was good, though not exact, vividly remembering facts and general circumstances though not particular words. He seldom forgot faces, even though names escaped his recollection.

Among other qualities, eminently useful in his high station, by which the Governor-General was distinguished, one of the most marked was his tact and management of men's minds, in soothing animosities, reconciling adverse spirits; and when differences proved irreconcilable, in conciliating to himself the good will of both the contending parties. Contrary to a practice too common in India, Lord Hardinge may be said to have been on excellent terms with almost every individual with whom he had to transact business. He expected every man to do his duty conscientiously, yet in marking his disapprobation of neglect or slackness, his manner was so kindly, gentlemanlike, and consistent as seldom to give offence. Many difficult questions were offered for his solution; and his arbitration was demanded even in personal quarrels.

Nor was Lord Hardinge's career less marked by moderation, we might almost say, by *modesty*, in his public as well as in his private capacity. The unassuming general order directing the proud march of the captured Sikh ordnance to Calcutta, when contrasted with the "Song of Triumph," which heralded the return of the gates of Somnath to Hindoostan, might be adduced in illustration of the former; and the latter was most conspicuous in the quiet and unpretending style in which he travelled, and which marked his daily rides. Lord W. Bentinck himself was not more unostentatious; and often, even when in the neighbourhood of the enemy, Lord Hardinge might have been observed riding about with a single attendant.

His habits were abstemious and regular. He was liberal in his hospitality; no day passed in which visitors did not sit at his excellent board; and twice or thrice a week large parties were given, to which all strangers were invited. He was at first surprised at the independence of the Indian service, but freedom of opinion when allied to due subordination was too congenial to his nature to win disapproval. We have said that Lord Hardinge was considerate and kind, and we repeat that he was so to all, whether distant or around him. His letters and orders were always courteous and gentlemanlike; never betraying anger, or forgetfulness that those addressed were gentlemen, and that even if wrong in particular cases their motives may have been right, or that their previous services may have deserved well of the head of the Government. All this is undeniable, but we fear it is equally true, that many who partook of Lord Hardinge's hospitality left his house annoyed rather than pleased. They considered themselves intentionally slighted, because the Governor-General had not separately addressed his conversation to them. Wounded vanity is hard to deal with, and we believe that had Lord Hardinge been able more frequently to divert his mind from cares of State to the frivolities around him, he would have been what is called a more popular man. On our own experience we can testify to his desire to be affable and attentive to his visitors. He was always indignant if his staff appeared to fail in their duty to guests; but it was not always easy for an elderly man, worn down with labour from early dawn, to remember the especial case of every pompous field officer or self-complacent civilian. To take wine and say a civil nothing was seldom omitted, but the special remembrance of each individual's peculiar case was often wanting. This we know gave offence, especially to those who, having applied for private audiences, were refused them, but invited to dinner.

This refusal of audiences also offended many. Lord Auckland gave them, but regretted it, and recommended Lord Ellenborough not to do so; but his Lordship was more ready of speech and more at home at a *levée* or an evening party than was Lord Hardinge. We are, however, of opinion that both were quite right. Audiences waste much time: they give advantages only to the forward and presuming and to parasites of the Presidency and Simla. Every man can tell his story by letter or *vivâ voce* to the Private Secretary. If there is much in him, it will not require an audience to elicit it; his name, character, and particular merits are better known at Army and Government head-quarters than in any other service in the world, and Lord Hardinge was the last man in the world to intentionally neglect an individual, high or low, who had in any manner, by courage or by ability, distinguished himself; indeed, by his hearty and cordial converse, he soon won his way to such men's hearts.*

In Europe, Lord Hardinge's duties required the smallest modicum of official correspondence, and up to his sixtieth year he had little or no practice in writing; but restricting himself in his minutes, memoranda, and letters, as in his speeches, to facts, and attempting no

* What we have stated relates more especially to all cases of application for private interview, with reference to the obtainment of personal favours, connected with any of the services. As regards individuals, who have worthy objects to promote, unconnected with any of the regular services, a relaxation of the rule, under proper restrictions, might be at once politic and beneficial.—H. M. L.

sort of display, the products of his pen may be placed without disparagement by the side of those of any statesman of his day. Clear and distinct in his perceptions, he has always desired to master every subject before him, and would never be satisfied with slurring over questions imposing even the necessity of perusing voluminous papers on matters often affecting only the particular interests of an humble individual, but which he perceived did involve *a principle*.

This was a notable and a valuable feature in his character. He took large views of all questions. He saw them as Governor-General; looked on them from the arena of Europe, as affecting England as well as India, and not as referring to a particular class. Such men are needed for this country, and it is on this account we consider that, as a general question, India can be best supplied with Governors-General from the British senate. Large and enlightened views, influenced but *not warped* by local experience, with ability, is what is wanted in India. The due admixture of European and Native talent is one great secret of good Government; a no less one is the introduction in all places of fresh minds and fresh talent from the mother country.

Because Lord Hardinge was always cordial and kind to his secretaries, some have jumped at the conclusion that he was unduly influenced by them. Far otherwise. He was ready to hear the opinion of every man who had a right to give one. But no Governor-General ever more decidedly took his own line, and chalked out his own course, than did Lord Hardinge. He is understood to have usually drafted most of his own official letters of importance, as indeed seems to have been the practice with Lord Ellenborough, and many of his predecessors. Lord Hardinge's quick perception at sixty enabled him readily to master matters to which his previous habits had been alien, and to which he had before paid little attention; moreover, his experience on the stage of Europe enabled him often to throw new lights on the most abstruse Indian subjects.

Accustomed, as a constant attendant, for twenty years, of Parliament, to turn night into day, he found no difficulty in reconciling himself to Indian habits, and not only to be stirring with the dawn, but as an almost general rule to be at work one, two, and three hours before daylight. It was this practice that enabled him to get through so much business and to appear more or less at leisure during the day. On an average, however, he could not have worked less than ten hours a day.

He was regular in his rides and walks, and took much exercise; pacing his room or verandah he would discuss questions of interest with his advisers and secretaries, and often with chance visitors, or those he met on the road. Many of the younger as well as older members of the service, in no way connected with his own staff, have thus been honoured with his cordial and even familiar conversation on the most interesting European as well as Asiatic questions, and it was thus he elicited opinions on Indian subjects, and obtained an insight into the characters and merits of individuals. On such occasions, it was no uncommon speech for him to make. —"So-and-so must be a fine fellow, every one speaks well of him;" or "It must be true, or some one would say a word in his favour."

Much has been said and even written of Lord Hardinge's dispensation of patronage. We are among those who believe that the last four Governors-General all dispensed theirs with scrupulous honesty; none more so than Lord Hardinge. Like other mortals he has erred, but his nominations have been made carefully and with perfect good faith. As in duty bound he has considered recommendations from the Court of Directors, where they were in behalf of deserving individuals, in the same way that he has recognized the superior claims of the sons of distinguished officers; but in the whole circuit of his appointments we know scarcely an instance of his putting a man into a wrong place, and not one of his wilfully doing so.

We happen to be able to narrate the real circumstances of four of his most important nominations; two of which were at one time unreasonably arraigned.

Lord Hardinge may have originally thought that there was one other officer in the army who would have made a better Adjutant-General than Colonel Grant, but he considered his strong claims, his long departmental experience, his excellent business habits, his recent gallant services in the field, his severe wound, and last, perhaps not least,—but by no means *the* ground of the appointment as some would say—his connection with the brave Lord Gough, and confirmed him in the appointment in which he had officiated throughout the war. We know that he is now perfectly satisfied with the choice he made, and we are not sure that if he had to choose again he would not give the *first*, instead of the second place to Grant.

Mr. John Lawrence was known throughout the Bengal Presidency as a practical, clear-headed, and energetic officer, who had for years, as magistrate of the turbulent city of Delhi, enjoyed the confidence of all ranks. When passing through Delhi, the Governor-General admired his bold, frank manner, and was pleased with his activity in forwarding supplies, carriage and stores to the army, as well as with the cheerful, manly tone of his conversation and correspondence. Before Colonel

Lawrence's arrival on the frontier, Mr. John Lawrence was acordingly sent for to be employed in a judicial capacity in the Cis-Sutlej States; but the Lieutenant-Governor, remarking that he could not be spared at such a time from Delhi, sent up another civilian, who was considered a good judicial officer. Some disappointment and even disapprobation was expressed at what Mr. Thomason had done; and when, at the expiration of the war, a commissioner was required for the Jullunder Doab, Lord Hardinge again selected him, and has assuredly had no reason to regret his choice; nor has a single voice ever pretended to assert that he has failed in his duties, while those who know him say there are few better civil administrators in India. No man is more satisfied of this than Mr. Thomason.

Colonel Gouldie is our third instance. We doubt if the Governor-General had seen him twice when he made him Auditor-General of the Bengal army. Colonel Gouldie had been for many years a pension paymaster, and had acquired a high character as a man of business. He joined the army, and was found to be a good soldier, a shrewd, sensible man, however employed. This Lord Hardinge ascertained from various sources. We have it from an honourable man that he was casually asked by Lord Hardinge what was Colonel Gouldie's character, and that when he answered favourably, his lordship replied, "that is much what Colonel —— and Major —— said," mentioning persons equally unconnected as our informant with Colonel Gouldie. At the time we refer to, Lord Hardinge had recommended Gouldie to the Court of Directors for the appointment; though some months later, when he was sent for to be told of his selection, he had not the slightest idea of the purpose for which his presence was required.

In the same manner Mr. H. M. Elliot was selected as Secretary to Government in the foreign department. For a whole year preceding the vacancy, Lord Hardinge would ask, in conversation, all sorts and degrees of persons as to Mr. Elliot's character and ability. Thus, without—as far as we are aware—ever having seen him, he selected the man whom the voice of the services voted the best qualified for this important ministerial office.

We might adduce a dozen other instances equally to the point. Every man cannot have his wishes, nor perhaps all his deserts; but it may be fairly asked, where was the high influence, or what is called the interest, of Littler, Currie, Elliot, the three Lawrences, Thoresby, Wheeler, Campbell, Mackeson, MacGregor, Birch, Colvin, Sage,* Benson, Gouldie, Edwardes, the four Abbotts, the Bechers, Lumsden, Holmes, Napier, MacLagan, Taylor, Beadon, and a host of others whose names Lord Hardinge probably never heard of before he reached India; before they approached him officially, or were presented to his notice as suited to certain offices?

Although we have already exceeded the limits usually allowed to a single paper in a Review, we must not altogether omit mention of the cordial reception given to Lord Hardinge by all ranks of the community of Calcutta on his Lordship's return from the North-West Provinces. Commendatory and congratulatory addresses poured in on him, and the warm expressions of the commercial, civil, clerical, and military community of the metropolis of India, will be found not only

* We readily bear our testimony to Colonel Sage's zeal and ability, we wish we could add to his urbanity and considerateness. There are many abuses in the Department of Public Works, but they are more likely to be remedied by the Military Board, working *with* and through Executive Engineers, than by irritating a body of zealous and honourable officers.—H. M. L.

to bear out the anticipations with which we opened this essay, but our own statements may possibly appear cold and heartless when contrasted with the glowing and affectionate terms in which they recorded their sentiments.

At the meeting of the inhabitants of Calcutta at the Town Hall on the 24th of December, a letter from the Bishop was read by the Chairman, regretting that indisposition prevented him from attending the meeting, and in warm and energetic terms proposing that a statue be voted to the retiring Governor-General, towards the expense of which the writer expressed himself ready to subscribe £200. We can only find space for the following portion of the letter :—

"To no one of our greatest Governor-Generals was such a task assigned by Providence, as was allotted to Lord Hardinge. His victories at the moment of conflict were only equalled by his discretion in avoiding all previous causes of irritation, and by his moderation and wisdom in the use of his success.

"None of our bravest Governors had the happiness of conveying, and at once, to a fierce and tumultuous population, such wide-spread blessings, social and moral, as the Punjab has already received.

"Nor can I forget the other services of my Lord Hardinge, the honour he has shown to the Christian religion on all occasions, his prohibition of the continuance of public works on the Lord's Day, his encouragement of Col. Lawrence's Benevolent Asylum at Kussowli, and the impulse he has given to public education by instituting periodical examinations into the learning and good morals of the candidates for employment. In fact, Lord Hardinge has crowded into one short administration all the services of the highest order, both military and civil, which have commonly been divided amongst several much longer ones."

Several Natives took the opportunity at this meeting, in enthusiastic terms, to express their gratitude to Lord Hardinge for the benefits he had conferred on India, and, entirely approving of the address, as far as it went, proposed to add to it the following paragraph :—

"We cannot, on the occasion of your Lordship's departure, refrain from expressing our grateful admiration of the lustre which your beneficent policy in the encouragement of education, your resolute adherence to peace until war became inevitable, and your paternal solicitude for the welfare of the people entrusted to your charge, have shed on your administration. Brief as your sojourn has been, you have represented the high-minded benignity of the British sceptre no less than its majestic splendour, the peaceful virtues of the Christian statesman no less than the indomitable courage of the British warrior, the humanizing influences of British ascendancy no less than the invincible force of British arms."

Some discussion ensued, the only difference of opinion being as to whether the sense of the proposed additional paragraph was not expressed in the address already prepared. With the consent of all parties, it was finally determined to insert a few words, exhibiting the purport of the amendment in the original address. We give the document in full as presented on the 28th, placing the additional paragraph between brackets :—

"To the Right Honourable Lord Viscount Hardinge, G. C. B., &c., &c., &c.

"My Lord,

"The inhabitants of Calcutta addressed your Lordship on the occasion of your return to the Presidency, and declared their sense of the distinguished services rendered by you to this country. In acknowledging that address your Lordship expressed your conviction, that a pacific course was the one best calculated to promote the honour and interests of Great Britain and the welfare of the people of India. We feel that in this belief your Lordship commenced your administration, and that it influenced you until war became the necessity of self-defence. We can desire no happier future for India and England than that this sentiment should prevail with our rulers, and no more glorious achievements, when forced into the field, than those which, under Divine Providence, have won imperishable honour for our arms on the banks of the Sutlej.

"We cannot permit your Lordship to lay down the high office of Governor-General of India, and quit these shores, without repeating our admiration of your distinguished career. History perpetuates the memory of great public benefactors, and its pages, which have already recorded your Lordship's early services to your country, on the most desperate field of modern times, will glow with the brilliant addition made to them after an interval of thirty-six years, the greater portion of which has been subject to the ordeal of public life.

"[In the same pages, and in the traditions of a grateful people, will live the recollection of the wise measures by which you have encouraged education, and contributed to the permanent improvement and happiness of those committed to your charge.]

"We desire, my Lord, to have and preserve in Calcutta some personal memorial of one who has received the highest honours from his Sovereign, and the thanks of his countrymen, while ruling this great empire: we desire it, my Lord, as a testimony of our respect for your private and admiration of your public character, and as a legacy of deep interest to those who will come after us.

"We have, therefore, to ask that your Lordship will permit a committee to place itself in communication with you for the purpose of carrying out the object we have in view, and it remains for us only to bid your Lordship farewell, and to convey to you our earnest hope that it may please the Almighty to bless you with years of health and strength, to enjoy the honours you have nobly won, and to deserve yet further the gratitude of your country, by enforcing in the Senate that principle of enlightened rule which recognizes peace as the surest guarantee for the prosperity and happiness of mankind."

In an appropriate and feeling reply, Lord Hardinge expressed his gratification at the handsome testimony of the approbation and personal regard of the inhabitants of Calcutta, and in the course of his speech thus gracefully recommended cordiality and unanimity between the two great classes of the community:—

"It is also very flattering to me to observe that this address has been agreed to by the united voice of the European and Native inhabitants of this great city, the capital of Her Majesty's Eastern Empire; and I may allude to this fact, because I am impressed with the belief that the happiness of the Native population depends upon the existence of a thorough identity of interests among all classes of the community. By the encouragement of such a feeling, our power will be more firmly consolidated, our national character more pre-eminently exalted, and our influence more beneficially exercised in promoting the prosperity of British India."

The *Friend of India*, of the 30th of December, in echoing the sentiments of the community at large, thus concludes an elaborate notice of Lord Hardinge's administration:—

"But we must draw this lengthened sketch of Lord Hardinge's career to a close. His brief administration has been crowded with events of the deepest interest and importance. To it appertains the distinguished honour of having extinguished the last enemy left to us between the Himalaya and Cape Comorin, and removed the apprehension of future hostilities. Though his Lordship has been engaged in large military enterprises which have terminated in making the will of the British Government as paramount in Peshawur, as it is in Jessore, no one has dreamt of threatening him with a Parliamentary inquiry. His measures have been characterised by so much justice and moderation as well as vigour, that although they have resulted in an extension of territory and influence which Lord Ellenborough himself might have envied, he has not roused the outcry of party hostility. He has reduced the numerical strength of the army without weakening our means of defence; and he delivers the empire to his successor with an excess of income over expenditure, and in a state of such tranquillity as to inspire the hope of large resources for the future triumphs of peace."

Before his departure, Lord Hardinge must also have received the reports of the speeches made at the parting dinner given by the Court of Directors to Lord Dalhousie, and in them had an earnest of the greeting that awaited him in England. On the occasion referred to, the Premier of England, addressing the Governor-General elect, expressed his conviction "that he would show, as his immediate predecessor, Lord Hardinge, had shown, that resolution in administering justice, forbearance towards all neighbours and foreign powers, attention to the arts of peace, and sedulous care for the improvement of the internal condition of India, which are compatible with the utmost spirit, the utmost courage in repelling any aggression that may be made —meeting and conquering those who choose to constitute themselves the foes of the British empire in India."

The Chairman of the Court of Directors, himself a distinguished member of the Bengal Civil Service,* at the same dinner, when proposing the health of Lord Hardinge, eulogized him no less than Lord John Russell had done.

Thus, amid the plaudits of the people whom he had ruled, and already stamped by the approbation of the home authorities, closed the administration of Lord Hardinge.

We bid adieu to his Lordship with every hearty good wish. He found India held by a discontented army, threatened by invasion, and almost bankrupt. He, in all senses, righted the vessel, restored confidence to our ranks, to our allies, and our dependants; replenished the public purse, tranquillized the frontier, and brought peace and security to the long distracted Punjab. He had his reward; but the title and the pension which he earned were but a small portion of his recompense. His best reward was in the conviction of his

* Mr. Henry St. George Tucker.

own noble heart that he had honestly and bravely done his duty; that he left behind him more than a hundred millions whom he had largely blessed by enlightened and just measures; and that, returning to his native land, he was regretted by those he left behind, and warmly welcomed by men of every shade of opinion, as the pacific warrior, the happy statesman; the man who, in reality, "brought peace to Asia!"

THE INDIAN ARMY.

[WRITTEN IN 1855-56.]

RECENT discussions and events have proved, to the dullest understanding, the necessity of military reform throughout the British army. The evidence before the East India Committee, the Report of the Promotion Commissioners, and, finally, Roebuck's Crimea Report, have laid bare deficiencies, and shown that, with the best physical and moral materials in the world, with the bravest and the strongest men, the most chivalrous officers, and the largest resources of any nation, ancient or modern, Great Britain is wanting in almost all the requisites of an efficient army. Our meaning is well expressed by a friendly critic, Baron Bazancourt, in his "Five Months in the Camp before Sebastopol:"—

> "The English, those soldiers whom it is impossible to disturb in the midst of the battle, those human walls which may be pierced by the heavy fire of the enemy, but never beaten down, experienced a great misfortune at the commencement of the expedition. A defective internal administration decimated their forces more effectually than war. There was amongst them an amount of demoralization of which I cannot give the terrible account. The soldiers lay down before their huts looking sad, sullen, and exhausted. The horses died by hundreds. Inkerman had decapitated the head of the army. The vice of an improvident organization devoured the rest. It is the war in Africa which has preserved us. We owe our safety to our habits of encamping, and to our expeditions into the interior of countries. The necessity thus incurred of making provision for the smallest details, has been of the greatest utility to us in the Crimea."

India is England's Africa, if she knew how to avail herself of its opportunities. But such is not the case.

Here we have our camp life, and our expeditions; how many benefit thereby? Hundreds of officers, especially of the royal army in India, with every opportunity, go through their career, live and die, in the most child-like helplessness. They have no object, or at least the very smallest, to a worldly mind, for exertion. They are accustomed to have everything done for them. To be fed, clothed, barracked, encamped, all without a thought on their part; when, therefore, a necessity for using their senses arises, they are like babes. All goes wrong. European soldiers are exposed in long useless marches, in the hottest months, are paraded and sometimes even made to march during those months in full dress cloth clothes. Sepoys, in their lines, are equally ill dealt with. Much hardship, and even many deaths, are the result. A good deal has been done to remedy the most glaring evils. Reform is afoot: but after a hundred years' experience of Indian warfare we are still nearer the A B C than the Z of a sound, practical, military administration. We neither clothe nor arm our troops according to common sense. They are not even rationally fed. The sepoy is perhaps the best paid soldier in the world, and, the large majority of them, the worst fed. The European is at times too highly fed. Eating and drinking, rather than heat or cold, send him to his grave. In the matter of finance, thousands are spent uselessly to-day; lives are sacrificed to-morrow to save a few rupees. We might interminably run on and offer scores of examples; mortality-bills and bills of expenditure. At present we can only glance at the bare facts. There notorieties need no examples for Indian readers.

The startling disclosures of the *Times'* correspondent, and of the Crimea Commission, for a time turned attention to India; and the Press, usually little prone to do justice to the Indian army, all at once found a panacea for all Crimean and home shortcomings in Indian officers and Indian arrangements. East India Company's servants at once rose to as undue a premium as they had shortly before been, and are already again, at an unfair discount. A Bengal civilian was offered the post of Commissioner in the Crimea Commissariat inquiry, and the same able and energetic gentleman might have been the superintendent of the Smyrna Hospital. Indian contingents were called for. Certain leaders of public opinion would have sent elderly subadars and sepoys to the Caucasus, or the Crimea; and some would have done still worse, and have transferred bodily many of our European battalions from India to the seat of war. Even our hitherto very worst department, the commissariat, was suddenly, and for the nonce, trumpeted into fame, and it required Sir Charles Trevelyan's personal knowledge and matter-of-fact evidence to convince the British public that they would not gain by superseding Mr. Filder by one of Jotee Pershad's protegés. The names of some excellent soldiers were introduced into the discussions. Cheape, Steel, Stalker, Edwardes, Mayne, and Chamberlain obtained due praise; some others more than due. But the hot fit passed. India is again forgotten. Another Cabul, or another Sebastopol, is required to remind England of India's existence. In the interim, out of the 6215 officers of the Indian army, two or three dozen, some good and many bad, have been permitted to take part in the great European struggle, although there are scores, nay hundreds, of the best who would gladly join, and who might, under proper arrangements, be temporarily spared. We fear that the chief permanent result will be a considerable increase to our present stock of self-conceit. We forget that, on a small scale, we have had our own Balaklava and our own Scutari a dozen times over; and that from the days of Hyder Ali down to those of Akbar Khan, Providence only has saved our armies from destruction by hunger and thirst as well as by the sword. The exposures by the Press of incompetency, neglect, and cruelty in the Crimea, have done good. The eyes of England being on the hospitals, the harbours, the tents, and the bivouacs of the army, it will hardly again be exposed to the scenes of 1854 and 1855, that struck so much horror into every British heart. To have got rid of the fine gentlemen who do not like real soldiering, is itself a gain. To have obtained a commander possessed of physical strength, is a greater.

We are by no means so certain of the good effect of English discussions on Indian affairs. The gross ignorance with which everything Indian is discussed in England is well exemplified in the mention, during these discussions, of Brigadier Mayne. Few Indian officers have been more before the public, during the last fifteen years, than Mayne. Yet the Press, while lauding his military qualities, must needs dilate on his experience with wild tribes, and in raising irregular levies; the fact being, that he never raised a single troop or company, and that all his experience has been with as civilized soldiers as any in India.

But to our subject—the Indian army. Both the writers, whose historical works are professedly reviewed in this article, go over the same ground—the British conquest of India, from the earliest days down to the settlement of the Punjab. Mr. St. John chiefly sketches political, while Captain Rafter restricts himself to military events. Both praise the army and, in the main, the Government of India; but while Captain Rafter (a *nom de guerre*, we presume *) would knock away the "twenty-four stools" that have worked out the present glorious consummation, Mr. St. John, more logically, advocates the maintenance of a system which, in his opinion, has worked so well.

Captain Rafter professes to have been in India, but it would be difficult to elicit the fact from his book. Both writers have evidently crammed, with the purpose of cramming their readers. Country gentlemen and members of Parliament will accordingly be as often misled as instructed when they seek for information on controverted subjects from their pages. The old jog-trot is followed. There is no original information, and little of any sort in either book but what is superficial. Captain Rafter's book, though dedicated to Lord Gough, omits the battles of Ramnugger and Sadoolapore, and makes Agnew and Anderson retire to "a small fort outside the town" after the treacherous attack on them at Mooltan. Neither writer has gone much further for his facts than Mill, Wilson, Thornton, Malcolm, and Orme. Captain Rafter seems never to have heard of Williams, Broome, Buckle, or Begbie; nor is Mr. St. John acquainted with Prinsep, White, or other well-known writers on politico-military events.

The Synopsis of Evidence taken before the Select Committee of the House of Commons in 1834, is a mine of information, and the man who understandingly studies it, and the first and second Reports of 1852, will rise from them with more knowledge of Indian affairs than he could obtain from all the published abstract histories, Gleig and Macfarlane included. We say *understandingly;* for the subject of India, in any department, is not to be taken up as mere holiday amuse-

* Apparently an erroneous supposition.

ment. The figures in the Blue Books would frighten Babbage. They have given us a dozen headaches. But the less abstruse matters discussed require previous knowledge to enable the reader to separate the chaff from the grain—to appreciate the sound sense of a Colonel Alexander or Grant, and the nonsense of a Sir W. Cotton or a Sir E. Perry.

For instance; Sir E. Perry is an able English Judge and an enlightened reformer; but he made holiday trips into the interior, and therefore presents himself as *personally* acquainted with the wants of India. Himself unversed in any Indian language, he would introduce English into Courts where the judge alone understands it, where the mass *never* can do so, where the smattering that may be attained by a few attorneys or others would give them an unfair influence were such a proposal carried into effect. Sir Erskine's proposed re-distribution of the army and transfer of it to the Crown was, however, an interference of a different sort, involving a more immediate danger. He would have better evinced his wisdom by showing more modesty in the discussion of a question so foreign from all his previous pursuits. With respect to Sir W. Cotton, one anecdote will express our views regarding his Parliamentary evidence. Being asked on Committee by Lord Gough whether men of the Concan "are not so peculiar with regard to their castes?" he replied, "No, they are not; but now we get Bengal men of a caste that we prefer very much, called the 'Purdesee' caste; if they had any caste before they came to us, we never heard of its interfering in discipline." We much doubt whether either the gallant interrogator or respondent knows what is the caste of the Concan men, or even whether they are Hindus or Mahommedans. They certainly do *not* know that "Purdesee" means foreigner, and that the Bombay "Purdesee" is simply the Brahmin and Rajpoot of the Bengal army. Indeed they are entered as such, to the number of 6928 in Mr. P. Melvill's Table, at page 11, of his second examination.

In a previous essay we have afforded some information relating to all branches of the Indian army. We profess here to offer few new facts; but, with the aid of the mass of evidence before us, to correct some errors, and to sketch the present and past condition of the army, and also to point out many points in which its efficiency may be improved without increasing its expense. Costing now eleven millions a year, or little short of half the revenue of the country, the army cannot be increased without risk of bankruptcy. Reform and adaptation, not numerical increase, then, are required. Reform in the French rather than in the English fashion; not in pipe-clay details, but in arms, accoutrements, and drill; above all, in tone and *morale*. In putting not only the right sort of soldier of *all ranks* and *creeds* in the right place, and giving him an object and a motive for simple duty, but offering him inducements to zeal and exertion. In short, to substitute to a certain extent, rewards for *merit*, in lieu of for *old age*. Our remarks must necessarily be desultory, and will touch the prejudices and even the interests of many. They will, therefore, not be popular; but we trust they may be useful.

We have vainly sought for exact detailed states, at different periods, of the Indian army, in Blue Books, in histories, in army lists, as also from private sources. Captain Rafter quite misleads his reader. He gives two European regiments, instead of *three*, to each Presidency, though a third was raised a twelvemonth before his book was published. He calls all the Engineers "Royal Corps."

What he means by "twelve regiments of irregular infantry" and "sixteen of local militia" in Bengal, we are at a loss to imagine. The expression, "militia," smacks of his book being a "get up" in Paternoster Row. Unfortunately we have no militia in India. All are mercenaries—the most faithful in the world, but still mercenaries. The men who fought against us under Mahratta and Sikh banners are now our trusty soldiers. They are ours to the death, so long as we keep covenant with them. Their salt is their country and their banner. We cannot expect and do not deserve more: we have done little to induce *personal* attachment in sepoys or in any other class. The time, we hope, is coming, when both will have greater reason than at present to fight for love of our supremacy.

The evidence before Parliament has scarcely assisted us more than Captain Rafter has done; we have puzzled ourselves for very many hours over the Blue Book figures and tables, but have not succeeded in reconciling the statements of the different authorities or even the evidence of the same individual at different times. We have, therefore, concocted a table for ourselves, which will be found on the other side of the page.

Tabular Statement of the Army of India in January 1856, *including all and Irregular Corps officered from the Line ; also*

Presidency.	East India Company's Commissioned Officers.	Regiments of Her Majesty's Cavalry.	Her Majesty's Infantry.	European Troops Horse Artillery.	Native Troops Horse Artillery.	European Battalions Foot Artillery.	Native Battalions Foot Artillery.	Irregular Artillery Men.	Gun Lascars and Gun Drivers.	Engineers and Sappers.
Bengal . . .	2,907	1	14	9	4	6	3			1,200
Madras . .	2,019	...	4	6	...	4	2			1,369 (Madras and Bombay)
Bombay . .	1,289	1	4	4	...	2	2			
Total Corps, &c., &c. .	...	2	22	19	4	12	7			
At an average of . .		700	1,100	140	110	337	640			
Total strength	6,215	1400	24,200	2660	440	4,044	4,480	1,530	7,490	2,569

Grand Total . . . .

Of the 6215 officers, 782 are medical. Invalid officers are not included, but simply those on the strength of regiments. Police Battalions and Police Horse are not included, but only corps included in Army Lists. The one weak corps of Cutch Horse is counted with the two *strong* regiments of Scinde Horse as a total of three average corps. In the same way two

Her Majesty's and the Honourable Company's Troops; all the Contingent. the Field Regular and Irregular Guns attached.

East India Company's Regiments European Infantry.	Regular Regiments Native Infantry.	Irregular Regiments Infantry.	Regular Cavalry.	Irregular Horse.	Veterans. European.	Veterans. Native.	Ordnance and Commissariat, &c., Warrant and Non-Commissioned Officers.	Subordinate Medical. European.	Subordinate Medical. Native.	Guns. Regular.	Guns. Irregular.
3	74	41	10	31	368	...	Europeans.	...	320	198	78
3	52	6	8	4	304	2,041		...	17	138	24
3	29	8	3	6	28	483		...	235	78	0
9	155	55	21	41						516	
1,000	1,100	930	450	580							
9,000	170,000	51,150	9,450	23,780	700	3,424	300	339	652	...	...
.	.	.	.	.	.	.	.	.	.	323,823	

and three corps or detachments are occasionally clubbed. The grand total 323,823 includes 48,519 European officers and soldiers; and 275,304 natives, 516 field guns, as also a small mountain train, are attached. Three hundred battery guns and as many mortars might be brought into the field within a month.

We submit this account to our readers with much confidence, as containing a nearer approximation to the total strength of the Army, and even of its details, than any other published document.

In preparing the above table we have derived assistance from Mr. Philip Melvill's evidence, but have not always been able to ascertain his meaning, nor are we satisfied that his figures are always correct. Most of ours are taken from the Army Lists. Mr. Melvill gives no details of the contingents, but clubs them at 32,000 men, which is above their strength.* We have entered them in our table, with other Irregulars, under their several heads, Artillery, Cavalry, and Infantry. It will be observed that we estimate the Army at 323,823, which though differing in detail, closely agrees with Mr. P. Melvill's total of 289,529, added to 32,000 contingents. Our total strength includes 1400 Dragoons, 24,200 Royal Infantry, 2660 Horse Artillery, 4044 Foot Artillery, 6215 officers of the Company's Army, 9000 Company's Infantry, 700 veterans and 300 Ordnance, Warrant, and N. C. Staff, making a total of 48,519 European officers and soldiers. The 275,304 natives include 2569 Sappers, 4480 Foot and 440 Horse Artillery, 9450 Regular and 23,780 Irregular Cavalry; also 170,000 Regular, and 51,150 quasi local or Irregular Infantry,† and 516 guns, are attached, 138 being Horse Artillery.

This vast army occupies about 1,350,000 square miles

* Since writing the above we have observed that Mr. Melvill reckons the Guicowar and Mysore contingents as part of his 32,000, and as being on the same footing with the Gwalior and Hyderabad contingents; but such is not the case. The two latter are disciplined bodies, officered by English gentlemen; the others, especially the Guicowars, are neither officered nor disciplined.—H. M. L.

† They are more regular than the regular battalions of Clive's time, and indeed differ little from the regulars except in having only three officers instead of twenty-four. Few of them can correctly be called local.—H. M. L.

of country, and protects and overawes about 150 millions of people. There is, therefore, about one soldier to 465 of the population, but so unequally divided, that in the Punjab the proportion is one to 200, whereas in Bengal it is one to 3000. Intermediately and in the south, it varies according to the circumstances of the country, a single regiment being here and there stationed at long intervals, but more frequently a brigade with cavalry and guns being located together.

The army as above detailed, does not include the Punjab Police battalions, the Scinde, and other organized Police, altogether numbering at least 16,000 drilled, and well armed, soldiers; most of them quite equal to average Irregulars.* To these may be added about one hundred thousand *ordinary* Police and Revenue peons, the "Idlers" of Sir Charles Napier. He estimated the number in the Bengal and Agra Presidencies at 158,000; but the correct number is 59,000, and in the Punjab 11,000. In somewhat similar proportion 30,000 will be the number for Bombay and Madras. If to this hundred thousand, we add the village police throughout the country, an array of numbers equal to the whole strength of the army might be made. And if we count, as our predecessors the Moguls would have done, or as any European Government but our own would do, the armies of Native States situated *within* our limits, we may nearly complete the full million, and rival Xerxes of old, or the Czar of today. That we allow the village police of Bengal to be breakers, instead of conservators of the peace, is surely our own fault. If they commit dacoitees and overawe landholders and planters, and act energetically *against* the law, *for a motive*, they *can* also, for a motive, fight

* We have taken no account of the projected Oude contingent and Bengal Police battalion.—H. M. L.

dacoits to maintain the law. Whole districts in the North-Western Provinces filled with the brethren of the fighting classes of Oude have never, during the last seventy years, seen a British sepoy. Sir George Clerk, no mean conservator of the peace, in his evidence before Parliament, considered it quite feasible to make use of the 30,000 to 40,000 hereditary village police of Bombay, now set aside, though still enjoying service lands.

In regard to native armies, when we were comparatively weak, they fought on our side. The Nizam helped cordially at Seringapatam. Less cordially different Mahratta chiefs have at times done so. The Rajpoots were more true to us than we were to ourselves during Monson's retreat. Sikh contingents served at Bhurtpore, and in the Nepal hills. The Sikh army, in its worst days, helped us to force the Khyber, and a portion even accompanied us to Cabul. The Goorkhas periodically offer their services, and Golab Singh's regiments have, on two occasions, fought valiantly by our side in Hazara. Above all, the Bhauwalpore Nawab fought our battle when the weather was thought too hot for us to fight it ourselves. Bearing these facts in mind, we would steer a mean course between those who would have made over Delhi and Agra to the Rajpoots during the Sikh war, and Sir Charles Napier's alarm of the Goorkhas, of Hyderabad, Golab Singh, and the Burmese. Indeed, we are of opinion, that all but the last might without difficulty be induced to aid in the conservation of the public peace.

The expense of the army, including the dead-weight, is eleven millions a year, or nearly one-half the revenue of India. To increase it, as many suggest, would be to risk bankruptcy. It already exceeds, by 158,000, the strength when Lahore and Gwalior had large hostile armies at our very doors; and is 30,000 in excess of the highest numbers during the Burmah and Sikh wars. Allowing, then, the police in all its branches to do ordinary police work, as in good hands it is amply able to do, we have the army to support it and to watch a sea-girt frontier, whence nothing can touch us, the Nepal and north-west borders where we are scarcely less safe, and to owerawe the rabble portions of the Hyderabad army, and deal with Sonthal and other half-armed savages, and even less-formidable discontented chiefs.

For these purposes our means are most ample, if we are true to ourselves. In the words of the first Punjab Report:—

"It is not open war that is to be guarded against (at Lahore), but secret intrigue, and outbursts of small bands of desperate men: against the first, the best remedy is a mixture of the different arms, with a large sprinkling of Europeans; for the other, irregular horse, and such infantry as, unencumbered with baggage, can be under arms and in movement at an hour's notice."

"One thousand (1000) men (half cavalry, half infantry), and two guns, put in motion within two hours of the news of a disturbance reaching any of our stations, and able to traverse the country at the rate of twenty or thirty miles a day, will do more to secure the peace of the Punjab than the tardy assemblage of armies. Indeed, we do not hesitate to state that our anxiety is rather on account of the number of troops, and the system on which we understand they are to be located, than of any deficiency of force."

The above passages entirely express our opinion. There is nothing in the length or breadth of the plains of India that could for an hour stand against such a force. Had such an one been put in motion at the outset of the Sonthal insurrection, the whole affair would not have lasted as many weeks as it has months. Had the ten thousand men that had been told off on the north-west frontier to meet disturbance promptly marched on Mooltan, in 1848, there would probably have been no siege, or, at least, the affair would have been as insignificant as it proved momentous. Decisive and energetic measures have never yet failed, though contrary courses have often brought us very near destruction. Arcot, Plassey, Buxar, Assaye, and Laswaree, tell their own tales, as do Baillie, Monson, and Elphinstone theirs. With less means than Monson, Goddard successfully performed twice his task. By a bold front Goddard marched across the continent of India, and carried everything before him. Monson, by distrusting his troops, by retreating when he ought to have advanced, drew Holkar after him, and lost his army. A few hours' stand, or a single march in the right direction, would have saved Baillie. A three-mile movement would have preserved Elphinstone, even after months of insane delusion. The very first day he taught the Affghans their game. Instead of attacking the rabble, who had murdered Burnes in the city, he called in his detachments and kept close within his intrenchments, letting nothing but hunger move him. A single regiment would have dispersed the mob on the first day. For three days the very men who afterwards destroyed our army supported Mackenzie and Trevor in the city, and eventually aided their retreat. Thus it will always be. Providence helps those who help themselves. Those who don't, need not look for friends anywhere, especially in the East. Lords Hardinge and Gough won Ferozeshah by holding their ground during the night. Lord Gough lost the fruits of Chilianwalla by *not* following the same course.

Rome conquered the world by never yielding a foot, by never confessing herself beaten, by rising with renewed courage from every defeat. We require such fortitude more than Rome did. As yet our tents are only pitched in the land. We have a numerous and a noble army, but six-sevenths of it are of the soil. We have *one* fortress in all India. We offer no inducement to extraordinary fidelity, even while we place our magazines, our treasuries, and our very throats at the mercy of any desperado. While we English are thus reckless, we, both at home and in India, are more easily panic-stricken than, perhaps, any brave people in the world. Not only does a Cabul, or a Chilianwalla, strike terror from one end of the country to the other, but a simple murder, a Sonthal or a Moplah outbreak, has scarcely less effect. With few exceptions *there is no preparation to meet sudden danger. There is the most helpless alarm when it does occur.*

Russia did not wait until she was attacked, to fortify Sebastopol, Bomarsund, and a hundred other points. She *will now* lose character if, at the *present* juncture, she fortify St. Petersburgh and Moscow. Let us profit by experience. Let us put our house in order. We know not how soon a coalition may press Britain as Russia is now pressed. While the war lasts there will be no undue economy; but should peace occur to-morrow we run the risk of reverting to the old apathy, that left the whole coast of England undefended, and only thirty guns in the isles available for field service at the very time we were expecting war with France.

Let us not be misunderstood; we are no alarmists. We only testify to what we have witnessed during the last twenty years. Our disgust was often great at what we did so witness. History testifies to the preceding eight years. We have vividly before our eyes the terror of Madras when Hyder Ali's horsemen swept its suburbs. The alarms caused by the failures of the first Nepal campaign; also those by supposed Mahratta combinations, and by Pindaree incursions, by Murray's and by Monson's retreats, by the occupation of Furruckabad, and the beleaguerment of Delhi, and, lastly, by our four failures at Bhurtpore. Even greater, though utterly without reason, was the panic at Calcutta at the outset of the first Burmah war. Chittagong was reported in flames. Bankers asked to be allowed to send their cash to Fort William, and Burmah war-boats were reported on the salt-water lake; and all this because the Calcutta militia ran away at Ramoo. These are historical facts. Nor were the whisperings of alarm less loud on the occasions of the murders in 1848, or when, in the ensuing year, six Malay-like Sikhs sold their lives in an onslaught on a whole European regiment at Lahore. Or, on each Moplah affair, though the number of fanatics concerned was scarcely more numerous than in that of Lahore. Finally, our readers will remember how the murders of Mackeson and Connolly, and the attack on Mackenzie, were received. The first was supposed to be connected with a simultaneous rise at Peshawur and invasion from the Khyber; the others, as the forerunners of the assassination of all Europeans.

It must be pleasant to our enemies, and amusing to others who watch our arrogance and insolence in ordinary times, to observe the dastard fear with which many of our numbers receive such events. The loud talk, even in mess-rooms, of general insurrection, the loading of pistols, and the doubling of sentinels. Such acts are all wrong. They tend to produce the very danger that is feared. It is right *always* to bear in mind that we are but encamped in the land. We are dwelling "in the tents of Shem." We have yet to prove the permanence of the encampment, whether it is to be rudely broken up in blood, whether to be a Mogul, "Oordoo," a Mahratta, or a Sikh "Lushkur," or "Chaonee;" or whether, after a fertilizing and blessed rule of centuries, we are voluntarily to hand over regenerated India to her own educated and enlightened sons. But whatever be our and India's destinies, our obvious duty is to avoid all *unnecessary* occasion of danger, at the same time *always* calmly and unostentatiously to stand to our arms. The spirit of Wellington's and Cromwell's words should be our motto, and always in our hearts, "Trust in God," "Keep your treaties," and "Keep your powder dry."

To such of our readers as are disposed to tax us with exaggeration in the above rough sketch, we recommend a glance at recent newspaper statements regarding Connolly, Mackenzie, and the Sonthal disturbances. Above all, let them read Sir William Napier's pamphlet of 1854 on the Dalhousie and Napier controversy. They may then blush for British officers. It is difficult to know whether William Napier believed those incendiary and dastardly reports. If he did he was as credulous as his gallant brother when the latter perceived danger from Hyderabad, Burmah, and Cashmere. Such records of our shame, however, abound in the newspaper correspondence of the Affghan, Scinde, and Sikh wars. Wellington and Raglan were equally molested by scarecrows; and according to the accounts from our own ranks, Spain should have been lost, and the army before Sebastopol destroyed. The public enunciation of such opinions is by few; the talkings and murmurings are by many. Even brave men—men ready to lead the storming party, or to die at their posts—consider themselves privileged to talk in strains they would never permit in the ranks under them; strains that must weaken their own influence, and might even endanger their own lives.

We freely admit that, with the march of civil improvement, much has been done, during the last few years, to improve our military position. But, in the words of Napoleon, moral is to physical force as three to one, and moral strength is not *altogether* at the bidding of Governor-Generals, Commanders-in-Chief, or subordinate leaders. But, to a great extent it is. The army at Candahar *never* lost heart, because Nott kept his. MacLaren's brigade, intended for Ghuznee, failed even to reach Khelat-i-Ghilzie, because MacLaren never *expected* to carry out his orders. It did not require a Xenophon to do so. Havelock, Monteith, Richmond, Mayne, MacGregor, Broadfoot, Pottinger, MacKenzie or Backhouse, with many others engaged in Affghanistan, would have saved not only Ghuznee but Cabul. The futile attempt of MacLaren did mischief. It added to the previous discouragement of our own people; it gave courage to the Affghans. The fact is notorious. Mahomed Akbar had failed in an attack on the citadel of Cabul held by Shah Soojah; but the same night, hearing of MacLaren's retreat, he renewed the assault, and succeeded. With Cabul also fell Ghuznee, and Khilat-i-Ghilzie was left to its fate, for Craigie to make a defence not often surpassed. The counsel of a few brave hearts saved Jellalabad after their own Government had abandoned them.

It was the moral depression of Wilde's brigade, added to the shameful manner in which it, a body of four sepoy battalions with a hap-hazard brigadier and brigade-major, taken from their own ranks, without a single other staff officer, without carriage, commissariat, guns, or cavalry, was sent to Peshawur, that not only prevented its reaching Jellalabad, but nearly caused its own destruction in the Khyber. The Blue Book records Sir Jasper Nicholl's opinion—"I have yet to learn the use of guns in a pass." On this wondrous conclusion, a general who, four-and-twenty years earlier, had himself done good service in a mountain country, or rather, we suspect, on the preconceived opinion that Jellalabad *must* be lost, acted. It would have been more honest, sensible, and humane, to have boldly refused to permit a man to cross the Sutlej. *That* chapter of Indian military history has yet to be written. Kaye's work, admirable as it generally is, has not done justice to those concerned, but has done very much more than justice to the Commander-in-Chief. Few officers have been worse treated than the gallant and unfortunate Wilde. As brave a soul as ever breathed, he was driven, broken-hearted, to his grave.

We might adduce scores of such examples, bad and good, from past Indian history, of the effect of prestige and of leading; of good and of bad conduct, by the very same men, all induced by individual example, or by the moral effect of circumstances. No soldier is more open to the influence of all the above causes than the sepoy. He has a wonderful opinion of the "Ikbal" of the Company. He has also a keen perception of the merits or demerits of his officers. He loves the memory of the commander who has led him successfully; and, in extreme old age, will talk of the subaltern who was kind to him and shared his dangers.*

In the track of Monson's retreat, we have repeatedly heard an old subadar recount the doings of his own corps, going over not only the names of his own officers, but of others with whom he was not immediately connected. Telling how nobly Lucan died in covering the

* Malcolm's anecdote of the old native officers, always taking their sons to salaam to the pictures of Coote and Medowes in the Town Hall of Madras, but of their making a distinction in favour of the former, is an example of the advantage of long intimacy with sepoys. Sir William Medowes was an admirable soldier. On the breaking out of the American war, being transferred from a corps he had long commanded, he called for volunteers to accompany him, and every man stepped out. Such an officer must everywhere be loved, but probably he could not talk to natives, and therefore lost one important engine of influence. Sir Eyre Coote was perhaps as badly off in regard to the languages, but he had more knowledge of the habits of sepoys. Let us not be told that Hastings and Clive could not converse with natives. They were giants: rules are not for such.—H. M. L.

retreat through the Mokundra Pass; how the 12th N. I. was destroyed in covering the passage of the Bunnas River. History corroborates the old man's tale, and tells how the sepoys bade their officers keep heart; "we will take you safe to Agra." Captain Rafter records that "out of 12,000 men, scarcely 1000 entered Agra, without cannon, baggage, or ammunition." The guns dragged by bullocks were, *of course*, lost in a country which in the rains is a quagmire; but our author *has*, unintentionally no doubt, exaggerated the tale of misery and disaster. Never was more devotion shown by a mercenary army. With Holkar at their heels, slaying them like sheep, or sending them in noseless, or otherwise maimed, to terrify their comrades, and on the other hand, offering them service with the prospect of high command in his own ranks; there were scarcely more desertions from the sepoys' battalions than there have been from the British ranks at Sebastopol.

Monson's affair was one, *entirely*, of trust and of prestige. Affairs were ill-managed, but the sepoys stood by him as by Matthews and Baillie, because they looked to the Company's Star;, because in all points they trusted and respected the Government. In those days it was not unusual for the pay of the troops to be six, twelve, and even twenty months in arrears. The army was then numerically not half its present strength; but our character as soldiers was superior to what it is at present. Strange, that after we have conquered all around, we should have lost weight with our own people. Monson was a brave man and somewhat retrieved his own *personal* character at Bhurtpore; but the effect of his retreat nearly negatived all Lord Lake's victories.

Hector Munroe, Coote, Ochterlony, Adams, Malcolm, and Munro were men of a different stamp. With them there was confidence on both sides. In full reliance on his troops, Ochterlony, with sepoys alone, succeeded where royal officers and royal troops had failed. Gillespie's prompt gallantry rescued Vellore, though the same general, by impetuosity at Kalunga, sacrificed his own life and virtually lost the campaign. It would be a pleasant task to tell of Arcott, Onore, Masulipatam, Korigaum, and Setabuldee. We point to them simply as illustrations of the happy effects of mutual trustfulness. We might also with advantage glance at other and more recent affairs of opposite complexions. We shall, however, not, on this occasion, do so.

The moral of our dissertation is to take advantage of the present crisis in Europe, and, while we have no *present* cause of alarm in India, to take warning from the past. Much we repeat has been done. Much rottenness has been swept away. Many departments have been reformed. Some portions of the empire have been put in good state of defence. Less expensive but equally efficient bodies of troops have been raised, thus combining economy with efficiency. Above all, some steps have been taken to give us Commanders-in-Chief, having the use of their limbs and with their senses about them. We are not henceforward to have the dregs of the lives of gallant veterans who, during health and strength, were never entrusted with important command; nor are we to have as generals of division and brigade, men whose only guarantee of efficiency is old age, whose very existence is often a token of their never having earned command, who have kept themselves in clover, during the legitimate years of working life, and thus, while generous souls have sunk in the struggle, survive to win the prizes.

Another and more urgent step is wanted. There must be a bar against the command of regiments being the reward of thirty and forty years of incompetence. We can even do better with bad generals, than with bad regimental officers. Inkermann was won by the individual action of regiments, not by the strategy or tactics of generals. Most of our Indian battles have been so won. The appointments of Generals Anson and Grant are auguries of good. There may be abler and more experienced commanders, but both have common sense, the use of their limbs and of all their faculties. Let them see that their subordinates enjoy similar advantages. Neither Wellingtons nor Washingtons are expected, but it is not therefore necessary we should wait till the quantity of sense and strength that officers have been endowed with, has evaporated, before they are employed in command. No such absurdity is perpetuated in ordinary life. No brewer or baker waits till his workman is superannuated before he promotes him to the post of foreman; a pension is the fitting reward for old age. Some officers now in command, to the injury of the service, were good men and true twenty years ago,—others were never fit for a corporal's charge; and only in a seniority service could have escaped from the subaltern ranks. Chief Judges, Residents, and Commissioners, are not the oldest men in the service. Metcalfe, Jenkins, Elphinstone, Clerk, and Munro performed good service when under thirty years of age. On the bench, if anywhere, age is wanted, or at least is not an incumbrance. We reverse the order —we have young judges and old divisional and even regimental commanders. We have boys on magisterial benches, hoary age commanding Light Horse.

We implore the attention of all the authorities at home and in India, to these glaring inconsistencies. Lord Hardinge, Sir Charles Napier, Lord Gough, all testify to the necessity of a change. *No one denies it.*

Honour will be to him who, notwithstanding the outcry that will follow, will change the system that has brought irregular troops into fashion, to the disparagement of Regulars, thus averring that three selected and comparatively young officers are preferable to a dozen or sixteen haphazard ones, commanded by such men as are generally found at the head of regiments of the line. Some system must be devised, by having the whole army in one general list; or by having regiments of two, three or four battalions, or by striking off inefficients, and by admitting the transfer of officers from one corps to another, to *secure* the command of regiments to those, between the ages of thirty and fifty, who have at least not given *proofs* of incompetency. There are men now commanding regiments *known* to have greatly injured, if not ruined, more than one corps, and who are working hard to destroy the credit of their present charges. We have heard the new Commander-in-Chief of the Madras army regret the *necessity* of putting such men in command. We confess never to have been able to perceive the *necessity*. It has been a custom rather than an obligation, and the sooner it is abrogated, the better for the Indian army.

Let officers rise to rank much as at present by seniority; but drive inefficients to resignation by positively refusing them command. Let there be tests for every grade of authority. Let no officer obtain the command even of a company until he has *proved* his qualification. The present tests are altogether insufficient. The examination should be systematic, and not dependent on the whims of commanding officers or examiners. Graduated for each rank, it should *oblige* each officer to evince *moderate* ability and *moderate* application. All men are not intended by nature for soldiers. The sooner incapables find out the mistake of their parents in having put them into the wrong line, the better for themselves and for the service. In no army are higher qualifications required. Is it good that *one* single individual officer should be a laughing-stock to his men? They are nearly fifty to one of us. Our staff should be good—the best *procurable*, or it must be more than useless—mischievous, nay dangerous.

On this the most important question concerning the army, we desire to suggest no specific rules, but simply, though most earnestly, to recommend those of common sense. Let a mixed committee of officers from the three Presidencies be appointed to consult and report on this, and other matters, and let their report be published, and, after discussion, be acted on, as far as possible; but unhappily there is less lack of information than of desire or ability to act on it. Some twenty years ago such a committee did report on artillery matters, and made many excellent suggestions, few of which have to this day been carried out.* General Patrick Grant tells us, in his evidence before Parliament, that cavalry matters were also, though less formally, reported on many years ago, but still the strife goes on between Regulars and Irregulars, as to straight swords, sabres, spears, carbines, pistols, bits, and saddles. All this is bad. There is a good and a bad way for everything, and what is good for one Presidency is good for another. Shafts and poles, Bengal system and Royal system, are *not all* best. The best ought to be insisted on for all. And so with cavalry. If an Irregular is, as Sir Charles Napier and

* The present Emperor of the French, then the exile Louis Napoleon, in his treatise on Artillery, called attention to the labours of that committee.—H. M. L.

others insist, the most efficient soldier, it is foolery to pay double the money for an inferior article.

But, whether by a committee or any other authority, let the vital questions be settled. Respect as far as possible present incumbents, by giving them time to meet examinations, &c.; but, at *any* cost, rid the service of notorious incompetents, and prevent incapables from obtaining command. If the cry be, "vested interests," and "men will not enter the service on insecure terms," we answer that able and energetic men are most likely to enter a service that encourages ability and energy. We dont want the mass that join the army simply as an easy provision. For England's glory and India's safety, we are better without such. We would not deprive Directors of patronage, but the tests at home should be much higher, and, as already suggested, should be continued up to the rank of Field Officer, as the rule now obtains in H. M.'s Service.

There must be a Staff Corps; whatever may be its inconveniences, they will be less than those that now obtain. The French "Etat-Major" might, to a certain extent, be our model. The rewards of the staff should not be on such a scale as to prevent good officers desiring to stay with their corps. When commands are open to them after fifteen or twenty years, instead of after thirty and thirty-five, there would be more content in the regimental ranks; without contentment there can hardly be efficiency. In proof of the present prevailing spirit we annex, verbatim, an extract from a recently-received letter, from an officer of ability who has done good service to the State, and who obtained command of his regiment after about twenty-five years' service.

"As to the service, I have long since ceased to take any interest in it; for however hard I may work, or however much I may know or do, I find myself not one bit better off than the fool who knows and does nothing; therefore, beyond doing exactly as I am told, I do nothing.

"You will, I dare say, laugh when I tell you I never mount one (a horse) but to go to parade, and this I consider a great bore, and never go out of a walk."

The above, if not a favourable specimen of the spirit of the writer, is at least the honest opinion of an able officer who has been more than usually fortunate. We could match with it a similar letter, received from a captain of a different Presidency, of nearly equal standing, who is yet several years from a command. Ten or fifteen years ago, both these officers were full of zeal and energy. They were of the Chamberlain and Jacob school rather than of the race of incapables. Chamberlain and Jacob would be as they are, after thirty years of subordinate regimental duty.

The Native officer question is only second to that of the European. With efficient commanders there would soon be efficient subordinates, but to expedite matters and to prevent tyranny, perhaps convulsions, extraneous help and Government authority are required. In this, as in other matters, perfectly different systems obtain, not only at different Presidencies, but in different regiments of the same Presidency. In Bombay and Madras, the merit-fostering rule is followed; in Bengal all sorts of rules and systems obtain. There *is* authority, though not very explicit, for promotion by merit, and provision is made, by increase of pay after terms of seven years, for the superseded, but recent orders have directed differently. The consequence is, that commanding officers do much as they like. One finds reason for promoting all the old, another all the young. One pesters and persecutes the veterans, another objects to the smart fellows who "can drill the regiment as well as any officer, and who wear trousers as neat as the adjutants." These are the extremes. Discipline suffers, and deserving Native soldiers of all ranks suffer, and are often driven with disgust from the service.

We confess to a decided preference, notwithstanding all the objections of Lord Hardinge, Sir Charles Napier, and other high authorities, for the Madras and Bombay systems. We allow it to be dangerous to bring forward young energetic native soldiers, to the rank of subadar and there to stop, and that it would be, *on the present system*, safer to have subadars of sixty rather than of thirty years of age. But it is the danger of the power-loom over the fire-side wheel; the danger of the steam carriage over the poney chair. Where is to be the end of our fears if we shirk efficiency in dread of our own tools turning on us? It is our obvious duty to put the right man in the right place, *and to keep him there by self-interest*. We desire no such radical change as to put armies, or even very important posts, or detachments, under Native officers. We desire not the Carthaginian, or the Mogul, or the latter Roman systems, but to a certain extent, that which influences the autocratic Governments of Russia, France and Austria. Surely we can afford as much license as they can. If Asiatics and Africans can obtain honourable position in the armies of Russia and France, surely Indians, after tried service of a century under England's banner, are entitled to the same boon—nay, justice. We desire no extremes. We would not, as Austria did in the Hungarian war, place our magazines in the enemy's hands. We would avoid risking them in questionable ones. We would not, as in our own early times, by undue temptation, turn honest soldiers into traitors,* but we would not drive

* Mahommed Issoof's is a case in point. He was more useful than most of the European officers in the early wars of the Carnatic. Faithful, gallant, and enterprizing, he conducted sieges, defended posts, and earned supplies and reinforcements, at critical times, through the enemy's country. But he was tempted beyond his strength. He was put in

them from our service or, worse still, permit them to remain in it in sullen discontent. If among the 6000 European officers such feelings prevail as we have shown in the preceding extract, have we any right to expect that among the 275,000 natives of the army, they do not exist to a much greater extent?

This subject is too much pooh-poohed or altogether blinked. If the correspondence of Native soldiers was as patent to us as that of our European comrades, we should better understand their feelings. Those who do associate with them can testify to the disgust of the very best at their present position. The Bengal Baboos of Calcutta, and the Parsees of Bombay are among our best-treated and most-contented subjects. The latter highly-enlightened class is a loyal and useful section of the community; and some of its legal members have recently been appointed to high office; as have also some of the Bengal Baboos. These latter however are not contented. They complain that the highest salary allowed to their class is 1200 rupees a month, and that very few positions of 1000 rupees, 800 rupees, and 600 rupees, though many of 250 rupees a month, are open to them. Native civil officers of the higher grades are remunerated throughout the provinces at somewhat the above rates. In every district are to be found half a dozen, whose salaries average 250 rupees, with two or three on 400 or 500 rupees a month. Exceptional cases run up to 800 and 1000. The latter are still too few to command honest devotion. More prizes, and some of them of greater value than any yet conceded, are wanted.

Such, however, as they are, they greatly exceed those of the Native army. The largest pay obtainable in an

possession of a fort, and made a renter of the surrounding district. In such times, what Native could have stood such a test? Some Europeans could not.—H. M. L.

army of 275,000 soldiers of the soil is 300 rupees a month, and we do not know more than three men enjoying such pay. The Hyderabad pay of a ressaldar, which is the title, in that province, of a Native cavalry commandant, used to be 413 rupees, but it has recently been reduced to 300. Jemadars of troops (virtual ressaldars) have also been lowered from 165 to 150, the rate of ressaldars throughout the Bengal Irregular Cavalry. The pay of a subadar in the regular army is 67 rupees a month, with 25 rupees additional, making 92 rupees, to *one* subadar in every regiment, as subadar Major. *This is the highest bonâ fide pay enjoyable by an infantry soldier.* When *marching*, he receives fifteen rupees batta, which seldom covers his extra expenses. The "*Moniteur*" constantly recounts the rewards of bravery, in all ranks, of the French army. To one private soldier, "for keeping his place in the ranks when badly wounded." To another, "for being the first in the breach;" to a third, "for saving his captain's at the loss of his own legs, by throwing aside a live shell." To a fourth, "for helping to extinguish the flames around the magazine." Such matters, if not wholly overlooked in the British army, are not so noticed as to excite emulation or create any hearty desire to do likewise. What rewards have been given to the subaltern's party which for half an hour, last November, stood on the top of the magazine of the Light Division, covering it with saturated tarpaulins, while all around was on fire, and while shells and rockets were falling thick on every side? But, nearer to ourselves, what reward has been given to the sergeant of the Pegu magazine who, last year, heroically performed a similar feat? Such men are the real heroes of an army. Any fellow can charge *with* a crowd, or can stand between his comrades, to be mowed down or ridden over. He seldom can help himself. Many, in such positions, would run away if they could: they cannot, and they come out of the fray, heroes. But the soldier who, with no excitement before him, courts death, in the path of duty, deserves more especial honour—indeed all the honour, and all the reward, that can be bestowed. It is true that in the British army after every battle, strings of names are submitted for brevet rank and honours. There is seldom a response in any man's heart to the accuracy of those lists. Lord Gough got brevet rank for one officer for carrying, "orders through the hottest of the fight," though he was not in the battle at all: for another for "leading a brigade," though he was in bed. Some of our readers will also remember his Lordship's favourable mention of the gallant brigadier, who, he said, "manœuvered skilfully in the rear." Sir Charles Napier was the first of our generals who mentioned a private soldier in his despatches. How rarely has the good example been followed, even in the Crimea! Napier's and a very few other cases excepted, we do not remember ever seeing a native soldier, *in orders*, though we could narrate scores of instances of individual valour. Of a naick and six swimming the Buri Gunga in the face of the enemy; of a single trooper carrying a despatch through the enemy's lines, at Setabuldee; of two troopers in open day, fathoming the ditch at Bhurtpore; of a ressaldar leading his single troop through Shere Singh's cavalry at Mooltan; of another, on the frontier, carrying his into the midst of twenty times their number, though covered by a bank. None of those men were held up to the admiration of their comrades. Descending to the ridiculous, we recollect a lady telling us that she had parted with her husband, going to Affghanistan, with some comfort, "as Ram Singh, the pay havildar, has promised to cover him in action, and Ram Singh is a big man." The captain came back safe, whether by Ram Singh's "*ikbal,*" we cannot say.

The nearest approach to the French system, in the Indian army, is "the Order of Merit." It is open to all ranks of the Native army for "individual gallantry" in the field, or in the attack or defence of a fortress. But, though its numbers are not *positively* limited, there are so many restrictions to its obtainment, that "the decorated" are so few as to be hardly discoverable. The order is divided into three grades. The first is only obtainable by those who have *already* won by *individual gallantry* and, step by step, the second and third grades. The badge of the first grade is a gold star with inscription—"The reward of valour." The decoration of the others is of silver, with a similar motto. All are pendant from a dark blue ribbon with red edges. With a very large acquaintance, with the Native army, we do not recollect having seen a dozen silver stars. We cannot recollect seeing *a single golden one.* Double pay is attached to the first grade, two-thirds increase to the second, and one-third to the third. These are substantial advantages to the clod of a sabreur, to the sentinel whose sinews would never have earned him a front place in the Akhara (gymnasium); but what reward are they to the adventurer whose sword, under a different régime, would have carved out for himself a principality? None. They are a mockery, ending as they do, at utmost, in extreme cases, in double pay; that is, to a ressaldar, in three hundred rupees a month, —or if he have *also* obtained the first class "Order of India" on sixty rupees additional, at fifty or sixty years of age. But *how* the first class, "Order of Merit," and *double pay* are to be obtained, we are at a loss to imagine.

He is a lucky fellow who has *one* chance "of individual valour" that is accepted, by his surviving comrades, that then satisfies the reporting Committee; that afterwards passes the ordeal of the Military-Auditor General, whose duty is, *not* to reward valour, but to watch the public purse, at all hazards; and, finally, that is sanctioned by Government. Three times has this full process of proof to be gone through, before the subadar major can obtain 92 rupees a month, added to his original ninety-two, or the ressaldar 150 + 150 = 300.

The Order of Merit, moreover, gives no handle to a man's name. The brave man is still the simple havildar, ressaldar, or subadar. In a country where words and looks are even more valued than rupees, though a hero, he is not a bahadoor. On the other hand the title, though a military one, is freely conferred on Native civilians and traders, of no better blood, and is arrogated by black and white of all ranks.

But there *is* an order that *does* confer rank and title—"The Order of British India." It is divided into two classes, each of a hundred members, the first restricted to subadars and ressaldars, and giving the title sirdar bahadoor, with two rupees a day increase of pay; the second to native officers, generally, with the title of bahadoor and one rupee a day. The decoration is a gold star, pendant from a blue ribbon. Though awarded only for good service, it is virtually the reward of old age; indeed, the wearers are mostly invalids at their homes.

The pay, including batta, of a jemadar of regular infantry (lieutenant), is 24½ rupees a month, havildar (sergeant), fourteen; naick (corporal), twelve; sepoy, seven. The pay of the sappers and native artillery is the same as infantry; both should be higher; that of the regular cavalry is considerably so.* Sepoys after sixteen years' service, with good conduct, get one rupee extra, and after twenty years two rupees; or, in all, nine rupees a month.

Such are the temptations we offer the military populations of India, and to the northern adventurers who still occasionally find their way, through the passes, and who would do so, in numbers, were there moderate inducement. The mistake is in treating all alike: in attempting to have one dead level, and still expecting active zeal and fidelity. The astonishment is that, under the present system, we should have so much of both. Present rules cannot last. They are against nature. Ninety in a hundred sepoys have every reason to be delighted with the service. Several of the remaining ten are satisfied. One, two, or three *are thoroughly, and dangerously, discontented.* The reason is plain. They feel they have that in them which elsewhere would raise them to distinction. Our system presses them down. The throne of Hyderabad is held by the descendant of one such adventurer. That of Oude is, or rather was, by another Hyder Ali, Ameer Khan. The first Holkar and the first Scindiah were such fellows as are now in our ranks, if indeed the Koorme slipper-bearer, and the goat-herd would have been received into our high-caste ranks! Golab Singh, and Runjeet Singh's grandfather, were military adventurers. Several of the generals in the Sikh service, as also some of the most powerful amils in Oude, were, originally, sepoys in our ranks.

*			IRREGULAR CAVALRY.		
Subadar Major	Rs.	150	Ressaldar	Rs.	105
Subadar	„	80	Ressaidar	„	80
Jemadar	„	32	Naibs	„	50
Havildar	„	20	Jemadars	„	45
Naick	„	16	Kote Duffadars	„	33
Trooper	„	9	Duffadar	„	28
			Sowar	„	20

Troops have a ressaldar and a ressaidar, alternately.

Those outlets FOR RESTLESSNESS AND ABILITY ARE GONE; OTHERS ARE CLOSING. It behoves us, therefore, now more than ever, to give legitimate rewards, and as far as practicable, employment to the energetic few, to that leaven that is in every lump—the leaven that may secure our empire or may disturb,—nay, even destroy it.

In early days, when Europeans *fancied* themselves more dependent on Natives than at present, they were not only more courteous, kindly, and considerate to them than they are now; but posts were then open to them that, of late years, have been closed. Mahomed Issoof's case, already mentioned, was an extreme one. In those times, Native civilians were over-paid. English civilians were denied honest wages. With few exceptions, all were accordingly dishonest. There was no check, no restraint. The tables were suddenly turned. Europeans were made honest by *honest treatment;* natives were driven to worse roguery than before, for bread. During the last twenty years, our eyes have been gradually opening in regard to Native civil establishments. If all have not been made honest, the right measures have been taken to make them so. The service is already greatly reformed. It is because the authorities seem still in the dark, regarding the *necessity* of improving the condition of the higher soldiery, that these remarks are offered. Let the sepoy soldier be treated as the civilian is; that is, let there be openings for the gentleman—for the hero. The ordinary sepoy *is amply paid.* He has even been pampered and petted. The extra battas and the donatives that he has received, have done him harm, and induced greed. We have been running fast on the shoal of the Sikh army,—of the Legionaries, the Janissaries and the Mamelukes. The many are usefully provided for, but honours and rewards, present and future, are still wanted for the few.

In what has been done to raise the condition of Native civilians, Government has been influenced by the best motive, the good of the country, the purity of the judgment seat. In what we advocate there is even a nearer interest, one that swallows up all others.

It is not easy to suggest the details of our proposed scheme; but there are points of it, open to every understanding. In the Punjab are six battalions of police; commanded by native officers. Excellent soldiers all. Some of these corps were in the Sikh service, served with Pollock's army and again under Edwardes. Two or three of them are doing frontier work; all are fully equal to average irregular battalions. Their commandants, with most of the responsibilities of command, receive only 200 rupees a month, or one-fourth the pay of a European officer in a similar position. The latter too rises to be a general, may find himself successor to Morrison, Casement, Pollock, Littler, Gilbert and Low in the Council Board. The old Native officer lives and dies a commandant on 200 rupees,* or retires on half the amount. "Lives and *rots* without hope" is the expression we once heard a comparatively young ressaldar use regarding himself. The sons of the commandant have *no opening*. They would have entered the Sikh service, as subadars, or even in their fathers' rank; if they enter ours, it must be as privates. We say, give such commandants about *half* the pay that Europeans get, and let their sons, if qualified, enter the service as jemadars, and let those of other Native officers have *some* advantages above the ordinary recruit.

Let also the officers of a certain number, say one, of the irregular corps be *entirely* Natives. A European brigadier commanding every two or three such, looking

* Present incumbents, some of them colonels in the Sikh service, receive their old rates of pay—400 or 500 rupees a month.—H. M. L.

to the *pay*, discipline, tone, &c., doing, in short, much the duty, and having the same military authority, as captains of police in the Punjab have, though interfering with details less than they do. Give in *all* irregular corps half the Company's allowances to the subadars commanding companies, who should do all the duty of captains *except* paying the men. This important duty should always be performed by a European officer *in the presence* of the commanding officer, or second in command. No room should be left for scandal or discontent. Raise also the pay of subadars from 67 rupees a month to 140, or about one-third that of captains *doing the same work*. Raise proportionally the pay of jemadars. In all corps of the line let there be no *Native officers*. Their position is anomalous and absurd. In the Bombay army there are seldom sergeant-majors or quartermaster-sergeants, because they clash with the Native officers. The Bombay authorities are quite right. It is absurd, and might prove worse than absurd, giving twenty men, "all good drills" and all "wearing tight pantaloons," commissions, and then allowing them to be bullied by vulgar uneducated Europeans, *without commissions*. The anomaly, and the heart-burnings, will be removed by having the European officers and sergeants with the stricter discipline, or rather with the more English practices, in one set of regiments; the Native officers with the looser, *the French system*, in others. By removing Native officers from corps professedly commanded, and officered by Europeans, though too often *really managed* by havildar majors, opportunity would be given to the European officer to look into the interior economy of his regiment or company. Seldom is anything of the kind done at present. So long as all is smooth and quiet on the surface, few inquiries are made. All may be rotten below; the jog-trot is followed—a mine may be ready to be sprung, for all that nine-tenths of the officers would know. *Many do not know the very names of the men of their own company.*

No great expense need be incurred in carrying out the proposed arrangement. There are plenty of regiments, an excess of men, scarcely a deficiency of officers. We repeat that organization and adaptation, mainly, are wanted. Let the one hundred and five infantry corps of the line be *gradually* converted into a hundred and twenty five service, and thirty veteran corps. Let 18 of the present 24 officers be removed from each of the 30 veteran regiments, and be divided among the 125 service ones, leaving the three field officers with one *selected* captain and two *selected* subalterns, in all six European officers. Omitting two field officers as generally absent, four officers will thus remain, *all being selections.* This would leave 540 officers available for service corps, which number, increased by eighty-five, would provide five additional officers for each, and thus increase their strength to twenty-nine. Allowing then nine for field officers, and for absentees, on private and medical leave, twenty officers, or two for each company, would be present with each service regiment.

The scheme involves the disposal of all staff officers in a staff corps, also eighty-five additional officers, and one hundred promotions to rank of captain. The proportions of the relative ranks we would thus suggest for the 125 regiments, would be three field officers, as at present, eight captains, twelve lieutenants, and six ensigns, instead of six, ten, and five, as now. And attached to each of the thirty veteran corps, three field officers (only one to be present), one *selected* captain and five *selected* subalterns.

To make this or any other scheme work, the service,

not individuals, must be considered. Incompetent field and other senior officers *must be rigorously* set aside. None incapable should be at the head of *any* corps, regular or irregular, service or veteran. There is no knowing where exigencies may arise. The Calcutta militia and the Ramgurh battalion should have as good officers and as *good arms* as the frontier regiments. There is at least no excuse for their being badly armed. It is very bad economy to send a soldier into action with any but the very best muskets in his hand. Incapables may be shelved as seconds in command, but they had better be sent home, even with a brevet step. The title of major or lieutenant-colonel will do no harm as long as it be not accompanied by authority. Old men, with their senses about them, and with the use of their legs, may command veterans, but there should be a limit to the age, even of such incumbents. The now pending orders as to vacation of staff commands are anomalous, and, if they be decided against brevet officers, will be absurd. To replace a man of fifty by one of sixty is indeed a novel mode of regenerating an army, wanting, above all wants, new blood, life and energy. Commands of *all* corps should be given to the *very best* officers available. Their staff should be strictly selections. These should be posts *of high honour*, and of considerable emolument. The veterans should have all the advantages of other corps of the line, the men being older and the Company's officers being Natives. Such corps will be available for *all* home service, that is, service within the Provinces, and will be specially valuable, if *treated with honour and consideration*, for guards on forts, magazines, and treasuries. Majors and captains should obtain brevet rank for three years' command of regiments. Subalterns of ten years' service and captains of twenty should receive one-fourth increased pay. Half batta should be abolished. It is an injustice and an inconvenience, and costs on the one hand, as much as it saves on the other.

A large proportion of the expense thus suggested may be covered by a reduction in tho strength of companies, throughout the service, and by departmental clippings; but supposing the balance of expense to be half a million a-year, which would be its utmost limit, we hold that such a sum would be well expended in making a more contented and a more efficient army. It is not a *very numerous army,* but *a really efficient and a contented one,* that is wanted. Much of the duty still performed at Bombay, and some that is done elsewhere, by the army, might with advantage be made over to the police so as greatly to relieve the ranks. Indeed, the military might be entirely relieved of escorts, jail guards, &c.

Officers should serve five years in the line before being eligible for the staff, the examinations for which, *in every department,* should be strict. Those for civil and political employ should involve the tests in the languages required of interpreters. At Madras, Tamul should be a requisite.* Exchanges should be permitted between regiments, even of different Presidencies, also between cavalry and infantry up to the rank of captain. It is ridiculous to keep a man, who cannot ride in a mounted corps. Good may be derived from exchanges, harm cannot. The armies of the Presidencies should, as at present, be kept separate with separate commanders of the forces, but with one Commander-in-Chief, relieved from the Bengal command, for all. Proper emulation, and some check, is caused by these

* Mr. P. Melvill shows that 2500 Madras Sepoys cannot express their wants in Hindustani.—H. M. L.

separations. Rates of pay have already been almost entirely assimilated. For future incumbents there should be no differences. The great question of simplifying and making plain to all ranks, what is their pay under all circumstances, has yet to be resolved. Whoever effects the measure will save much discontent, if not some mutinies.

The arrangement for the supply of Native officers will be the most difficult part of our proposed arrangements. From the hundred and twenty-five service corps of the line, let old havildars be transferred for promotion to veteran battalions for home duties, and the younger to service corps for frontier and *Sonthal*-like work. The veterans, we repeat, should be corps of honour, manned by sepoys of good character above forty years of age, or of weak and worn constitutions, from all other corps, and officered by subadars and jemadars of similar stamp, from the same quarters. The Native officers of irregular corps should be partly from their own ranks, partly young picked men from the line. Unless they are so selected, and unless they are unmistakably good men, commanding officers of irregulars will often pester their lives out. Their berths will not be worth holding. The utmost honest care will be required in making selections for transfer. We repeat, that to all these corps, veteran and irregular, *first-rate* European officers must be attached; four to the first, five to the others. Their names to be borne on the strength of the staff corps.

As a *general* rule we would require every sepoy to serve a certain period in the ranks. Consideration should also be paid to seniority, to cleanliness, smartness, and soldierly bearing, rather *than to literary acquirements*. Too much stress is now laid on reading and writing; we ought to remember that the military class, as a body, despises study. Time, at least, should be given them to get over their prejudices. Recent orders on this subject are very unpalatable to many of our best soldiers. Indeed, very few of our worthiest old warriors would be now ressaldars and subadars if they had had to pass present tests. They should not be educated *above* their positions. To add literary attainment to Pathan and Brahmin pride of birth, and still to keep Brahmins and Pathans under serjeant-majors, is a grievous mistake. There are sepoys in the Bombay army who translate treatises on drill and tactics. This is hardly safe. Havildars, unqualified for promotion to either of the above classes of corps should, on retirement, after certain terms of good service, receive a step of rank. The present system of invaliding is defective. The Madras and Bombay armies invalid eight and ten years earlier than is the practice in Bengal. With them almost any man is passed after fifty years of age, and so it generally should be. Few Native soldiers are fit for *field* service after that age, though many are up to all garrison duties at sixty. In Bengal the term for invaliding should be shortened; but at the same time there should be more check on malingering for pension after fifteen years. Veteran battalions would be a check. They exist already in Madras and Bombay; but Bengal, which most wants them, has none.

The higher prizes for the very select have now to be considered. They should as of old, be commands of Hill forts, and jaghirs. Also, as at present, titles of honour and pensions, &c., but on increased scales, commensurate with the present British position, where we gave hundreds when subordinate to the nabobs of Arcot and Bengal, we should, now as successors of the Mogul, give thousands. The practice, however, has been rather reversed. Jaghirs, that were once perhaps too freely dispensed, are now *entirely* withheld. An able and deserving public servant, ambitious to possess what, above all else, a Native desires, viz.: a bit of land of his own, has now hardly a road to its obtainment but by plotting to subvert our rule. At least, so it may easily seem to him. Why oblige such conduct? The labourer is worthy of his hire,—the faithful servant of his reward. Why make him, at least in heart, a rebel, because he thinks Government an ingrate? We, intentionally, personify Government. Every Native does so. The general, colonel, commissioner, or collector is, to him the Government. He perceives the great powers for mischief in the hands of such an official; he cannot credit that he has no power to reward. He, accordingly, thinks him ungrateful. Much good service is thus lost; much bad feeling engendered. It matters little in the calm; it might matter much in the storm. Are calms so lasting, storms so rare? The objections to giving estates appear to us of no weight. Under the present settlement of estates there is protection to the cultivator. At worst the old soldier would not be harder on the ryot, than are the *Jotee Pershads* who are fast buying up villages throughout the Provinces. Or, if jaghirs be denied, let some of the zemindaries be purchased by Government and reserved, either in fee-simple, or as zemindaries, as the great rewards to the faithful soldiers of the higher ranks. Such grants need not, as a rule, be in perpetuity. Two or three lives will be a long vista to the old trooper or sepoy. *Five hundred rupees in such form* will go further than a thousand in any other. We beg attention to the fact; we write of what we know.

In the same spirit we could name a hundred forts, or other posts, which could, with perfect safety, be entrusted to Native officers, and would be prized by them as honourable retiring berths. Titles and honours are cheap; they cost nothing and are greatly valued. Medals to the mass should be abolished. Decorations are brought into contempt, when worn by individuals, or by whole regiments known to have run away, or even when largely distributed to those who were not under fire. The "Order of Merit" and that of "British India" should be largely extended, and should be open to Europeans and Natives of all ranks. There should be two branches of each, one civil and the other military. Titles should be attached to the higher grades; pecuniary grants to, at least, all the lower. There would be difficulties in the way. In what scheme are there not difficulties? The first Napoleon found no insuperable difficulties in his selections for the Legion of Honour. We doubt if either Napoleon ever decorated a notorious coward; that is, one who had given proof of cowardice. So it might be with us. The army itself can sufficiently judge such questions. After each action, let a hundred or thousand decorations be adjudged. No difficulty will be found in ascertaining who are best entitled to them. There may be heart-burnings and dissatisfaction; there cannot be more than at present. Half the value of a decoration is lost to A. B. and C., when it is also worn by D. E. and F.

We have much to say on many other points, but must reserve most of our remarks for another occasion. The great, the vital question is the officering of the army. We have roughly sketched our scheme—roughly, but we hope sufficiently to explain our meaning. Sir Charles Napier, a general of decided ability and of large experience, who had led both Bengal and Bombay troops into action, has declared that the present system is canvassed in every guard-room. To a certain extent this assertion is correct, and the fact bodes no good. Sir Charles advocated the introduction of Natives into the covenanted ranks of the army, but he would have found it difficult to carry out his scheme; caste, food, a hundred causes, will, for a half a century at least, present such amalgamation. The difficulties far exceed those of entrance into the civil and medical services, and in them they are not small. But, if all that ought to be done cannot be done, there is no reason why we we should sit still and wait until obvious rights are clamoured for; until, in a voice somewhat louder than that of the European officers, in the days of Clive, the "excellent drills" and the "tight pantalooned" combine to assert their claims. What the European officers *have* repeatedly done, may surely be expected from Natives. We shall be unwise to wait for such occasion. *Come it will, unless anticipated.* A Clive may not be then at hand.

Those who have watched events, or have studied Indian Military History, can distinctly trace almost all past murmurs and mutinies, we might indeed say *every one*, to some error or omission, trivial or great, of our own. Pay has been the great stumbling-block. Whether in Bombay, Madras, or Bengal, doubts as to the intentions of Government in regard to pay have been at the bottom of most mutinies. In Bengal such affairs have generally been exaggerated, while in Madras and Bombay they are kept quiet, if not hushed up. We confess to preferring the quiet system—washing dirty linen at home: the linen should, however, always *be* washed, somewhere and somehow; quietly, but fully.

This motive to mischief should be disposed of *at once.* It should not be in the power of any stupid commander or paymaster to refuse what Government had conceded. The Bombay rule of auditing *all* bills before payment is good; and preventing retrenchments, shuts one door of dissatisfaction. But even at Bombay, a plain unmistakable code is wanted in addition even to "Jameson's." One has repeatedly been attempted, but has always failed of accomplishment. Amusement might be derived from the narrative of the failures, if the results were less grave. We look anxiously for the very long promised Bengal Code, but fear disappointment. An officer who had scarcely done any regimental duty, with a regular corps for twenty years, aided by two young artillery officers, however clever, was not the fitting president, and they were not the fitting members, of a committee to prepare a code for all branches of the Bengal army. We strongly recommend that the new code, with all others extant, of the three Presidencies, be made over to a committee of mixed artillery, cavalry, and infantry officers, and that a code for *India* be prepared, in which *every* question, involving the rights of individuals, of all branches of the three armies, should be distinctly and unmistakably laid down in the briefest way consistent with clearness. Such a code would be more valuable than three more European regiments, or than five hundred miles of rail.

The other chief cause of mutiny is religion—fanaticism. Hitherto it has been restricted to Mahommedans. Hindus are content to be let alone. The faithful not only desire to proselytize, but go out of their way to annoy their neighbours with their ceremonies. On two or three occasions we have witnessed Mohurrum processions ostentatiously drawn up opposite a Christian church during Divine service, and there drumming lustily. The late Bolarum affair, like most Indian questions, has been taken up with party spirit. Brigadier Mackenzie possesses much of the Covenanter spirit, and Mrs. Mackenzie's book is unpopular (we hope *not* Mrs. Mackenzie, objectionable as are many parts of her work); therefore we fear the attack upon him was accepted, in some quarters, in a controversial spirit. But having read much on the subject, we cannot discover what legitimate offence was given, and fully approve the order which sentences all directly connected with the murderous attack on Mackenzie to condign punishment, and all responsible to be dismissed the service. The Hyderabad contingent, of all classes, is a distinguished body, but the Deccan Mahommedans, pretty generally, are fanatical and insubordinately disposed, beyond anything to be found elsewhere in India, except, perhaps, at Patna and on the Peshawur border. Witness Colonel Davies's murder in 1827, and the more recent mutiny of the 4th Madras Cavalry. Davies, like Mackenzie, was a fearless chivalrous fellow. Their cases were even more alike than their characters. On the impulse of the moment, the comrades of the murderers avenged Colonel Davies's death, but the murder was approved of by the Mahommedans of that day and neighbourhood, and the ringleader's grave shortly became a place of pilgrimage and a resort for Mussulman devotees. The attack on Mackenzie was also by fanatics, and was, perhaps, more premeditated. Mackenzie issued a perfectly legitimate order; it was disobeyed. His mistake was in *personally* interfering. The error nearly cost his life, and may yet do so. His wounds were frightful, few men could have survived them. His dauntless spirit sustained him. However, this and other matters of the kind should make us more than ever cautious against real offence. A cap, a beard, a moustache, a strap, all in their time have given offence. *All on pretence of religion.* But by a little management, by leading instead of drawing, almost anything may be done. The man who would not touch leather a few years ago, is now, in the words of a fine old subadar, "*up to the chin in it.*" But the same old fellow begged that the leather might stop there, and that leather caps might not *be tried.* In the corps of which that old gentleman was a worthy member, leather cap-straps had been accepted *gratis*, in preference to paying an anna or two for cloth ones. We mention the fact as showing what may be done with men who have all but mutinied because the Grenadiers were told to occupy the Light Company huts: and at another time because they *thought* they had been prohibited taking their bedding to the guard-room. Tact and management, *not Brahminism*, in officers, are wanted. Hindus and Mahommedans can respect real Christianity. They certainly do *not* respect Anglo-Hindooism.

Sir William Gomm's farewell order tells how much has recently been done for the European portion of the army. Barracks are improved; gardens, libraries, and other sources of amusement will soon be as plentiful as they used to be scarce. Little more is wanted than to *prevent* individual commanding officers nullifying the good intentions of Government, by keeping sickly men in the plains, and sending bad characters in their places to the Hills; bullying the men, torturing them with stocks, cloth coats, and hot weather drills—in short, making what are called *smart* regiments at the expense of the men's very lives. Railroads, waggon trains, and steamers should now prevent Europeans being moved between April and November. Too much is heard of the sun (*not from them*) when they are wanted for field service, but when there is no such necessity they are too frequently exposed, even in April and May. Brigadiers and generals of divisions, as well as regimental officers, should be held responsible for such cruel follies. The European soldier is, after all, our stand-by. We are delighted at every unattached commission that we observe given to a Company's European soldier. Like his officer he has more *average* emolument than his comrade in the Royal ranks, but like him is debarred great reward. Until lately, commissions were not open to the soldiers; yearly, we hope, they will become more common. With such rewards, and with rational pursuits open to the men, the tone of the barracks will rise. Drunkenness, we trust, will yet be the exception rather than the rule. Chunar should be abolished; it is a discredit to us.

We will no further enter on the vexed question of cavalry than to remark that we generally support Captain Nolan's views. We mis-arm and mis-dress the trooper, bit and saddle his horse as if the object were not to hold and ride him, and then we wonder that the same trooper is no match for a comparatively feeble and ill-mounted Asiatic horseman. The complaint made in India is equally rife in Africa and in the Caucasus. A recent French writer observes that one Arab is good for three French dragoons. We ourselves have witnessed one Indian horseman dealing with three English dragoons. The annexed extract from Spencer's "Crimea" shows that to repulse Circassian cavalry the Russians are obliged to bring guns to bear on them:—

"In other situations, on the banks of rivers or open places, they are equally dangerous, provided their inimitable cavalry can act; for, should they unexpectedly surprise a Russian army, a charge from these terrible horsemen is a most disastrous affair. They then sweep down upon them like a living avalanche, and invariably throw the front and rear into confusion, cut them in pieces, and disappear before the artillery can be brought to play upon them."—Page 327.

There can be little doubt that the Regulars have been over abused and Irregulars unduly bespattered with praise. The comrades of the men who rode at Laswaree,

Delhi, Setabuldee, and Meanee, only want good leading and good management to ride through any Indian cavalry. The disappearance of "the small speck of French grey" at Setabuldee, amid the host of Arabs, rivals Unitt and the 3rd Dragoons at Chilianwalla, Ouvrey at Sobraon, and the Light Brigade at Balaclava. Why is it that one British regiment, the 3rd Dragoons, for instance, always covers itself with glory, while others go through campaigns unheard of? The men, materials, all but the leading, is the same! To talk of all the Irregular Cavalry as heroes is as absurd as to call all the Regulars cowards. We *personally* know many brave men who ran at Purwandurrah. That story also has yet to be told. The leaders were brave men, but they were not good Native cavalry officers. *No man can manage well or lead successfully men whom he dislikes.*

We would not convert a man of Regular Cavalry into Irregulars, but we would have three regiments of Company's dragoons in lieu of six of Regular Cavalry. All others should stand, but they should be dealt with much as we have proposed for the infantry. The Native officers should be collected in three or four out of the twenty-one regiments, with *bonâ fide* power and pay, as troop officers; but to those corps four *selected* officers should be attached. Every trooper should be permitted to fit his own saddle, and adapt his bit to his own horse. Lancers should be abolished, and the tulwar, the weapon of the Indian horseman, should be allowed, as also a carbine and one pistol, to each trooper. It must be borne in mind that they are light horsemen, *not* heavy dragoons.

Most of the Irregulars are good of their kind. Some very good, some bad. Some of the officers cannot ride; some cannot talk to their men, others do so only to abuse them. Some of the regiments are overwhelmed with debt; and yet burdened with bankers, and with all sorts of tomfoolery in dress. In short, there is little system, and no uniformity in the service. One regiment wear kettles on their heads, others wear cocked hats. Few wear their own sensible turbans that will stop a sword-cut and keep their faces cool. An inspector is wanted; not an old Royal dragoon officer, but a first-rate Irregular officer—a Jacob, a Chamberlain, an Anderson, a Daly, or a Malcolm. A man, in short, who will go on common sense principles, keep the men out of debt, insist on rational uniform and rational treatment. Such as the Irregulars are, there are very few instances of their misconduct, and then only when greatly over-matched; indeed, unfairly tried. They are a most valuable arm and deserve every consideration. With such an arrangement as above proposed, and five rupees added to the pay of the men, a noble body of horsemen might be secured to the Government, and fitting employment offered to the numerous broken-down families, now muttering curses against us, in the streets of every large city in Upper India. Lord Gough, Sir Charles Napier, and almost all Irregular Cavalry officers, recommend the increase, even on the terms of reduction of strength of regiments. If thirty rupees is necessary for the Scinde Horse and for the Hyderabad (in the Deccan*) Cavalry, twenty-five is surely so for the whole body. In scarce times the Irregulars have not bread. In war time they *must* plunder for subsistence. Sir Charles Napier thought they must do so in peace. What more need be said? If more be required, let us add that each of these horsemen is a soldier gained from the enemy's ranks.

* Until lately the Hyderabad Cavalry received thirty-three Company's rupees a month.—H. M. L.

ARMY REFORM.

[WRITTEN IN 1856.]

Our last essay abruptly closed with some meagre mention of the cavalry. We propose now to continue our rough notes on the most urgent wants of the army, especially on those which most easily admit of remedy: to tell of all its wants would require a goodly volume. It is, however, consolatory to think that the most glaring defects are not only on the surface, but can be removed without difficulty. Their remedy only requires the exercise of ordinary common sense, *in the appliance of materials ready at hand*, and a very slight pull at the purse-strings; indeed *proportionately* a less pull than would be required to insure the life of a healthy soldier. An expenditure of three or four per cent. on the present eleven millions, and placing the right man in the right place, would do all that is required—would convert a discontented into a contented army; an immoveable into a moveable one; would put it beyond the power of any section of the military community to beard the Government; perhaps to destroy it.

We pretend to no panacea for all military evils, to chalk out no military Utopia, but simply to bring before the public, in very brief form, the experience of all ages in all departments; to show that men of like creeds, influenced by like motives, and moving under like conditions, *will* combine; that they have always done so in every clime. Further, that creed and colour are to be greatly nullified by slightly-varied conditions. Above all, that every man, whatever be his country, creed, or colour, has his particular ambition, and that such ambition varies, not only with general creed, colour, and country, but with individual temperament, constitution, and circumstances. That the ambition of very few European soldiers is limited, in their old age, to abundance of cheap grog at Chunar, Cuddalore, or Dapoulee. That, though many sepoys would delight to retire and smoke their hubble-bubbles under the shade of their village trees, yet that their ranks contain many fit for higher destinies, panting for them, and sullen at their non-obtainment. Such are the objects of our past and present essays. To help the Government by helping its servants; to induce the former to effect the usual insurance on its property, and prepare the fire-engines before the house is on fire; to urge on each individual his own particular duty. Some of our readers will doubtless remark, that we are propounding mere truisms which everybody knows. Everybody *does* know; but what authority *does* act on the knowledge of the foregoing facts? *Are* the right men everywhere in the right places? Is the army as efficient as it might be? Is it in any rank contented? A dozen more such questions might be answered by all honest men, in the negative. If such be the case, we request attention to what we have said in the preceding essay, as also to the following remarks. We are quite aware that they are loosely, perhaps illogically arranged. Our facts, however, are beyond question; and we feel that our inferences are not strained. We accordingly propose to hammer both facts and inferences into the public, in our own rough way, until they have at least a trial.

In military matters the Government of India starts on wrong principles. *Strict* seniority never secured efficiency in any department, in any country. It has only been by superseding the seniors, after the first bungling campaign of each war, that the British army has escaped great disaster. To a less extent the example has been followed in India, where the remedy was much more wanted. Why not prevent war by preparations? *Si vis pacem para bellum.* Muskets and accoutrements, cannon and munitions are all prepared during peace. It would be considered a crying shame for arms to be kept unpolished, belts uncleaned, lines, barracks, and magazines to be slovenly and dirty; but what is all this to having at the heads of armies, divisions, brigades, and regiments, men less efficient than nine-tenths of those under them? To have age and comparative inefficiency in all posts of authority. To drive the Cromwells and Washingtons from our ranks, and in lieu of them, to place the Whitelockes, Englands, and Elphinstones in command!

That this parallel is not exaggerated, every man with an eye to see and an ear to hear can ascertain for himself. He may discover, as we have done, a corps of *Light horse* in which nearly every trooper is close on fifty years of age. The old gentlemen paint and dye to such an extent, and are so well set up, that casual observers might easily mistake a "*boodha*" for a "*puckha juwan.*" He may talk to subadars and jemadars, sixty and even seventy years old. He may perhaps, have served under a commander-in-chief who could not mount or sit upon a horse; perhaps his own commanding officer can do neither. When he has thus cast his eye around, he may contemplate the Jacobs, Chamberlaines, Maynes, Malcolms, Taylors, Edwardeses, Lumsdens, Cokes, Nicholsons, and others, who, however, favoured *above* those of their own standing, still chafe at their positions, still feel that they have not their fitting places, and that a seniority service is not the service for them. With regard to the many Singhs and Khans, Syuds, Begs and Tewaries, who, with even more reason, —because their attainable position is much more subordinate—pine in the ranks of the army, such men, one after another, leave its service. A lieutenant-colonelcy would have retained Washington in the British service. An accident detained Cromwell in England. Men of kindred spirit are not so easily obtained that, when found, they should be scorned, or lightly set aside. Clive conquered and saved India. Individuals have, probably several times since preserved the country.* An individual may also, any day, bring it to the verge of ruin; nevertheless scores of individuals, not one of whom would have been intrusted in his youth, health, and strength with the charge of a mill, by a sensible cotton-spinner, during a disturbance, are now placed in commands, where their incompetence may any day blow a spark into a flame that may cost hundreds of lives and millions of money. We might go even further, and show that some of these men have, at every stage of their career, *proved their incompetence*. That as young or middle-aged men, they have been set aside or superseded, to have, in their old age, commands thrust upon them, and to be pushed into authority, even on the frontier, to the hinderance of distinguished officers. Such men also are frequently supported by commandants of regiments of kindred spirit and physique. The latter, *of course*, recommend, for promotion to commissions, the *oldest* Native soldiers, the grounds of election

* Forty years ago Metcalfe wrote, "Often has the fate of India depended on a single army; often again may the fate of a great part of India depend on a single army." He lived to verify his words.

being that old men are *the most inoffensive, the least dangerous*. What would the cotton-spinner, or the mill-master, say to such a system? Why, that the Indian Government deserve to have an inefficient army.

But to return to details. The closing remarks of our last essay referred to the Cavalry. We have since made minute calculations, and find that the cost of Irregulars and Regulars is about three to seven against the latter. We have not the means of estimating the proportion of pensions, but are satisfied that the differences would make the ratio fully equal to three to one. That is, fifteen hundred *more efficient* horsemen, *for light horse duty*, could be obtained for what now maintains five hundred. What possible reason then is there for delaying a day, to commence modifying the cavalry to the extent recommended in our last essay? No individual, black or white, need be injured; whilst the Government and the army, and many individuals, would greatly benefit. A few words of warning, however. Let not *half* our scheme be taken. Let not a mongrel system be introduced, or rather continued. Every man, high or low, cognizant of the whole system, allows that the pay of the majority of Irregulars is now too low. Lord Dalhousie allowed it. Sir Charles Napier not only recorded the fact, but fixed thirty, instead of twenty, rupees a month for the troopers he himself raised. He paid Native officers proportionally. Let then twenty-five, or at the least twenty-four, rupees be the horseman's pay; and, what is equally important, let pensions be raised to the footing of the line. With such increases, the expenses of *reformed* Irregulars will hardly exceed half that of the present Regulars.

We beg those who object to our proposition, to consider what it costs themselves, throughout the year, to keep a horse with gear, accoutrements, &c. Let them then bear in mind, that the sowar has to provide for bad as well as for good seasons, and for dear as well as for cheap localities; for Candahar, with grain at a seer the rupee; as well as for grain countries where thirty and forty seers may be obtained. Government allow mounted officers thirty rupees a month for each horse; few gain materially by such contract; and yet twenty is given to the trooper, who ought not to be materially worse mounted! Of this twenty, after deductions for the remount-fund, clothing, gear, washing, watermen, barber, &c., there is not, we firmly believe, a sowar in the service who receives more than seventeen, to feed himself, his family, and his horse, and to provide arms, a tent, and a hut! Fix, then, twenty as the sum to *be actually paid to each man,* every month. Let the balance, whether four or five rupees, be retained in the commandant's hands for remounts, clothing, &c., and be accounted for every six months. If commanding officers are fit for their berths, they should be able to arm, mount, and equip their regiments better than individuals can. One hundred and fifty rupees is now the usual price of a remount. Where such sum is insufficient—which in some parts of the country is occasionally the case—the unfortunate sowar, already perhaps burdened with debt, has to give the difference, possibly thirty or fifty rupees, from his seventeen rupees monthly pay. He is thus swamped for life. The proposed scheme would prevent the *necessity* of debt, and would enable every sowar to ride a three-hundred-rupee horse.

"Bargeers," as now constituted, should be entirely abolished. No respectable man will take service as a bargeer, who, when away from head-quarters, is little better than a servant to the owner of the horse. Nine bargeers out of ten, of this class, are disreputable fellows. Let the head of a respectable family have as "bargeers" whatever number, within moderation, of his relations he may wish to bring with him. There is no danger of *their* being made servants of, or of their chief making money out of them. He will neither be willing nor able to do so. Each man will receive his full Government pay; the chief being contented that they, being his assamees, are dependent on and look up to him as their head. He is thus able to control his young relations, to keep them from being extravagant and to restrain their debaucheries, &c. If it be objected that we advocate the old system of *brotherhoods*, and throw undue power into the hands of Native officers, we deny the imputation. Limit the number of "bargeers" as at present, but encourage *good* men to introduce their kinsmen into the ranks. Government is thus strengthened; the enemy weakened.

No Native banker should on any account be allowed. Many regiments do without them; there is no reason why all should not: they only encourage extravagance and debt.

Our scheme, then, for the mounted branch of the army, is, for Bengal, two regiments of European dragoons, and six of regular cavalry, *all fully officered;* with similar proportions for the other Presidencies. The rest of the cavalry, under whatever names, irregular, contingents, legionaries, &c., to be designated "Hindustani Horse," on not less than twenty-four rupees a month; three-fourths of the regiments to have each three or four European officers; the others to be commanded by natives, and to have a brigadier* over every two or three regiments. An inspector is part, and not the least important part, of this scheme. He should be an officer of experience, temper, and discretion, answering, as far

* The brigadier to be paymaster: that is, *bukshee* and deputy inspector.

as possible, the description given by Lieutenant Jervis, of an efficient cavalry commander. Indeed, such men only should command cavalry regiments, and from the best of them brigadiers (bukshees) should be selected. A Wellington makes an army; one man *can make or mar* a regiment or a brigade.

If there have been repetitions in the above remarks, the importance of the subject demands them all. The question involved is, whether by reforms, consonant not only to the spirit of the age but to the genius of the Hindustani horseman, increased contentment and increased efficiency are to be given to the whole mounted branch of the Indian army; the expense demanded to meet the required change being only about twelve lakhs, or £120,000 a-year.

We are quite aware of the financial necessities of the State, and therefore would not throw away a rupee. But bad cavalry are worse than none. If, then, there be not means to meet reforms, let the strength of regiments be reduced sufficiently to provide the necessary funds. Four hundred efficient and contented troopers would, in war or in peace, be very preferable to five hundred discontented, badly-equipped, and badly-horsed sowars.

Regiments, though weak in numbers, would be efficient and safe. Hundreds of expectants, all prepared for Jacob's ordeal of "a stiff leap on a bare-backed horse," would always be ready for the ranks of a popular service. In a month, under the proposed system, the Hindustani horse might be increased by a sixth, and in three months be doubled. Such a service would give bread in comfort to the poor soldier of fortune, and would afford a chance of honour and competence to the Native gentleman. The system would, at least, not drive them from our ranks to Cabul, or to any native service; there to introduce our discipline, and, as has often been the case, to turn our own weapons against ourselves.

Let it not be said that the writer of these remarks has a personal interest in Regulars or Irregulars. He has just the interest, and no more, in the cavalry question, and in army reform generally, that has every loyal British subject in India. It is his interest that the army, in all its branches, should be both safe and efficient. Every man is not born a soldier, much less a trooper, nor are horses to be had for the asking. Care, selection, and timely arrangement are scarcely less requisite for organizing cavalry than artillery. We lift our voice loudly *in the calm; that it may not be needed in the storm.*

One word more on this point. The *Calcutta Review* has furnished during the last thirteen years, ample facts and ample theories. Let Government make selections and lay them before three of their best and *least-prejudiced* cavalry officers, with orders to carry out details. To fix the arms and accoutrements, for both regular and irregular cavalry, and once for all, to set at rest all controverted questions. We are quite convinced that this scheme carried out, *in its full spirit,* would give the Indian Government the *best light horse in the world for Indian purposes;* we might indeed add for Asiatic purposes.

Regarding both cavalry and infantry, we have another suggestion to offer, viz., that the recruiting-field should be extended. Oude should no longer supply the mass of our infantry and regular cavalry; indeed, twenty years hence, it will be unable to do so. The Punjab, Nepaul, and the Delhi territory should be more largely indented on; as should the whole North-West Provinces, and the military classes of Bombay and

Madras. Hardy men, of fair average height, not giants, are wanted for light horsemen. The Zouaves and Goorkhas prove that the biggest light infantry are not the bravest. We have too long tilled the same fields.

If proof were wanted that abundance of Sikhs are ready to enter the ranks, Captain Rattray has settled the point. When Sikhs volunteer for Bengal on police-pay, they will assuredly accept better service in better climes. Already have they fought on the Irrawaddy, and volunteered for the Crimea. But assuredly the right plan has not yet been followed, for getting the best Sikhs. As usual, extremes have been tried. On annexation, of the 40,000 or 50,000 Sikhs thrown out of employ, scarcely a tenth were taken into British pay. The Punjab Irregular Corps were even restricted to ten Sikhs a company. All of a sudden, within two years of the issue of the above restriction, the enlistment of two hundred Sikhs in every regiment of the line was authorized. This was, indeed, going to the other extreme. Fortunately, the measure failed, or the Sikh *punchayut* system would probably have been introduced into the British ranks. Some few Native infantry regiments, stationed in the Punjab, did boast of having enlisted "a hundred or more" fine Sikhs, "who had fought against us in every battle of both campaigns." This was just what might have been expected, but what ought to have been avoided. The older Sikh soldiers should have been sent to their homes, and encouraged to expend their energies at the plough. Their young kinsmen should have been enrolled in *irregular* regiments *throughout India*, and should thus have been gradually introduced to British discipline. There was too much of the leaven of insubordination in the Sikh army, to make the sepoy ranks fitting places for the old khalsa, or even for their sons. Time, new scenes, and strict discipline, under officers acquainted with their virtues and their vices, were wanted. The ship has, however, righted itself. The *Hindoo* prejudices of commanding officers have kept the Sikhs aloof from many regular corps, and driven them out of others. Some gentlemen wished to cut their hair, forgetting that the very essence of Sikhism lies in its locks. Other officers found Sikhs dirty and troublesome; others, probably, unable to get young recruits, hesitated to enlist the veterans of Sher Singh's army. The result is, that the Bombay army has ceased to enlist Sikhs, and that in the seventy-four Bengal infantry regiments, there are scarcely three thousand of that faith. We believe we should be nearer the mark, were we to say half that number, for some Sikhs have abjured Sikhism, others have been driven out of it, and not a shadow of encouragement has been given to counteract the quiet, but persistent opposition of the Oude and Behar men.

That such opposition is no small obstacle to the introduction of new classes into the army, all experienced officers know full well. Even the determination of the present Commander-in-Chief at Madras, when commanding the Hurriana Light Infantry, eighteen years ago, did not enable him to carry such a measure. He tried to introduce into its ranks the hardy "Aheers" and "Ranghurs" of the Province, but failed; we have it from his own lips; the Rajpoots and Brahmins bullied the new levies out of the corps.

We are tempted to give another anecdote. A corps of the line, within our observation, that has about four-score Sikhs in its ranks, possesses only one Sikh non-commissioned officer, and him of the lowest rank. We asked the reason why the Sikhs had not their proportion of officers. The reply was, "Why, the naick is the luckiest soldier in the Bengal army." Be it remembered, that this luckiest fellow in the Bengal army has served the period which entitles a civilian to a seat in council. This is luck indeed; to be a corporal on about a pound sterling a month, after ten years' service. He is a *remarkable* man, has attracted the special attention of his officers; otherwise he would to this day have been a sentinel. Had he similarly outstripped all his compeers in the Punjab service, or in any Native service, he would now have been, *at least*, a commandant, perhaps a colonel, possibly a sirdar, or even a rajah. In the Russian, Austrian, or French service, he would most likely be a decorated captain or field officer. In the sepoy army, he is a corporal! To complete the story, the officer commanding the company, in which was *one* of the batch of Sikhs to which we refer, begged that *this one* too might be made a naick. The reply was, "What has he done that he should be put over the heads of the whole Bengal army?" If that man be lucky, he will be a corporal ten years hence! Such is the inducement, to the finest infantry soldier in India, to enter the British ranks.

The whole system is wrong. In a few years the survivors of those Sikhs will be simply low-caste Hindus; they will have learnt to object to mess together, and in all points will be as helpless and as subservient as Brahmins or Rajpoots. The plan to be followed, to get and to keep the best soldiers throughout India, and to *quietly* oppose class against class, and tribe against tribe, is to have separate regiments of each creed or class, filling up half, three-fourths, or even more of the commissioned and non-commissioned ranks from their own numbers. Thus there might be Brahmin, Rajpoot, Aheer, Goojur, Meena, Ranghur, Patan, Mogul, Malay, Goorkha, and Sikh regiments, as also

Chumar and Sweeper ones. Each to have a sprinkling of other castes or tribes, stout fellows, with *more* than their proportion of promotion, and therefore able to hold their own. Say, in a corps of Brahmins, a hundred Rajpoots, and as many Mahommedans. In one of Sweepers, a couple of hundred Mahommedans. Similarly with Sikhs and Goorkhas, a sprinkling of Hill Rajpoots and Moslems. Such dilutions will be sufficient to prevent, or at least to bring to light, internal disaffection; while it not only cuts off sectarian influence, but unostentatiously opposes class to class and party to party. We have not a doubt that, thus organized, the low-caste man, who, under present influences, is the mere creature of the Brahmin, would as readily meet him with the bayonet, as he would a Mahommedan. There might still be many regiments composed much as at present, only keeping the very high, and very low castes more apart.

Some people will say that Brahmins will not act with low-caste men. We happen to know better. In the Bombay army Sweeper subadars command Brahmin sepoys. We ourselves have seen Bheels and Meenas, Grassias and Patans, Aheers and Rajpoots, all shoulder to shoulder, all working well and amicably together, notwithstanding that the first two tribes eat carrion, and are classed little, if at all, above Mehturs. We are aware that such arrangements are only to be carried out by tact and determination. In a certain Bheel corps the Grassias and others combined to refuse to salute the first Bheel who was promoted to the rank of a subadar. The commanding officer, having seated the Bheel on a chair by his side, called in the whole company, asked each individual his intentions, ordered him to salute the Bheel and pass on. The Hindustanis did so; *three* Grassias refused. On the instant they were discharged.

There was no more hesitation; the Bheel subadar ever afterwards was duly obeyed.

It is, however, well known that low-caste men give most trouble about caste; that the Sweepers of the Bombay and Madras armies are more fanciful than the Brahmins and Rajpoots. Religionists, too, whether Hindoo or Mahommedan, whether Syuds, or Brahmins, or Swamees, influence only the mob; they do not touch each other. They should therefore have their energies, as far as possible, confined to their own classes.

Under somewhat such arrangements as above suggested, there would be no scarcity of Sikhs or Goorkhas in the ranks, nor, indeed, if desirable, of Malays, Moplas, and Arabs. At present few *original* Goorkhas enter the British service, simply because it is not worth their while. It was recently shown, in the *Calcutta Review*,* how a thousand Goorkhas had been enlisted in a week. The same means are open any day to Government. Let a popular officer be sent to raise a corps of Goorkhas in communication with the Resident at Khatmandoo. Let three-fourths of the native commissions, &c., be given to Goorkhas, and there will be no scarcity of recruits. There must, of course, be good management; but the ice once broken, there will always be a fair proportion of Goorkhas in the British ranks.

In Oude the Punjab mistake has been reversed. Oude has long been the Alsatia of India. In that province were to be met, even more than at Hyderabad or at Lahore, the Afreedee and Euzufzye of the Khyber, the Belooch of Khelat, and the Wazeree of the Sulimani range. There also congregated the idle, the dissipated, and the disaffected of every native State in India. Added to these were many deserters from the British ranks. Yet the contingent of twelve thousand men

* Article, "Sir Charles Napier's Posthumous Work."

has been almost wholly filled from the old Oude army. The reason assigned for the different line of conduct is, that the Punjab was conquered, but that Oude fell in peace. In this there is a fallacy, little understood, but not the less a fallacy. Proportionally few of the instigators of opposition at Lahore, and in the Sikh army, were Sikhs. They were British subjects, many of them British deserters. The general feeling of the Sikhs was hardly hostile; many of the Sikhs were friendly—decidedly so, compared with the Hindustanis in the Punjab service.

The king of Oude employed 59,000 soldiers; his chiefs and officials at least as many more. Of these vast numbers, one-fifth at the utmost have found employment in the police and irregular corps. Yet these levies, with half-a-dozen regular corps, form the whole army of occupation. This seems a grave mistake. Why not at least make a change? Why not move some of the Punjab regiments that have been keeping watch and ward on the Indus for seven years to Oude, and send some of the king's people to the north-west? The king had some 8000 artillery. Of these about 500 may have obtained employment; the rest, old and young, are on the world. Surely if there was danger in employing Sikhs in 1849, it would be well to remove some portion of the levies from Oude, where such materials for mischief still remain. In the province are 246 forts, besides innumerable smaller strongholds, many of them sheltered within thick jungles. In these forts are 476 guns. Forts and guns should all be in the hands of Government, or the forts should be razed. Many a foolish fellow has been urged on to his own ruin by the possession of a paltry fort; and many a paltry mud fort has repulsed British troops. Forts and intrenched posts, moreover, notwithstanding all Sir Charles Napier and other great authorities have said, are the bridles and the main safeguards of all, especially of conquered, countries. Spain confirms, indeed all Europe and all history confirm, this opinion. Gibbon imputes the downfall of the Roman empire, among other causes, to the facts that—

"In the vast extent of the Roman empire there were few fortified cities capable of protecting a routed army, nor was there any person, or family, or order of men, whose natural interest, unsupported by the powers of Government, was capable of restoring the cause of a sinking party."

The latter portion of the passage hits the British Government. Hitherto it has made no interest with the people; it therefore the more needs an efficient and contented army.

The eighty or ninety thousand disbanded Oude soldiers are the brethren of the British sepoys. In one sense this makes them more dangerous, in another more safe. *All* will expect much from Government, most too much. Future tranquillity will greatly depend on the manner in which justice, firmness, and kindly consideration are combined in Oude arrangements. We simply recommend forethought, moderation, and common sense for Oude, for all new countries, indeed for India generally.

No troops, regular or irregular, should remain for ever in one province. They should move every three or four years; not at one step from Peshawur to Calcutta, as is sometimes the order; but step by step, from one end of the country to the other. All these are very obvious truths; they are, however, not the less disregarded. While on this topic we commend to the attention of Oude, Punjab, and Nagpore administrators Gibbon's 43rd chapter, on the rebellions of Africa, when among other events—

"Two-thirds of the army were involved in the guilt of treason; and eight thousand insurgents, assembling on the field of Bulla, elected Stoza for their chief, a *private soldier* (the italics are ours), who possessed, in a superior degree, the virtues of a rebel."

Volumes nine and twelve of the *Calcutta Review* have largely dwelt on the history, the services, and the necessities of the Bengal artillery. Intending shortly again to enter in detail on the artillery question, we need here only cursorily refer to that arm. Except at Guzerat, the Indian army has always been greatly overmatched in guns; and as British commanders have ordinarily delighted to attack in front, the loss of life has been proportionally great. By reversing the rule at Guzerat, the enemy was smashed at little cost. With very few exceptions our proceedings have been similar in the conduct of sieges. In 1825–26, at Bhurtpoor, close to the Agra magazine, and with the result of the first siege before our eyes, the army nearly ran out of ammunition, and was not over-supplied with guns. The tardy and insufficient supplies on the Sutlej will be in the memory of many, even though Lahore and Umritsur were expected to resist. Indeed Hatras is the only fortress against which the army went altogether prepared. The result was success after a few hours' shelling. Those were the days when Lord Metcalfe lifted his voice to urge the authorities to expend shot and shells rather than human lives. European lives, at least, are more expensive than ordnance ammunition.

We recently showed that 506 field guns are attached to the Indian army of 323,823 men, being one gun to 630 fighting men, instead of to 500 as, *at the lowest calculation*, should be the equipment. Jomini and other eminent writers give *three* guns to a thousand men as the needful proportion. It is true, as Jomini remarks, that Napoleon conquered Italy with 50 guns, while he failed in Russia with 1200. It is not the less true that his batteries of 50 and 100 guns won him several battles. There is really no excuse for insufficient or inefficient artillery in India, and yet the proportions here are below the standards of all armies. Moreover, of the 506 existing field guns, 102 are what is called irregular; that is, have, at the utmost, one officer to six guns. To some few no officer is attached. Such guns can never be as efficient as other batteries. Two officers, at least, are absolutely required to each battery. We are glad to perceive that a second officer has recently been appointed to each Punjab one. In other quarters seconds are equally required. An irregular battery is an absurdity. It is truly childish hazarding the efficiency of six guns on the life and energy of a single officer. Horses should be given to all remaining bullock batteries. What are called "post guns" are as liable to move as any others within the provinces; their being unable to do so might, on occasion, be disastrous.

We quite agree with the late Sir Charles Napier that the foot artillery is sacrificed to the horse: we do not agree as to his remedy. Horse artillery are as requisite to act with cavalry, as foot artillery with infantry. The whole of the artillery should always be kept up on the amplest scale, and on the most efficient footing. Notwithstanding all the idle talk of Sikh guns and Sikh practice during the Punjab war, the Indian artillery is unmistakably superior to all that can be brought against it. All the field batteries should be nine-pounders, as all but one, and "the mountain train," are in Bengal. Indeed we would have half the horse artillery of that calibre, and keep a nine-pounder equipment for *every* troop ready at the nearest magazine. The change from sixes to nines of the Royal artillery, just previous to Waterloo, may have saved that glorious day. The nine-pounders did at least greatly help to win it. Two or three elephant field batteries should be kept up at points on the trunk or railroad, whence they could be made most generally available.

In a former essay we remarked that 300 battering guns, with as many mortars, might be turned out of the Indian magazines in a month; we should like to think that every magazine could move a second-class train in a fortnight. We are aware that the present Inspector-General is quite alive to the subject. We desire to strengthen his hands. Why are there not Inspectors of Ordnance at Madras and Bombay? And why is not the School of Instruction at Meerut put on a really efficient footing? Half the object in moving the Bengal Artillery head-quarters to Meerut has been lost by petty savings. The artillery is one of the last legitimate fields for retrenchment.

The next increase in artillerymen may, with advantage, be partly Golundauze. They are admirable soldiers, die at their guns, never join in disaffection, scarcely ever in discontent. Regarding Golundauze, there has been at all the Presidencies more than the usual see-saw of the Indian army.* In Calcutta, a hundred years ago, *Foreigners, Papists*, and natives, were prohibited entering the arsenal. Half a century later, the Bengal artillery were stronger in natives than in Europeans. A few years afterwards, as the tide of suspicion again rose, whole battalions of these fine fellows were discharged, and driven for bread into the enemy's ranks. Again the Golundauze were increased, and again reduced. Sometimes mixed up with Europeans, at other times placed on their old formation. Then, again, Lascars were largely employed, good fellows in their way, but not to be put on a par with, still less in the place of, Golundauze. These unnecessary changes, and, above all, the reduction of pay to the level of infantry, have affected the confidence and the efficiency of the Golundauze. The same style of men are not now enlisted in

* See Broome's, Buckle's, and Begbie's volumes.

any Presidency as formerly; and should Golundauze be again required in a hurry, they will not be as easily recruited as of old. In all Native armies the artillery are the best and trustiest men. They are always true to their guns; they worship them. But artillerymen are not made in a day, nor is it either prudent or economical to teach sepoys to work guns in substitution for short numbers of Golundauze. The latter can better and more safely do infantry duty than infantry theirs. Serving the vent, sponging and ramming are only the A. B. C.'s of an artilleryman's work. But under any circumstances, when Golundauze and sepoys are paid at exactly the same rates, why put extra temptation in the way of the larger body? A thousand Golundauze cost no more than as many sepoys. The more is the pity. They should be taught to consider themselves a separate and selected body. No sepoy should touch a gun. The Golundauze should be in numbers amply sufficient for all post guns, with large reserves to take their share in siege operations.* Their number should not exceed the European artillery, but, whatever the number and proportions, let the Golundauze receive *the one extra* rupee. It would be good economy. We repeat that our arrangements are for the storm as well as the sunshine—for the possibility of a Russian army at Herat, simultaneously with an American fleet off Bombay. But, whether in peace or in war, the more the several arms are kept apart, the better. Perpetual *ordinary caution* in this matter, as on other points, prevents occasional spasmodic alarms, which alarms again put mischief into men's minds.

* The reserve artillerymen are altogether insufficient. At every siege from Seringapatam to Mooltan artillerymen were in battery two nights out of three, often many successive nights. At Sobraon, the men of three troops worked the heavy ordnance until their ammunition was expended, and then joined their own six-pounders.—H. M. L.

The fame of the Indian artillery is world-wide; there is no finer. The Bombay men are not behind their Bengal and Madras comrades in *esprit de corps* or soldierly qualities. Why does not some Bombay artilleryman follow the example set by Captain Buckle and Major Begbie, and record the services of his regiment? Such compilations are valuable. Indeed every corps should have its history. What better stimulus to the young soldier than to read the record of his brethren's services? Such memorials, too, would tend to draw together officers and sepoys. In the regimental "*Tuwareekh*" they would have something in common; the honour of the corps would then be more palpably in the keeping of each individual. No deed of personal bravery of the youngest sepoy or drummer boy would pass unrecorded. Each might hope to live in history.

The Bengal army is largely indebted to Major Broome for his excellent history. Its tone is admirable and its painstaking research most praiseworthy. We sincerely hope the Major is at work on its continuation, and that the three armies will at least take as many copies as will cover his expenses. It is not creditable to any regiment to be without his first volume; nor could any person desiring to acquaint himself with early British-Indian history have a better or more impartial guide.

Engineers and sappers, even more than artillery, ought to be kept in full strength. Sappers are not used in public works to the extent they might be. The men should not have the disbursement of public money, but should be liberally rewarded according to their zeal and abilities, as sappers are, when employed in England on the trigonometrical survey, &c. By such peace duties engineer officers, sergeants, and native sappers are kept in training, and, while largely aiding the works of peace, are preparing themselves for war.

A few words on the calling of military engineers at the three Presidencies. In war their duties are important, and in sieges they are the virtual commanders. It was the joke of the camp how Cheape kept the nominal commander at Mooltan informed, from day to day, of the work he intended should be performed. Irvine's, Abbott's, Waddington's, Smith's, Napier's, Baker's, Tremenhere's, Scott's, Durand's, and Thomson's services, during recent campaigns, are in the memory of our readers. Still more valuable are the services of such men during peace. A Cotton, a Boileau, a Napier, or a Cautley, is worth a brigade. This is the only portion of the army that *pays* at all seasons. So few civil engineers of ability consider it worth their while to come to India, that all civil engineering is virtually in the hands of the military. We are not quite clear that this is the best arrangement, but under improved management it may be made very much more effective than at present.

Promotion has recently been good in the Engineers. In the higher ranks they are nearly ten years a-head of their sister corps—the Artillery; but they are still numerically weak for the work required at their hands. The consequence is, that there is more poaching on their domain than on any other. The artillery, with reason, scream when people even talk of posting infantry officers to field batteries; but the engineers obtain little sympathy when some of their best berths are monopolized by outsiders. Nor, indeed, should we pity them were better men put over their heads—were Cautleys, Maxwells, Prices, Balfours, and Longdens to be had for the asking; but such is not the case. By all means let the best man be selected for every berth in every department; but be sure he is the best, before trained and able men are superseded. Far be it from us to join the cuckoo-cry in favour of individuals. There are plenty, without our aid, to advocate the cause of the incompetent; our voice is for "the right man in the right place."

Engineer officers are the *élite* of the service. They are the *selections*, and generally very fair selections, from the mass of Addiscombe. The energies of many are, however, damped by the treatment they meet in India. They win the race, but obtain not the prizes. The latter are too often reserved for the sluggard and the incompetent. Few engineer officers would select the engineer corps for their own sons.

Great pains are taken at home to qualify the young engineer officers for the important and arduous duties which they are called upon to perform in India. The great error, however, is in so calling on them at too early a period after arrival. This may, in a measure, account for cracked and broken bridges, for unfinished and ill-made roads, and for high rates. While yet apprentices, and while ignorant of the rudiments of the language and of civil routine, they have heavy responsibilities thrown on them, and are put to deal with the veriest rogues in India.

Every young engineer officer, on arrival in India, should be sent to the head-quarters of the Sappers and Miners, now also the head-quarters of the corps; and he should not be withdrawn on any grounds or pretence until he had passed at least one year of probation with the corps; had attended the schools regularly, and been well instructed in the technical language and practice of sapper-engineering duties as conducted in India. Most young officers could, during this year of probation, pass the P. H. examination, and this should be made a *sine quâ non* for their employment in any independent substantive charge. The rule is enforced with regard to officers of other branches of the services appointed to the Staff, and it is only fair and proper that the same rule should be extended to the alumni of the engineer department. Few young officers, when they have once quitted the sappers, after their few months' sojourn with the corps, ever rejoin it, unless, perhaps, on active service in the field. Thus, unless grounded in the vernacular phraseology of their craft, and instructed, on their first arrival, in the various processes of their duties, as conducted in India, it is perfectly certain that they will not acquire these very important and necessary qualifications in after-life; while as builders and civil engineers, their talents will remain hidden, or lose half their value, until a competent knowledge of the vernacular language shall enable them to communicate their knowledge in language intelligible to the people of the country. Our advice is, thus to instruct them well, then to trust them largely, and pay them liberally.

The abolition of the Bengal and Bombay Military Boards was a grand measure. But the rubbish has not yet been all cleared away. Commissary-generals, inspector-generals of ordnance, and chief engineers must have more authority; must each respectively be put into a position assimilating more to that of the old Boards than each now fills, before the new system can be expected to work smoothly. Chief engineers must not be made mere postmen and clerks to local governors. They are the most scientific and among the ablest and most zealous officers in the service. Their positions should be of high honour, considerable authority, and great comfort. At present this is far from the case. The sooner the matter is righted the better. We commend the subject, as also the following anecdote, to the attention of the Secretary in the Public Works Department. We might tell many such tales.

Some three years back, a sanatory measure urgently

recommended by a medical officer, involving an expense of six hundred rupees, was reported. The immediate superior, a person of high rank, authorized the measure, and the local officer carried it out. Sanction was quickly obtained from the Supreme Government; but a greater than Lord Dalhousie, the auditor-general, had not been consulted. A few words in red ink, negatived his lordship's order, and the bill was made over to the Military Board. After many months the Board passed and sent it to the military accountant for adjustment. In due course, the cash was paid. After a considerable interval, however, the military auditor-general *again* interfered, and retrenched the full amount. *Again* was the matter referred to the Supreme Government, which passed it on to the Local Government, and after six months more it was finally sanctioned, and the retrenchment recovered through the local chief engineer. Thus, during more than two years, some forty official letters had been written, and innumerable copies been made for one authority or another; and during all this time, the zealous officer who had expended his private means, in the cause of humanity, was out of pocket £60. Such delay could not now occur, but six months or more of the delay in this very case, did take place during the present order of things, and we believe that with a less energetic officer than the local chief engineer, twelve months more might have passed before the cash had been recovered.

Much reform is still required in the Commissariat. As yet, in some quarters at least, confusion and expense seem rather to have been increased than diminished, by recent changes. In the cattle department, for instance, the new arrangements were inaugurated by the sale of the greater part of the public stock. Under such circumstances, only nominal prices were, of course, obtainable; but scarcely were the elephants, camels, and bullocks sold, than out came an order to re-purchase. The fortunes of some rising "Jotee Pursads" were accordingly made at Government expense. We know not whose was this see-saw move, but such was the fact. We refer specially to sales at a certain large station, and we have reason to believe that, throughout the Bengal Presidency, sales, re-purchases, discharges, and re-enlistments followed each other, quickly. Such has always been the East India Government's fate in war time. This was a peace measure.

Half the commissariat expenses during war is attributable to such doings; to alternate haste and delay; above all, to untrustworthy agency. War is expected, or a movement is to be made in any quarter, whether within or without our limits. At once the market is up, *not* for the contractors, but for the Government. The former, *practically*, have the benefit of the earliest intelligence. They buy at twenty seers for the rupee, sell at ten; and again, after a few weeks or months, re-purchase the accumulated stores at fifty. Jotee Pursad's trial proved how cattle contracts were managed. But reform has now commenced. The great contractor has himself arranged for a small retaining fee, to hold some thousand cattle available for the public service. This is a good move. On this principle, contracts for all commissariat necessaries should be made. In our opinion, they can be most cheaply effected by civil officers; the commissariat officers looking only to quantity and quality. Let Local Governments, through their most efficient civil officers, contract with monied men, to supply at fixed points, within given periods, certain quantities of grain, cattle, &c., and let a given proportion be always kept available, under special restrictions, for the contractor's own purposes.

We propose that these arrangements be made by civil officers, because *they* ought to have most influence in the country; ought to know the soundest traders; and to be able to make the cheapest bargains. The commissariat should look to the terms of contracts being kept, and should manage all details; a few *well-paid* inspecting officers, men not above their work, and accustomed to such matters, with *well-paid* Natives under them, will suffice for all the suggested duties. A single active officer could ordinarily supervise a Province. *No sergeants*, and very little inferior European agency, should be employed in the department. The temptation is too great. If the officer does his duty, little subordinate supervision is required. The *legitimate* work of sergeants can be better done by Natives. The *legitimate* work of gentlemen should be done by gentlemen, trained to the work. Some of them, at least, might be mercantile men from England. Indeed, we are disposed to think, that the commissariat might advantageously be altogether a civil establishment, as is now the case in the Royal army; but our Indian "Mr. Filder," should be, at least, a K.C.B., and so be hoisted well above the vulgar depreciation of the commissariat service, so general through the Peninsular and Crimean wars.

The commissariat must be a well-paid and respectable body; every responsible official having the status and pay of a military officer. But there should be no irresponsible agency; contractors should be strictly kept to contract work, and not permitted, by their money-influence, to overshadow and bully, even the chief commissariat officers.

By our scheme, *very small* annual payments will give Government the command of markets at all times; instead of, as at present, leaving it in every difficulty, at the mercy of its own *nominal* servants. Retaining fees may, in many cases, be almost nominal. Monied firms gain so much in credit by Government contracts, that they can afford to deal for small profits. Their stores will be laid in at harvest-time, and by sale of half or three-fourths at sowing time, they will at least cover their own expenses, having their full retaining fee as profit. Similarly, by being permitted, within limits, to work the cattle they keep up, they can afford to charge the merest trifle. Such a scheme would involve clashing, some must necessarily occur at first; but lieutenant-governors and the commissary-general could *easily* stop all that. A few severe examples would suffice. And as long as inspectors and receivers, European and Native, are paid sufficiently well, to make it *worth their while* to be independent of contractors, but at the same time to do their duty to them, as well as to Government, all else will work well. Officers enough are now in the department, to do the needful. Numbers might even be reduced; but pay and position should be raised. Zeal and ability should be the sole passports to promotion in all ranks. Let also venality be promptly and severely punished, and all will soon be smooth. We repeat that much has been done in this department. To simplify accounts and insist on their being promptly rendered, would be immense points.

A transport train should be established; one combining the virtues of Sir Charles Napier's baggage-corps, and of those recently employed by the Allied armies in the Crimea. Hints may also be taken from the Russians; from their wonderful organization and application of resources. Organization and military discipline in this department, are as requisite as in any other branch of the army. Economy and efficiency will both be thus best secured. An Indian army can never move like a European one; but still there is very much that can be effected, *if officers will set the example.* There was no more necessity, as *was* the case, for a lieutenant-colonel to take three elephants and double-poled tents, and glass doors, to Candahar, than for him to have taken the Crystal Palace. Neither was it necessary for subalterns to take dressing-boys, and deputy dressing-boys, and butlers, with their assistants, &c., throughout those campaigns.

Mr. Kaye has recorded that Sir John Keane's army was accompanied by five non-combatants for every soldier. In such a country *every* man should have been armed, and the camp-followers should not have exceeded the fighting men. It is all nonsense to say that the present system is necessary. It is not. General Pollock had not half General Nott's number of followers; nor were such proportions found necessary during either the first or second Burmah war. Three or four servants will suffice, for a time, for each officer. They, and indeed all ranks, should have as good cover, over their heads, *as circumstances admit of;* but it is nonsense to expect to carry all *peace-luxuries* into war. Indeed, the attempt to do so, too often leads to the abandonment or failure of *necessaries.* There should be a director-general of baggage, with deputies, and assistants for divisions and brigades, as in continental armies. They should be stern men, of somewhat Napierean views, with authority to burn all extra baggage, and all burthens of overloaded cattle. Those who remember Burmah, or who bear in mind the passes of Affghanistan, *crammed* with cattle and human beings, even as poppy heads; who remember grain at a rupee a seer, and water nearly as scarce as beer, will feel with us, that the very existence of armies should not be risked to give Cleopatra sofas and fresh bread to gentlemen whose services, at best, are ill worth such price.

With a staff corps would, of course, come more efficient staff establishments in all departments. Good regimental officers who had studied their profession, in all its arms, would then, as in the continental armies, be attached to the *Etat Major*, and according to their more special qualifications be distributed into the adjutant and quartermaster-general's and other departments. No one will pretend that the best man is now selected for either of those important branches. We cannot indeed be said to have a quartermaster-general's department at all. We never had. The present heads are striving to make up for departmental deficiencies, but the whole department requires regeneration and extension; in short, radical reform. Assistant quartermaster-generals should be the eyes of divisional commanders, not merely their aide-de-camps; still less should they be gentlemen at large, occasionally, in fine weather, marching with large perambulators along high roads.

We have suggested the formation of a staff corps. A word as to details. The French *Etat Major* is a distinct corps, admission to which is only obtained, as in the engineers and artillery, by a special education, and when this has been completed and the requisite examination passed, by a fixed period of regimental duty, with each of the three arms of the service, in the grade of subaltern. Adverting to local peculiarities, we would require an officer to serve from two to four years with his original corps: when armed with a certificate that he thoroughly understood his regimental duty, was physically active, zealous, and intelligent, he should, after passing the interpreter's examination in the languages, be admitted into the staff corps. No man is thoroughly fit for staff duties without such qualifications. He should, in addition, pass for a particular department.

First. Adjutant-General's, Military Secretariat, and Judge Advocate-General's Department.

Second. Quartermaster-General's and Survey.

Third. Civil and political employment.

Fourth. Army Finance Departments, as pay, audit, commissariat.

Fifth. Miscellaneous, as military police, baggage, &c., &c. Government to fix tests for each department.

High proficiency in other branches might permit the P. H. to be substituted for the interpreter's test in individual cases; but we look on a thorough colloquial knowledge of the languages, next to good judgment, the very first qualification for a staff officer. Half the *contre-temps* and violences that occur between Europeans and Natives, are occasioned by mutual ignorance of language. Book learning is less required; but ability to read accounts and sepoys' letters is important. Many civilians never acquire the power, and are accordingly much at the mercy of their own moonshees. Good colloquial knowledge, acquired by free association with all ranks, will render other lingual attainments comparatively easy. By such processes the staff corps would possess soldierly officers, qualified by study for every branch of duty, whether civil or military. After passing the interpreter's examination, and being furnished with a certificate of proficiency in his regimental duties, the staff candidate should then be sent to do duty for one year with each of the other branches of the service, his name being struck off his original regiment, and enrolled in the staff corps. A staff man would thus have done from five to seven years' regimental duty, and be about twenty-four years of age, before being eligible for staff duty. He would have fairly won his spurs, and would then be available, according to qualification and the test he had passed, for any department.

It will be observed that we have thrown the whole civil as well as military staff into the staff corps. We have done so deliberately, and after much consideration, as agreeing with Lord Hardinge,* that it is useful to have officers qualified for both civil and military duties on the strength of the army.

Such is the Oriental system, which is too much overlooked, or even despised. Orientals put a man of energy and ability to the front, whatever be his antecedents; whether he were a slipper-bearer or a pipe-bearer, a slave or a son of a slave, a pasha or a son of a pasha. In troubled times and places, at least, they put such a man in authority with *full power*. On the other hand, Englishmen, judging by English rules, split up and separate offices, thereby puzzling Natives where to look for justice, and often obliging officials to waste half their time in forms and squabbles. England has no need of Rome's fears. The most popular Governor-General would not be followed in rebellion by a single regiment. Yet Rome won and held the world under consuls and pro-consuls. Even the jealous Augustus armed his governors "with the full powers of the sovereign himself. It was reserved for Constantine, by divided administration, to relax the vigours of the State."†

We do not altogether advocate Roman powers for British officials, although there cannot be a doubt that half Sir Charles Napier's success in Scinde is attribu-

* Evidence before the Lords.

† Gibbon, Book xvii.

table to his despotic powers. A fool so armed will get into a mess; but a man of ordinary judgment will consult others where he is himself deficient, and by prompt action will cover a multitude of defects. For the next fifty, or hundred, years there must be non-regulation provinces and military civilians. Indeed, we would always have them, and uncovenanted officers also, were it only for a stimulus to civilians, and a fillip to routine practices.

Thus, according to qualification, men would be posted to civil and political berths, to the adjutant-general's, quartermaster-general's, finance, supply, baggage, law, and other departments.

They might rise regimentally, as vacancies occur, in the staff corps, or being originally appointed in that corps, according to army standing, they might be promoted at fixed periods, so as to reach lieutenant-colonelcies in twenty-five years. Or present incumbents might be promoted on the day on which each would have obtained *each* step had he remained with his original regiment. The regimental rank being secured, each departmental step would only be *won* by efficiency, by hard work, and by keeping pace with the times. The regimental pay might be as that of the engineers; separate staff allowances being allotted as at present for each office, *and a fresh test required on each departmental step up to certain periods*. If men became lazy or apathetic, they might be restricted to small inoffensive berths; or if physically or mentally qualified, be sent as juniors of their rank to do duty with a corps of the line. After two reports, at intervals of six months, of continued apathy they should be discharged, pensioned, or invalided, according to the circumstances of each case. There would be no more difficulty in disposing of each case than of that of the late Colonel Davidson, of the engineers. To place incompetence on the shelf, and to employ men in positions according to their talents, is following common sense rules. Thus, a captain might be commissary-general, a field officer his deputy. Other posts would be similarly filled.

It strikes us that some such arrangements provide, as fairly as is practicable, for all circumstances, and would not be difficult to work. They would effectually *check*, if not altogether prevent, jobbery; would give all young *working* officers an object to work for, and still would not altogether shut the staff doors to regiments. The scheme would, at least, put down the present cry of favouritism, and thus induce comparative contentment. If it did no more than allay present restlessness, much good would be effected.

The corps would be large or small, according to the necessities of the service, and would, like other regiments, annually receive drafts to fill up vacancies. Our scheme will be called incomplete, because it does not shut the staff door *entirely* to regimental officers. This is intentional. All men do not ripen early. A very efficient regimental officer may be idle during the first three or four years of his service, or his education may have been neglected. Such a man, if of commanding talent or energy, should not be lost to the *Etat Major*. Ochterlony, Barry Close, and other eminent staff officers, would have been excluded from high employment by such a rule. The arrangement would, however, lessen the necessity of drafts from the line. After its formation, one captain and two subalterns from each regiment should be the utmost allowed on the staff. Most of these would probably go to irregular corps. They should, however, be available for all staff posts, remaining on the strength of their original corps. In fixing the strength of regiments and battalions, allowance should be made for these three absentees, and for one in four absent on furlough, &c.

Calculating, then, the staff to eventually require six officers for each of the 219 regiments and battalions in the service, and 657, or half the number, to be attached to the staff corps, the expense will be in round numbers a quarter of a million sterling. At least half of this would, however, be civil charges, as pay of men *ready on emergency for military duty.*

A delicate point remains. Are the staff to be eligible for command? The recent order, making the command of a regiment and certain posts the only roads to a full colonelcy, implies that such is the present intention. The rule does not work well, and has already put bad juniors over good seniors. Its tendency is to exclude from eventual command many of the very best officers in the service—men who have risen by their military merits. We feel that we can argue this point without prejudice. In discussing it we have no purpose to answer but the good of the State. The question is not what is best, or even fairest, for this or for that individual, but what is best and fairest for the service: whether in a great calamity—and Government should always be ready for one—the public, and, above all, those immediately concerned, would place most confidence in soldiers like Broadfoot, Jacob, and Edwards, or in hap-hazard seniority commanders. Whoever would have preferred Xenophon to Menon, or Pottinger to Elphinstone, must vote with us. It is doubtful whether Xenophon was a soldier* at all when he was raised to command on the shields of the soldiery. Herat proved Pottinger to have been a thorough soldier, though he was far from being what is called a clever man. Washington was a militia man and a surveyor; Cromwell a country gentleman. *They* were all *born* soldiers.

* Rollin calls him a young Athenian: Plutarch says Cyrus gave him a commission.—H. M. L.

The staff corps must then correspond with the *Etat Major*. Its colonels must come on the general gradation list, it being always optional with Government to keep men to their gram bags, law books, &c., or to put them in command of brigades. General Huyshe, one of the most efficient officers in the Bengal army, rose to his majority in the commissariat; and General Lumley, one of its best adjutant-generals, was transferred from the head of the commissariat to be adjutant-general. The command of European regiments is given to the smartest officers. Huyshe commanded one, and Colonel Swatman, who also rose in the commissariat, now commands another: we mention these names and dwell on the question because we daily hear it said, "So-and-so can know nothing of his duty, he was all his life in the commissariat, &c." We particularize the commissariat as being a department perhaps less soldierly in its character than others. The quartermaster-general's and survey departments are among the best schools for war, as are many of the duties of the military collector and magistrate. They are akin to Wellington's hunting parties; they improve the *coup d'œil*, sharpen the perceptions, and give opportunities of display of courage, hardihood, and resource. Five to seven years of mixed military duties, in early life, would instil into soldierly civilians all requisite details. It is not by three times a day seeing soldiers eat their rations, or horses twice a day eat their gram, nor is it even by, year after year, driving fuzes and portfires, or by marching round barrack squares, that officers learn to be soldiers, much less to be generals. Such avocations are rather the necessary drudgeries of the profession; with hasty spirits, they cramp rather than foster eminent attainments. The soldier in heart will keep up his military knowledge, wherever or however he may be placed. He will also avail himself of opportunities to take part in battery practice, and in field exercise; nor will his steps be unfrequently turned towards the regimental parades, hospitals, and target practice. *He* will enjoy such avocations, while many regimental men expend their energies in execrating them.

In short, we altogether deny that the officer who has passed his life in small regimental details, and in performing Dundas' eighteen manœuvres, or any one else's twenty-eight, is likely to prove a better commander in field or in garrison, than the one who, with from five to seven years' practical military education, has early distinguished himself above his fellows as a soldier; and, in later years, has been knocking about the country as a quartermaster-general, a surveyor, a magistrate, or a collector. We even question, whether the individual of like antecedents, whose wits have been sharpened by the duties of a military lawyer or commissariat officer, will not, as a rule, be as efficient as the man of regimental details. We argue on the rule, *not* the exception. There are undoubtedly excellent regimental officers and very bad staff men. Facts however bear out our argument. Among the highest names in European warfare, are those of men who performed little regimental duty. In the Indian ranks, also, the Pollocks, the Notts, the Gilberts and the Cheapes of the present day, did as little battalion drill, as did the Malcolms, the Munros, and the Clives of old.

We are very far from decrying the school that produced Colin Campbell, Henry Havelock, Markham, Franks, and hosts of good soldiers in the Company's ranks. We simply aver with all confidence, that there is nothing erudite, nothing difficult in Dundas, nor in more modern books of manœuvres; on the contrary, that any dolt may learn his battalion drill, and even the Light

Infantry manœuvres in a few weeks; that many do so, and are little the wiser; that they are practically as great dolts as ever, and that not one out of a dozen of them could get a brigade out of Hyde Park, much less manœuvre it before an enemy. No; it is not elementary knowledge, such as barrack life, or regimental parades can give, that is most essential to a commander. It is *good sense*, energy, thoughtfulness, and familiarity with independent action. Above all, it is that coolness under all circumstances, that enables a man to apply the full resources of his mind, and without *fear of responsibility*, to act upon his own judgment. Few will deny these obvious truths. Then, in all common sense, let not at least working men be *excluded* from command, and those hoisted over their shoulders, who have neither studied their profession as these have done, nor had their opportunities. Such practice would deprive Government, perhaps in its necessity, of the military services of its *best*, or at least of its most accomplished soldiers.

In all we have propounded, we are borne out, not only by Asiatic practice, but by the practice and theory of the Continental masters of war. We have already more than once referred to Jomini; we do so again, as his words are very apposite to our argument. He tells us that a chief commander of artillery should be a good strategist and tactician, a man who could consult with the commander-in-chief, and bring into play, at the most effective moment, not only the reserve artillery, but half the guns attached to divisions. This is common sense, but is not what is learned at Dum-dum, Meerut, the Mount, or Ahmednugger. Those head-quarters turn out excellent practical artillerists, but few strategists or tacticians. We quote in more detail Jomini's views as to the requisite qualifications of a commander-in-chief, also his opinion as the arm whence he may be best drawn. The translation or rather paraphrase is our own.*

"A general must be a man of great mind, of a moral courage which leads to great resolutions, of *sang froid* or physical courage which overcomes dangers. Knowledge is only a third-rank requisite, but is a powerful auxiliary. Vast erudition is not here meant. It is necessary to know little, but to know that little well, and to be well grounded in principles."

* * * * * *

"The question has often been agitated, whether command should be given to the general long habituated to the management of troops, or to generals who have risen in the *Etat Major*, and, though learned in war, have been little habituated to handle troops. It is indisputable that a general may be able to combine operations, and carry on war on a large scale, who never led a regiment against the enemy. The great Condé, Frederic, and Napoleon, are examples."

Jomini proceeds:

"It cannot be denied that a man from the *Etat Major, as well as any other*, may become a great Captain, but it will not be from having grown old in the functions of quartermaster,† but *because he possesses the natural genius for war.* A general of like character from the cavalry or infantry will be equally fit for supreme command. *Individual qualities* will be everything."

"In coming to a decision, all points must be considered, and a medium taken. A general from the *Etat Major*, from the Artillery, or from the Engineers, who has held the command of a division or corps d'armee, will have, other points being equal, a *superiority* over the general who understands the conduct of only one arm, or of a special corps."

"In brief, a general who has *thought much on war*, that is, has studied war, will be qualified for command. A great and comprehensive mind *is, above every other quality*, necessary for a commander-in-chief. Lastly, the union of a wise theory with a great mind will constitute the great captain."‡

Such are the dicta of one of the ablest, and most practical, military writers of the present age. Of one who was the chief of Ney's staff, and who is supposed to have inspired his genius. Of one who, even as a traitor to the side on which he had so long fought, was so much respected as a soldier, by the Emperor Alexander, that he made him an aide-de-camp, and put him at the head of an army. Jomini advocates all we urge.

* Precis de l'art de la guerre, par le Baron de Jomini. Paris, 1837, pages 604 and 605.

† In the Russian army, for which Jomini wrote, the quartermaster's department combines the general staff.

‡ Jomini, part i., pages 110, 111, and 112.

Genius is heaven-born. Strategy, tactics, and all else must give way on occasion. A general must *understand* rules and principles, but not be the slave of them. Neither rules nor principles require the term of a life to learn. He must have moral and physical courage, and ready aptitude to apply his resources. These qualifications are somewhat akin to genius. They *are* to be cultivated, though not to the best advantage under dry routine. The India Government has seldom the power of selection from generals who have commanded divisions. It is limited to select between commanders of regiments, and men who, like Generals Patrick Grant and Cheape, and Colonels Tucker and Birch, though of known ability, not only never led a regiment into action, but never commanded one for a day.* Or the selection may be extended to a third class, to men distinguished in youth as soldiers, but afterwards employed as civilians; to the Broadfoots, Edwardes', Lakes, Bechers, and Nicholsons of India; to the Hardinges, Raglans, and Cathcarts of the Royal Army. The importance of the subject tempts us again to quote Jomini:—

> "A general instructed in theory, but destitute of *coup d'œil*, of *sang froid*, and of skill, may make a fine strategic plan, but fail in every law of tactics *when he finds himself in presence of an enemy*. His projects will then vanish, his defeat become probable. If he has force of character, he may diminish the bad results of his check: *if he loses his head, he will lose his army*."

Few soldiers in India have witnessed much strategy; but many have witnessed the failure of tactics *in the presence of the enemy*, aye, and every day witness it on their own parade grounds, when "adjutants' regiments" in the hands of routine lieutenant-colonels and majors, even though they may "have never been on leave for a day for thirty years," are clubbed up and tortured in every conceivable way. [The men who never go on

* General Grant is the exception, but the corps was irregular.

leave are not the best officers. All work and no play makes Jack a dull boy.] The card system fails. The man who *never reflected* in his life cannot be expected to reflect on an emergency. An inequality or contraction of ground puts him out; the unexpected appearance of a crabbed brigadier flusters him; the whirlwind rush of a Sir Charles Napier down the line, frightens him out of his senses; cards, manuals, catechisms, and all other helps are forgotten, and the unhappy field officer is like 'a babe in a wood.' He loses his senses, and is alike the laughing-stock of his sable soldiers, and of his younger countrymen. Is such a man,—and there are scores of them,—the fitting leader of a brigade through the Bolan or the Khybur; up the Persian Gulf, or to China or Burmah? Yet they are the men so sent, daily so selected. Can such men be expected to preserve their senses in the presence of the enemy? That such men have not lost armies is no fault of the present system, but is attributable to the courage and skill of subordinates, and to the *Ikbal* of the company. But let not Providence be too long tempted. Rome lost her Legions when commanded by generals who were soldiers only in name. Napoleon's words to his brother Louis at Toulon apply to our argument. Standing in midst of the corpses of 200 grenadiers slain through the ignorance of their commander, at the assault of an impregnable side of Fort Phuron, he observed, "If I had commanded here, all these brave men would be still alive. Learn Louis, from this example, how absolutely necessary instruction is to those who aspire to command others."

We have dwelt so much on the mischiefs of routine and strict seniority, and on the evils of having decrepit or incapable officers at the head of troops, that it behoves us to offer some remedy for present evils. We know that the seniority system cannot be uprooted altogether, nor indeed do we desire to uproot it. Seniority must be the basis of Indian promotion, but seniority may be, and must be, helped over the stile.

In the first place, then, let us earnestly deprecate the threatened closing of the invalid establishment. As Sir George Pollock deposed before the Lords, it has often been grossly abused, but so have other establishments. Army head-quarters, and the doctors between them, ought to be able to prevent gross abuses. Invalid officers ought to be employed, as they usually have been at Madras and Bombay, in duties commensurate with their powers. It is by leaving them as gentlemen at large that malingering is encouraged. Our objection to the abrogation of the establishment is, on the double ground that present incumbents have a sort of right to its advantages, and that it is a safe outlet for incapables. This latter is surely a substantial reason for its maintenance. What matter, whether a man be unwilling or unable, so that he *do not perform* his duty? His disease may be real, though not apparent. It is, indeed, a grievous disease, to prefer idleness and inaction to moderate work. It is surely then better to shelve such diseased gentlemen in *small* civil posts, requiring only an hour or two's daily work,* than to have them at the head of companies or regiments. In garrison duty, with veterans, commanded by good officers, they may also earn their bread. We pray then the authorities to let the invalids stand, but to employ them as above suggested. The alternative is to allow invalid officers to cumber the regular ranks. Commanding officers are men with bowels, and such men will not drive respect-

* Few such sinecures exist in India; but our argument is, that there *are* quasi-civil posts which indifferent soldiers may creditably fill. Pay and pension and post offices are among them.

able incompetents, with families, out of their corps, to starvation. The pension establishment, in lieu of the invalids, would be starvation to many.

But we have a more substantive proposal to make. A scheme for an unattached list for the armies of India, prepared with a view to relieve the service from the weight of seniority, now lies before us, and *as far as it goes*, it seems well suited to effect the object. We therefore notice it at length.

First, let us glance at the measures which have been adopted by the Court of Directors during the last twenty-five years, to improve the condition of their officers.—In 1832, the Court expressed themselves desirous of remedying the then stagnant state of promotion, and of providing for the comfort of their officers on retirement. They intimated their willingness cordially to encourage the institution of retiring funds, and informed Government that they were prepared to bear the increased charge of retired pay that would be consequent upon the establishment of funds at the three Presidencies. They sanctioned the remittance of the retired officers' annuities through their treasury, at the rate of two shillings the Sicca rupee, and the grant of six per cent. per annum, on the balances of the several funds. The number of retirements, however, were limited to 24 per annum, for the three Presidencies, and the amount of the annuities to be given in each year was fixed at £7750.

Schemes for retiring funds were prepared, but none were approved of. After waiting a reasonable period, the Court resolved themselves to provide for the object contemplated, by enlarging the retiring regulations. This was effected in 1836. Officers were then for the first time permitted to retire after certain fixed periods of service instead of, as formerly, according to their rank. In 1837 these new regulations were still further enlarged, and a colonel's pension was sanctioned for all officers, whatever might be their rank, after 32 years of actual service in India; lieutenant-colonel's pension, after 28 years; major's pension, after 24 years; and captain's pension after 20 years. This enlargement of the retiring regulations was not productive of any real advantage to the service. Mr. Philip Melvill, in his evidence before the Lords in 1852, says—

"The first and great effect (of the new system of retirement) has been to soothe the feelings of the officers with regard to the rate of their retiring pension; they know that, however unfortunate they may be as compared with others in regimental rise, a fixed rate of pension is secured to them; the healing effect of this change has been most beneficial."

He further says,

"The number of retirements is increasing, as a necessary consequence of the additions made from time to time to the number of European officers, but the percentage is much the same; it is less than two per cent. from all causes, whether retiring on full or half pay, or resigning without any pay, and it has been much the same for the last thirty years."

He gives the number of officers who are entitled to retire on full pay at 1098, of whom 557 are entitled to retire on the pay of a rank superior to that which they had actually attained. The aggregate establishment of European officers in 1834, he states to have been 4084, and 5142 in 1852.

We give below an abstract* return, showing the

* Abstract return of retirements in the Bengal army from 1834 to 1853, showing the branch of the service to which the retired officers belonged.

	Colonels.	Lieutenant-Colonels.	Majors.	Captains.
Artillery	0	10	12	21
Engineers	0	4	3	1
Cavalry	0	3	6	27
Infantry	0	33	60	169
Invalids	0	4	21	32
Irregular Cavalry unattached	0	0	0	1
Ordnance Commissariat department	0	0	0	1
	0	54	102	252

number of officers who have retired from the Bengal army for the twenty years commencing with 1834 and ending with 1853. The retirements in the artillery, and engineers, and in the medical service are more numerous, in proportion, than those in the cavalry and infantry. This is caused, no doubt, by the existence of retiring funds in those branches of the service. In 1849 a fund called "the Majors' Bonus Fund," was established in the infantry of the Bengal army, and existed until the end of 1851. It offered no fixed bonus on retirement to lieutenant-colonels, nor was there any certainty that a bonus would be available at all to a lieutenant-colonel wishing to retire. It therefore fell to the ground.

The "Unattached Senior List" scheme now before us, is more of the nature of a superannuation fund, than of one of mere purchase. Unlike the superannuation funds of the civil and medical services, it does not propose to remove the annuitants from the service altogether, but simply raises them as it were a step, to make way for others: leaving their services available to the Government, if they have any physique remaining. But we must let the proposal speak for itself.

It sets out by showing the average length of service on promotion of the infantry officers of the armies of Bengal, Madras, and Bombay, in October, 1853, which are as follows:—

	Colonels.	Lieut.-Cols.	Majors.	Captains.	Lieutenants.
Bengal,	43.76	32	28.03	13.42	4.74
Madras,	39.39	31.32	26.53	12.80	4.33
Bombay,	39.29	31.23	27.78	12.24	4.60

The average ages, therefore, of officers, assuming that they entered the army at 17, must be, colonels on promotion to that grade, 58 years; lieutenant-colonels, 48 years: majors, 44 years; captains, 29 years; and lieutenants, 21 years. The length of service of the junior officers on promotion varies very considerably. In the Bengal army, there were, in 1853, majors who, on promotion, had served but 18 years, and majors of 35 years' service. In Madras, the most fortunate major of infantry was promoted in 14 years, and in Bombay in 13 years. The most unfortunate officers of that grade, in those Presidencies, were of 34, and 33 years' service respectively. Amongst the captains of the three armies, last promoted, the most fortunate were of 7, 8, and 9 years' standing, those who were most unfortunate, had been subalterns 26, 20, and 17 years. In Bengal, the average rate of promotion from grade to grade, is given as follows:—

	Years.	Months.
Ensign to Lieutenant	4	10
Lieutenant to Captain	9	10
Captain to Major	11	9
Major to Lieut.-Colonel	5	10
Lieut.-Colonel to Colonel	10	2
Total years	42	5

which corresponds very nearly with the average length of service of the colonels of the Bengal army as given before.

In order to better this wretched state of promotion, it is proposed "that a certain number of the senior colonels of each branch be placed yearly on an unattached list, and promotions made in their room, as in the case of death vacancies."

To carry out this proposal it is suggested that a fund be formed somewhat similar to the Annuity Fund of the civil service, or to the Medical Retiring Fund. The chief difference is, that the army retirements would be by strict seniority, and not by voluntary withdrawal, as in the services above named. To exhibit the working of the fund it is explained with special reference to the Bengal infantry.

It is proposed, *First*,—That the number of colonels to be placed yearly on the unattached senior list shall not exceed nine, or such number as the Court of Directors may sanction.*

Secondly. That the pay proper or British pay, and the colonel's allowance of the unattached officers shall be paid as at present by Government, and the promotion to the ranks of major-general, &c., and to the honours of the Bath, shall be open to all officers on the senior list, as in the case of unattached officers in the Royal army.

Thirdly. That the cost of the senior unattached list be borne partly by the Government, and partly by the army. The former to defray the amount of British pay of the unattached officers, and the latter to provide annuities for them, equal to their colonel's allowances.

Fourthly. That the terms of payment of the annuities, payable at the India House to be solicited from Government, be similar to those now granted to the civil and medical services, namely, an exchange of two shillings for the Company's rupee, and interest at the rate of 6 per cent. per annum on all appropriated capital.

* For the whole Indian army, the number of officers to be placed yearly on the unattached list would be :—

Bengal	Infantry	9	
"	Cavalry	1.153	
"	Engineers	0.461	
"	Artillery	1.384	
			11.998
Madras	Infantry	6.333	
"	Cavalry	0.923	
"	Engineers	0.230	
"	Artillery	0.807	
			7.293
Bombay	Infantry	3.807	
"	Cavalry	0.346	
"	Engineers	0.230	
"	Artillery	0.576	
			4.959
	Total per annum		24.250

The value of an annuity of £650 (colonel's allowance) at 6 per cent. is calculated for the various ages from 60 to 76. For the former age, the cost would be Rs. 53,293, and for the latter Rs. 30,914. To provide these annuities it is proposed to levy contributions from the several grades of the service, the chief payments being made by the senior ranks as they gain most by promotion. In the grades of lieutenant-colonel and major, a fixed sum is required for each step. The maximum subscription of a lieutenant-colonel is limited to two months' difference of pay between that grade, and the grade of colonel, that is, to Rs. 500, and the minimum is fixed at $\frac{1}{80}$th of the above sum, or Co.'s Rs. 6-4. All other subscriptions in the grade of lieutenant-colonel, are in arithmetical proportion to the above sums, and according to the standing of the subscriber. The maximum subscription of a major is limited to one and a half month's difference of pay, namely, to Rs. 300, and the minimum to Rs. 3-12. All junior grades to pay a donation on promotion. Captains on promotion to major, 8 months' difference of pay, or Rs. 2500. Lieutenants on promotion to captain, 4 months' difference of pay, or Rs. 500; and ensigns on promotion to lieutenant, 2 months' difference of pay, or Rs. 100. These contributions are expected to yield as follows:—

	Rs. as.	
Lieut.-Colonels . .	500 + 6—4 × 40 =	20,250
Majors	300 + 3-12 × 40 =	12,150
	For each step, Rs.	32,400
		9
	For nine steps, Rs.	291,600
25 Captains promoted at	2500 is . .	62,500
40 Lieutenants promoted at	500 is . .	20,000
50 Ensigns promoted at	100 is . .	5,000
	Yearly Income, Co.'s Rs. .	3,79,100

This sum will insure nine annuities yearly, to Colonels above the age of 69 years, or seven annuities, should the ages of the annuitants be below 69, but not under 60. The total payments that would be required from any one officer, in passing from Ensign to Colonel, would be

	Rs.
As Lieutenant on promotion . . .	100
As Captain on promotion	500
As Major on promotion	2,500
While passing through the grade of Major .	4,404
While passing through the grade of Lieut.-Colonel	10,125
Total Co.'s Rs. .	17,629

Under the present system, the average period of service in the grade of Lieutenant-Colonel, is 10 years and 2 months, which gives $7\frac{3}{4}$ steps a year as the rate of promotion: by adding 8 steps to the above, a Lieutenant-Colonel would pass through that grade in 5 years. Majors are at present 5 years and 10 months in passing from Major to Lieutenant-Colonel: eight additional steps per annum, would push them through the grade of Major in 3 years and 7 months. Ensigns are, on an average, 25 years 5 months in attaining the rank of Major regimentally. Eight additional line steps per annum, would be equal to one regimental step in ten years. The regimental officer would therefore gain two regimental steps by the line promotion in his run to Major more than he does at present, and for his greatly-accelerated promotion would pay but Rs. 3100.

Such is the scheme before us. Its promised advantages are so great that we cannot imagine any officer refusing it his support. It appears to be free from the objections which have been urged against purchase in

Her Majesty's service. No unnecessary supercession of old officers by young and inexperienced boys, whose only recommendation for promotion is their ability to pay for it, would occur. The cost to individuals would not be out of proportion to the increased income that would follow the several payments. The rise would be equally felt by all, and Government would derive even greater benefit than the officers themselves, by having at their disposal in the higher grades men physically fit for service, The average age of colonels would not in the course of time exceed forty-seven years. Lieutenant-colonels would be placed in command of corps at forty-two, and the lower grades would feel the benefit of a senior list in equal proportion.

During the first years of its existence the cost of a senior list to Government would be trifling. The financial result ought not, however, to prevent its adoption, if it offer, as we believe it does, the means of making the armies of India, as regards their European commissioned officers, really efficient. Supposing the mean duration of the lives of the officers removed to the senior list to be nine years. This will give $9 \times 24 = 216$ annuitants as the maximum of the senior unattached list for the three Presidencies. The ultimate cost, therefore, to Government would be

$456\frac{1}{4} \times 216 =$	£98,550
To which add the difference between 4 and 6 per cent. as the donation interest on £908,712, the value of 216 annuities	18,174
Making a total of	£116,724

or eleven lakhs of rupees a year for the whole Indian army; that is, one-hundredth part of the cost of the military establishment of India, as at present constituted.

We are given to understand that the scheme is before Government. We beg their support. It received the cordial concurrence of the late commander-in-chief, and has met with the concurrence of many experienced officers, the letters of several of whom lie before us. We trust that it will receive that consideration from General Anson which the subject deserves.

Let a mixed commission be appointed to inquire into the state of promotion. That now sitting in England will not benefit the Indian army. The system of promotion in India being by seniority alone, requires a separate investigation; and without some such special inquiry we despair of effectual improvement. We fear we have been tedious, perhaps unintelligible. The great importance of the subject demands the time and attention of our readers.

From general, let us return to special necessities. Among the burdens of the army—indeed, of the Indian services—are paper forms and returns. They weigh down men's souls. The medical department, which has always been a step-child, peculiarly suffers. The doctor must often neglect his patients to enable him to send in his papers, and prove why he gave No. 1 three eggs and a chop, and No. 2 a pint of ale and two ounces of brandy. Such things, at least, are managed better in the Royal army. There a surgeon enjoys the reasonable confidence due to his position and profession. The East India Company's doctor is treated as a quasi-peculator. All this must, in a great measure, be imputed to the fact of the service having few influential friends. The boards have no proper influence; they can retard or prevent ameliorations, but can seldom further good measures. How can a board of the oldest of the old surgeons be otherwise? Age is the practical, though not the ostensible, qualification. A change in *names*, and nothing more, has been recently effected. Senior and junior members of an effete board were converted into a physician-general, a surgeon-general, and an inspector-general of the *same* board, with identically the *same* duties. The inspector-general inspects no one! In the Royal army the titles and duties are more appropriate; one director-general supervises all: and a right good supervisor Dr. Andrew Smith seems to have been, notwithstanding the abuse heaped on him last year. If others had evinced half his forethought, and had done their duty as he did his, many of the dreadful tales of 1854-55 would have been spared. Inspectors-general are as Indian superintending surgeons. Deputy-inspectors are superintending surgeons of divisions—a rank and office much wanted in India in the field, if not in quarters. All these appointments go by age; indeed, almost by incompetency. The *form* of selection has, in two cases only, been gone through. Men like Kennedy, Dempster, and James McRae are selected for *war service*. They evince indomitable energy, cool courage, and great skill. Their operations are carried on under fire. They stand fast when crowds of fighting men break through their doolies and over their amputating tables. They endeavour to make up for the misconduct of others. What is their reward? A bare mention in the Gazette with the crowd who have, as above hinted, roughly interfered with their duties; no honours, no rewards, await them on return of peace; they sink to regimental charges. We are wrong. Jemmy Thompson was, in his old age, knighted, and three or four surgeons, for past services, were made Companions of the Bath. These inaugurations were somewhat akin to the recent creation of field-marshals in honour of Sebastopol. All this is very bad. The man who works, who hazards his own life to preserve others, whatever be his position or department, should be honoured, and otherwise rewarded, and that *promptly*. There ought to be special professional rewards. Men like McRae and Dempster ought to be Knights of the Bath, and be placed in positions putting them above pecuniary care. The former good man and good surgeon has several sons, and cannot get one of them into the service in which he has behaved so well and ably! True, he was specially thanked after the second Punjab campaign, and told that *no* man in the whole army of twenty-five thousand men had done the State better or more useful service; but for years he remained unrewarded. The fact is, that, as in the Royal service, there is little, if any, professional stimulus or reward for the practical surgeon. Lord Dalhousie, just previous to departure, as far as lay in his power, did McRae tardy justice in placing him at the head of the Calcutta Medical College.

We might name many surgeons, far down in the list, who merit special reward, and yet are unrewarded. Dr. John Murray, of Agra, can hardly be said to be unrewarded; but his reward and position are the private fruits of his public and private ability and energy. The late cholera crisis at Agra bears witness to all. His case at Aliwal so peculiarly exemplifies our argument that we must narrate the circumstances. Murray was then assistant-surgeon attached to the troop of horse artillery. Heaps of wounded lay around, but there was no field surgeon; neither were there sufficient amputating instruments. Several large boxes, however, full of all requisites, were lying at the post-office, addressed to the superintending surgeon at Ferozepore, eighty miles distant. No one dared to open them. The postmaster probably objected to such *felony*. Murray, unable to inspirit his seniors, went at the boxes like a man; no, like a woman, like Miss Nightingale at the Balaklava store-room. Hatchet in hand, he got out saws, knives, plasters, lint, and tourniquets; told his brethren to help themselves, each giving a receipt for what he took (the canny Scot here peeps out). He then went to Sir Harry Smith, and got him to name a field surgeon; but the nominee refused the responsibility. Murray then accepted it himself, worked hard, got the wounded under cover, and doubtless saved many lives. What was his reward? Why, that the Auditor-General deducted his horse artillery pay, and refused to pass his field surgeoncy allowance on account of some informality—perhaps, because he was an assistant-surgeon. The essential part of the story we know to be correct. He did the work, and was thereby out of pocket.

We have also a story of a different sort to tell. About that same period an old surgeon arrived within a few miles of where lay nearly a thousand sick and wounded soldiers, belonging to a brigade to which only a single surgeon, or assistant, was present for each regiment. He came to be superintending surgeon, but could not take up his new office, pending some arrangement. How did he pass the interval? Why, in entire idleness, a march or more from the sufferers, although he was urged to lend a hand! We can vouch for this fact. It occurred under our own eyes. Yet Murray lost his pay by his exertions, and is now simply a civil surgeon; while his senior who thus acted never suffered in pocket, more than in feeling, by his cruel apathy, and is now comfortably out of the service.

The medical staff of the army is altogether insufficient, and hitherto it has not been well supported by the recently-appointed class of sub-assistant-surgeons. The move in their favour was a good one, but has not yet ripened to good fruit. We are well pleased that assistant-surgeoncies are now open to natives of India; but for some years it will be moral, not mental, capability that will be found most deficient. In no profession are conscientiousness and high moral worth more required than in the physician and surgeon. More Native doctors are greatly wanted, and those in the service have insufficient motives for exertion. Some of them are most deserving men. A few can operate for cataract, extract calculi, &c. We strongly recommend grades being established, rising on strict examination, from present rates, 25 and 30 rupees, to 50, 70, and 80 rupees a month. Also, that schools for the professional education of such persons be established at Bangalore, Poonah, and Lahore, as already exist at Agra and Hyderabad.

Pay should also be proportioned to work and responsibility with the higher classes. Every assistant-surgeon has, on arrival, to do duty on subaltern's pay with an European regiment, or at the Presidency General Hospital. His aim is accordingly to move as soon as possible. Some stay hardly a month, and are then comfortably settled in civil stations, or in the hills. Others are knocked about from regiment to regiment. We have known an instance of a young assistant-surgeon being eighteen times moved within as many months, ending with having to take a wing of an European regiment two hundred miles in the month of May and June, after having just brought a similar detachment a similar march in April. We recollect another young medico dying of heat and exposure when similarly employed. The assistant-surgeon with an European regiment has exactly the same duty to perform as the surgeon—the same responsibility *for his portion* of the corps. He is not, like a subaltern, under minute orders. He acts every hour, in matters of life and death, on his own responsibility. He should receive, at least, the same staff pay as if in charge of a Native corps, and thus have a motive for remaining at his more responsible post. At an apparent first expense money would thus be saved, inasmuch as valuable lives, now sacrificed by changes and by inexperience, would be preserved. Constant changes do no one good; they damp all zeal, and vitally hinder all efficiency.

Medical officers in charge of corps should have full authority, however, to *draw* for all necessaries for the sick. Thus trusted and sufficiently supplied with European medicines, which is not always the case at present, they would endeavour to keep down expense by using indigenous drugs, many of which are valuable; and all of which are cheap, and procurable in every bazaar. Surgeons should be assisted by efficient well-paid stewards, as is the case in the Bombay army. They should not be teased with mere business details about bread, sago, saucepans, and flannel gowns. It should be quite sufficient in such matters for them to satisfy the superintending surgeon, that they have not wasted the public money. Dooly-bearers and other hospital servants should all be enrolled, well-paid, and eligible for pensions; their not being so has cost many a wounded man his life. The scum of the earth will go under fire when there is a pension for heirs. Non-combatants can hardly be expected to expose themselves without such provision. Mule-litters, horse ambulances are much required on service. Every corps should have *two* educated medical officers; European corps *four*. We remember an officer proposing to *prosecute* Government for putting his precious limbs into the charge of a very worthy and deserving man, who, however, was only an apothecary. On the other hand, we knew another who preferred the apothecary to the doctor.

Our remarks on this division of our subject have been somewhat full, because we deeply feel its importance both to humanity and to the Government's good name. Every European, and Anglicized native, in India is a missionary. Each individual has the opportunity, within his sphere, of doing great good or great evil; of setting a good or a bad example. He is a light on a hill. Surgeons are specially so. The subaltern deals with a hundred men, the doctor with a thousand, and if he have a spark of philanthropy, will minister extra-officially to hundred of others. Some do to thousands. Such men are ministers of mercy to the most wretched; give light to the blind; relieve the leper, heal the sick, and greatly smooth the path of the aged to the grave. They should be cordially assisted by Government. Every medical man should have a *carte-blanche* to open dispensaries for the poor, under check, as to medicines, *only* of their immediate professional superiors.

The truth of our sentiments as to the prospects of Indian army doctors is demonstrated by the fact that the candidates for employ, at all the recent examinations in London, have been hardly as numerous as the vacancies awaiting them. The well-educated young doctors of England have discovered the East India Company's service *not* to be the best field for talent and energy.

Did space permit, we should have much to say on the morality of the Indian army. The Native portion gives no trouble. No soldier ever existed more patient, more sober, more obedient than the Hindoo sepoy.

The Hindustani Mahommedan has more energy, but is scarcely less tractable under a firm but considerate commandant; both classes offer examples for any army. A petty theft, an occasional religious brawl, and a less-frequent murder, originating in revenge, form the full catalogue of serious crime. In some regiments years glide by without a necessity for severe punishment.

The European soldier is a different creature, and requires a stricter discipline. The day of great severity has happily passed away; the day when the remedy for every error was the lash. The law of kindness has however yet to be tried. Let British soldiers be dealt with as reasonable beings. Relieve them from espionage, keep them strictly to their duty, but let them have all reasonable indulgence when off duty. Let Jacob's scheme be tried with European soldiers, as with Native horsemen, with rifles, and with cannon. We are glad again to quote Jacob's words:—

> "The attempt to govern English soldiers by fear of bodily pain is as wise as is the cramping of our men's bodies by absurd clothing and accoutrements. * * * * Appeal to the highest and noblest faculties of man."

Jacob thinks that fifty thousand *élite* English peasantry and yeomen in the ranks, treated, and trained, and armed on rational principles, "would be a match for a world in arms." Again we go very far with Colonel Jacob, and heartily wish he were "the Lord Panmure" of India.*

* Since the first part of this article was in type, we have fallen upon the following extract from the *Times*, relative to the efficiency of the Enfield rifle and its advantages over artillery. This experiment goes far to support Colonel Jacob's views on this subject, more especially when it is considered that Jacob's rifle is a more deadly and larger-ranging piece than the Enfield rifle:—

"An interesting experiment took place lately at the School of Musketry at Hythe. Some condemned tumbrils and gun limbers having been lately procured from Woolwich, on Monday morning last one of each of these was taken to the target practice ground. To the tumbril were attached six horses with riders made of framework, covered with canvas, and stuffed with straw; the whole the size of life. About the gun-carriage were stuffed figures representing men unlimbering and bringing the gun into action. At a distance somewhat beyond 600 yards from them, about sixty of the men under instruction at the School of Musketry were drawn up in two divisions, the one extending in skirmishing order, the other supporting.

Barrack married life is one of the greatest military difficulties. The expense of keeping and moving large numbers of women must always be a bar to the positive encouragement of matrimony. On the other hand, the improved health and steadiness of married men, should be considered in all calculations of expense, and should at least modify its discouragement. We agree cordially with a recent Bombay reviewer,* that "the percentage system of indecency, and the rejection of all beyond the percentage (six, on embarkation), should at once be knocked on the head."

With him we urge that, whatever be the number of women allowed, they should be cared for and dealt with as *Christian females*. At present, they are hardly allowed to be respectable; they are not treated as if they were. A shawl, a bit of cloth, separates families. Obscene language ever rings in their ears, obscene sights are constantly before their eyes. The result is too often what might be expected, and then the cry is, "the nasty creatures, the hypocrites, the liars." That some respectable women do *live and die* in the barracks *is* a standing miracle. Great should be their reward!

On board ship and at depôts, where most attention is required, least is often given. We have known women

One round was first fired by the front rank only of the skirmishing party, which may have consisted of about twenty men, and the result was that a bullet had passed through almost every horse, as also through many of the riders and men employed at the gun. The support was then ordered up to reinforce skirmishers, and the whole fired three or four rounds in skirmishing order, which completely riddled horses, riders, and footmen. The party was then closed on its centre, and retired to a distance of above 800 yards, when volleys were fired at the supposed artillery, first by sections, then by sub-divisions, and finally by divisions, the whole with an accuracy perfectly wonderful. The experiment clearly proved that, in the hands of well-skilled soldiers—men who, having been taught the principles of rifle-shooting theoretically and practically, have obtained a perfect confidence in their weapon—the Enfield rifle must prove more than a match for any field guns of the present day."—*Times*.

* Bombay Quarterly, No. VI.; article, "Military men and their dress."

sent in open pattemars, from Scinde to Bombay, in company with bachelor soldiers, without the slightest arrangements for privacy. The hourly scenes at most depôts are too disgusting for description.

The principle of the *Patcherry*, or cottage system, for married soldiers, obtaining in the Bombay Presidency, is good, but is badly carried out. Many of the buildings are altogether unfit to be occupied by Europeans, when the thermometer is 100° and even 110°, as is often the case during several months of the year. But the principle is good. Indeed we see not why the *Patcherry* system should not be extended to bachelors of good characters. Let two, four, ten, or more friends, under joint responsibility for good conduct, mess and live together, whether in detached cottages, or in partitioned-off apartments of present barracks. The sober and the pious man might then, at least, live unmolested by the jeers and ribaldry of his dissipated comrades. We throw out the hint to the authorities. A distinguished officer, who advocates the measure, has told us that in Scinde he has often, in his rides in the jungle, come upon threes and fours of the 78th Highlanders at prayers, or reading their bibles.

Considering their circumstances and temptations, the early age at which they leave home, and the little check on irregularities by regimental authorities, the morality of the officers of the Indian army is good. It is at least on a par with that of corresponding classes in England. It is superior to that of the Colonies. In many quarters there is much earnestness of purpose, much that is thoroughly good. Gross and open immorality is now most rare: as rare, as forty years ago it was common. While, however, in many corps there is an excellent tone, while in such the commandant considers and treats the subalterns as his wards, and while the elder officers set an example of sobriety and gentlemanly conduct to the younger; in others, the whole atmosphere of the regiment is clouded by opposite influences. The proceedings of courts-martial, as occasionally published, let the public behind the scenes in such matters. And what more uncertain and even whimsical, than the fiats of such courts? A Lieutenant Barnes at Bombay is acquitted of blame for virtually declining to do duty. A Major O'Grady at Madras, is "severely reprimanded" for denouncing his commanding officer before the young officers of the mess, as "an old fool" and "a d—d jackass." Within a few weeks of these two awards, Lieutenant Patterson, a young officer of previously-unstained reputation, is dismissed the service for an act of gross violence certainly, but perpetrated on the impulse of the moment, under gross provocation. We are of opinion that two of these sentences might, with advantage, have been reversed, and that the award on Lieutenant Barnes was erroneous. He was undoubtedly guilty of the crime of which he was charged, however he may have been provoked to it, and doubtless he was grievously provoked.

Although then the army is not so bad as Sir Charles Napier and some recent writers depict it, there is, in many quarters, much that needs reform. H. M.'s 46th Regiment prove that full messes are neither the most moral, nor the most gentlemanly; but in India, as a rule, the largest messes are the most respectable. Major O'Grady set a bad example to his younger brethren, but it is where a number of idle young fellows get together, without the restraining voice of their seniors, that vulgar quarrels and immoralities mostly occur.

The remedy, *again*, is efficient commanders to regiments. At whatever cost to the State, and at whatever pain to individuals, let there be a *soldierly* man, of *good sense*, at the head of every corps, and let his authority be supported. Better that his authority be in excess, than that he should lack power. For the rest, and from the higher authorities, a medium course between that of Sir William Gomm and Sir Charles Napier is needed. The violent tirades, the hollow and insincere compliments, the biting and damning invectives of Sir Charles are not wanted. Neither Europeans nor Natives require *severity;* they *do* require *firmness.* The soft showers, the kindly and well-meant platitudes of Sir William are therefore as little to the purpose as were the thunder torrents of Sir Charles.*

Judicious, without afflictive, discipline is required. Such as, while reminding officers that they must always be gentlemen, will equally impress on gentlemen, that they are and must be soldiers. In Bengal the latter reminder is most necessary. We will not assume the invidious task of deciding where the other is most wanted; in what quarter Mr. Arnold's and Mrs. Mackenzie's caps best fit.

Such discipline and such surveillance as we advocate, will be approved by most good officers. Throughout the services the materials are excellent. Some of the best working blood of England is in India. The sons of the middle classes, that have won and raised England's Oriental empire, will maintain it against all comers and all odds. The task may be easy or hard, according as each individual performs his part.

As one example is at all times more effective than many homilies, we commend to our readers the "Me-

* Each general, in his parting address, well epitomized his own administration. Each evidently wrote his own farewell greeting.—H. M. L.

morials of Captain Hedley Vicars, H. M. 97th Regiment,"* who, after a short but brilliant career, died a hero's death in the trenches before Sebastopol. Stern soldiers wept at his death: many recorded their lamentations. One sentinel wrote, "as our adjutant, he was loved by every one in the regiment, and as captain of No. 4 Company, he was more so by his company."

Officers of all grades and arms, from Lords Panmure and Raglan downwards, lamented his fall. One, a kindred soul,† who at the age of twenty was adjutant of the 97th Regiment, and twice fought his way into the Redan, on the fatal 8th of September, and was there found, "far advanced on that red ground lying by a cannon, in the sleep of death," thus wrote of Vicars the day after the death of the latter in a private letter to his *own* mother:—

> "Such a death became such a life,—and such a soldier. The most gallant, the most cheerful, the happiest, the most universally respected officer, and the most consistent Christian soldier, has been taken from us by that bullet. * * * I had fondly hoped that we should live to go home, and that I might bring my dear departed friend to you, and proudly show him as a specimen of what a model soldier should be. * * * Noble fellow! he rushed in front of his men, and his powerful arm made more than one Russian fall. * * * How he fearlessly visited and spoke to the men in the worst times of the cholera! but, as he told me, he got his reward; for the soldiers' dying lips besought blessings on his head. * * * Our men got great praise for the fight last night, but *who would not go anywhere with such a leader?*"

Yes, we can vouch to all who will "go and do likewise," that such a man, the soldier's friend, the brave in battle, the gentle in peace, will be followed to the death by every British soldier and by every sepoy. Sympathy, kindness, and gallantry are nowhere more appreciated than in the Indian army.

We are happy to perceive that, for once, peace has not thrown the home authorities off their guard. There

* James Nisbett and Co., Berner's Street, London, 1856.

† Lieut. Douglas Macgregor, H. M. 97th Regiment, nephew of General Paul MacGregor, and cousin of Lieut.-Col. George MacGregor, Bengal army.

can be no lasting peace. The time has not come. The war of principles has yet to be fought. Russia *must* have her revenge, and America *must* try her strength, her gigantic frigates, and her ten-inch guns: we are accordingly delighted to observe that the *peace* establishment is to be 140,000 men, on a footing admitting of speedy increase: above all, that twenty thousand artillery-men are to be maintained.

We regret, however, that nothing was done, on the treaty of peace, to control Russia in Asia. We are aware that there were difficulties; but the right of having a Consul at Meshed and trading vessels on the Caspian might have been obtained. Information on Central Asian matters is greatly wanted. Insensibly and almost by a *coup-de-main*, the Russian empire has been extended for *thirteen thousand miles* across the whole Continent of Europe and Asia, and for twenty degrees over America. Curbed to the south and west, Russia has not waited an hour to push forward her soldiers, her sailors, her savants, her engineers, and her labourers to the Caspian, to the Aral, and even to the mighty Amoor. Her old policy will now, more vigorously than ever, be pursued, and though the dream of a century will never be realized, her position in Persia will speedily be strengthened, and posts will be established in Central Asia and even in China. Bomarsunds, if not Sebastopols, will arise at Orenburgh, Astrakan, and Astrabad, perhaps even at Balkh and Herat. The wave has receded, to return with redoubled force, though at a different angle.

Such has ever been and will be Russia's policy. There will be no Russian invasion of India, nor probably will the tribes be impelled on us. The latter now understand our strength; Russia has long understood both our strength and our weakness. There will be no foolish raid *as long as India is united, in tranquillity and contentment,* under British rule. Russia well knows that such an attempt would only end in the entire destruction of the invaders. India *has been* invaded some forty times, but always by small armies, acting in communication with domestic parties. A small Russian army could not make good its way through Affghanistan; a large army would be starved there in a week. The largest army that could come with Affghanistan and Persia in its train, would be met at the outlets of the only two practicable passes, and while attempting to debouche would be knocked to pieces. A hundred thousand Anglo-Indian troops might, with the help of railroads, be collected at each pass in as few days as it would take an *unopposed* Russian army weeks to traverse them. Hundreds of eight-inch guns would there be opposed to their field-pieces. The danger, then, is imaginary. Herat is no more the key to India than is Tabreez, or Khiva, or Kokan, or Meshed. The chain of almost impenetrable mountains is the real key to India. England's own experience in the western passes, and in the Crimea, have proved the absurdity of the tale of Russian invasion. No, the dream is idle: England's dangers are in India, not without; and we trust that it will be *in India* they will be met, and that there will be no *third* Affghan campaign. Such a move would be playing Russia's game. We are safe while we hold our ground and do our duty. Russia may teaze, annoy, and frighten us by her money and by emissaries. She may even do us mischief, but she will never put foot in Hindostan.

What America may venture, sixty years hence, when her population numbers a hundred millions, and when vessels of ten thousand tons ply the ocean, is another, and may possibly be considered a wilder question. But that America *will* strive for Oriental sovereignty is certain. She is welcome; there will be room for centuries, for the whole Saxon race. Let England work out her destiny, let her govern India for the people, and, as far as possible, by the people, and neither England nor India need fear Russia or America, or both combined.

To recapitulate. Our object is, to direct attention to Wellington's dying legacy, and to our greatest living warrior's equally solemn enunciation,

> "Woe to the nation that forgets the military art! Woe to that nation —woe to that nation which heaps up riches, but which does not take the precaution to defend them."

Such were the impressive and truthful words of the hero of Kars, on the day he landed in England; such the warning addressed by him to the thousands who hailed his return. And the lesson his words inculcate, based as it is on a mournful experience, cannot be too often or too earnestly urged upon the minds of those who truly and unselfishly love their country. Let us not for ever learn *only* from disaster. Let us use our opportunities.

To conclude: Our recommendations are, to have one strong fortress in every province, and a redoubt in *every* cantonment. All may be of mud, at very moderate expense. No man, black or white, to be permitted merely to cumber a muster roll, a cantonment, or a battle field. Only the young and middle-aged to be in the *service* ranks. Elderly men to be in garrison, and in veteran corps, *commanded by hale and efficient soldiers*. Old men to retire to their homes. Similar rules for European officers and soldiers, as for Natives, without favour or affection. It is sheer madness, on the plea of economy, mercy, or aught else, to keep inefficients, from whatever cause, in the *service* ranks. It is worse, it is a crime, to keep such men in authority, high or low. Their fitting places are the invalids, the pension list, the clubs, their English hearths.

Legitimate outlets for military energy and ability in all ranks, and among all classes, *must* be given. The minds of subadars and resseldars, sepoys and sowars, can no more with safety be for ever cramped, tramelled, and restricted as at present, than can a twenty-foot embankment restrain the Atlantic. It is simply a question of time. The question is only whether justice is to be gracefully conceded or violently seized. Ten or twenty years *must* settle the point.

Our view is also, that regiments *professedly* officered by Europeans should be *really* so, that officers should *really* do the duty they profess to do. That the work should not be left to havildar majors and pay orderlies. We accordingly propose that at least two European officers per company be posted to each of such regiments; that there be no Native officers, unless indeed one Anglicized jemadar (as ensign) be attached to each company, to learn his duty as a captain (subadar), when he may be transferred as such to a regiment officered by Natives.

We further propose that certain cavalry and infantry regiments be wholly, and others partially, officered by Natives.

That the veteran service be made one of honour and comparative ease.

That honorary rewards be increased, and that pensions be given earlier, and, in particular cases, on a more liberal scale. Whether pensions be by deferred annuities, or as at present, there can be no better safety valve to the service than the pension establishment. Comparatively few attain it; all look to it. The vista is long, and the cottage in the distance, *very* small; it is nevertheless the day and the night dream of thousands. To the Native soldiers, *home* is not, as with Europeans, a simple resting-place after life's task is done; it is the return to, and union with, the relatives and friends of earlier years. The whole domestic existence of the sepoy is limited to the few years of pensioned and furlough life. His peculiar customs deprive him of such happiness while in the ranks.

The scientific branches of the service to be kept complete on the most liberal scale. This is the best economy. Sappers and artillerymen will, on an emergency, make fair infantry, but sepoys cannot reciprocate the obligation, nor is it perhaps expedient that they should be taught.

The numerical strength of the European troops should never be less than one-fourth of the regular Native army. One-third would be a better proportion. Year by year, the proportions have decreased, though the contrary would have been the wiser policy. Familiarity nowhere engenders reverence. A hundred years ago a company was looked on by the enemy as a regiment is now, and yet at Seringapatam, the proportion of Europeans was very much greater than it has been during more recent wars.

The arms and accoutrements of all, but especially of the Europeans, should be of the very best description. Our infantry arms at Sebastopol were better than those of the Russians. The Minié rifle probably saved Inkermann, as the change from six to nine-pounders may have saved Waterloo.

A staff corps to be formed of officers who have served from two to four years with their own arm, and for at least *one* with every other. The staff not to be *exclusively* drawn from this corps. Examinations to be required for *every post*, and for *every grade*, up to given points. Staff corps men, as others, to undergo such examinations. Literary attainments to be slightly considered; *military science, rather than mathematics,* to be the desideratum. In short, strictly *practical and professional* knowledge with soldierly bearing, and good characters, to be the main points. We are quite sensible of the difficulty: the public service, not the welfare of individuals, is the point at issue.

Another of our suggestions is, quietly and unostentatiously to oppose class to class, creed to creed, and interest to interest. We have also argued, that this can be best done in the army, not as at present, by a mixture of sects in each regiment, but by separate regiments, each consisting chiefly, though *not entirely,* of a single sect.

Annual "Chobhams," and "Aldershotts" to be established at each Presidency, where officers, soldiers, and sepoys should be taught to work, *as before an enemy;* to make gabions and fascines: to dig and delve; to throw up works; to attack and defend them. In short, for two or three months of every year, soldiers should have the opportunity, as far as practicable, of learning what war is, and should also learn to take care of themselves in the field in all weather.

On somewhat the principles above enunciated, and with one *unmistakable Pay Code* for all India, the army * might be made doubly efficient for war or for peace, at an expense hardly exceeding half a million in excess of present expenditure. Officers would no longer

* We have purposely left untouched the question of *one* army or *three* armies, or of a general amalgamation with the Royal army. But in whatever hands the Indian army remains, its officers should be available for service *throughout the world.* All the arguments that apply to the necessity of a *large* field for selections for Indian army staff apply equally to the Royal troops. Free employment *for all,* and liberty of exchange between the Queen's and Company's troops should be the rule.—H. M. L.

doubt their own men,* the men would have less reason to complain of their officers. The latter would do what they hardly now profess to do—they would look into the details of their regiments and companies, not leave them to Native officers whom they despise, or to non-commissioned Natives, who have no legitimate authority. Each man, high or low, in each class of regiments, would have his place and his duty. Each man would accordingly have more contentment. The staff appointments from corps being few, and regimental commands being earlier obtainable, and *given by merit* as much as by seniority, there would be fewer and less loud aspirations for staff employ. The contentment of the officers would alone go far to content the sepoys. Pleasure and pain are catching. The murmurs of messes quickly reach the quarter guard, as do contrary feelings. We conclude with our oft-repeated remark, that it is not a numerically strong army, but a contented one with efficient officers, that is wanted. Our duty is now done; let others do theirs, and a reproach, possibly a danger, will have been removed.

A paragraph in the *Delhi Gazette*, announcing that the Oude authorities are disposed to dispense with the service of the regular regiments for Lucknow, tempts a few further words of caution—though we do not altogether credit the newspaper report. The earliest days of annexation are not the safest. Be liberal, considerate, and merciful, but be prompt, watchful, and even *quietly* suspicious. Let not the loose characters floating on the surface of society, especially such society as Lucknow, be too far tempted, or trusted. Wellington's maxim of "keeping the troops out of sight," answered for Eng-

* We refer especially to such times as those of the Madras Mutiny.

land; it will *not* answer for India. There must be *trusty* bayonets, within sight of the *understandings*, if not of the *eyes*, of Indian subjects, before they will pay willing obedience, or any revenue. Of late years, the wheels of Government have been moving very fast. Many Native prejudices have been shocked. Natives are now threatened with the abolition of polygamy. It would not be difficult to twist this into an attack on Hindooism. At any rate, the faster the vessel glides, the more need of caution, of watching the weather, the rocks, and the shoals.

Felix quem faciunt aliena pericula cautum.